M000268563

LAUNDRY

THE HOME COMFORTS
BOOK OF CARING FOR CLOTHES AND LINENS

CHERYL MENDELSON

Illustrated by Harry Bates

SCRIBNER
New York   London   Toronto   Sydney

CONTENTS

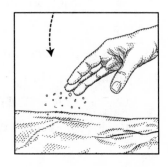
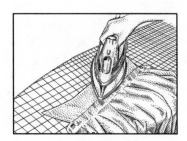
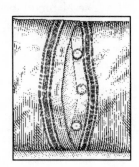

AUTHOR'S NOTE

This book contains material on laundering and the use and care of fabrics in the home originally published in *Home Comforts: The Art & Science of Keeping House* (1999), a general work on housekeeping nearly 900 pages long. *Laundry* unites in one convenient volume the long segment of *Home Comforts* called "Cloth"—which was devoted entirely to laundering, laundry products, and fabrics and fibers—with related discussions from other parts of *Home Comforts* on subjects ranging from mending to bed linens and carpets.

The material has been updated where recent developments have required changes in the original. I have also written a new introduction and a new chapter, expanded the index, here and there reorganized for increased clarity, and made other changes throughout, all with the goal of creating a comprehensive, practical, humane, and readable book on modern home laundering and the domestic use and care of cloth and linens.

PREFACE

How to Do the Laundry

Laundering is easily explained. Indeed, the basic steps of laundering have not changed for at least a century and a half.

Every week or so, when enough of your clothes and linens are soiled to make doing a wash worthwhile, you gather them all together in one place and separate them into loads, or heaps on the floor, of items that can safely receive similar laundering. Paying attention to fiber content and care labels, you sort them according to their color and dye-fastness, the type of cloth they are made of and the way they are made—their sturdiness or fragility—how dirty they are and what the dirt is, and other characteristics, watching out for stains and especially hard-to-remove soil as you go. These difficult spots you treat immediately, either with liquid detergent, a paste of detergent powder and water, or a product specially manufactured for the purpose. Once the loads are separated and stains treated, you wash the clothes in sudsy water that is cool, warm, or hot, depending on the kind of cloth. Sometimes, one or more garments need hand-washing, whether because they are so delicate or because they are not colorfast or are prone to shrinking or for some other reason. Most, however, you wash in your washing machine, one load after another. Then you dry each load, either in your dryer or on a clothesline, drying rack, or hanger. After the laundry is dry, some people will iron wrinkled things smooth. Garments and linens that will not be ironed—all of them, in many households—are hung or folded. All are then replaced in closets and drawers or on shelves, ready to be used again. At regular intervals, you repeat this series of steps—storing, using, gathering, sorting, washing, drying, ironing and folding, restoring. It's simple.

Why, then, is this book more than four hundred pages long? Because each of these steps is a place where you can trip. The potential causes and kinds of missteps are remarkably numerous, and there are countless opportunities to fine-tune your methods. The more you know and the greater your experience, the fewer money-, time-, and labor-consuming errors you will make. A book like this cannot confidently claim to have included *every* fact or technique that someone might look for, but its pages are crammed with facts, some for beginners and others for experts, that will be useful in someone's laundry. No one needs to know all of them. Many are about fabrics or linens or clothes or laundry facilities completely unlike yours. Some are geared toward standards that are irrelevant to your circumstances or possessions. For just as good cooking includes everything from hamburgers on your grill to Julia Child's Crêpes Courées et Flambées, so laundering can be done either in a perfectly satisfying rough-and-ready way or with elegant finesse—or something in between. What is best for your household depends on your own time, resources, needs, tastes, tolerances, goals, and belongings.

INTRODUCTION

Laundering is part of everyone's life because clothes and linens are indispensable to comfort, health, and beauty. In spite of this, a massive de-skilling of the population in matters of cloth and its domestic care began in the last decades of the twentieth century and continues at an accelerating pace today. This is a trend worth resisting.

Contrary to nudist fantasy, the clothed body, in all but a very few circumstances, is more comfortable than the naked one. In hot weather, cloth prevents perspiration from irritating your skin and running into your eyes and mouth. A sweaty-wet cotton T-shirt cools you more than going shirtless, and it also protects you from sunburn. Clothes, after all, are ingeniously engineered cloth constructions designed to guard us from the discomforts of our environment: frostbite, scratches, bruises, mosquito bites, poison ivy, splinters, and a thousand other hazards. What we wear can simultaneously shield us against unwanted looks and touches and entice wanted ones. We wrap ourselves in cloth to stay warm and comfortable during the long hours of sleep, we lay it on our floors and wrap it around our furniture to cushion our limbs and feet while walking and sitting, and we drape our windows with it to regulate light and air for our comfort. Cloth does all this for us, and at the same time it is an astonishingly fertile means of expression for our aspirations to beauty, sociability, and individuality in our lives.

Because clothes and other fabrics are among our most intimate and prized possessions, the old maxim, who loves the end loves the means, applies forcefully to the arts of caring for and choosing cloth goods. Everyone, no matter how rich or poor or domestically uninclined, can not only benefit from acquiring laundry skills and learning about fabrics but will also find considerable satisfaction in doing so.

Appalachian Know-How

My interest in the subject of laundering and cloth comes from home, which for the greater part of my childhood was a farm in Greene County, in the southwestern, rural Appalachian part of Pennsylvania. This region was in many respects "backward," and we children were taught so in school. All through the fifties, when, we learned, much of the nation was suburban, affluent, automated, and leisurely, we seemed stuck in the nineteenth century. Television reception in the hills was spotty to nonexistent. Outhouses were still common. My best friend had an outhouse and no bathroom—let alone a laundry room—and her mother did the wash by hand in a tub. In my own great-grandmother's house, there was no running water except what was provided by a pump that sat in the middle of her kitchen, with one of those handles you jacked up and down until the water gushed.

My mother had an agitating washing machine with an electric-powered wringer that you fed clothes into by hand. My grandmother and great-grandmother, however, did laundry almost the same way that people did in the nineteenth century, in tubs in the cellar, except that they also had electric wringers—dangerous, hungry beasts that tended to pull in and crush hands and fingers along with sheets and shirts. But the automatic wringers were enormously laborsaving, which you will appreciate if you will try, with unaided muscles, to wring just *one* sopping bedsheet or bath towel dry enough that it does not drip.

The night before wash day, my grandmother gathered tough-to-clean items, such as work and play clothes, and put them to soak in hot sudsy water. On Monday morning, she separated the rest of the laundry into loads, looking out for stains; she used milk on ink, rubbed grease spots with sand, and cleared fruit stains with lemon juice. After attending to stains, she put the loads into a tub of hot sudsy water in which stood a washboard. There they soaked for a while; then she scrubbed them by hand or stirred and beat them with a stick. After the clothes were washed (and bleached and blued) and wrung, she put them in the rinse tubs, then through the wringers again. Finally, shirts, cotton dresses and skirts, and handkerchiefs were dipped in the starch tub (which contained powdered starch dissolved in boiled water—in increasing amounts depending on the degree of stiffness desired). I learned how to do all this on summer Mondays, helping mother or grandmother through the wash, so that on sunny days our backyard, like those of all other respectable citizens, were aflap with snowy sheets and colorful shirts on clotheslines. In a rainy spell or in winter, they hung on lines strung in the cellars, which were dark, airless, and humid even without wet laundry.

Was this fun? No, indeed. It was quite as cheerless and exhausting as it sounds. You don't know dreary if you have never had to slither between cold, wet sheets hanging in a dank, dark, moldy cellar. Supper on Monday night was always Sunday leftovers because the labor of laundering, in addition to all the other necessary chores of farm life and child care, left no time or energy for fresh cooking. I hated wash day. Everyone did. In the nineteenth century, they called it "Blue Monday." Monday was wash day because laundering, followed by ironing, was so physically draining that it was best to do it immediately following the Sabbath rest.

But mine was not a normal childhood of the fifties, when, as I was enviously aware, the more typical family watched *Leave It to Beaver* at its leisure while the laundry happily tumbled and swished in fully automatic washers and dryers. Even a few of my more fortunate Greene County friends had those machines. In 1957, my grandmother was the first in the family to acquire an automatic dryer, and I remember eight or nine of us crowding into the kitchen to examine this marvel. In the 1960s, we, too, finally had big gleaming-white machines, washer and dryer both, churning and rumbling in a real laundry room located not in the cellar but in a warm, airy light nook on the ground floor. As a teenager, I appreciated the blessings of household laundry automation with the same level of fervor that a nineteenth-century housewife might have. I took pleasure in the ease of the modern methods that had conquered the beast and its dismal reign of exhaustion, bone-crushing wringers, and clothes that turned moldy in the damp cellar before they dried.

When my family moved on to modern suburban and urban life, like so many others who had made that journey before us, we took with us what we knew, and we really understood what modern laundry technology was saving us from. Having used our muscles to do what the machines did under those metal lids, we knew intimately the effects of soaking, the difficulties of removing blood and grease, what makes things look white and what fades dyes, and what cold and warm or hot temperatures do to various kinds of cloth. Perhaps surprisingly, we also knew about laundry chemicals—when you would need acid, when base, when a solvent—because we had relied heavily on these to reduce our labor. We understood the difference between detergents and soap, Tide versus Rinso and Ivory Snow flakes. We knew about hard water and water softeners and bleaches. On our cellar shelves, we had stored gentle soap (both cake and flakes) and a cake of harsh soap, a mild and a strong detergent, washing soda, chlorine bleach, mineral spirits or a drycleaning solvent, ammonia, powdered bluing, and powdered starch. For gentle acids (lemon or white vinegar), we ran up to the kitchen, for rubbing alcohol, up to the bathroom.

To all this, we added the general knowledge of fabrics and fibers that were common in a sewing society that was, in some instances, only a generation or two removed from cloth-making in the home. My own maternal grandmother used linen sheets that she had woven and hemmed as a girl in Italy. In Greene County, some attics still held spinning wheels, insurance against the time when disaster might require us to make cloth again. My girlfriends and I learned to embroider, sew, and knit early in childhood. Our absolute favorite pastime, into which we poured extraordinary passion, was making doll clothes. In the process of stitching up hundreds of sometimes gorgeous, occasionally ingenious little garments, we developed a comfortable, intuitive knowledge about fabrics, fibers, finishes and weaves, and thread counts—what worked and what did not, and what we had to ask for at the company store when we went with our dimes and quarters to buy pretty scraps of cloth: best quality muslin 140 thread count, 180 percale, polished cotton, new wool, size 50 *mercerized* thread, a book of sharps, a paper of pins.

Because we had grown up learning the basics of fibers, weaves, finishes, and dyes, we all eventually developed an easy acquaintance with the effects on these of different laundry products and procedures. Such knowledge was then part of ordinary adult competence for most women and many men. For each person, it amounted to a private patchwork of what their parents taught them, bits of science picked up here and there, and countless private experiences and observations. Subjective considerations—such as whether you or a family member perspired more or less or tended to feel warmer or cooler than others, or had more or less sensitive skin—factored subtly into the choices of dress, bed linens, and furnishings. Cultural considerations, what you got used to in your home and society, also entered in, usually unconsciously. The Inuit's habitual and accustomed comfort requires something different from ours, even when we happen to live in the same climate. Because skill in using and caring for cloth interweaves so much that is subjective and traditional with hard, objective facts, it is as much art as science.

Of course, we can learn many useful facts from scientific experts on textiles, fabric design, chemistry, or home economics. But scientific facts, indispensable as they are, are unavoidably put to use through a medium of private taste, household traditions, and domestic habits that are passed down and around over generations. Ultimately, the real experts on home laundering are home launderers, and it is as likely to be true today as it was a hundred years ago that home laundering gives most people better results than professional laundering.

Little that people knew about laundering and home fabrics fifty years ago is out-of-date today. Some new fibers and fabric finishes have been introduced, but with few exceptions the old ones, those your grandparents and great-grandparents used, are also still in common use today. What is really new and different are our machines and tools, the scientific technology that changes how we use what we know and permits us to launder and care for treasured and important cloth possessions without physical strain.

Today, aside from cooking, which I like almost too much to consider work, laundering is my favorite kind of housework. It requires just enough physical involvement to give the satisfying and all-too-uncommon experience of work that unites head and hand. Ninety percent of laundering success is knowledge and experience; 10 percent is physical action and skill. It is sensually pleasing, with its snowy, sweet-smelling suds, warm water, and lovely look and feel of fabric folded or ironed, smooth and gleaming. Best of all is the anticipation of feeling good or looking good in garments and linens restored to freshness and attractiveness through one's own competence and diligence. And during most of the work, especially folding and ironing, you can permit your mind to wander among its own thoughts or you can listen to music or the news or books on tape. You have a chance to enjoy quiet entertainment while being productive. These modest, quiet, private pleasures are valuable even though they are nothing that there ever could—or should—be a buzz about. Nor should we permit advertisers and marketers to invade or exploit this or any arena of domestic life by making it a matter of fashion, display, and buying. Expensive laundry products, machines, aids, and facilities can be attractive and fun to own, but, if you cannot afford them, remember: They are not in the least necessary for doing the laundry well and taking pleasure in the work.

How to Use This Book

In the chapters that follow, I record, enlarge, and occasionally correct the learning about fabrics, fibers, and laundering that came to me from my parents and grandparents. I pass on my own family tradition especially for the benefit of those who did not learn one in their own home. But the book is also for those who did absorb a family tradition and will enjoy supplementing and comparing theirs with someone else's. And I include up-to-date facts about laundering and new kinds of cloth that will be useful to everyone, whether novices or experts, who would like to increase their knowledge without resorting to forbidding texts full of diagrams, jargon, and chemical terms.

This book is not intended to serve as a miscellaneous collection of tips and hints. Although you will find hundreds of tips in it, the book is structured as a book of *systematic* explanations, of fundamentals, whys and wherefores, and unabbreviated ways of doing things. Briefer, more casual approaches to the subject have their uses and their place, but my goal is to provide a thorough home reference book for people who like to know *why*. Tips and hints are used most successfully by those who are most knowledgeable because they can fit the tip into an organized mental context. The person who best wings it, the one who invents the most efficient and fastest shortcuts, is the expert, the experienced hand—not the beginner.

Laundry is divided into three parts. Each part, indeed each chapter, can be read separately, or you can read the book straight through, as you wish. The book is designed to be used both as a reference work, permitting a reader to dip in here or there at will, or, for people who like to read about housekeeping (the way some people like to read about food or travel), as a unified, connected exposition. To find the subject you are interested in, check the Contents or look it up in the Index. In any event, I suggest you read through the Contents and leaf casually through the book just to get a feeling for the way it works.

In Part I, I explain laundering, starting with gathering, storing, sorting into loads, and a discussion of care labels (how far they can or should be disregarded), then progressing through washing, drying, ironing, and folding. Machine and hand-washing, and machine, clothesline, and other methods of drying are all covered, along with the pros and cons of relying on commercial laundries or hired help in the home. These chapters also include a great deal of advice on stain removal; the chemicals of the laundry (laundry detergents, bleaches, softeners, and other products); sanitizing (killing germs, mites, and nits); laundering tricky items; and common laundering problems and their causes and cures.

Part II is about using and storing certain kinds of fabric goods in the home. I begin with some general guidelines on selecting household fabrics. Bed linens and bed dressing are thoroughly discussed, including information on which fibers, weaves, and thread counts in sheets are most comfortable, durable, and launderable, and such useful details as standard dimensions of table and bed linens. I try to arm the reader against some expensive and countercomfort fads in buying and using contemporary linens. Choosing and caring for textile furnishings—upholstery, draperies, and rugs—are also covered, along with some simple methods of mending. In the final chapter, I offer suggestions on keeping good closets for clothes and linens.

In Part III, I explain the basics about cloth and textile fibers. I canvas all common weaves and fabric types—from plain weave, twill, and satin to houndstooth, crepe, gingham, poplin, serge, batiste and lawn, oxford cloth, and more—teaching how to name and identify them and to know which is better for given purposes. In Part III, you will also find a description of each type of fiber commonly used in clothes, linens, and home furnishings—cotton, linen, silk, wool, hemp, and other natural fibers along with polyester, nylon, the rayons, and the rest of the synthetic and man-made fibers. For each type of fiber, I provide information on judging quality, comfort, rational uses, typical weaknesses and strong points, and detailed care characteristics. In addition, Part III includes simple explanations of the finishes and dyes fabrics are subjected to, and how these affect their laundering and care as well as their suitability in various uses.

Let me caution readers against deciding too quickly that the material in Part III does not interest them. It contains much useful lore about things you love. Did you know that wool actually warms when wet? Did you know that resin treatments that make cottons less wrinkly also weaken them so that they wear out faster? Part III provides a great deal of similar information that is useful, even indispensable, in the laundry. And, I hope, it also helps to reawaken us to the part of the physical world that we experience most intimately—on our skin—and reacquaints us with it in a way that makes us more at home in our homes.

PART I

ABOUT LAUNDERING

1

Gathering, Storing, and Sorting Laundry

Laundering at home vs. sending out the laundry . . . Reducing the amount of laundry in your home . . . Scheduling; how often you should launder; laundry day . . . Deciding when clothes need washing; clothes hampers . . . Why we sort before laundering . . . Care labels; the rules of sorting; sorting by washing method, color, level of soil, potential for damage; compromises in sorting . . . What counts as white; more about sorting colors; bleaches . . . How to test for colorfastness . . . Pretreating and other prewash preparations

The automated home laundry is a great boon to comfort and happiness. Yet more and more people, caught in the terrible time-squeeze of the modern home, think of it only with abhorrence. I suspect they have not thought through the drop in their standard of living that would follow if all the fabrics in their home had to be sent out for laundering. In any event, like so many other kinds of modern housework, home laundering is much more a matter of knowing than of doing a lot. Once you know how, home laundering is little trouble and provides great benefits.

Should You Send Out the Laundry?

Centuries ago, well-to-do city dwellers sent their laundry to the country, where there were rivers to wash it and fields in which to spread it in the sun for drying and bleaching. Aristocratic French families at the end of the seventeenth century sent their soiled linens all the way to the sunny Caribbean for laundering. By 1900, the custom of sending the laundry out (or sometimes of having a laundress come do it) had been adopted by other classes and was widespread. This system had some inconveniences—lost or poorly laundered clothes, damage, stains, clothes and linens that could not be used because they were away being laundered—but these were overridden by its great benefits. One hundred years ago, laundering was highly labor-intensive and required elaborate facilities for washing and drying, including boilers, wringers, and mangles, a whole collection of irons and ironing equipment, drying contraptions of various sorts, and ample space indoors and out. Few city families could supply all this muscle power, time, equipment, and space—or know-how—so out went the laundry, or, in some cases, in came the poor laundry women.

Then came automatic washing machines and other improvements for home laundries, and the private home again took on sole responsibility for the job. Commercial laundries disappeared by the hundreds. That is why some feminists who wish to relieve women of the burdens of housekeeping have bitterly complained that home laundering is a case of a battle once won and then lost again. The calls for once more giving up home laundering, now that women have gone out to work in such numbers, have become louder and louder. In my view, home laundering is so easy, convenient, inexpensive, and successful that it is here to stay for most of us. For some, however, sending it out would be the best thing to do.

If you are single and working long hours or are part of a two-career family with children, you may sometimes find that this is a good choice for you. I know from experience that when you are tired and stressed from work, nothing cheers you up like someone delivering bundles of crisp, clean laundry. I also know from experience, however, that commercial laundries do not do nearly as good a job as you can at home, cause much faster wearing and fading of clothes and linens, and will rarely give the individual attention to cherished garments or expensive linens that you will. Commercial laundering means that you have to give up either having especially nice things or trying to keep them looking good, and you suffer the same inconveniences it caused a century ago. The garment you desperately need for a trip cannot be retrieved from the bowels of the laundry establishment until the appointed day, and even then maybe not. Special sheets or extra towels unexpectedly needed for company may be gone. Cracked buttons, discoloration, fading, and loss are still common.

The greatest problem for most people, however, is the large expense of sending the laundry out. It costs much, much more than doing the wash at home, even when the laundering services are mediocre. To have it done with anything approaching the delicate attention to individual garments and laundry problems that can be offered at home costs more than most people, even some who are relatively well off, can afford. (Because dry cleaning costs even more than commercial laundering, most of us choose some kind of laundering over dry cleaning whenever possible.)

Many people can afford the occasional use of good commercial laundries, however, and taking advantage of this possibility when you must work extralong hours or when you or your children are sick or when there is a series of meetings you must attend at the time when you would ordinarily be laundering, can be such a boon that it is worth dipping into your emergency nest egg for this service now and then. Using commercial laundries only occasionally rather than regularly has the additional advantage that it causes less overall wear and tear on your clothes than habitual commercial laundering. Another option is to use commercial laundering services for some portion of your laundry; dress shirts are the classic choice here because they almost always require heavy ironing. Just sending out the shirts saves a significant amount of time and causes a minimum of inconvenience. (But be sure to stock more shirts in the wardrobe than you would find necessary if you were doing them at home.)

You can also have someone come to your home to do your laundry, but you must take care to pick a conscientious person who knows how to do it, for the damage caused by sloppy or ignorant laundering can be immense. You might try asking the prospective employee to describe his or her laundering procedures. Questions about care labels, bleaches, permanent-press cycles, and drying temperatures tend to smoke out areas of ignorance. Even when you hire someone who understands laundry basics, however, you cannot expect the same kind of knowledge and attention you would give the task yourself; nor can you expect to pass along everything you know—about your clothes, linens, and fabrics as well as about laundering—especially if you have limited time to devote to training someone. And if you are going to sort, pretreat, and do a few hand-washables yourself, you are not going to save much time

REDUCING LAUNDRY

You can reduce the amount of laundry you have to do each week by taking any or all of the following steps:

Hang towels to dry carefully after each use.

Instead of putting lightly worn outer garments in the clothes hamper, spot-clean them (if necessary), let them air, and hang or fold them neatly.

Wear T-shirts, dress shields, camisoles, or slips under shirts, blouses, and dresses.

When you clean, cook, or do other messy jobs, protect clothing with smocks or aprons.

Use good bed manners to save laundering of bed linens and blankets: Avoid lying or sitting on the bed wearing street clothes; and always wash at least your face and hands before getting into bed. Make up your bed in the traditional way described in chapter 15, "Beds and Bedding," pages 213–20.

by having someone else do the rest, which, after all, does not take much time. What it takes is your being at home for a few hours at a stretch so that you can change loads and remove loads from the dryer. You can be doing many other things while the laundry proceeds.

There are many people who truly cannot manage to be at home for a few hours. More often, however, the hours are available, but doing the laundry is felt to be a strain and a bother in a busy life. When this is the case, the cause is often a lack of experience and know-how combined with the absence of a routine that includes laundering. Habitual conduct takes the least effort, and doing what is habitual soothes rather than stresses. Know-how reduces the amount of attention a task takes and the amount of annoyance you experience in carrying it out, which enables you to focus on other things. Know-how in laundering also enables you to make the things you care about look good and last long.

Scheduling

> "Ain't no use havin' soap an' water if you ain't got my ingredient.
> . . . I'll whisper it. . . . It's . . . dirt. . . . Get it? . . . D-I-R-T. Dirt."
> —UNCLE BALDWIN IN WALT KELLY'S *Pogo*

Laundry Day: How Often Should You Launder? In most households, doing laundry only once or twice a week is more effective and efficient than doing a load or two every day, and that is because the first step in preparing to do laundry is to accumulate an adequate stock of dirty clothes and linens to wash. It is inefficient and ineffective to run washers and dryers with very small loads; clothes come cleaner if washed in medium or larger loads and if articles of different sizes, large and small, are mixed loosely together in a load. (See chapter 4, "Laundering," page 56.) This sort of mix will also help prevent the load from becoming unbalanced. (When the load becomes unbalanced, the washing machine may automatically shut down or dance wildly across the floor.) Clothes dry faster, too, if the dryer has at least a medium fill. Moreover, if you wait until a good stock is accumulated, you will have fewer temptations to give some items improper treatment by washing them with a load of dissimilar items.

On the other hand, the accumulation of laundry should be small enough to be completed in a reasonable amount of time, and each laundry day should be fairly close in time to the last one—a week or less. The longer the dirt stays on fabrics, the harder it is to remove. In many instances, articles should receive interim treatment to prevent permanent staining or discoloration. Dirt, particularly perspiration and many food stains, also weakens fabrics, causing them to deteriorate, fade, or turn yellow. Mildew and odor are more likely to develop if laundry sits unwashed for a while; mildew can permanently discolor fabrics. And, of course, the sooner the laundry is washed, the sooner the clothes and linens are available for using again.

Choosing one day a week when most of the laundry is always done will go far toward making laundry easier to do while keeping life pleasant and orderly. One may choose to do a smaller wash of similar items on a second washing day—say, toddlers' clothes or towels and linens or other items requiring relatively uncomplicated treatment.

Households in which all adults work full-time out of the home may prefer to have two laundry days (or evenings), a major and a minor one, or in households with lots of laundry, two roughly equal laundry days. If you are going to have two laundering days, you may help yourself to stay organized by doing a different kind of laundry on each day—for example, towels and linens on one, clothing on the other. Cleaning day, when you strip the beds and put out fresh towels, is also a good day to wash towels, sheets, tea towels, tablecloths, and other household linens. Clothes may be better done on a separate laundering day from linens and towels because they are usually more complicated to sort and tend to. If you do any ironing, you will find you stay more organized, and the clothes stay fresher, if you do it as soon as possible after washing, or even while you are washing.

It is possible to do small amounts of laundry several times a week or every day. This system actually tends to work best in large, highly organized households, particularly those in which someone stays home to keep house. But it also tends to be adopted as a kind of default system in more disorganized households where no one stays home. Frequent laundering geared to the needs of the day makes it hard to get properly sorted and balanced loads. Besides, this method never gives one a sense of repose, freedom from an accomplished chore. Nor does it lead one to form expectations and habits in accordance with what clothes and linens will be available for use at a given time. And because it requires you to attend to the laundry so frequently, it is a system that tends to break down, creating disorder and crisis and more frustration. The system of doing laundry once or twice a week depends on having a stock of clothes and linens that will last a week and be adequate for occasional emergencies as well—but this is usually a condition easily met in the era of inexpensive fabrics. Some people manage to have even fewer, but longer, laundry days by stocking extra-large quantities of clothes and linens, a satisfactory procedure so long as proper stain-removal procedures and pretreatments are used on stored soiled clothes. Centuries ago, the difficulties of laundering meant that in some large, wealthy households linens were washed only annually or semiannually. These households held astonishing stores of linens, dozens of sheets and tablecloths, for this was necessary to get from one rare laundering day to the next. (See chapter 15, "Beds and Bedding," for a discussion of adequate stocks of linens in modern households.)

CLOTH CARE ROUTINES

An overall routine for the care and cleaning of clothes, linens, and other fabrics in the home might or might not resemble the one below. Use anything that works for your home, and ignore the rest.

DAILY

Put soiled clothes in hamper and hang up or fold worn but still wearable clothes

Put out fresh kitchen linens (dish towels, dishcloths, tablecloths, napkins) if necessary

Check bathroom towels and change if soiled or not fresh-smelling

WEEKLY

Change bed linens and bathroom towels

Do laundry

Do one minilaundering (in households that prefer two laundering days)

Iron (if you iron)

Send out and pick up dry cleaning

MONTHLY, SEASONALLY, OR INTERMITTENTLY

Change and launder underbedding (mattress covers and pillow protectors or under-covers) and washable covers, comforters, quilts, and blankets that you leave on the bed while you sleep

Dry-clean nonwashable spreads and covers

Wash or sun and air pillows

Briefly straighten up closets

SEMIANNUALLY OR ANNUALLY

Dry-clean nonwashable blankets, quilts, comforters, and spreads (or more often, as needed)

Remove out-of-season clothing from closet, clean and store it, replace with seasonal clothing (in spring and fall)

Give or throw away or make into rags unused or worn-out clothing, linens

Shampoo rugs, upholstery, and throw pillows

Wash or dry-clean curtains and draperies

Gathering and Storing

When Do Clothes Need Washing? All new clothes, sheets, and other household fabrics that are launderable should be washed once before they are used. After this, wash launderable clothes, linens, and household textiles when they look, feel, or smell dirty. Even if they look fine, you should launder them if you know that they have accumulated dirt and dust, because particulate dirt and dust will contribute to wearing them out. Particles of dust cut into cloth like tiny knives, weakening it and rendering it susceptible to holes and tears. Perspiration, food, and other substances that get on clothes during wear cause deterioration or discoloration in many fabrics.

On the other hand, because laundering and dry cleaning also age cloth, you should avoid resorting to them too frequently. Most of us today do tend to over-launder simply because laundering is so easy; children find it much easier to deposit a barely worn garment in a laundry hamper than to hang it nicely for airing or fold it neatly for the shelf. Of course, if you have perspired heavily in a garment, you must wash it before wearing it again, and what used to be called "body linen"—underwear and other intimate clothing—always needs washing after just one wear. But if you get a spot on a fresh garment, try washing or cleaning off just the spot with plain water or a commercial spot remover or a cleaning fluid (unless the garment is a silk or other fabric that may water-spot or unless the spot cleaning may leave a ring or faded spot—test your procedure first in an inconspicuous area). And rather than throw the shirt you wore for an hour into the laundry hamper, put it on a hanger and let it air, then replace it in your closet for wearing again. Brush and air clothes and blankets, especially woolens, after use. Sometimes you can simply wipe down wools and synthetics with a barely damp, white, nonlinting cloth to keep them clean longer. (If you do this, be sure to air them until they are absolutely dry before replacing them in drawers or closets.) Wear T-shirts under dress shirts, and use camisoles, slips, or dress shields under blouses and dresses. By these means, you can often keep launderable garments free of visible soil and heavy perspiration so that they remain fresh enough for two or more wearings before laundering. If you are on a tight budget, all this is even more important for clothes that must be dry-cleaned.

Clothes Hampers. As clothes and linens become soiled through regular use, collect them in a clothes hamper or other receptacle. Let towels and other damp articles dry before you put them into the hamper, and place the hamper in a dry room, not in the bathroom (unless you have a bath suite with a dry room separate from the shower and tub). Stored damp laundry may mildew or become malodorous, and the odor can taint the air in the room where they are stored. Gathering soiled laundry in an airy container, such as a wicker or woven basket or hamper, will help avoid this problem. (You can sprinkle baking soda in a hamper to deodorize it as well; the soda can go right into the washing machine, as it is a gentle detergent booster.) Lidded baskets of wicker or similar material with a polyurethane coating are a good choice for hampers; air can enter through the interstices, and the smooth coating protects clothes from being snagged and the container itself from being damaged by moisture.

Very greasy, muddy, or heavily soiled clothing should be stored separately if there is any danger of the soil getting on other articles in the hamper. Fine and delicate items should also be stored separately for laundering so as to avoid their coming into contact with soil, odors, snags, or anything else that might harm them. A smooth cloth sack that will breathe and can be hung in some convenient place (not your clothes closet) works best. Later on, these items are laundered separately to protect them from harsher cleaning methods that they will not easily withstand.

Sorting the Laundry

> The laundry-maid should commence her labours on Monday morning by a careful examination of the articles committed to her care, and enter them in the washing-book; separating the white linen and collars, sheets and body-linen into one heap, fine muslins into another, coloured cotton and linen fabrics into a third, woollens into a fourth, and the coarser kitchen and other greasy cloth into a fifth. Every article should be examined for ink or grease spots, or for fruit or wine-stains.
> —*Mrs Beeton's Book of Household Management,* 1861

Why Sort? Sorting is the process of separating soiled clothes and linens into heaps or piles such that all the articles in a pile can safely receive similar laundry treatment—similar washing methods, washing products, water temperature, washing vigor and duration, and, usually, drying methods, times, and temperatures. Sorting the laundry has become more complicated than it was for Mrs. Beeton (who wrote what became the bible of British housekeeping for more than half a century) because there are new fibers, finishes, and fabric constructions to deal with. Even care labels may seem to complicate matters instead of simplifying them. I recently counted ten different sets of laundry directions included on the care labels of the clothes included in one medium-sized load (out of three loads washed that day in my home). Drying instructions add even more complications. If you tried to obey each care label to the letter, you might end up with thirty or forty laundry loads on every laundry day. As a result of these complications, a kind of minicrisis of sorting has developed in which the old rules no longer seem to work, and the standard consequence of a breakdown in rules and values has ensued: the youth have become skeptical and nihilistic. They do not believe it is possible to figure it all out. They do not sort their clothes for laundering, and they sneer that sorting makes no difference.

But they are wrong. You can still figure out how to sort, and if you don't sort, over time your clothes will suffer the subtle or not-so-subtle bleeding of dyes that turns all light-colored clothes dull pink or dingy gray, along with shrinking, pilling, tearing, and other problems. Damage can be mild or immense. The bad effects of undesirable laundering habits are often cumulative and long-term. You will not necessarily see them at once; they may appear over weeks and months. Some people know very well what is the cause of their pink undershorts and towels and sheets of uniform dinginess, but they believe that their time is so short that bright, attractive colors, good fit, and unpilled knits are luxuries that they cannot afford. Doing laundry well, however, takes little more time than doing it poorly, and endless shopping to replace goods that prematurely look bad or function badly takes far more time in the long run. Besides, when you find something you like, you want it to last. Most of us cannot afford to buy whatever we want whenever we want it, even assuming that another shirt just like the ruined one could be found.

Care Labels. Chapter 2, "Carefully Disregarding Care Labels," tells you how to interpret and follow care labels and provides explanations of terms and symbols used on care labels. Sorting clothes properly requires knowing what their care labels say. The care label warns you against procedures that will likely do damage and tells you a safe way to clean the garment. If reading a lot of care labels seems onerous and you are not accustomed to it, be assured that as you gain experience, you come to know your own clothes and linens. Eventually, you will read care labels only when you first buy and launder things, as you get into the habit of keeping this kind of information in mind. If you, like me, choose to second-guess care labels, it is virtually guaranteed that sooner or later you are going to wreck something. Ignoring care labels has led me to turn a crisp linen suit into a limp rag and to shrink a chic rayon/acetate crepe dress so severely that I was unable to pull it on over my shoulders. When this happens to you, be prepared to shed philosophical tears and blame no one but yourself. And consult chapter 2, "Carefully Disregarding Care Labels," for suggestions on reducing the risks of care label defiance.

Rules of Sorting. Once the laundry has been gathered, sort it into piles according to these five rules:

1. sort according to the appropriate wash cycle or procedure based on fiber and fabric type,
2. sort by color,
3. sort by level or kind of soil,
4. sort according to whether some clothes will cause other clothes to pick up lint, snag, tear, and so on; and finally

5. make sorting compromises, as necessary and safe, to create a reasonable number of good-sized loads.

Wash pairs and sets (socks, gloves, sheets, pajamas, etc.) in the same load. If you wash one piece of a matched set without the other, you will end with unmatched sets because items fade differently and subtly alter in color depending on what other items are in the load they are washed with and how often they are washed.

First, Sort According to Wash Cycle or Procedure Based on Fiber and Fabric Type. Separate washable clothes and linens, in accordance with their fiber and fabric type, into four piles corresponding to the four basic laundering cycles or procedures: regular, permanent-press, gentle machine-washing, and hand-washing. As you sort, follow Mrs. Beeton's advice: look for stains and spots and pretreat them. Note that although there are four basic procedures, most of us use only one or two on any given laundry day. Thus this step in sorting typically, but not always, amounts merely to separating out a few items that need some sort of special treatment. The basic procedures are explained more fully in chapter 4, "Laundering," but here is a summary of which clothes get which treatment:

Regular machine-washing. Normal or regular washing treatment is appropriate for sturdy white and colorfast cottons and linens that have not received antiwrinkling treatments or other finishes that need special protection. Close plain and twill weaves and sturdy knits, such as T-shirts and underwear, diapers, towels of all sorts, wrinkly sheets, work clothes, play clothes, and sportswear ordinarily receive laundering on the regular cycle of the machine. (See "The Regular Cycle," pages 52–53, in chapter 4, "Laundering.") In my experience, many, if not most, households still wash most of their clothes on the regular or normal setting.

Permanent-press machine-washing. Permanent-press, wrinkle-resistant, durable-press, or "easy-care" cotton, linen, and rayon fabrics, together with blends of these, get washed on the machine's permanent-press cycle, as do most garments made of some synthetics: polyester, nylon, some spandex, and blends containing such fibers. (See "The Permanent-Press Cycle," pages 53–54, in chapter 4.) Generally speaking, when laundering blends, choose the most conservative laundering treatment required by any of the fibers present in the blend.

Gentle machine-washing. The gentle cycle is used for fine cotton knits, machine-washable silk, wool, acrylic and modacrylic, some spandex, triacetate, some washable acetate, viscose rayon, and blends and items with linings containing them. Laces, netting, fringed items, embroidery, fine lingerie, loosely knitted or loosely woven articles, and other fine, sheer, or delicately made articles of any fiber need gentle washing. This cycle is also proper for sheer weaves such as cambric or lawn; satin weaves and other weaves with floats (these will snag and abrade easily), irregular surfaces, low yarn counts, or open or loose weaves of any sort in which there are spaces between yarns (because these are prone to snagging and shrinking); washable laces; articles with fragile or loosely attached trims, ties, or decorations that might get pulled off in vigorous washing; anything unusually susceptible to abrasion, pilling, or snagging; and many specialty items, including nonwoven materials or those bonded with various adhesives. (See "The Delicate or Gentle Cycle," pages 55–56, in chapter 4.)

Hand-washing. Hand-washing is usually best for some washable acetate, washable delicate acrylics, silks, wools, rayons, some cotton knits, and especially fragile, old, or other delicate articles. The difference between this group and the previous one is only a matter of degree. Especially delicate fibers and fabric constructions and fabrics that have become fragile through age should be hand-washed. Panty hose and stockings are safest washed by hand, too, but you can try putting them in the machine on the gentle cycle in a mesh bag if you are willing to risk occasional snags or runs. (See "Hand-Washing," pages 61–64, in chapter 4. Machine "hand-wash" cycles are also discussed in that section.)

When sorting by fiber content and construction, do not forget that some washable garments are made of two or more fibers or constructions that might ordinarily get two or more different treatments. If so, always choose the more conservative. For example, if a dress has a delicate, sheer top but a sturdy cotton skirt, give it gentle treatment. If a shirt is a cotton/polyester blend, wash it as though it were polyester. Pay attention to linings, trim, buttons, and similar parts of a garment that might require treatment different from the rest.

Remember: Although there are four basic laundry procedures, you may use only one or two of them on any given day. I rarely use more than two—regular, and either gentle machine-washing or hand-washing.

Second, Sort by Color. Once you have sorted your laundry into piles according to the cycle or procedure best suited to its fiber type, divide each of those piles into color-compatible groupings. The basic color groupings are these: all white, mostly white (prints with a white background, towels with a colored stripe at the border), and light, medium or bright, and dark colors. As much as possible, wash things of the same hue together. Separate out bleeding colors for separate washing or for washing with like colors, as necessary. You should also divide the color piles into those that will and those that will not receive some sort of bleaching. Generally speaking, white and colorfast colored articles made of bleachable fibers are the components of the wash that can benefit from bleach of some sort.

Third, Sort by Level and Kind of Soil. Separate out of the foregoing piles any extra-heavily soiled articles or those with heavy grease, mud, or other soil. If you live in the city, as I do, you will have to do this very rarely—perhaps only when your child has a muddy day at the playground or if you have cloth diapers to wash. Articles with heavy or unusual soil and stains, particularly greasy or oily ones, must be washed separately from clothes without such soil (and sometimes from each other) for two reasons. First, there is a danger that the heavy soil will be redeposited on more lightly soiled clothes or that serious stains will spread to other items in the wash. White and light-colored clothes are particularly susceptible to turning dingy, gray, or yellow if washed with heavily soiled items. Second, heavy and unusual soils usually demand special, more vigorous treatment to which you may not wish to subject your ordinary wash. Stronger treatments cause faster wearing and fading and are inappropriate for many fibers and fabric constructions. Diapers should be laundered only with other diapers, using a presoak and sometimes a double wash as well.

If you have serious infectious illness in your home, you may also wish to wash the clothes, towels, and linens of the sick person separately. I know elderly women who tell me that in their day you would also have separated handkerchiefs, bed linens, and body linens from table linens; it would have been considered unsanitary to mix them up. No one does this anymore. Only diapers still are (and should be) washed separately as a routine matter. But keeping germ-laden materials separate when a household member has a serious infectious illness is not a bad idea.

Get off as much of the soil as possible before inserting the clothes into the washing machine, scraping it off with an old table knife if necessary, or rinsing briefly by hand in a separate basin or laundry tub. Scrape or rub off mud from garden clothes and gloves. (On washing cloth diapers, see pages 126–27.)

Fourth, Sort According to Whether Any Items Will Cause Other Clothes to Pick Up Lint, Snag, Tear, and So On. Separate out of each of the foregoing piles any clothes that might mechanically damage or spoil the appearance of other clothes in the load. Again, if your laundry is at all like mine, potentially damaging and linting articles are rarely a problem (at least since my son disdained buckled overalls and I gave up my chenille bathrobe). This category includes items that produce lint or pick up lint easily and those with heavy buckles or clasps, zippers that might catch lace or ribbons, or other features that might cause damage. What is dangerous is relative to the other clothes in the load. A buckle or clasp might tear chiffon, lace, net, or other open weaves but not denims. Clothes and linens that produce lint include some towels and other terry-cloth items, especially when they are new; flannel; chenille bedspreads or bathrobes; and rags or fabrics that are fraying. Clothes and linens that will attract or hold lint include those that develop static electricity (polyester, acrylic, nylon, and other synthetics primarily) and pile fabrics like corduroy and velvet. Linting fabrics should be washed separately from any of these that would show the lint badly. For example, dark clothes will show white lint far more than white or light ones will. Note that household furnishings such as washable draperies, small rugs, and slipcovers often produce lint and should almost always be washed separately.

Fifth, Make Compromises! After you have completed sorting by the foregoing rules, you may find yourself with one or more loads consisting of a single item or too few items to make up a good load. In that case, make compromises. Compromises are occasional choices made in the interests of efficiency. Engaged in too often, they will eventually spoil your clothes and linens. If you have time and hand-washing would not be too difficult, consider separately hand-washing one or two items—the shirt that bleeds, the one unbleachable white item—that do not belong with a load according to the foregoing criteria. Here are some guidelines for making effective sorting compromises:

- Combine bleach-fast, nearly-all-white prints with pure whites (excluding orlons and nylons) and treat all as you would the pure whites. But see the discussion of whites, colors, and bleach below.
- Wash synthetic and natural-fiber whites together, giving them all permanent-press treatment. Synthetic whites that receive permanent-press washing can usually take bleach, even if they do not need it. So if you would have used bleach on the natural fibers and you can confirm (by checking labels or testing) that the synthetics can take it, use bleach.
- If color, colorfastness, and soil type do not preclude it, include items that can take more strenuous treatment in a load that is to receive less strenuous treatment. For instance, colored cotton T-shirts that are only lightly soiled could be given permanent-press or gentle treatment now and then, even though ordinarily they require stronger washing techniques. Or put nylons and polyesters that you would ideally give permanent-press treatment in the gentle cycle to wash, making sure you use a cold rinse (and adjust the drying treatment too).
- When an article is not heavily soiled, combine it with any color-compatible load that is to receive milder or less vigorous treatment.
- Wash light coloreds with bright coloreds, or bright coloreds with dark coloreds. Watch out for bleeding dyes.

More About Whites, Colors, and Bleach; Testing for Colorfastness

Whites and Nearly Whites. What, for sorting purposes, counts as white? "White" means white. Off-whites and creams are not whites, and neither are mostly white prints. Whites are best washed only with other fabrics that are all white. For the sake of making up a load, however, you may occasionally compromise this principle according to the guidelines sketched below. White or light nylons and orlons—orlon has not been made since 1990, but some is still in use—will pick up any faint hint of color in the wash water, even the all-but-invisible taint of pastels, and may become dingy or gray. If this happens, it may be quite difficult or impossible to restore their original whiteness. With other fibers, however, such an accident is often reparable. (See also chapter 9, "Common Laundry Mishaps and Problems," page 136.)

If you have a number of whites with an occasional touch of color, it is best to wash them in a load made up of other such items. However, washable articles that are white except for some colorfast colored trim may often be treated as whites for sorting purposes—for example, men's athletic shorts made in white cotton with colored piping, sheets or pillowcases with edges sturdily satin-stitched in colored or black thread or with colored embroidery, or white dish towels with a band of colorfast color at each hem. Any color on such items is almost always fast to detergent and water; if it were not, there would be no way to launder it without tainting the white with the color of the trim. (Unfortunately, you may occasionally find that you have purchased just such a ridiculous item. I once bought a child's bathing suit, marked "Machine-washable," whose red stripes, after being immersed in ordinary chilly lake water, proceeded to bleed enthusiastic-red on its blue stripes and on white beach wraps and continued to do so after any number of immersions. Such an article should be returned to the retailer or manufacturer.) Other items that may occasionally be treated as whites for sorting purposes are colorfast prints that are mostly white with a little color—a white shirt with fine pinstripes, a sheet with pastel flowers, or white pajamas strewn with colored balloons. But test all of these for colorfastness to detergent and water before adding any to a white load. (Testing is explained on pages 21–22.)

Bleaching Whites and Mostly Whites. The appearance of whites and mostly whites can sometimes be dramatically improved with the use of bleaches. Almost all colors that are fast to detergent and water are also fast to oxygen bleach, which can practically always be used safely. For more information on using bleaches, see "Bleaches" in the Glossary of Laundry Products and Additives at the end of chapter 4. When mostly white items (white with a colored border, piping or trim, or mostly white prints) are also fast to chlorine bleach, they usually benefit from an occasional bleaching with chlorine bleach or an activated oxygen bleach. (Use the tests for bleach-fastness on pages 21–22. Remember that the color in a white-background print might be fast to hot water and detergent but not to bleach.) In my own household, almost all such fabrics are chlorine-bleachable, including towels, children's print cotton knit undergarments, pajamas, and shirts. Remember that low labeling (care labeling that prescribes more conservative treatment than is necessary) is common on white and mostly white cottons and linens. On most washdays I use bleach, including chlorine bleach, on several articles whose labels proscribe it, without the slightest damage, and many of these have been receiving chlorine bleach now and then for years. However, using any kind of bleach when the care label says not to is risky; some all-white fabrics should be bleached neither with chlorine bleach nor with all-fabric bleach. You must always test. Even when your test shows no damage, you must think about the long-term effects and possible forms of damage that will not show up right away; there are many reasons (besides the possibility of causing the colors to run) why such an instruction might be included.

Even if you use a chlorine bleach on articles with bleach-fast colors only occasionally, you may nonetheless notice over the long run that this makes the colors fade more quickly than they otherwise would. This result may be acceptable in many instances or, at least, it may be preferable to the alternative of dingy, yellowed, or grayish-looking clothes. If you are not prepared to accept any degree of increase in fading, do not use chlorine bleach on these articles. Try an oxygen bleach instead.

Off-whites and pastels will lighten if you regularly subject them to chlorine bleach, and they may eventually turn white. Never bleach one piece of a matched set and not the others. Nonetheless, you can occasionally wash very light bleach-fast pastel or cream-colored cotton sheets or an off-white cotton blouse that has become dingy or gray with whites that are being chlorine bleached. This treatment usually helps remove the dinginess. But do not do this if you would object to a lightening of tone in pale colors. And do not include white nylon or orlon in such loads.

Light, Bright, and Dark Colors. When you sort colored clothes for laundering, divide the loads initially by color intensity, separating the laundry into light and pastel colors, medium or bright colors, and dark colors. Even clothes that are theoretically colorfast may lose a tiny bit of color each time they are washed. That tiny bit of color from, say, a navy blue shirt will be invisible if deposited on a forest green skirt but it could muddy a pastel yellow one. Hue matters too. You will keep colors most clear and true if to the greatest extent possible you wash like colors together—oranges with reds, bright blues with purples, navy with black, light tan with cream. This is a principle that must be compromised to some degree each time you wash.

Separating Out Clothes Whose Dyes Bleed Color. Care labels that say "Wash separately" or "Wash with like colors" should be taken very seriously; articles that lack care labels should be carefully tested for colorfastness before washing. Instructions of this kind indicate that the dyes in the articles are likely to bleed during laundering and give an ugly, unwanted coloration to all the clothes washed in the same load. The story behind the labels, however, is slightly complicated. Some dyes that bleed will do so to some extent—sometimes greatly—every time they are washed; others will bleed only very little, but visibly. Those that bleed greatly should always be washed separately. Those with dyes that visibly bleed very little should be washed only with like colors. Many other items, such as towels, have dyes that bleed the first two or three times they are exposed to water, or to water and detergent, and then stop. These items are actually colorfast; the fabrics are simply giving up excess dye on the first few washes. (A good manufacturer will make this clear on the label by instructing you to wash the article separately or with like colors for two or three washes only.) If your care labels simply say "Wash separately" or "Wash with like colors," be observant. Retest the garments after two or three washes to see if they are still bleeding color.

Denim, madras, and fabrics dyed with vegetable or "natural" dyes are among those that bleed color their entire lives. Fluorescent colors, too, tend to pose problems. (You should not treat fluorescent dyes with stain removers unless you have first tested them.) Blue denims, whose notorious fading is sometimes valued and sometimes deplored, depending on the current fashion, continue to bleed a little color even if they are "stonewashed" or "prewashed" when you buy them. New blue jeans that have not been prewashed or faded should be washed only with very dark blues and colors darker than the jeans— deep brown, charcoal, black. You may safely wash blue jeans that have faded to light blue with medium-color loads, always keeping in mind that the more closely you can match the colors of any colored load, the better—that is, it is best to wash the blue jeans with medium purples or grays or greens.

Madras garments are supposed to fade, and one is supposed to prize the changes in their looks as the different colors in them fade and merge over time. They must always be washed separately.

If you have a garment that will bleed or if a care label advises you to "Wash with like colors" and you lack any like colors, you are going to have to wash it alone; this may mean by hand if your washer cannot accommodate a very tiny load without coming unbalanced or wasting too much water and energy (something to think about when you are buying clothes and linens).

Remember that many dyes tend to fade more over the lifetime of the garment when you use hotter water, stronger detergents, and stronger bleaches. Preserving color and getting the cleanest wash are goals that have to be balanced.

If you have a washing disaster involving dyes that bleed, try the suggestions on page 136 in chapter 9.

Bleaching Colored Clothes. For dinginess or grayness in colored clothes, use an "all-fabric" or oxygen bleach. Many colored clothes, especially prints, are also fast to chlorine bleach. Test first to ensure that all articles in a load are fast to whatever bleach you are using.

Pretreating and Other Prewash Preparations

Once the laundry is sorted, final preparations for washing are done as follows:

Pretreating. Pretreat stains, spots, and heavily soiled areas either while you are sorting and making loads or, if the problem is likely to be hard to remove, as soon as possible after the garment becomes soiled or stained. Pretreatments are often especially useful on cuffs, collars, the undersides of sleeves that have rested on desks or papers all day, and the area at the waist that leans against a table or desk edge. Pretreatments are particularly important for oily stains and areas that take up body oils on synthetics, and the cooler the wash temperature to be used, the more important they are. (See "Pretreatments and prewash stain removers" in the Glossary of Laundry Products and Additives at the end of chapter 4.)

To pretreat, rub a little liquid detergent or spray or rub a pretreatment product or stick on the soiled area. You can also rub the area with a paste of detergent and water or pure bar soap (one that contains no moisturizers, medications, or dyes); dampen the area first when you use either of these treatments.

If there is any question as to the safety of a pretreatment substance, it should be tested on an inconspicuous area of the garment—on the wrong side of a hem or on a seam allowance. Simply apply the pretreatment product to the test area, wait ten minutes or so, and then check for ill effects: staining, fading, bleeding, or other problems. If you have done a good deal of pretreating, you may not need as much detergent in the wash water as you would otherwise have used.

Test fabrics for colorfastness and bleachability on an out-of-sight area.

Preparing the Clothes. Some commonsense precautions are necessary to prepare the clothes for the machine or washtub:

- Turn inside out any blue jeans or other articles that may fade or whose color may abrade (if you wish to prevent that); also turn inside out articles made of synthetic fibers, knits, and other articles prone to pilling or that have poor abrasion resistance. The creases of cotton fabrics that have received resin treatment to prevent wrinkling are particularly vulnerable to abrasion. Turn corduroys inside out to avoid wearing down the pile and to reduce lint. Heat-transfer, pigment, or other prints that might rub off will also be safer turned inside out. But remember that turning a garment inside out can make it hard to get heavy soil or stains off the protected right side; sometimes you will want to omit this step for the sake of a cleaner outcome.
- Check pockets, cuffs, pleats, and folds for coins, keys, crayons, pens, tissues, papers, lint, and so on. Hard objects, such as coins and keys, can damage the smooth surfaces of the washer and dryer tubs, leaving rough places that might snag, tear, or abrade clothes. Crayons and pens can mark much of the load. Tissues, paper, lint, and the like will adhere to the laundered clothes and prove troublesome to remove.

- In a mesh bag, place hosiery, articles that tear and snag such as lace, articles with fringe that might fray, tangle, or become detached, and small items that might otherwise get lost. A zippered pillow cover or a pillowcase with the opening secured can be used in place of a mesh bag. (Contrary to what you may have heard, small items like baby socks are never actually sucked down the drain pipes, which have filters to prevent this; they disappear into sleeves, pant legs, and dresses and are folded, unnoticed, into towels and sheets.) Hosiery can get twisted or knotted or can snag on almost any rough surface. Heavily soiled pieces may not wash clean, however, in a mesh bag. You may have to hand-wash them.

- Pins should usually be removed before washing because of the possibility that they will rust or that the pinned fabric will tear. Cuff links, buckles, and other metal attachments pose the same dangers—and the additional danger, according to washing machine manufacturers, that they can damage the enamel inside the machine—and, if possible, should be removed. Buckles on sturdy fabrics that will not be harmed by pins could be fastened inside pant legs instead. Or, if you can, place such potentially hazardous items in mesh bags for laundering.

- Tie together sashes or other long pieces that might knot and tangle the wash. Button long sleeves to each other or to shirt fronts to prevent them from tangling. Fasten bras. Pin things together only if you are certain that the pin will not rust and that the fabric around the pin will not tear during the wash. Some people like to pin little items to a bigger one, such as a towel, to be sure that they are not lost, but do this only if you are sure that it will not tear. Again, the easiest solution is to remove sashes and similar items and tuck them into a mesh bag for laundering.

- Mend tears and tighten loose buttons before laundering. Tears will grow larger and buttons may come off and be lost in the wash.

- Remove detachable decorations, linings, buttons, and other trim or attachments on a garment that are not washable. Of course you can do this only if you know how to reattach them. If sewn-in linings are not washable, few of us are up to undertaking to remove them and sew them back in later; such garments should be dry-cleaned. If you are astonished to learn that someone might go to the trouble of removing and then resewing a delicate button or piece of lace trim for the sake of laundering something safely, the perspective of the nineteenth century may help. Good washing practice then called at times for taking a dress apart entirely for washing or other cleaning and sewing it back together later! Removing collars, buttons, or lace for laundering was commonplace.

- Check each load for matching: does it contain any pieces that belong in sets? If so, add the missing pieces, even if they are clean, so that all will fade to the same degree. Always wash sock mates together, too, or they may become different colors.

TESTING FOR COLORFASTNESS TO LAUNDRY PRODUCTS

When you are worried about an item's colorfastness, you should usually test its fastness to any substance with which you plan to launder it: bleach, boosters, pretreatments, stain removers, and even detergents if they contain bleach or other additives that raise questions in your mind. Some dyes will run or fade in a solution of water and detergent but would not be affected by plain water; some will bleed when you use hot water but not warm. Some will bleed in a pretreatment solution or in bleach but would not run in a solution of mere detergent and water. Test with hot or warm water if you will be washing in hot or warm water; the action of oxygen bleaches and some other laundry additives is greatly increased in hotter water.

Pretreatments and stain removers sometimes have special ingredients that can cause some dyes, especially fluorescent dyes, to run, so be particularly careful to test neon pinks, electric blues, and other fluorescent colors.

Choose an inconspicuous area for testing, such as the wrong side of a hem or on a seam allowance, so that if your test leaves a spot, it will not show. Be sure to lay the cloth in such a way that the solution does not penetrate through to visible areas.

Recipe for testing fastness to detergent. Follow the directions on the product. If there are none, mix one teaspoon of dry or liquid detergent in a cup of warm or hot water (whichever you will be using). Apply enough solution to soak a small hidden area of the garment and wait for a few minutes. Then press the area with a clean white cloth, tissue, or paper towel to see if any color comes off. If color comes off or if you perceive a color change on the garment, it has failed the colorfast test. If you perceive nothing, rinse and let dry, and observe again (because it may look darker while it is wet). If you see no color change, it is colorfast to your detergent at the temperature of the water you will use.

The quick, easy, less reliable way to test is to make a cup of water of the proposed temperature, add a teaspoon of detergent, and dip a corner of the fabric in it. If the water turns color, the fabric is not fast to the detergent in water of that temperature.

Recipe for testing fastness to chlorine (sodium hypochlorite) bleach. Use the method recommended on the product. Or add one tablespoon of chlorine bleach to ¼ cup water. Apply the solution to a hidden area, and wait one minute. Then blot the spot dry with a clean white cloth, tissue, or paper towel. If color comes off or if you perceive a color change on the garment, it has failed the colorfast test. Look for yellowing and other changes as well. If you want to be very sure there has been no color change, rinse the item and wait until it dries to draw conclusions, as sometimes it is hard to tell while fabrics are wet.

Recipe for testing fastness to oxygen bleach and other wash additives. Follow the instructions on the label for testing. If there are none and if the product is not a liquid, mix it with enough water to get a solution somewhat stronger than the one you will have in the washing machine, making sure that all of the product is dissolved. Apply enough solution to soak a small inconspicuous area of the garment. Or, if the product is a liquid, simply apply a little, undiluted, to an inconspicuous area of the garment. Wait ten minutes and then look for any changes of color, fading, bleeding (press a clean paper towel to the area), or other damage. Then rinse and let dry to be completely sure there is no change.

When testing an activated oxygen bleach, be sure to read and follow the manufacturer's instructions, which may specify a more concentrated testing solution and a longer exposure time than is usually called for.

2

Carefully Disregarding
Care Labels

*Inaccuracy of many care labels, low labeling . . . FTC regulations;
how to interpret care labels . . . What the care label means when it is
silent, when it gives warnings, when it does not mention ironing,
when it prescribes no bleach or non–chlorine bleach; what care labels
do not have to tell you . . . When to disregard care labels and when
not to . . . What to do when the care label procedure causes
damage . . . Glossary of Care Label Terms and Symbols . . .
Appendix, Extracts from FTC Regulations on Care Labels*

Following Dr. Seuss's example, I feel obliged to warn the reader that this chapter is dangerous. It contains advice on when and why you might wish to disobey that fundamental law of the modern laundry: "Follow the instructions on the care label!" Those of you who are beginners should follow the care labels unless it is clear you have nothing to lose—for example, when the garment looks so awful that you are never going to wear it again in its present state anyway and there is no way to remedy it if you limit yourself to care label instructions. Even then, you have to think of your chagrin when someday you find out that you could have saved it by trying another remedy that you had not known about. If this sounds too frustrating, follow that care label, or hand the problem over to a professional. Otherwise you risk the destruction of your fabrics, their colors, or their appearance. I have given garments to my dry cleaner saying, "Try anything. It's ruined as it is, so I won't blame you if you make it even worse."

Those of you who are not beginners should also be prepared to accept the risks, because in this area no one can offer you certainty, least of all someone who has never even seen the fabric or problem you are dealing with. First survey the risks (including the possibility that you might render a wearable garment unwearable) and decide if you can accept failure. Remember, if it is a T-shirt, this means merely a little money and some inconvenience; if it is an expensive cashmere sweater, this could leave you with quite a hole in your pocket and nothing to wear this weekend.

The Uses and Limits of Care Labels

All wearing apparel (except footwear, gloves, hats, and other head and hand coverings) and piece goods used for home sewing of apparel sold in this country, including imported clothes and piece goods, are subject to the care labeling rules promulgated by the Federal Trade Commission. These rules require the manufacturer to attach a permanent label to each garment telling the buyer how to clean it. The regulations mandate that the label tell you at least one form of regular care, either washing or dry cleaning, needed for the ordinary use and enjoyment of the product, and that it warn the buyer against procedures that the buyer might assume are safe if in fact they would result in damage to the product or others being laundered with it.* The instructions on the label must cover trim, lining, buttons, and any other permanent part of the garment.

Surveys show that most home launderers pay attention to instructions on care labels, and textile and laundering experts unanimously advise you to follow care labels. If you do not, you run the risk of ruining your chances of a refund or replacement, for if you follow improper laundering procedures, any damage is likely to be considered your own fault. This seems fair enough until you look at some of the practicalities.

Every home launderer will have had plenty of experiences like my own with care labels. Among my son's new school clothes one year, for example, were two 100 percent cotton knit shirts, one in green and one in red, made by different manufacturers and bought at different stores. I would have bought neither of them if I had bothered to read the care labels, which specify treatment that is not the most practical for the clothes of the active son of busy parents: "Wash separately, cool water. Dry flat." One of the shirts bled dye at every washing, even in cool water; it faded quickly and accumulated some oily stains that were impossible to get out with cool water. The other shirt never bled dye at all, not even in hot water, never faded, and shrank just enough to fit per-

---

*In a few instances, the care instructions may appear on a hang tag or package rather than being permanently affixed to the garment. This is true of reversible clothes whose appearance might be ruined by a visible label. It is also true of garments that can be cleaned by any normal methods without harm. In the latter case, the hang tag must show this statement: "Wash or dry-clean, any normal method." This means that you may wash and dry at hot temperatures, use all types of bleaches, including chlorine bleaches, and dry-clean with any ordinary solvents. If a product cannot be cleaned by any method, the manufacturer is required to attach a label saying so, for example, "Do not wash, do not dry-clean" or "Cannot be successfully cleaned."

fectly, even after repeated tumble drying on low heat. Its care label instructions were flat wrong, but there was no way to determine this without bringing it home and experimenting; it looked just like the other shirt, which really did require separate washing.

For another example, I have an oversized, white cotton T-shirt that I bought in 1986 whose care label says, "Machine-wash warm. No bleach." I have machine-washed it in hot water hundreds of times, usually with chlorine bleach. It has hardly shrunk at all, and although it became comfortably soft and thin after more than a decade of good wear, it still looked white and attractive, and only developed holes when it turned eighteen. Overcautious labels when it comes to bleaching appear to me to be more the rule than the exception. But the problem is the opposite when it comes to ironing. My family's closets are full of shirts that lack any care label instruction as to ironing and nonetheless require regular ironing to look presentable.

Then there are those irksome care labels on ordinary sheets and towels that counsel utterly irrational caution. Towels, for example, which have been available for decades with profound colorfastness (colorfastness to withstand even chlorine bleach), now frequently have labels that advise you to wash them separately, wash them cold, and—hard to believe—to tumble dry on low. Of course, everyone will ignore this, because towels would take forever to dry on low. And, I hope, everyone will leave in the store looking decorative all those bath towels that require cold or separate washing or have any places or parts that shrink in a hot dryer. For everyday use, hold out for towels that can work hard, receive stain treatments and laundering that sanitizes (when necessary), and cause you no trouble. There is no reason in the world why toweling cannot be beautiful and practical too. But, of course, if buyers do not hold manufacturers to reasonable standards, manufacturers will certainly not hold themselves to any.

As an experiment, you might try (as I once did) sorting your laundry according to the exact instructions on the care labels. Because practically no two articles are labeled identically, even if, in quantity, you have only clothes enough to make up three or four good-sized loads, you might end up sorting them into at least three times that many loads. No experienced home launderer actually washes twelve or more loads instead of three or four. Thus we all become care label skeptics, routinely defying their instructions.

Inaccurate labeling and "low labeling" (labels that prescribe more conservative care than the garment really needs) are both quite common. Nonetheless, some of our skepticism about labels is in fact mistaken. We might fail to recognize that a label is accurate if, for example, a garment labeled "Dry-clean only" seems perfectly all right after being laundered. The effects of laundering may become apparent only after the third or fourth wash, and those effects may include shrinkage, fading, weakening, or the loss of beneficial treatments and finishes. By the time you discover that the label was right all along, it is too late to save the garment.

In other cases, a garment's care label simply cannot give the whole picture. Knowledgeable readers will appreciate, given how complicated a fabric's cleaning story can be, that manufacturers should not be faulted for not getting all the nuances on a square inch or two of care label. Moreover, what constitutes the "best" treatment will in some respects turn on the goals and skills of the person who will apply it: Is longer wear or whiter appearance more important? Is expense any object? Is the buyer a skilled and willing ironer?

A care label is intended to help you launder safely and effectively by giving you some simple guidelines. Care labels are not intended to do away with your need to know, more or less, what you are doing when you putter around in the laundry. I have often wondered whether we would be better off if we had regulations that required manufacturers to inform us about the characteristics of the products instead of the rather authoritarian care label system that asks us to obey simpleminded instructions blindly without giving us any hint of the reasons behind them. But because there is no likelihood that the system will change anytime soon, you are often going to find yourself wanting and needing to use laundry procedures other than the ones that are recommended on the labels.

There are three main reasons for sometimes ignoring care labels. The first is that you want to do a better job than you believe is possible with the recommended treatment. The second is that you believe you can safely and effectively clean the garment with less trouble or expense than the care label treatment would require. The third is that you want to wash in one load clothes whose care labels would require different treatment. Before you can decide to ignore a label you need to be able to make educated guesses about whether an alternative procedure is safe. This requires being able to spot potential problems and decide when the risk is worth it. You must also be prepared to accept the loss when you guess wrong. I repeat: If you are a novice, just follow the care labels. The less you know, the greater the risks of doing anything else. Sooner or later, however, every novice develops an instinct for fibers, fabrics, and laundering, and discovers for himself or herself when the risks are small enough to justify taking a chance.

The FTC Regulations: What Care Labels Do and Do Not Tell You

The glossary at the end of this chapter sets forth definitions of certain standard terms and symbols that are permitted on permanent care labels. If you do not know the meaning of the terms or symbols on your clothes' care labels, consult the glossary (see page 34). Better yet, photocopy it and tape it to the wall or put it on a bulletin board in your laundry. Although the discussion that follows often talks about what care labels "say," the labels may use symbols, words, or both so long as the instruction is consistent with FTC rules. The heart of these rules, the provisions governing washing and drycleaning

ITCHY LABELS

Sometimes labels are made of stiff, scratchy material that irritates the skin—especially children's sensitive skin. If you cut the care label off and you think you need it as a reminder, pin it to a bulletin board in your laundry with a note saying, for example, "Manufacturer X's striped T-shirt." Better, but more trouble, is to reattach it to the garment, with firm stitching, someplace where it is less irritating, say at a side seam within a couple of inches of the bottom hem. Some manufacturers have begun to print the care instructions directly on the fabric of the garment. In my experience, this method is long-lasting and convenient as well as more comfortable.

instructions, are set out in the appendix at the end of this chapter, pages 36–37, following the glossary.

The Meaning of Silence. Most care label instructions you will encounter are straightforward, but some have implications that are not so obvious. Often, it is what the care labels do not say that creates confusion. For example, when both dry cleaning and washing are safe for regular use on a product, the rules do not presently require the manufacturer to say so on the care label. Rather, under the rules as they now stand, "the label need have only one of these instructions." Thus, a label that says merely "Dry-clean" means neither that you can nor cannot wash the article without harming it. ("Dry clean only" does mean that washing will harm it.) And if the label says "Machine-wash," you have been told nothing about whether it can also be dry-cleaned or whether dry cleaning would harm it. The manufacturer is required neither to recommend an alternative method if it would be safe nor to warn you if it would not be safe. Despite requests by consumers, consumer interest groups, laundry product manufacturers, and the EPA, in 2000 the FTC refused to amend its rules to require washing instructions on all articles that could safely be washed.*

Sometimes, however, silence on a care label means that, in some respect or other, anything goes. For example, a label that says nothing about washing, drying, or ironing temperatures means that any temperature is safe. A label that says nothing about bleach means that all household bleaches are safe and can

---

*In 2000, the FTC also decided not to amend the rule "at this time" to include an instruction for professional wet cleaning on garments that carry a drycleaning instruction. (Wet cleaning is an environmentally favorable cleaning technology that uses water instead of drycleaning solvents and is safe for a wider variety of fabrics than normal laundering.) And it revised water temperature definitions to make "hot" mean 112°F to 145°F (45°C to 63°C), "warm" mean 78°F to 111°F (31°C to 44°C), and "cold" mean up to 86°F (30°C). Prior to this amendment, "hot" meant water up to 150°F (66°C), "warm" meant 90°F to 110°F (32°C to 43°C), and "cold" meant water up to 85°F (29°C). See chapter 4, "Laundering," pages 65–67.

be used regularly. "Machine-wash, tumble dry" means that any temperatures for washing and drying and all types of household bleach may be used.

Warnings. The words "only," "do not," and "no" are always warning words on care labels. Warnings mean that harm is likely to ensue, in one or more washings, if the instructions are not followed. For example, if a label says "Dry-clean only," the word "only" makes this a warning against machine washing; and the instruction means that machine washing will be harmful. If the label says "Wash with like colors" or "Wash separately," despite the absence of obvious warning words, you are being warned that the article is not color-fast and may bleed dyes onto anything washed with it. There is also an implicit warning against a stronger alternative when a care label specifies a gentler one; for example, a label that prescribes warm water is implicitly warning you not to use hot, even though no explicit warning words are used. Note, however, that the FTC rules require the manufacturer to warn you only about harmful aspects of the recommended treatment. A label that says "Machine-wash" need not tell you whether or not dry cleaning will harm the garment, but it must tell you if bleaching would.

Ironing. If a label says nothing at all about ironing, that is supposed to mean that no ironing is needed to "preserve the appearance" of the garment. But this provision of the rules, so far as I can tell, is routinely ignored; many garments that require ironing have care labels that do not mention ironing. Presumably, manufacturers think that telling people they have to iron would not be a big selling point.

Bleaching. If a label says "No bleach," this does not mean that the article will stay white or bright without bleach, or that bleach is unnecessary. Some garments that are marked "No bleach" do not stay white without bleach. You may infer only that the manufacturer is telling you that all types of household bleach can reasonably be expected to harm the product in one or more washings.

If regular use of chlorine bleach would harm the product but regular use of a non-chlorine bleach would not, the label must say "Only non-chlorine bleach, when needed." This instruction seems to tell you that you are to use a non-chlorine (or oxygen) bleach only when the product starts to look dingy, but—whatever the instruction is really intended to mean—in practice this would often be a mistake. In general, non-chlorine bleach is effective only when used regularly to prevent a dingy appearance from developing and can do little to remove it when it has already developed. Nonetheless, the manufacturer, it seems, has no lawful choice but to give you this exact wording, misleading as it may be, if it wants to warn you against using chlorine bleaches but not against other types of bleach. This required wording is misleading in another way, too: it does not allow for cases in which "irregular" or occasional use of chlorine bleach might do no harm.

What Care Labels Do Not Have to Tell You. You should not assume, when you read a care label, that the manufacturer is trying to give you the least expensive or the best or even both of two equally good sets of care instructions. The rules do not require this, and care labels very often do not do so.

When care labels give warnings, they are not required to explain what danger is being warned against, how big a danger it is, or how likely the danger is. Care labels never tell you why one procedure is recommended rather than another, whether it is because a garment might fade, shrink, pill, or go limp or shapeless, whether invisible finishes may dissolve, and so on. Care labels do not tell you whether the product has received wrinkle-resistance or other treatments or whether any instructions on the label are there to protect a finish. Manufacturers are not required to tell you on care labels how much shrinking you can expect, nor when instructions are geared toward preventing shrinkage.

Care labels are not required to tell you when starch or sizing is necessary to restore the crisp appearance of a garment, or when ironing should be done when the clothes are damp. Apparently, they are also not required to give instructions on the use of soaps or detergents, softeners, bluing agents, boosters, and the like, and they rarely do, except, occasionally, to advise the use of mild soap or detergent.

At the present time, care labels are not required on gloves, hats, handkerchiefs, neckties, shoes, and similar items of attire, or on sheets, mattress pads, tablecloths, blankets, towels, rugs, upholstery, and many other textile products used in the home. Wisely, manufacturers almost always include care labels on towels, linens, and other textile goods even though they are not required. When care labels are absent, as sometimes happens on imported towels and linens, you have to rely entirely on labels describing fiber content—which are, fortunately, required by the Textile Fiber Products Identification Act for all domestic and imported textiles—and use care procedures appropriate to the fibers. (See Part III.)

Disregarding Care Labels Carefully

Those who wish to at times defy care labels will find that their best protection from frustrating laundry errors is understanding fabrics and fibers. (See Part III, chapters 19, 20, 21, and 22, for general information about fabrics and the care procedures appropriate to fabrics made of different types of fibers.) If you wish to launder or clean in a way other than the one recommended on a care label, you should be aware of the general nature of the fiber and construction you are dealing with and what is generally safe and effective in laundering such a fiber and construction, even though particular articles may have to be treated differently. To try to figure out whether the garment is actually launderable or cleanable in the way you intend, you should look for hints on the care label, on hang tags, and on fiber content labels, and you should examine all parts of the garment—its trim, linings, interfacings, buttons, and so on. Consider the weave and the yarn construction. Before proceeding, test for colorfastness, yellowing, and the like. Ask sales personnel whether they have any experience with the type of garment in question. Manufacturers may recommend a given procedure for a variety of reasons that you can only guess at.

Here are some specific ways in which it often pays to depart from care label instructions. Following these guidelines, you may sometimes ruin something, but in the long run your laundering is more effective and more efficient.

- Use chlorine bleach on white fibers that are bleachable in principle, such as cotton, linen, or polyester. (To learn about a fiber's bleachability, see chapter 21, "The Natural Fibers," and chapter 22, "The Man-Made Fibers and Blends.") Always test first, watching for yellowing, color change, or other negative effects.
- If home testing indicates that chlorine bleach is safe, use chlorine bleach on colored articles.
- Launder, by hand or machine as seems best, articles whose care labels say "Dry-clean," when they are of a type or construction that typically is launderable. This calls for judgment and is only for the experienced.
- Wash polyester and nylon in warm or hot water, although labels recommend cold, so as to get better cleaning. (Use a cool-down rinse to reduce wrinkling.)
- Use lukewarm water on washable wool sweaters and silks when care labels call for cold or cool.
- Use warm water rather than cool to wash colors that fade, choosing cleanliness over color preservation. (But be sure to wash clothes that bleed separately from others or with others of like color, as appropriate.)
- Wash colorfast and white closely woven cottons and linens (not knits or loose weaves) in hot or warm water, although labels recommend warm or cold.
- Wash sturdy cotton blends and synthetics (not those containing viscose rayon, acetate, or other delicate and heat-sensitive fibers) in the regular cycle or permanent-press cycle when the label says "Gentle" or "Delicate." (Make sure there is no likelihood of pilling or tearing.)

You can also depart from care label instructions in the direction of being more cautious rather than less so. The usual reason to do this is to combine a stray item or two with a larger load, by giving it a less rigorous treatment than it could safely take. For example, you can

- Wash or dry clothes at cooler temperatures than care labels direct.
- Wash or dry clothes with shorter or gentler agitation and spin cycles than care labels direct.
- Wash clothes with milder laundry products than care labels direct.

- Wash clothes without bleach that could safely be bleached.
- Hand-wash clothes whose label says to machine-wash.
- Dry flat or hang dry clothes whose labels permit tumbling dry.

The potential cost of using milder or gentler or cooler treatments is that clothes may not come as clean or may take longer to dry. Over time, dirt retained in the fibers weakens them and makes clothes appear gray and dingy or even feel unpleasant. However, the effects of retained dirt are not going to show up if you occasionally or infrequently make this compromise, for the sake of fewer loads. You would probably never wish to wash heavily soiled children's play clothes in cold water with mild detergent, for they simply will not come clean. But play clothes with moderate soil that you usually give strong treatment to would probably do fine if they were occasionally washed in warm water with permanent-press clothes on the permanent-press cycle—especially if you have pretreated any stains or heavy soil marks.

When Not to Disregard Care Labels

If you are in the habit of ignoring care labels, you will minimize your risks if you know that some care label instructions should never or rarely be disregarded. Here are a number of situations in which you *should* obey care labels:

For General Reasons
- Obey care labels on garments made by manufacturers whose care labels you have found reliable or important in the past.
- Obey care labels that are carefully written or provide a lot of detail. In my experience, this unfailingly indicates a degree of attention to proper care that is a sign of the instructions' importance and reliability.
- Obey care labels on expensive garments that you cannot afford to damage or replace.

For Reasons Related to Construction of Garment, Fabric, or Yarn
- In laundering specialty items, of whose construction and materials you know virtually nothing, follow care labels carefully. For example, always follow care labels on materials that are flocked, glued, furry, or otherwise unusually constructed.
- Generally, obey care label instructions on upholstery, rugs, quilts, draperies, and down-filled or feather-filled articles such as pillows, comforters, and sleeping bags. Not only are these things expensive, but they often have constructions or treatments that require special care. Remember that curtains and draperies, particularly those made of very loose weaves or silk velvet, are often not washable.
- Obey care labels on highly tailored items, especially those made of delicate or expensive fibers such as linen, silk, or wool.

- Never ignore "Dry-clean" or "Dry-clean only" instructions on crêpe—especially silk or rayon crêpes, which may shrink dramatically—or on other high-twist yarn constructions or low-twist yarn constructions. (Shrinkage of up to 50 percent can result if a fabric made of highly twisted yarns is immersed in water.)

For Reasons Relating to Fiber Content
- Obey care label instructions to dry-clean dressy, glossy silks.
- Obey drycleaning instructions on any crisp, tailored, or heavily sized linen or cotton garments. Never launder tailored linen suits unless the care label permits it.
- Obey all care labels on fiberglass!
- Never ignore instructions to use gentle treatment on rayon, acetate, or fabrics of delicate or fragile construction (open weaves, netting, lace).
- Never ignore instructions to use mild soap or detergent or cool water with silk or wool.
- Never ignore instructions to dry-clean acrylic or modacrylic, as this may be prescribed because the garment has a water-soluble finish. Laundering might cause a loss of softness.

For Reasons Relating to Dyes and Finishes
- Never ignore laundering instructions for any garments with special or unusual finishes.
- Never ignore laundering instructions on items treated with flame retardants to render them flame-resistant; this may harm the flame-resistant finish.
- Never ignore care instructions on water-repellant articles; this may render the article non–water-repellant.
- Pay attention to instructions concerning temperatures for washing or drying wrinkle-resistant, easy-care, or permanent-press garments or you may get wrinkling.
- Never ignore instructions to wash separately or with like colors unless you have thoroughly tested to be sure that a garment will not bleed. (And always follow care labels of colored or printed silks.)
- Obey care labels on fabrics that have been treated with nanotechnologies or other stain- and shrink-resistance treatments. Otherwise you may inadvertently destroy or mask the effect of the treatments.
- Obey lyocell (Tencel) care labels, which may be designed to protect anti-wrinkling or antishrinking finishes.

When Instructions Relate to Bleaching
- Obey care labels that forbid bleaching on wool, silk, leather, mohair, spandex, and nylon fabrics; on fabrics with colors that run; and on any colored fabrics that you have not successfully tested for bleachability. Obey care labels about bleaching on any fabric or finish that is not generally bleachable.

When Instructions Relate to Ironing and Drying
- Never use a hotter iron than a label instructs without carefully testing it first in an inconspicuous area to be sure that the fabric will not scorch, glaze, or melt.
- Drying instructions should almost always be obeyed. Although knits whose care labels say to dry flat can often be tumbled dry on low, even low-heat drying is likely to result in some shrinkage. This might be tolerable if you expect and allow for it.

What to Do When the Procedure Recommended by the Care Label Causes Damage

If an article is damaged when you launder or clean it in accordance with the care instructions, the FTC recommends that you return the article to the retailer who sold it to you. The FTC suggests that if the retailer refuses to "resolve the problem," ask for the name and address of the manufacturers and write them a letter. "In your letter, fully describe the garment and give all the information that is on the labels and tags," advises the FTC. "Estimate how many times the garment has been washed or dry-cleaned and give the full name and address of the store where you bought it." You can also get in touch with the FTC, and you should definitely do so if the manufacturer fails to give you a satisfactory resolution. Write to Correspondence Branch, Federal Trade Commission, Washington, DC 20580; or call 202–326–3693. The FTC will not attempt to resolve your grievance, but the information you provide it "may reveal a pattern or practice requiring action by the Commission. You may be contacted if the FTC decides to investigate."

In my experience, however, retailers and manufacturers are almost always happy to make an exchange or refund.

GLOSSARY OF CARE LABEL
TERMS AND SYMBOLS

Machine-wash. Use washing machine, hot, warm, or cold setting. See the note on page 27 of this chapter for the temperature ranges meant by "hot," "warm," and "cold."

Machine-wash, warm. Use washing machine, warm setting. (Hot water should not be used.)

Machine-wash, cold. Use washing machine, cold setting. (Hot or warm water should not be used.)

(Note that the absence of any instruction concerning bleaches or ironing should be interpreted as meaning that all commercially available bleaches may be used on a regular basis without harm, and that no ironing is necessary to preserve the appearance of the garment.)

Hand-wash, cold. Wash by hand in cold water. (Machine-washing and warm or hot water should not be used.)

Only non-chlorine bleach. Non-chlorine bleach can safely be used when needed. (Regular use of chlorine bleach would harm the product.)

No bleach. [Do not bleach.] Use no bleach. (All commercially available bleaches would harm the product when used on a regular basis.)

Tumble dry. High, medium, or low dryer temperature setting can safely be used.

Tumble dry, medium. Medium or low dryer temperature settings can safely be used. (The hot setting should not be used.)

Tumble dry, low. Low dryer temperature settings can safely be used. (The hot and warm settings should not be used.)

Iron. High, medium, or low iron settings can safely be used.

Warm iron. Iron on a medium temperature setting. (The hot setting should not be used.)

Cool iron. Iron on the lowest temperature setting. (The hot and warm settings should not be used.)

ASTM GUIDE TO CARE SYMBOLS

Wash	Machine Wash Cycles							hand wash	Warning symbols for laundering
	normal	permanent press	delicate/ gentle						do not wash
	Water Temperatures (maximum) symbol (s)	(200F)(160F) 95C 70C	(140F) 60C	(120F) 50C	(105F) 40C	(65F–85F) 30C			do not bleach
									do not dry (used with do not wash)
Bleach		any bleach when needed	only non-chlorine bleach when needed						do not iron
Dry	Tumble dry cycles						line dry/ hang to dry		Additional instructions (in symbols or words)
	normal	permanent press	delicate/ gentle				drip dry		do not wring
	Tumble dry heat setting	any heat	high	medium	low	no heat/ air	dry flat		do not tumble dry
Iron	Iron—dry or steam								in the shade (added to line dry, drip dry, or dry flat)
	maximum temperature	200C (390F) high	150C (300F) medium	110C (230F) low					no steam (added to iron)
Dryclean	Dryclean—normal cycle			do not dryclean	Dryclean—additional instructions				
	any solvent	any solvent except trichloroethylene	petroleum solvent only		short cycle	reduce moisture	low heat	no steam finishing	

Reprinted, with permission, from
1997 Annual Book of ASTM Standards

Copyright 1996 American Society for Testing and Materials
100 Barr Harbor Drive West Conshohocken, PA 19428-2959

This figure illustrates the symbols used for laundering and drycleaning instructions. As a minimum, laundering instructions should include, in order, four symbols: washing, bleaching, drying, and ironing; and drycleaning instructions should include one symbol. Additional symbols or words may be used to clarify the instructions.

APPENDIX

Extracts from FTC Regulations on Care Labels

(1) Washing, drying, ironing, bleaching, and warning instructions must follow these requirements:

(i) Washing. The label must state whether the product should be washed by hand or machine. The label must also state a water temperature—in terms such as warm, cold, or hot—that may be used. However, if the regular use of hot water up to 145°F (63°C) will not harm the product, the label need not mention any water temperature. [For example, "Machine wash" means hot, warm, or cold water can be used.]

(ii) Drying. The label must state whether the product should be dried by machine or by some other method. If machine drying is called for, the label must also state a drying temperature that may be used. However, if the regular use of a high temperature will not harm the product, the label need not mention any drying temperature. [For example, "Tumble dry" means that a high, medium, or low temperature can be used.]

(iii) Ironing. Ironing must be mentioned on a label only if it will be needed on a regular basis to preserve the appearance of the product, or if it is required under paragraph (b) (1) (v) of this section, Warnings. If ironing is mentioned, the label must also state an ironing temperature that may be used. However, if the regular use of a hot iron will not harm the product, the label need not mention any ironing temperature.

(iv) Bleaching.

(A) If all commercially available bleaches can safely be used on a regular basis, the label need not mention bleaching.

(B) If all commercially available bleaches would harm the product when used on a regular basis, the label must say "No bleach" or "Do not bleach."

(C) If regular use of chlorine bleach would harm the product, but regular use of a non-chlorine bleach would not, the label must say "Only non-chlorine bleach, when needed."

(v) Warnings.

(A) If there is any part of the prescribed washing procedure which consumers can reasonably be expected to use that would harm the product or others being washed with it in one or more washings, the label must contain a warning to this effect. The warning must use [the] words "Do not," "No," "Only," or some other clear wording. [For example, if a shirt is not colorfast, its label should state "Wash with like colors" or "Wash separately." If a pair of pants will be harmed by ironing, its label should state "Do not iron."]

(B) Warnings are not necessary for any procedure that is an alternative to the procedure prescribed on the label. [For example, if an instruction states "Dry flat," it is not necessary to give the warning "Do not tumble dry."]

(2) Dry-cleaning.

(i) General. If a dry-cleaning instruction is included on the label, it must also state at least one type of solvent that may be used. However, if all commercially available types of solvent can be used, the label need not mention any types of solvent. The terms "Drycleanable" or "Commercially Dry-clean" may not be used in an instruction. [For example, if dry cleaning in perchlorethylene would harm a coat, the label might say "Professionally dry-clean: Fluorocarbon or petroleum."]

(ii) Warnings.

(A) If there is any part of the dry-cleaning procedure which consumers or drycleaners can reasonably be expected to use that would harm the product or others being cleaned with it, the label must contain a warning to this effect. The warning must use the words "Do not," "No," "Only," or some other clear wording. [For example, the dry-cleaning process normally includes moisture addition to solvent up to 75 percent relative humidity, hot tumble-drying up to 160°F, and restoration by steam press or steam-air finish. If a product can be dry-cleaned in all solvents but steam should not be used, its label should state "Professionally dry-clean. No steam."]

(B) Warnings are not necessary to any procedure which is an alternative to the procedure prescribed on the label. [For example, if an instruction states "Professionally dry-clean, Fluorocarbon," it is not necessary to give the warning "Do not use perchlorethylene."]

3

Washers, Dryers, and Other Laundry Room Equipment

Understanding how your washing machine washes . . . What goes on inside your washing machine . . . Which type of washing machine is right for you . . . Top-loaders, front-loaders, hybrids, high-efficiency machines . . . Be a washing machine skeptic; choosing a machine . . . Summary of cycles, the regular, permanent-press, gentle or delicate . . . Dryer cycles and options . . . Drying cabinets . . . Care and maintenance of laundry appliances . . . Useful furnishings and equipment for laundry rooms

You can launder more efficiently and effectively if you understand what goes on under the lid of your automatic washing machine when you close it. Most people do not. Many laundry failures and frustrations can be traced to the illusion that it is not necessary to know what the different cycles on washing machines do or why they are recommended for certain fabrics and fibers.

What Happens Inside Your Washing Machine. The type of automatic washing machine that most people in this country have in their homes is a top-loading machine that "agitates," or churns or jerks the clothes back and forth by means of a post in the center of the tub in order to wash and rinse them. As it drains the wash and rinse waters, it spins the clothes at ever-increasing speeds until the great "centrifugal" force of the spinning presses out so much water that the clothes do not drip, i.e., are "damp dried" when they are finally removed.

Other types of machines, those that tumble rather than agitate clothes, are growing in popularity. These have no agitator post and clean clothes by tumbling them in a turning barrel while causing sudsy water to be sloshed and, sometimes, sprayed through them. Different versions of tumbling, sloshing, and spraying are used by the various tumbling machines. Like agitators, tumblers spin the clothes to squeeze the water out of them until they are damp dried. Although most tumblers have a door on the front instead of a lid on the top and thus are called "front-loaders," there are several "hybrids" that use a variety of nonagitating washing mechanisms but have a lid on top like agitators. Both front-loading and hybrid tumblers are called "high-efficiency" (HE) washing machines, for reasons explained below. Both types of machines are referred to here as "tumblers" or "high-efficiency machines."

Which Machine for You? The increasing variety of types of washing machines available and features offered means that it is now more difficult to decide which machine is right for your household. Although front-loaders have been around almost as long as top-loaders, most people in this country have lived only with top-loading washers and are not familiar with many of the advantages and disadvantages of tumblers. (In Europe, the opposite is true.) For the average person, top-loaders offer two strong advantages: you can load top-loaders without bending and straining your back, and, more importantly, until recently, top-loaders were bigger and could wash far larger loads far more quickly than front-loaders. For most people, these factors were decisive. But things have begun to change.

In recent years, tumbling machines have become increasingly popular on account of their outstanding energy- and water-saving features. They offer faster spinning speeds, too, and faster spins mean that clothes come out of the washer far more dry and thus dry faster in the dryer, creating further energy savings and convenience. Tumblers often cost more up front, but depending on your laundry volume and your habits, you make up a good portion or even all of the excess cost in reduced operating costs over the life of the machine. For these reasons, they are called "high-efficiency" or HE machines.

American front-loading and hybrid models are no longer smaller than agitators; the different models have a range of capacities comparable to that of top-loaders. (European front-loaders continue to be smaller and slower than new American front-loaders.) And despite the ample capacity of new-model tumblers, they still use much less water and energy than old-fashioned agitating machines. Today's more stringent regulations on laundry appliance efficiencies, therefore, have tipped the balance in favor of tumbling machines for many home laundries.

Claims of superior laundry effectiveness are also made for tumbling machines—both by their manufacturers and by many users. Tumblers, they say, not only clean more thoroughly but they clean more gently, causing less wear and tear on clothes. Tumblers generally use more rinses than top-loaders, too, and repeated rinses are more effective at removing residues of dirt and detergent than one deep rinse.[1] More thorough rinsing is also better for sensitive skin and helps clothes last longer and stay cleaner longer. Because of their more effective washing and rinsing, some say that tumbling machines help decrease reliance on laundry chemicals such as detergent and bleach.

But new-model tumblers, unfortunately, are still slightly less convenient to use than top-loaders. They still tend to take longer to wash the clothes than top-loaders, although they offer various quick-wash options. You still have to bend down to fill front-loaders. You still cannot open some tumblers to add a forgotten item after the first couple of minutes of the cycle; nor do you have the same ability to fiddle with the length of washes or rinses as you have with agitators. Because tumbling causes more suds and uses less water than agitating, tumblers need low-sudsing HE detergents that at present cost more, although the prediction is that their price will come down. The new hybrids offer the convenience of top-loading but otherwise tend to have many of the advantages and disadvantages of front-loaders.

My personal experience is that although both tumblers and agitators clean well, my front-loader seems to be gentler and cleans better than my old top-loader. But I have never compared my new front-loader to an equally up-to-date top-loader. I do not notice that I use less detergent or bleach in my front-loader.

Be a Washing Machine Skeptic. General advice on choosing a machine is likely to miss the mark, but some factors that it pays to notice are not likely to get attention in consumer magazines. Keeping these in mind may help convince you that, if you cannot afford the fanciest new machine out there, it is probably nothing to cry into your pillow about.

- Some new machines are surprisingly pretty. You may need to exercise a little willpower to ignore a machine's looks until you have evaluated its practical qualities. Looks should come last on your list of desiderata even if your machine sits in a place where everyone can see it. Most machines do not offend the eye.
- New washing machines often have touchpad control panels that would not look out of place in the cockpit of a Boeing 757, but not everyone likes touchpad panels. They do not permit the same flexibility to shorten or lengthen washing times that you have when you can set a dial for the exact number of minutes you want the clothes to wash. My new front-loading machine, for example, lets you pick only, and exactly, 34, 29, 16, 10, or 5 minutes; you cannot choose, for example, 25, 20, 12, or 2 minutes. Even

more annoying, my presoak is set at 15 minutes, and I cannot lengthen or shorten it the way I could on my old top-loader.

- Watch out for pseudoadvances in washer/dryer technology. Many of the cycle options are about as useful as the fins on an old Buick. Do not buy without finding a human being or a manual or a website that can tell you exactly what each cycle does so that you can rationally decide whether an option is really helpful and worth paying for. How, for example, could a pet-bedding cycle—offered on one machine I looked at—be more than a bogus convenience when pet-bedding is not made of any single type of fabric or construction that a single method of laundering would fit? (I have seen polyester, wool, cotton, stuffed, unstuffed, knitted, and woven pet beds.) Besides, numerous cycle options are not necessarily efficient or convenient. See pages 44–45. And on some machines, you have to go through a confusing chain of menus to get to the option you want, and your manual may not make the route clear.

- The "stain" option on many machines should not impress you. This consists, typically, of stain-removal information plus an instruction to use the "stain" cycle, which may amount to just a presoak with laundry products that the machine directs you to use and an extra-long wash using the machine's fastest tumbling speed. In other words, the machine does nothing to remove stains that your old machine could not have done—except offer advice. Moreover, in many cases it is questionable advice. Suppose you have a bloodstain on a light-colored cotton shirt that you want to wash in a load of other, unstained, cottons. On my machine, you pretreat the stain as directed then set for stain cycle. This will result in cold-water wash and rinse temperatures (because cold is appropriate for bloodstains) plus a presoak and extra-long wash that the machine uses on all stains. But why should you subject your whole load to this very long, cold wash if everything but the stain really needs a warm or hot wash of shorter duration? Besides, many stains, even most, come out with pretreatment and need no extra wash time. Isn't it more sensible to remove the stain or to pretreat the stained item so that it is ready for normal washing than to subject the whole load to an abnormal, less than optimal wash? Ask yourself, finally, whether your washing machine's brain is really the most convenient and adequate source of information about the proper treatment for a stain.

- Some machines automatically sense the load size and adjust the water level accordingly. This is efficient, but it takes matters out of your hands. You cannot vary the density of loads by using a lot of water for just a few clothes (desirable under circumstances described in the following chapter) the way you could on an old-fashioned top-loading agitator.

- All new machines that I know of let you do warm or cold rinses, but on no new machine that I have seen can you do a hot rinse, which is unfortunate. That occasionally useful option was widely available on older machines.

- A water-heating element is available in many but not all new models. Water-heating is extremely desirable in a washing machine. It lets you do a really hot wash even when your hot water heater is set at 120°F for reasons of safety and economy. But be sure to ask just what heating options do and how and when; they are not all the same. Some do not heat the water to hot enough temperatures. Mine maxes out at 130°F, which is not as hot as hot washes should be for certain purposes. Be aware that Energy Star models (explained on page 43) often achieve their energy efficiencies by using lower water temperatures; one manufacturer, for example, offers "hot" water of 105°F, which care label rules deem merely "warm." Another model offers "warm" rinses of 30°C (86°F), whereas on a care label this counts as "cool." European models tend to give you much more heating power. Do not confuse a real heating element with another common feature called "automatic temperature control," which does not heat water but merely regulates the mix of cold and hot water entering the machine. This is useful; it can help keep water temperature at the temperature setting you choose. But it cannot make the water any hotter than what your hot water tap delivers to the machine. When choosing a machine with a heating element, keep in mind its implications for your energy costs. This feature costs something to use but it also enables you to have a hot wash without setting your water heater higher, which saves on your hot water heating bill.
- Some machines have several washing speeds. The ability to vary tumbling or agitating speed is extremely useful.
- Machines may have one, two, or more spin speeds, and different models reach different top speeds. Different spin speeds and high–spin power are highly desirable features. At least one manufacturer lets you turn a dial and go, in increments, from 400 to 1600 RPMs.
- Newer machines give you little choice about when to add detergent, bleach, softener, or other additives. You put them in the dispensers at the beginning of the cycle; the machine adds them when it is programmed to. This is convenient when you do not want to have to remember to come back and add softener or bleach, but annoying if you want to use something in a nonstandard way or if you forgot to put something in or changed your mind. The operating manuals, moreover, often will not even tell you when or how the laundry products are added to the load, which further reduces your ability to pinch-hit. (For example, some machines add liquid chlorine bleach in the last minutes of the wash cycle, and some add it in a rinse cycle.) If you want to know when laundry products are going in, you have to ask your dealer or call the toll-free customer service number, and even then, finding someone who knows the answer can take a chunk out of your afternoon. People who are trying to sell you a machine are much more willing to find answers for you than people who have already pocketed your money, so read the manual and ask the retailer plenty of questions before you buy.

DOE REGULATIONS ON
WASHING MACHINE EFFICIENCIES

In 2001 the U.S. Department of Energy issued new regulations governing clothes washers, requiring all new clothes washers to be 22 percent more efficient in their use of energy and water by 2004 and 35 percent more efficient by 2007. These environmentally desirable rules will result in huge national savings in water and energy with no loss, according to the DOE, in home laundering abilities. Both top- and front-loading machines can meet these standards, but high-efficiency tumbling machines, at least so far, tend to offer considerably more energy and water savings than top-loaders.

- If you are in the market for a new machine, in advance of shopping read up on performance, economies, and repair records in consumer publications and visit a variety of stores and websites. A complicated computerized machine is unlikely to have the long years of repair-free functioning that simpler machines have. Read the entire operating manual before you buy the machine. If the manual does not provide a toll-free customer information number, consider finding another manufacturer. Do not buy a fancy machine with a confusing or uninformative operating manual. Also be wary of a complicated machine with a very short operating manual; it may be equally short on answers and necessary information.
- Find a company or retailer whose representatives are well informed and willing to answer all your questions patiently. Be cautious about buying washing machines from people who are mainly good at making or selling DVD players and cell phones. You are best off buying from people and companies who really know how to do the laundry.

THE ENERGY STAR PROGRAM

When shopping for clothes washers and dryers, as well as other home appliances, look for Energy Star appliances. Energy Star is a U.S. government program that tries to encourage energy savings. Products that show the Energy Star symbol meet strict energy efficiency guidelines set by the EPA and the Department of Energy. Energy Star clothes washers use 50 percent less energy than standard washers, and full-size washers use 18–25 gallons of water per load, compared to the 40 gallons used by standard machines. Moreover, Energy Star washers spin clothes dryer, which means that they need less time in the dryer to dry, resulting in a further energy savings. You can find Energy Star machines of all types—top-loading (agitator-style), front-loading, or hybrid, i.e., machines without agitators that have a lid on top—but most are front-loaders and hybrids.[2]

Summary of Cycles. The sequence of events under the lid of the washing machine, the progression from washing action to rinses and spins until the machine reaches a final automatic stop, is called a "cycle." Despite a burgeoning variety of special options on new-model washing machines, there are still only three basic automatic cycles, answering to the laundering needs of the three major fiber groups. Novices should be sure to learn what each of these basic cycles is called on their own machines and to read the instructions for using them set out in the following chapter.

The normal, regular, or cottons cycle is for sturdy fabrics woven of cotton, linen, and other cellulosic fibers—fabrics, in other words, that can take heat and vigorous manipulation. Thus the regular cycle provides vigorous washing action and fast spin for drying; it is typically used with hot or warm water. See pages 52–53.

The permanent-press, wrinkle-free, or easy-care cycle is designed for wrinkle-treated fabrics, synthetics such as polyester and nylon, man-made fibers, and blends containing these. It consists of fast or medium washing action (depending on how many speeds your machine offers) and medium to slow spin (again depending on how many spin speeds there are); typically it is used with warm to cool water—because many synthetics cannot take heat—and a final cold rinse. The less vigorous washing action helps to reduce the pilling that many synthetics and blends are prone to, and the cold rinse and slower spin lessens wrinkling in these heat-sensitive fabrics, which, when warm, readily take the imprint of the shapes they are spun-dry into. See pages 53–54.

The gentle or delicate cycle is for washable silks and woolens—i.e., the protein fibers—for weak synthetic fibers such as acrylic or acetate, and for all fabrics of any fiber made in delicate constructions or weaves. The gentle cycle provides slow washing action and slow spin and is typically used with cool to warm water. Such procedures are usually necessary both for protein fibers and for articles of delicate construction that could easily be torn, stretched, or otherwise harmed by rougher treatment. See pages 55–57.

The manufacturers' decision many years ago to create three basic cycles, plus the means of varying them to fit special cases, was a wise one that answered real needs. More cycles would always have been possible; the ideal care for even similar laundry items is often different. But laundering is largely the art of making safe compromises, treating unlike things roughly alike so as to avoid the inconvenience and waste of having to wash too many loads and loads that are too small. If cycles are too numerous and too narrowly designed, you end up with too few items per load for efficient and effective laundering. See chapter 4, pages 56–57.

Recently, however, in an excess of marketing zeal, manufacturers have begun to fix what was not broken. Many of them now offer a fourth basic automatic cycle called, absurdly enough, "hand-wash." (See chapter 4, page 61.) Others have begun offering numerous "preset" cycles for everything from pet-bedding to sneakers, promising "no-brainer" laundering. So long as you can still easily find and identify the three basic all-purpose cycles and so long as the machine offers you the flexibility to vary these basic cycles as necessary to fit the characteristics of your particular load (colorfastness, degree of sturdiness, tendency to pill, and so forth), these extra preset cycles are harmless enough. But this is not always the case.

One manufacturer, for example, has broken up the three basics into nine, some of which are whites, normal, heavy-duty, delicate casuals, jeans, and wool. These are somewhat irrational categories that leave you guessing at what goes where and why. I consider jeans heavy-duty; and cotton whites were deemed "normal" on all washing machines for more than half a century. This same machine presets the "wool" cycle to a low-speed spin, which in my opinion is wrong more often than right. Presumably, on these machines you can concoct your own cycles—for washable wool or other fibers. That is some consolation, so long as you are not misled into thinking you do not need to. The machine cannot really make it unnecessary for you to know what you are doing. Besides, too many cycles may tend to create inconvenience and waste by inducing the inexperienced launderer to wash more, smaller loads, rather than fewer, larger ones with, say, jeans thrown in with other heavy-duty items. (Not all jeans bleed dye; even those that do present no problem for dark-colored loads or even bright colors after a few washes.)

If your machine does not have the three standard cycles, you can almost surely create them for yourself using their descriptions in this and the following chapter. You will find that you can wash nearly all laundry using these three cycles and that most of the time it is efficient and convenient to do so.

Dryers

In the past decade, while the home washing machine has been adding new features, dryers have changed little. They still tumble clothes in a barrel with heat and send moisture and lint through an exhaust pipe to the outdoors. You pick a temperature or fabric setting appropriate to the fiber content and construction of the fabric. All machines still offer timed drying periods. But because timed drying often leads to under- or overdrying, many dryers now also have "moisture sensors" as well. The moisture sensors let you set the machine to go until it achieves the degree of dryness (very, normal, damp, damper) you want instead of setting it for a specified time period. Most machines offer antiwrinkle options. For example, one keeps clothes tumbling without heat at the end of a cycle so that hot clothes do not get set-in wrinkles. Another offers a short warm tumble, followed by a cool-down, to freshen clothes wrinkled from a suitcase or from sitting in the dryer.

Drying cabinets are now being made by a couple of manufacturers, but drying cabinets are not new. I once lived in a century-old building that had a huge drying cabinet in the basement for the tenants' use. This convenience was a wall-high, built-in cabinet whose gentle, effective warmth was apparently derived from proximity to the building's boiler. Opening its doors pulled forth long rods on which to drape your wet linens and clothes. To see another sort of drying cabinet, one much like those today's manufacturers are offering, look at any late-nineteenth-century edition of *Mrs Beeton's Book of Household Management,* in the section titled "The Laundry-Maid," for a lovely engraving of a drying cabinet from Victorian England. It resembles an armoire with space both for drying on hangers and drying flat on pullout shelves of fine open grating, like an oven's—or as Mrs. Beeton says of hers, "clothes horses on casters running in grooves." This type of drying cabinet was metal-lined, heated by hot air pipes, and vented to carry off steam, so that the laundry room would remain free of "unwholesome vapour."

Today's drying cabinets, like Mrs. Beeton's, look like cabinets. They open to disclose hanging space and mesh shelves; you can hang things or lay them flat. You close the door and warm air circulates to dry the clothes much faster than in room temperature air. You can also steam and scent clothes in the cabinets to freshen and unwrinkle them.

Drying cabinets, if well designed, are practical and useful additions to any laundry room with space for one. Drip-dry items, sweaters, and knits would dry far more quickly hanging or lying flat in a drying cabinet. Lingerie would soon dry and be static-free without fabric softener. I have not used one of the new drying cabinets, but I can vouch for the very old ones. At the moment, drying cabinets tend to be rather expensive.

The low-budget alternative to drying cabinets is a drying rack that fits into the barrel of the dryer. You place wet things that you want to dry flat, without tumbling, on the rack and turn on the dryer. The rack stays stationary while the barrel turns, causing warm air to circulate around the wet things. (With the in-dryer rack, I use time-drying, not moisture sensor–drying, as the machine does not seem to sense the moisture of one stationary wet article.) Of course, you cannot fit much on one rack. If you would like to try such a drying rack, your machine will probably accommodate it whether or not its manufacturer makes them. Just make sure to ask when you buy (from appliance stores or—where you are less likely to get any answers—on the Internet).

Care and Maintenance of Laundry Appliances

Check your instruction booklet for maintenance chores for your laundry appliances. Some automatic washers have filters that need cleaning periodically. You should also wash out the dispensers and tub in your washer occasionally. First wipe out any dirt or lint particles with a damp cloth, then run the machine through a short wash cycle with laundry detergent and hot water, spin, and rinse with plain water. If you need to clean, sanitize, or deodorize the tub of an agitating top-loader, run it through a hot-water wash, rinse, and drain cycle with the machine set to its maximum fill; add chlorine bleach enough for an extra-large load (according to the label instructions) and all-purpose detergent. To sanitize your front-loading machine, add all-purpose detergent and the maximum permissible amount of chlorine bleach to your liquid bleach dispenser, set the machine for hot water, and run it through a short wash cycle. If hard water mineral deposits appear in your tub, use any commercial remover for these or try softening them with white vinegar.

Dryer filters need constant cleaning; too large a collection of lint causes the dryer to operate inefficiently and is a fire hazard. In addition to emptying the filter frequently between loads, you should clean in and around the opening in which the filter sits, as lint tends to collect in this entire area. Vacuuming there with the crevice attachment is helpful. The dryer exhaust system, including exhaust pipes or tubes and the outside exhaust hood, should be inspected and cleaned annually. Now and then, wipe the inside of your dryer with a well-wrung cloth dampened with a mild-detergent-and-water solution.

The exteriors of washers and dryers are usually made of baked enamel, which scratches easily but readily wipes clean with a cloth dampened in a solution of mild detergent and water or any mild, nonabrasive all-purpose household cleaner.

Useful Furnishings and Equipment for Laundry Rooms

Not only laundry appliances but laundry rooms as a whole have become subjects of fashion. Basement gloom and utility room dourness are out; laundry luxe is in. New houses have large laundry rooms with laundry gadgets, fancy faucets, huge televisions and stereo systems, lounging furniture, telephone, drawers, closets, shelves, hanging and drying racks, and more. The idea is that you spend enough time laundering, folding, and ironing to justify making your laundry, like your kitchen, as friendly and inviting as possible. It is an idea whose time came long ago.

As usual, Mrs. Beeton had something to say that bears on the contemporary discussion. She believed that the well-designed laundry should have not one but two rooms or possibly three. In one, you would wash—a process that in her day involved many tubs and water taps, boilers, rinses, clouds of steam, and washerwomen. The wash room would have drains for carrying off waste water and excellent exhaustion and ventilation. You would dry and iron and fold in another room, fitted up for those functions. But, even better, you would dry using a separate drying closet that would have exhaust pipes to carry off moisture. (See the discussion of drying cabinets above and in the following chapter.) This would permit ironing and folding in a room without "unwholesome" vapors of steam and heat and chemical fumes. Above all, Mrs. Beeton thought, you had to provide adequate ventilation.

If we plan to spend substantial amounts of time in our laundry rooms, we, too, should adequately cool and ventilate them because heat, steam, chemical fumes, and dust are problems even for the contemporary laundry. Laundry detergents and bleaches still produce chemical air pollution. Washers and dryers still heat and humidify the room—even if rows of steaming washtubs were much worse. And although our dryers are vented, they throw some lint and moisture into the air too. Laundry appliances are now quieter than ever. But for the foreseeable future they will continue to make at least a little noise.

For these reasons, I question whether it is wise to install laundry appliances in the kitchen or in other living areas if we can avoid doing so. I also wonder whether we should try to condition the air in the laundry room to make it healthy and pleasant enough to spend substantial amounts of time there, or should we, instead, take advantage of the freedom that our appliances give us of being able to get away from the heat, humidity, noise, and pollution of laundry. Maybe, in fact, we should have not comfortable and attractive laundry rooms, but quiet, well-ventilated, accommodating, and attractive ironing, folding, and mending rooms—laundry anterooms, so to speak, where these time-consuming but light and relaxing chores can be lightened with entertainments and cheerful, comfortable surroundings. In this room, you might have racks, shelves, tables, a mending kit, music, television, and all the other comforts and conveniences you like. If large enough, such a room could also double as an attractive sewing, general workroom sort of place. I suspect the latter would be my choice, if I had one.

All of these things, of course, are luxuries, second in importance to the necessities of a good washer and dryer, and plenty of hot water, cold water, fresh air, and light. But, if you have space, funds, and an inclination for a few such luxuries in your laundry room, the list of useful laundry room features below may spark your imagination.

Double laundry tub or sink with faucets

One or two small plastic basins

Small washboard

Indoor drying line

Drying racks, including a mesh one for drying knits flat

Drying rack that fits inside dryer

Drying cabinet

Hanging facilities, including a hanging rod, broad-shouldered hangers, and trouser and skirt hangers

Ample tabletop or countertop space for folding and stacking

Shelves for folded laundry

Shelves and cabinets for storing laundry products, stain-removal products and equipment, and mending equipment

Ironing board and iron, plus ironing aids such as a sleeveboard, press cloth, and a water-spray bottle

Clothes steamer

Windows providing good natural light for checking color compatibility of loads, colorfastness, success of pretreatment, color-matching sock mates, and so on

Small bulletin board with care label terms and symbols, notes on care for different articles, reminders, stain-removal charts, etc.

Clothes brushes and lint removers

Small sewing basket with scissors, needles, and several basic colors of thread for quick repairs such as reinforcing seams or tightening or removing buttons

4

Laundering

*Machine-washing . . . Presoaking . . . Regular, permanent-press,
gentle cycles . . . Making balanced loads that are the right size,
choosing order of loads . . . Starting up the machine, adding
detergent and other laundry products . . . "Hand-washing"
automatically . . . Hand-washing delicate things . . . Hand-washing
sturdy things . . . Water level . . . Water temperature . . .
Water hardness and softness, water softeners . . . Glossary of
Laundry Products and Additives*

There are four basic laundering procedures used in the home: the three basic machine cycles—regular or normal, permanent-press, and gentle—plus hand-washing. The first part of this chapter, "Machine-Washing," explains the nuts and bolts of loading and operating your machine. It begins with the most powerful laundry aid, presoaking, and an explanation of the best uses of the three basic cycles. (For a quick summary of what is going on in your machine during the three cycles, see pages 44–45 in the preceding chapter.) The second part of the chapter, "Hand-Washing," explains not only how to hand-wash delicates but also how to use muscle power on hard-to-clean sturdy items. In the third part, you will find practical information on making good use of the most important laundering tool of all: water.

Machine-Washing

The Short Version. After you have sorted your laundry into loads and pre-treated stains, you wash the loads one by one in your machine. First you set the machine controls properly for your load, choosing a presoak if desirable, the appropriate cycle, and, if necessary, selecting the load size. Depending on the options available on your machine, you may also need or wish to make separate adjustments to control the following factors:

- water or soil level
- the temperature of the wash water
- the temperature of the rinse water
- agitating or tumbling speed
- how long the clothes will be tumbled or agitated in the wash portion of the cycle
- spin speed
- number of rinses

If your machine has automatic dispensers, add detergent and, if you are using them, bleach and fabric softener to the proper dispensers. With front-loading tumbling machines, you then simply add the clothes, close the door, and start the machine. With top-loading agitating machines, it is best to let the machine fill with water and the detergent dissolve before putting in the clothes, closing the lid, and starting the machine.

Below, we consider these simple procedures in great detail, but in practice they take only seconds to accomplish.

Presoaking

Heavily soiled clothes, including diapers (which are washed separately from other garments), may benefit from presoaking or "prewashing." It is equally useful in machine or hand-washing, but this section is about presoaking in your machine.

Presoaking, which used to be called just "soaking," is a powerful laundering procedure that requires absolutely no labor, only foresight. The presoaking option on an automatic washer lets clothes sit in water to which have been added detergent (usually half again as much as you will use for the wash itself) and, if you wish and if appropriate for the load, an oxygen bleach or a presoaking product or both. Newer models automatically delay adding chlorine bleach until the appropriate time. (Do not use chlorine bleach with an enzyme-containing presoak product as the bleach will inactivate the enzymes. See the entries for "Bleaches" and "Enzyme laundry and presoak products" in the Glossary of Laundry Products and Additives at the end of this chapter.)

Presoaking in newer machines usually consists of longer intervals of stillness alternating with brief periods of gentle agitating or tumbling. After the presoak, without draining or rinsing, the machine enters its wash cycle. In some new-model machines, presoaking is automatically used on cycles called "stain" or "heavy duty" or similar names indicating vigorous, long washing. You can increase the cleaning power of any wash cycle by combining it with presoaking. If your agitating top-loader has no automatic presoak, you can simply let the clothes stand in their sudsy wash water for anywhere from fif-teen minutes to an hour before you start the wash cycle.

Presoaking is particularly useful for giving oxygen bleaches sufficient time to be effective. It is also the best way to clean and deodorize synthetic fibers, cure grayness and dinginess, brighten whites, and loosen ground-in dirt.

If you lack a presoak, stain cycle, or heavy duty cycle on your machine or if you want even more cleaning power than these offer, a double wash is another option for very badly soiled or stubbornly dingy clothes. Used in combination with a presoak, hot water, and strong laundry aids, it is the laundering equiva-lent of nuclear weaponry, so be sure your garments can take it. To do a double wash, you use two separate batches of wash water and add detergent twice. For the first wash, put in detergent and whatever bleaches, boosters, or other addi-tives you like, and set the machine for a quick regular wash of, say, five or six minutes (or as close to that as your machine gets). Use the hottest water and the most vigorous washing action that the fabric will take. Be sure you are pres-ent when the washing is finished and the machine has drained and spun off the wash water, because the next step is to stop the machine before it rinses and to reset it to the beginning of the wash cycle. Again add detergent, just as you would do if you were starting the load fresh, and wash again, this time letting the cycle run to its end. The first wash carries off the bulk of the dirt in the clothes, ensuring that the washing and rinsing in the second will be more effec-tive. Because of the extra detergent you have used in the second wash, you should do one or more extra rinses to be sure you have cleared it. Then feel the clothes; if they still feel soapy, rinse yet again.

The Regular Cycle

The vigorous washing action and high-speed spins of the regular or normal cycle are usually combined with hot water and all-purpose or heavy-duty detergent (an HE detergent if you have a high-efficiency washing machine). This cycle is suitable for sturdy cottons and linens, especially white ones, and for highly soiled work, play, and athletic clothing. Increase or decrease wash-ing time and detergent in accordance with the size of the load and how dirty or greasy the clothes are. Cold rinses are usually adequate, but, if you are not satisfied with the result, you can either do one or two extra rinses or try using warm-water rinses, which are modestly more effective at carrying off deter-gent and dirt residues. See "Water Temperature," pages 65–67. If you use cold water, use a liquid or a cold-water detergent. Please note that on some new machines, the fastest and most vigorous washing and spinning speeds are not used on "normal" or "regular" but on some other cycle intended for heavy-duty washing. Feel free to second-guess your machine and use these maxi-mum capacities whenever you think they would be safe and beneficial.

Hot water gets clothes cleanest, and most detergents and other laundry products are more effective in hotter water. Hot water best removes heavy soil and grease and keeps whites white. But it will also tend to cause more fading and more bleeding of colors that are not colorfast and more shrinking in clothes that tend to shrink, such as knits and loose weaves. Warm water is far more effective at cleaning than cool. See pages 65–67, below.

A presoak is highly effective on heavily soiled clothes that are to be washed on the regular cycle.

Bleach is often used for whites and colorfast colors on the regular cycle. See also the discussions of care for cotton and linen fabrics in chapter 21, "The Natural Fibers."

The Permanent-Press Cycle

The permanent-press cycle is usually best for the major synthetic fibers (nylon, polyester, and spandex), for permanent-press cottons and linens (also referred to as "easy-care," "wash-and-wear," "wrinkle-resistant," or "wrinkle-free" fabrics), and for blends of all these fibers. Please note that not all synthetics get permanent-press treatment. Acrylic, modacrylic, rayon, polypropylene, and acetate may require the gentle cycle, hand-washing, or dry cleaning.

The permanent-press cycle uses regular (vigorous) or medium washing action depending on the number of washing speeds your machine offers. If you wash permanent-press items on the regular cycle, it is best to use plenty of water so that the load is not crowded, and wash for a shorter time period than you use for sturdy cottons and linens so as to reduce abrasion and wear and tear on the synthetic fibers and their blends, many of which pill, and on resin-treated fibers, which are weaker than their untreated counterparts. (The shorter wash time is one reason why a presoak is desirable for permanent-press clothes.) Always set the machine for a final cool-down rinse—if the machine does not do so automatically—so that heat-sensitive fibers do not go into the spin cycle while warm or hot. This would set in wrinkles.

The permanent-press cycle uses a slower spin speed so that wrinkles are not set in to synthetic fabrics or permanent-press clothes by the spin pressure. Wash-and-wear fabrics, however, should not be spun at all. (These were once far more common than they are today.) Remove them from the washer after the rinse, roll them dry in a towel, and carefully hang them to dry. If this is not possible with your machine, consider hand-washing or, where possible, dry cleaning.

Ordinarily, when you use the permanent-press cycle, you will choose warm wash water but occasionally cold or, less commonly, hot—if for example, there are greasy stains and the fabric can take it. Ordinary all-purpose detergents are fine for clothes that receive permanent-press washing unless the care label says otherwise. Sometimes deodorizing detergents are advisable for odor-retaining synthetics.

To help reduce the pilling produced by abrasion during washing, any clothes that might pill should be turned inside out. In agitating top-loaders, you should also use more water than you would for a comparable load of cottons or linens so as to diminish the amount of rubbing against one another that the articles undergo. For example, fill the machine with water to the large load level when you are washing a medium-sized load or to the medium load level when you are washing a small load. And be sure to add the correct amount of detergent for the increased water level.

The downside of reducing the abrasion, of course, is that you also reduce the cleaning power of the wash because abrasion—rubbing together—is one of the things that gets out dirt. To get synthetic fibers clean, you will usually need to pretreat problem areas. Even with pretreatment, soil—especially greasy soil—and odor will often not come out unless you also give a long presoak in detergent and water as hot as the fiber can bear (which is often hotter than the care label indicates). Deodorant detergents, laundry boosters, and fabric deodorizers (Febreze or a similar product) are helpful because some synthetic fibers such as polyester, acrylic, and polypropylene tend to retain odors. When it is safe for the fabric, chlorine bleach also deodorizes effectively.* Warm water, rather than the cool that is often recommended on care labels, does a better job at getting odor out. If you are having odor problems on synthetics whose label recommends cold-water wash, try lukewarm water rather than cold; if that does not work, try warm or hot water—but never on polypropylene or other especially heat-sensitive fibers. Warm wash water, pretreating, presoaking, not skimping on detergent, and frequent washing all help to minimize problems in getting synthetics and permanent-press clothes clean and fresh.

Note that the old rule specifying regular-cycle laundering of whites does not usually apply to synthetic whites. Whites that are synthetic or wrinkle-treated probably will need the permanent-press cycle. Many white synthetics will stay white without bleach. If they do not, they often can take and will respond to ordinary household bleaches, but there are exceptions.

Fabric softener is appropriate for permanent-press clothes, but you need to use it only every two or three launderings. If you use it too often, you will get a greasy buildup. Softeners help diminish static and give a smooth feeling or "hand" as textile professionals prefer to say. Liquid softener is used in the final rinse; machines with an automatic dispenser will hold it until then. Softener sheets that go in the dryer are also good. Detergents that include softeners are not recommended; the softeners interfere with cleaning. On washing permanent-press cottons and linens and on synthetics and their blends, see also pages 349–50 and pages 369–70.

---

*Part III gives a profile of each type of fiber, synthetic or natural, that is used in clothes and household linens and fabrics, including detailed information on care of the fiber: whether it shrinks, is sensitive to heat or hot water, or can be damaged by strong detergents or other laundry products; what stains it is vulnerable to; which bleaches, if any, are safe for it; and much more. When in doubt, look up the fiber in Part III.

The Delicate or Gentle Cycle

Delicate or gentle laundering is the most variable of the washing machine treatments because the profiles of "delicate" fabrics are so variable. Sometimes, the gentle cycle is needed because of a garment's fiber content (machine-washable silk and wool, viscose rayon, acrylic and modacrylic, polypropylene, some spandex, and acetate), sometimes because of its delicate construction (lace, very sheer fabrics, loosely woven or knitted ones). The slow, short washes and spins typically used on the delicate cycle offer mechanical protection and reduced abrasion to delicate constructions, weak fibers, and fibers that weaken when wet. The cool to warm wash water, cold rinses, and mild detergents and soaps (preferably liquid ones or mild cold-water detergents such as Woolite when you are using cold water) protect fragile fibers and finishes from harsh chemical cleaning action.

It is helpful to be aware of why you are using gentle treatment so you can vary the delicate cycle effectively. For example, machine-washable acetate and viscose rayon need special treatment both physically and chemically. They need cooler temperatures, detergent that is gentle and works with cooler temperatures, and gentle washing action and slow spin. Knits of cotton, cotton/polyester, and rayon will shrink in hot water, but they rarely need mild detergent. An untreated white cotton dress with a fragile cotton lace collar trim may not be harmed by strong detergent or hot water, but it should receive brief, gentle washing action to be sure that the lace is not torn. Some linens might do best with gentle washing, hot water, and all-purpose detergent. Bleaches, too, are sometimes safe for fabrics that are not chemically vulnerable but are physically vulnerable, i.e., they need gentle agitation or spinning in order to minimize the risks of tearing or excessive wrinkling.

Agitation, tumbling, and spinning do not subject fabrics to the same kinds of stresses. Spinning or fast spinning should be avoided on some sturdy wrinkle-treated and thermoplastic fabrics only because it may set in wrinkles. Spinning exerts an enormous force on fabrics, which presses the cloth against the walls of the machine, squeezing out the water. Even very vigorous spinning is unlikely to harm many garments that would be badly affected by long, vigorous agitation. Quite often you will be able to use a fast spin in the gentle cycle; wool, for example, is so elastic that after hand-washing or gently machine-washing wool sweaters you can spin them dry in your machine using a medium or fast spin setting without fear of harming them.

More central to true gentle treatment is slow, gentle agitation or tumbling. Agitation is rougher than tumbling. It jerks and pulls fabrics. This forces water back and forth through the cloth, dissolving and lifting out dirt. It also abrades—causes a constant rubbing of one item against another which is part of what gets them clean. Agitation does no harm to sturdy cloth, but it can cause pilling on fabrics prone to pilling, as many synthetics are; it can weaken cloth with low abrasion resistance; and it can result in tearing of extremely delicate fabrics. Tumbling does all this too, but much less. In both agitators and tumblers, you can reduce abrasion and wear and tear on very fragile items by placing them in a mesh bag for laundering. (This also prevents very small items such as baby socks from being lost.) In agitators, use ample water to further reduce abrasion.

Besides these variations in why items need gentle treatment, there are all the ordinary differences between them in color, colorfastness, degree and type of soiling, and so forth. Because of this great variability, it is often unwise to wash all your delicates in one load. Some machines have a mini-basket. (See "Operating the Machine," below.) It is excellent for washing small loads of items needing a gentle wash. If yours does not have one, you may find it efficient to hand-wash some of your delicates.

Fabric softeners are advisable occasionally for synthetics that will receive gentle treatment. Liquid softeners are added to the final rinse water or, in some machines, are automatically dispensed at the proper time. Softener sheets are added to the dryer. See "Fabric softeners" in the Glossary of Laundry Products and Additives, pages 81–82. On washing delicate linen, see pages 333–34.

Operating the Machine

Making Balanced, Properly Sized Loads. As though you had not already expended a Solomon's store of wisdom in sorting your clothes, when you get to the point of putting them in the machine there are still other factors to consider. The physical size and composition of the load affects how clean your clothes come. Every load should be composed of a mixture of small and large items, because this mix produces the best action for cleaning and keeps the machine balanced. No load should be too small because the clothes should rub together to some degree to get clean. At a minimum, you usually need what your machine designates as a small load. Some washing machines have a water-saving mini-basket, a small tub that fits into the machine for doing very small loads.

Overloading can cause a smorgasbord of problems. Overpacked loads will not come clean. Water cannot circulate adequately or carry off soil when clothes are jammed together. Clothes will retain soil and soap, each of which will make them look dingy and weaken the fibers. Overloading can cause excessive linting and increased pilling and wear because crowded wash articles rub against one another too much. In top-loading machines, extra water is desirable for permanent-press, many synthetics, delicates, and machine-washable wool to reduce abrasion and, if the fabric is susceptible, pilling. About three dozen cloth diapers is as many as should be washed together in one load.

Overcrowding can also cause wrinkling. To get the most wrinkle-free wash possible, make sure the clothes have plenty of room to move in the water. Very large items like bedspreads, blankets, and sheets need more room to move in the washer than smaller ones. Permanent-press clothes and machine-washable knits will need more room to move in the water than other clothes to reduce or avoid wrinkling and abrasion, which can cause pilling. In top-loading agitator machines, in fact, never wash any load of permanent-press clothes that is larger than medium-sized, and always use the next larger water setting: use large for medium, medium for small. In tumblers, the water level is automatically set in accordance with how big the load is so that you cannot reduce abrasion by increasing the ratio of water to clothes. In general, however, tumblers cause less abrasion than agitators.

Gauge the size of your loads by seeing how full they make the machine before you add water, and carefully read your instruction manual on this subject. A typical top-loading machine uses the following scale for judging load size:

Small: ⅓ full, loosely loaded

Medium: ⅓ to ½ full, loosely loaded

Large: ½ to ¾ full, loosely loaded

Extra-Large: ¾ to completely full, loosely loaded

Manufacturers of tumbling machines usually advise that you can fill the tub but should avoid packing it tightly.

Once you are used to your machine, you will no longer need to load in clothes to see how full it is; you will be able to estimate this automatically as you sort.

Order of Loads. People who have limited supplies of hot water for washing will first wash the loads that require the hottest water: whites, cottons, linens, and heavily soiled clothes. Then they will do the loads requiring warm water, and finally those that take cold. Those launderers with plenty of hot water, which nowadays means most of us, can choose any order that is convenient. For my family, it is usually most efficient to wash first the clothes that take longest to dry—towels, thick bedding, and heavy denims.

Starting Up the Machine. Once the loads are ready, set the machine controls to the proper wash cycle, water or soil level or load size, temperature, and running time, designating a presoak or extra rinse or any other options you wish to use. (If your washing machine does not have an automatic lint cleaner, clean the lint filter before each use.)

Adding Detergent, Bleach, and Other Products. In machines with dispensers, add detergent, bleach, and other products to the proper dispensers in accordance with the manufacturer's instructions. They will be automatically added at the proper time. In some new machines, powdered bleach is to be placed in the detergent dispenser, but a separate dispenser is provided for liquid bleach. Pay particular attention to the instructions on proper use of liquids and powders; often, you are advised not to mix liquids and powders in a single dispenser. Note that in some machines, you can severely damage clothes if you overfill the liquid bleach dispenser; check your manual for the correct amount. Your machine may or may not have a separate dispenser for prewash or presoak detergent. Read your manual to see if using additional detergent for presoaks is recommended and, if so, how much; half the amount used for the wash is often suggested.

If you have a top-loading machine, fill the tub with water and add the detergent before you add the load of clothes. If you put in the clothes first and then fill the machine with water and add detergent, the detergent may not fully dissolve or be thoroughly mixed and you may get uneven cleaning or stains in spots where detergent sat on the clothes undiluted. At any time after an inch or more of water has accumulated, you can add detergent to the machine in the amounts specified on the boxes or bottles. You need more detergent if you are using higher water levels, no matter how little laundry you actually put in, since you want to create the right concentration of detergent in the water. Similarly, if you have a large- or extra-large-capacity machine, you need proportionally more detergent because it uses more water than a regular-capacity machine to do small, medium, or large loads. (See the detergent manufacturer's instructions.) You should also add more detergent if your water is extra hard, less if your water is extra soft. If you are doing a presoak, you should add up to 50 percent more detergent than would otherwise be called for or add a separate presoaking product. (Check instructions on your machine.) You can stir the water with a big wooden paddle or extra-long wooden spoon or run the machine for a minute, making sure that the detergent and other laundry products are completely dissolved and mixed; only then add the clothes.

Detergents may not dissolve readily in cold water. If you tend to have problems with undissolved detergent, try a liquid detergent or a detergent specially formulated for cold-water washing. Or first dissolve the correct amount of powdered detergent in a quart of lukewarm to warm water (the warmer the water, the more easily the detergent dissolves) and then add this to the machine.

If you would like to use fabric softener and your machine has an automatic

---

LIQUID VS. POWDERED DETERGENT

- Granular detergents, which rely more on builders for their cleaning power, are better at stains that respond to builders, like mud and clay. Liquid detergents, which rely more on surfactants for their cleaning power, are better at organic stains like gravy, blood, and grass.
- Liquids readily mix with cold water whereas powders, unless specially formulated, may not readily dissolve in cold water.
- Liquids typically cost more per load.

fabric softener dispenser, add the softener at the beginning of the wash cycle; it will be dispensed at the appropriate time. If you are adding softener manually, do this in the machine's final rinse. Do not use a dispensing ball in a front-loading machine. The tumbling will cause the softener to be released before the final rinse. (For a comparison of liquid softener and dryer softener sheets as well as for information on whether, when, and how to add fabric softeners, see pages 81–82.)

In top-loading agitators, bluing, water softeners, oxygen bleaches (which often contain bluing), and boosters should be added, and thoroughly stirred or mixed, when you add the detergent and before the clothes are loaded. Such products can be used in the presoak if you are doing one. (For more information on all such products, consult the Glossary of Laundry Products and Additives at the end of this chapter.) Years ago, before automatic or fully-automatic washers were used, bluing was added in the final rinse, but this is inadvisable in automatic washers because the clothes are already inside when you want to mix the bluing with the water. It is very important to make sure that oxygen bleach and bluing are thoroughly mixed into the wash water, or you can end up with light spots or blue streaks on your clothes. (These blue streaks can be cured. See "Bluing" in the glossary at the end of this chapter.) Never pour oxygen bleach directly on clothes. Oxygen bleach needs time to work; it will be more effective if you use it in a presoak or in extended washing, and, especially, if you use it regularly and with water as hot as the fabrics can bear.

When the detergent, oxygen bleach, and other additives are thoroughly dissolved and mixed, add the clothes, dropping them in loosely, one piece at a time, around the post. Do not string long objects around the post because this leads to tangling. (Fasten bras; place ties and other objects that may cause tangling in mesh bags.)

Follow the manufacturer's instructions for using chlorine bleach. For best results, chlorine bleach should usually be added only in the last few minutes of the wash period. This permits the additives contained in some detergents— optical brighteners, oxygen bleach, or enzymes—time to do their work; chlorine bleach can interfere with the action of all such additives. Allow about five minutes for the chlorine bleach itself to work. (See "Chlorine bleach" in "Bleaches" in the glossary at the end of this chapter.)

Most newer-model machines have liquid bleach dispensers that automatically delay adding the chlorine bleach until the proper time. If you do not have a bleach dispenser, manually add diluted bleach to top-loading agitating machines as follows: Mix the correct amount of chlorine bleach (see the manufacturer's instructions, paying careful attention to load size) with 1 to 1½ quarts of water; then stop the washing machine's agitation by opening the lid, pour in the bleach solution, and stir with a long wooden spoon or paddle. Close the machine to let it continue washing. You can add diluted chlorine bleach to top-loading agitators in this way at any point during the wash cycle when you can count on having a few minutes for it to work before the wash water

OPTIONS FOR ADJUSTING AND VARYING THE THREE BASIC AUTOMATIC WASHING MACHINE CYCLES

Water quantity. According to size of load (when not automatically determined by machine sensors). Larger, dirtier loads need more water. Permanent-press, wool, and fabrics that pill should be washed with more water than other clothes. More water also reduces wrinkling in permanent-press, knits. See pages 53–54, 56–57, 64–65.

Water temperature. Hot water is best for cleaning and sanitizing. Cool is best for lessening shrinking and fading. Use cool water for presoaking protein stains: for example, blood or egg. The cooler the water temperature, the longer you should wash/agitate the clothes and the more important is the presoak. See pages 65–67.

Water softeners. Helpful where water is hard (has high dissolved mineral content). See "Quality: Water Softeners," pages 67–68, 86.

Detergent. Larger loads, harder water, colder water, and heavier soil all require more detergent. If you do a presoak, you should use up to 50 percent more detergent than you would normally use for the load. Or add a presoaking product in addition to the regular amount of detergent proper for the load. (See "Detergents and Soaps" in the Glossary of Laundry Products and Additives at the end of this chapter.)

Detergent boosters. Boosters can help in cold water, hard water, or with extra-dirty laundry. (See the glossary at the end of this chapter.)

Bleach. Add to wash water for whitening, brightening, and cleaning. Chlorine bleach also sanitizes and deodorizes. (See "Bleaches" in the glossary at the end of this chapter.)

Bluing. Can help yellowing whites look white again. (See "Bluing" in the glossary at the end of this chapter.)

Length of wash period. Longer wash gives greater cleaning; shorter causes less wear and tear and abrasion.

Speed of wash action. Fast cleans better. Slow cleans more gently and causes less pilling. Delicates, permanent-press, and machine-washable wools need slower or shorter agitation or tumbling.

Speed of spin. Slower is gentler for very delicate articles. Faster gets things drier.

Additional rinses. Useful to avoid dinginess and premature wearing caused by detergent and soil residues incompletely rinsed out of clothes. Also useful when washing diapers or other clothes that go next to infants' sensitive skin (or anyone else's sensitive skin). Useful when using extra detergent or boosters or doing double washes to be sure extra cleaning product is completely removed. Useful for whites to be sure bleach and any other residues that might affect the fabric are removed.

Liquid fabric softener in final rinse. Reduces static, gives soft hand to synthetics, renders pile fabrics fluffier. Or use dryer softener sheet. (See "Fabric Softeners" in the glossary at the end of this chapter.)

Use of liquid starch in final rinse. Gives added crispness to cottons, linen, rayons. Or use spray product while ironing.

drains. (Front-loading machines do not permit manually adding diluted bleach to the tub after the machine has begun washing; you must use the dispenser.) Be careful to ensure that chlorine bleach is not splashed or poured directly on fabrics; this can cause holes, weakened fibers, or serious discoloration. Such splashing can occur when you are pouring bleach into your machine's automatic bleach dispenser, too. When using chlorine bleach, your goal is to ensure that the bleach is thoroughly mixed into the wash water and never touches dry clothes. If the bleach will be used when the clothes are not agitating, stir in diluted bleach with a wooden paddle or big wooden spoon to mix it well.

If a top-loading agitator washing machine becomes unbalanced during operation and rumbles or stops, open the lid and redistribute the clothes in a balanced manner, then close it again. The machine should start up automatically.

When the machine has finished a load, remove it for drying promptly. This will reduce wrinkling. Moreover, wet clothes will support rapid microbial growth; odors and even mold will develop if you leave wet clothes long enough. In warm weather, wet clothes can develop a sour smell overnight. If that happens, wash them again, for the smell will not come out during drying.

Hand-Washing

The care label regulations define hand-washing as "gently squeezing action." This action is what is being prescribed when a label tells you to hand-wash. Many new washing machines have a cycle infelicitously called "hand-wash," referred to in this book, reluctantly, because of the contradiction in terms, as "automatic hand-washing." The automatic hand-washing cycle is an extra-gentle one, named so as to convey that it is safe to use when care label instructions call for hand-washing. Typically, the automatic hand-wash cycle alternates periods of soaking with brief extra-slow wash action and a medium or slow spin. Sometimes it is simply a very short, very slow wash and spin. Usually, but not always, you use cold water for this cycle.

Hand-washing is most often advised because the fabric is so delicate, so weak, so prone to shrinking, or so weakened when wet that it could not take even gentle automatic washing and spinning without damage. Sometimes hand-washing is prescribed because a fabric loses dye so quickly that only the briefest immersion in water can be tolerated without serious fading. Automatic hand-washing is indeed safe for most articles requiring hand-washing, although, as we shall see, some articles are so very old, so extremely delicate, or so easily cleaned that the automatic hand-wash is not advisable. For instructions on washing vintage linens and similar items, see chapter 21, pages 350–51. But sometimes it is just more convenient and efficient to wash something with your own two hands—because there are not enough items to make up a load, because there are spots that need attention, or even because no machine is available. And sometimes you will want to hand-wash not because an article needs extra-gentle care but because it needs extra-aggressive treatment—something tougher than your washing machine can provide.

Hand-Washing Delicates. To hand-wash delicate items, usually you should immerse them for a few minutes in a basin of cool to lukewarm water in which some mild detergent or a specialty cleaning product designed for delicate fabrics has been mixed. See "Detergents and soaps, mild," in the glossary at the end of this chapter. If the hand-washing instructions on labels do not specify any particular water temperature, this means that any temperature—hot, warm, or cold—is safe. Keep dye-bleeding articles immersed for the shortest possible time, and use cold water.

The gentlest hand-washing, which should be used for panty hose and stockings, loose knits, lace, and other very fragile items, consists of patting the article until wetted with sudsy water, then softly squeezing it, forcing water through the fabric in the process, until the soil has been lifted. Silks, woolens, and rayons may be gently dipped up and down. Especially delicate items are simply immersed in sudsy water, soaked, and perhaps patted briefly. Delicates not vulnerable to abrasion may be gently rubbed against one another or against themselves. If delicates are heavily soiled, you might try a presoak or a pretreatment of just the heavily soiled spots with mild detergent when this is safe for the fabric.

Rinse with clear cold water, using the same technique as when washing, until all soap or detergent is removed. Several rinse baths may be necessary. The rinse is finished when the water no longer has a slippery feel on your bare hand. You may wish to use gloves when doing hand-washing to preserve your skin and the laundry too. If you don't wear gloves, remove your watch and rings and be sure that you have no rough fingernails. (You may want to apply a moisturizer to your hands afterward.)

Unless otherwise instructed, roll delicate hand-washed items in a towel to remove excess water. (If the garment bleeds, use a towel that you don't mind spotting.) Never wring delicate fabrics, many of which are very weak when wet. Wringing out clothes is much harder on them than spinning, tumbling, or agitating in the washer. Never wring wash-and-wear or permanent-press clothes, as wringing wrinkles them.

Delicates should usually be hung to dry or dried flat. (See chapter 5, "Drying the Laundry.") You can place them on a drying frame that provides a mesh for support while allowing air to circulate on all sides or on a drying rack in your dryer. (Set the dryer at the appropriate temperature—usually low or air fluff. I use time-dry with an in-dryer rack because the moisture sensor does not seem to sense a single stationary, wet item.) A drying cabinet is especially good for slow-drying items that should be dried flat. Or you can lay them on a clean, dry towel that does not bleed and will not be harmed if the garment bleeds. Knits and stretchy items should be blocked to their proper shape and dried flat to prevent stretching. See chapter 21, page 345, for more on blocking. To speed drying, turn an electric fan on the clothes. Dry delicates out of direct sunlight. For suggestions on washing old or other very fragile fabrics, see chapter 21, pages 350–51.

Hand-Washing Sturdy Articles. Sometimes you want to hand-wash something that is not delicate. You are in a hotel, it is midnight, and you need a garment for the morning. Or you have a muddy pair of toddler's overalls whose soil you do not want to contaminate the other clothes in a load, or perhaps you have one or two small things that are not worth running the machine for, or you feel that without individual attention a particular garment will not come clean.

Hand-washing can be vigorous as well as gentle. In fact, hand-washing can be much more harsh than anything your washing machine can do. If you are dealing with especially dirty clothes, hand-scrubbing, when the clothes are sturdy enough to take it, can be far more effective than machine-washing and sometimes is your only hope. The combination of physical action and chemical action is more effective than either alone, and the addition of heat (in the water) makes it even more so.

Use protective rubber gloves, ordinary laundry detergent (if appropriate to the fiber), and the hottest water that is suitable to the fabric, the soil, and that your gloved hands can bear. When it would be safe for the fabric, presoaking the item in extremely hot water before you scrub it is highly effective—using whatever detergents, boosters, bleaches, or pretreatment products are appropriate. Use only cold water, however, for articles that bleed, and never presoak these. Immerse them in water for the shortest possible time consistent with getting them clean. Of course, if you don't mind some fading—e.g., you're washing highly soiled blue jeans—hot water and soaking are fine.

To scrub a sturdy article, grasp the cloth in both hands and rub it against itself, concentrating on the areas with heaviest soil, perhaps the cuffs,

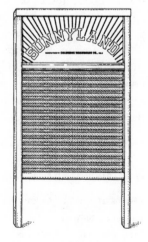

Washboard

knees, and collar. Alternate this rubbing with repeatedly immersing and swishing and squeezing the article in soapy water. This rinses away dirt that you have loosened by your scrubbing and gets you fresher soapy water to continue scrubbing with. If the water becomes too soiled, drain it and start over with fresh water and detergent.

If you find that you wash hard-to-clean sturdy items by hand more than occasionally, you might find it useful to have a small washboard (like the larger one your grandmother or great-grandmother had) to handle deeply ingrained soil in play clothes, gardening clothes, work clothes, or sportswear. Try this especially on mud, oil or grease, food stains, collar rings, and any other soil that resists coming clean in the machine. Just scrub the fabric up and down against the bumps on the washboard, occasionally dipping it in the water to carry off dirt and renew your suds.

If you do not have a washboard, you can scrub very hardy fabrics, such as thick denims or work clothes, with a small soft brush or toothbrush or against another cloth, such as a clean white terry towel, or scrub it vigorously against itself. All such procedures, while often effective, can be *very* hard on the cloth—harder than a washboard, whose surface is smoother. If you were to use them on more fragile items, you would probably get fraying, fading, or holes and tears.

When you can see that you have gotten the article clean, wring out as much soapy water as you can; then rinse thoroughly as many times as it takes to get out all the soap. When you are finished rinsing, wring the article as dry as you can. Novices might wish to know that wringing consists of twisting the cloth, grasping it at both ends with one hand rotated as far forward as it will go and the other as far back as it will go. Then reverse the rotation of your fists so as to tighten the twist, forcing out water. (Remember that these are techniques to be used only on sturdy hand-washables!) This takes muscles, and it is good exercise. After wringing, you may still want to roll the item in a towel, as you do with delicates, to get out even more water and decrease the drying time.

If the article will not be harmed, put it in the dryer on the proper temperature or hang it on a line. Otherwise, hang or dry flat as described in "Hand-Washing Delicates."

Never use these harsh hand-washing methods on delicate items, unless, of course, the soil or stain is so serious that the article will be unusable if it is not removed. In this situation, you have nothing to lose by trying progressively harsher treatments.

Water
How Much, How Hot, How Soft?

Quantity. Many newer machines automatically sense the size of your load and set the water level accordingly. In others, you have to choose the setting on your machine that is proper for the size of the load. Too much water results in poor cleaning because there is too little rubbing and abrasion. Too little water will also result in poor cleaning, along with poor rinsing, which means detergent and laundry-product residues in your clothes, dinginess, a harsh feeling, and itchy garments and bedclothes. Insufficient water also causes excessive abrasion and wears out your clothes prematurely. If you use too much detergent or other additives for the amount of water, you can get excessively high concentrations of chemicals on your clothes and damage them. The recommendations of the manufacturers of washing machines as to the amount of water needed for a certain amount of laundry are highly reliable.

Water Temperature. For the best laundering results, but not necessarily the most energy-efficient results, choose the hottest wash temperature that the fabrics will bear without shrinking, fading, or suffering other damage. Hot water cleans much better than warm or cool. The hotter the wash temperature, the better any laundry soap or detergent will work. Warm or cool water rather than hot, however, keeps many colors brighter and is less likely to cause shrinking. Some laundry products advertise that they work better than others in cold water. They may, but that does not mean that they would not work still better in warmer water. No matter what detergent you are using, hot water is always better than cold for cleaning oil and grease stains.

Hot, however, is not quite as hot as it used to be. The FTC has amended the care label rules defining "hot," "warm," and "cold." See the footnote on page 27. "Hot" now means temperatures between 112°F and 145°F (45°C to 63°C), whereas until 2000 it meant 120°F to 150°F. "Warm" now means 87°F to 111°F (31°C to 44°C) and "cold" means up to 86°F (30°C). The FTC did this, at least in part, because it assumed, not unreasonably, that people would think "hot" on a care label meant whatever showed up in their machines when they set them for "hot." But that may be not nearly as hot as they think it is. The water heaters used in many homes today are preset to 120°F at the factory (for safety and energy saving), and water cools on its way from the water heater to the washing machine inlet. "Hot" wash in these homes, therefore, is going to be considerably lower than 120°F, just as it will be considerably lower than 150°F in homes where an older heater is set to 150°F.

Thus 112°F to 145°F is more realistic as a prediction. But is this range really a good definition for "hot" in the laundry? No. There are cleaning and sanitizing jobs (see pages 147 and 151) that require considerably hotter temperatures. Compare the FTC's current standards with the laundry advice in the *Maytag Encyclopedia of Home Laundry* from the 1960s, which advises hot-water washing of 140°F to 160°F for best cleaning.[1] Hotter temperatures than 145°F are routinely used in professional laundries. And European self-heating washing machines offer you wash temperatures as hot as 200°F. (The FTC rejected the idea of adding an instruction about "very hot" water to the care label rule.) My grandmothers boiled their sheets and underwear, and my mother and her sister, telling me about this, got dreamy remembering how lovely and fresh those boiled linens were. (Do not try this at home unless you, too, happen to have a big copper boiler in your cellar made for the purpose.)

As though the changes to the care label rule definitions were not confusing enough, washing machine manufacturers, too, are redefining "hot," "warm," and "cold" to fit the temperature control and heating capacities of their newest-model machines, and their definitions are not the same as the FTC's, let alone my grandmothers'. Read your operating manual carefully to see what temperatures your machine defines as "hot," "warm," and "cold," because this varies among manufacturers. One company even uses different definitions of "warm" for wash water and rinse water, calling 86°F "warm" in a rinse and "cold" in a wash on the same machine!

The manufacturer of my machine, which heats the water only to a disappointing 130°F, promises approximately the following temperatures on "hot," "warm" and "cold" water settings:

Hot water: 130°F (54°C)

Warm water: 105°F (41°C)

Cold water: 65°F (18°C)

Another manufacturer's machine gives more options:

Extra-hot: 167°F (75°C)

Hot: 122°F (50°C)

Warm: 104°F (40°C)

Cold: 77°F (25°C)

The 65°F for cold that machines like mine guarantee is a minimum. No detergents will work properly in water temperatures below 65°F. (If the tap provides colder water, self-heating machines will warm it.) Washing your clothes in water as cold as 65°F can cause lint, poor cleaning, and residues of undissolved detergent. Granular detergents may not readily dissolve or mix into cold water. Keep in mind, too, the fact that the temperature of your cold tap water varies with the seasons and with geography. If you live in Florida, your cold water in August will be lukewarm; in northern Michigan, your cold water in January will be frigid indeed—below 65°F. And what your machine gives you as "warm" (unless you have a self-heating or temperature-regulating model) varies with the temperature of your cold tap water. On a day when your hot-water heater is set at 140°F and your cold tap water is 60°F, if you choose the "warm" setting on your washing machine you will probably get wash temperatures of about 100°F (which feels comfortably warm to the hand). This will provide good cleaning for much of your laundry, if less cleaning power than hot water. But if your hot water is 120°F and your cold is 40°F, your "warm" may be only about 80°F, which is considered cold under care label rules.

If your machine lacks both automatic temperature control and a heating element, it is worthwhile to acquire an inexpensive thermometer for testing your home water temperatures. You may find that there is a significant difference between what your heater is set for and what gets delivered at the faucet. Check the temperature at the beginning and at the end of the wash segment of the cycle, too, as significant cooling occurs while the clothes are washing.

Guidelines for Choosing Water Temperatures. Water temperature affects more than cleaning power. Hot enough water kills many microorganisms as well as dust mites and nits. See chapter 10. Colder water minimizes shrinking and fading, and it is better for presoaking many protein stains, such as blood. When dyes, fiber content, and construction are suitable:

- Use hot water for sturdy whites, pastels and light prints, diapers and soiled baby bibs and clothes, heavily soiled work, garden, sport, and play clothes; clothes and linens of those sick with infectious diseases; on oily or greasy dirt; dish towels and dishcloths, bath towels and hand towels, face cloths, pillowcases and sheets and other household linens; cleaning rags and cloths.
- Use warm water for permanent-press, colorfast brights, dark colors, and many knits.
- Use cold water to wash fabrics with dyes that run or bleed and fabrics that are lightly soiled; for soaking protein stains such as egg, vomit, or blood; for washing many delicates, knits, and other fabrics prone to shrinking; and for rinsing. (Use a liquid or cold water detergent.)
- Cold water is generally recommended for rinsing your clothes after they have been washed. Most home washing machines let you set your automatic controls for any temperature wash and offer you a choice of cold or warm rinsing. (With some coin-operated machines, you may have no choice as to rinse temperature.) Cold rinse water is adequate in all but exceptional circumstances. It is more energy efficient, even when you factor in the qualification that your dryer may take longer to dry clothes that have been chilled by the cold-water rinse. A warm rinse is a bit more effective at removing dirty, sudsy water from your clothes and linens. Try a warm rinse, or a couple of them, at times when you need especially effective rinsing— for instance, for the clothes or linens of someone with sensitive skin, for a delicate fabric from which you wish to remove all possible residues of detergents or other laundry additives, or if you are working on trying to remove dinginess or grayness or yellowness from whites.

Quality: Water Softeners. If you have hard water, you probably know it already: Your shampoo struggles to foam, and you may get mineral deposits around your faucets. It might still be useful to have your water tested to see just how hard it is so that you can make appropriate adjustments when you launder. Manufacturers have the following levels of softness and hardness of water in mind when they make their recommendations as to how much detergent or bleach or other product you should use:

	Soft	Moderately Hard	Hard	Very Hard
Grains/gal	0.0–3.5	3.6–7.0	7.1–10.5	10.6+
Parts/million or mgs/liter	0.0–60	61–120	121–180	180+

Many people install mechanical water softeners in their homes. These use ion-exchange resins to remove the minerals; they "exchange" the calcium and magnesium ions for sodium ions provided by the resins.

If your water is very hard and you have no mechanical water-softening system, you can add a packaged water softener to your laundry. Remember to use the softener in the rinse water as well as in the wash water. There are two varieties of packaged softeners: nonprecipitating and precipitating. Nonprecipitating types (such as Calgon) "sequester" the offending minerals and hold them in solution; the water remains clear. These usually contain polyphosphates. Precipitating softeners combine with the minerals to form a precipitate or residue that turns the water cloudy. The precipitate can stick to clothes or your washer. Precipitating softeners usually contain sodium carbonate (washing soda) or sodium sesquicarbonate. TSP and borax are both precipitating softeners. You can buy water softeners at the supermarket or your local hardware store. Be sure to follow the product instructions.

If your water is only moderately hard, you will probably need to do nothing more than use enough of a good detergent that contains water softeners. But in this case it would be better to avoid detergents that contain carbonates. (Read labels carefully.) The unpleasant potential effects of using a carbonate detergent if you have hard water include stiff, harsh towels; fading, dullness, dinginess, or graying; a white powdery residue on dark clothes; reduced wrinkle resistance in permanent-press clothes; increased abrasion; and buildup of crust in the washer.

To remove hard-water mineral residues from clothes, in a plastic container soak the clothes in a solution of 2 cups white vinegar to 1 gallon hot tap water for fifteen minutes. (Do not use a metal or other container that will be affected by the vinegar, which is a mild acid.)

In addition to using water softeners, try these strategies for coping with hard water: use a phosphate detergent; use hotter wash water; add more detergent and make sure it is fully dissolved before adding clothes; use more bleach;* and sort with special care, taking particular care to keep greasy or more heavily soiled clothes entirely separate from lightly soiled or delicate things.

---

*But see "Chlorine bleach" in the Glossary of Laundry Products and Additives, pages 72–74. Chlorine bleach may cause rust stains to appear on fabrics if your water contains a great deal of iron.

GLOSSARY OF LAUNDRY
PRODUCTS AND ADDITIVES

Acid. See "Vinegar, white." See also chapter 12, "Science for the Laundry," pages 172–75.

Alkali. See "Ammonia," "Borax," "Detergents and soaps," "Detergents and soaps, mild," "Trisodium phosphate," and "Washing soda." Laundering solutions of water and detergent typically are alkaline (have a pH greater than 7). See also chapter 12, pages 172–75.

Ammonia. Ammonia is an alkaline substance that can be used as a laundry booster. It will sometimes brighten a load of laundry and help detergent perform better. Add ½ cup of household ammonia to the laundry water before you add clothes. Do not add ammonia to any laundry water that has been treated with chlorine bleach: the combination of ammonia and bleach releases toxic fumes.

Average load. When a product label tells you to use a certain amount of detergent or soap for an average load, it is important to realize what it means by "average":

> 5–7 pounds of clothes
>
> Moderate soil
>
> Medium (moderately) hard water: 3.6–7.0 grains of minerals per gallon or 61–120 parts per million or milligrams/liter
>
> Average water volume: 17 gallons (64 liters) for top-loading washing machines and 8 gallons (30 liters) for front-loading machines

Observing my neighbors suggests to me that what detergent manufacturers consider "average," many people consider rather small. Thus detergent manufacturers are surely right when they say that one of the main causes of poor laundering is using insufficient detergent. If you use too little, the soil will redeposit itself and your laundry will be gray and dingy. If you use too much, however, your machine will not be able to rinse it out properly and your laundry will come out stiff and boardlike or may cause itching.

Baking soda. Baking soda is sodium bicarbonate ($NaHCO_3$), a white crystalline powder with chemical and physical properties that give it capabilities for gentle cleaning and deodorizing. See chapter 12, "Science for the Laundry."

- To deodorize and clean diapers, add ½ cup baking soda per 2 quarts of water in your diaper soak.
- To keep laundry hampers sweet-smelling, sprinkle in ½ cup baking soda.

The baking soda can be poured into the washing machine with the clothes, for it acts as a gentle detergent booster.

- Pour ½ cup to 1 cup baking soda in the washing machine with your detergent as a gentle booster and deodorizer.

Bleaches. Bleaching is the process of applying oxidizing or reducing agents to fabrics so as to chemically transform dark or colored materials in textile fibers into colorless, soluble ones that can be washed away. (*Oxidation* is the removal of one or more electrons from an ion, atom, or molecule. *Reduction* is the addition of one or more electrons. Both processes result in making stains colorless.) Household bleaches usually contain oxidizing agents such as sodium hypochlorite (chlorine bleach), sodium perborate, potassium monopersulfate, sodium percarbonate, and hydrogen peroxide.

Bleaching makes fabrics whiter and cleaner, which causes them to look brighter; chlorine bleaching also deodorizes and sanitizes them. But if used improperly, bleaches can fade dyes and weaken cloth. Different household bleaches vary considerably in strength. Strong bleaches can eat holes in cloth if accidentally splashed on it at full strength. Part of the art of laundering is learning to pick a bleach appropriate for the fabric, a process of weighing costs and benefits. One factor to be weighed in the balance is that bleach helps to remove dirt and detergent residues, which can also cause deterioration in cloth, and that a fabric that does not look good has also failed to "last."

When your eyes tell you that your clothes or linens are stained or heavily soiled or appear gray, dingy, dull, or yellow, you may wish to use bleach. Follow the instructions on the product's label. The process becomes intuitive as you gain experience with it. The product label tells you which of the commonly available chemical bleaches (discussed below) it contains. Advice on which bleach to use is included below.

Sunlight. In ordinary sunlight, nature has provided an effective bleaching agent that is gentler than chemical bleaches. Sunshine has a greater bleaching effect on damp fabrics than on dry ones, so if you want to bleach a cotton sheet, towel, or T-shirt, or a linen tablecloth, wash it and spread it out in the sun on a sheet or other clean white cloth, or hang it on a line. You can get slight results in one day, and more results in two or three. Sunlight can fade dyes, so, if you want to avoid fading, dry colored things in the shade. Prolonged exposure to sunlight, as with other bleaches, will cause fabrics to deteriorate. White cotton will yellow with prolonged exposure to sunlight, but the effect of moderate sun exposure on cotton is to bleach it. (Yellowing is not likely to be visible on colored fabrics other than pastel blues.) Vigorous laundering, especially with chlorine bleach, will usually take out such yellowing in white cottons.

Hydrogen peroxide. Dilute solutions of hydrogen peroxide can be used for household chemical bleaching. Hydrogen peroxide is an oxygen bleach. (The other oxygen bleaches convert to hydrogen peroxide in solution. See "Oxygen bleaches" below.) Hydrogen peroxide is recommended for bleaching delicate fabrics and washable white wool and silk and can be an important aid in stain removal. You can buy a 3 percent solution of hydrogen peroxide for various household uses at your drugstore; this is already dilute enough to be safe on fabrics, but add water if you wish. It comes in a brown bottle that is intended to keep it from deteriorating from exposure to light. Hydrogen peroxide loses its effectiveness over time.

Be sure to test for the safety of hydrogen peroxide in an inconspicuous area of the fabric before using it as a bleach. Soak fibers other than wool in the peroxide solution for thirty minutes. Wool can be harmed by soaking and should be removed after a few minutes. Rinse thoroughly.

Although you can, in theory, use any good commercial oxygen or all-fabric bleach for delicates and washable white wools and silks, all-fabric bleaches usually contain bluing, optical brighteners, laundry boosters, activators, or other additives. Plain hydrogen peroxide is desirable when such additives are not suitable for your fabric.

Oxygen bleaches. The household oxygen bleaches, also known as "all-fabric" or "color-safe" bleaches, include sodium perborate, potassium monopersulfate, hydrogen peroxide, and sodium percarbonate. All of these except hydrogen peroxide come in powdered form. When dissolved in water, the inorganic peroxide compounds they each contain convert to hydrogen peroxide (plus some residue, such as sodium borate or sodium calmite); this hydrogen peroxide is the actual bleaching agent. The hydrogen peroxide reacts with soil and organic materials, either rendering them colorless or breaking them up. This chemical bleaching action, in the strengths in which we use such products in our homes, is gentler than chlorine bleaching.

Powdered oxygen bleaches usually contain a number of other substances: builders and surfactants such as sodium carbonate, enzymes, optical brighteners, bluing agents, and perfumes.

Oxygen bleaches are safe for almost all whites, colorfast dyes, fibers, and fabrics. They should not be used on dyes that are not colorfast or on extremely delicate or old fabrics. There are some wools and silks for which they are not safe. They are said to be good for maintaining whiteness and brightness but not very useful for restoring whiteness once it has been lost. Thus you must use them regularly to reap their benefits.

Their effectiveness depends on four factors: temperature, time, concentration of the active ingredient, and pH of the solution. Oxygen bleaches need an alkaline environment to be really effective. Sodium carbonate, which is often added to commercial bleaches, increases the alkalinity of the wash-water solution. In addition, unlike chlorine bleach, which works at lower temperatures, oxygen bleaches need hot water—140°F or higher—to be effective. The typical load of laundry in this country, however, is washed at much lower temperatures. Activated oxygen bleaches, such as Biz, contain a chemical catalyst called an activator that significantly improves their functioning at lower wash temperatures. Activated oxygen bleaches are considerably more germicidal than nonactivated ones. Most oxygen bleaches sold in this country (unlike European products) are not activated, but some detergents contain an activated bleach, e.g., Tide with Bleach, Gain with Bleach, and Oxydol.

With all oxygen bleaches, the longer the exposure, the greater the effectiveness of the bleach. And the lower the water temperature, the longer you need to expose fabrics to oxygen bleaches. Thus presoaking or using an extended washing period when you use an oxygen bleach can greatly improve its effectiveness. (This is unlike chlorine bleach, which both works well in lower wash-water temperatures and completes its work within a few minutes, after which further exposure is not useful; see the discussion of chlorine bleach below.)

Despite their comparative mildness, oxygen bleaches can occasionally do damage when used on the wrong fabrics. If there is any question as to their safety, test them before using on an inconspicuous area of the garment (following the manufacturer's testing instructions). Test detergents that contain oxygen bleaches too. Oxygen bleaches can be used safely on fabrics that have received wrinkle-resistance resin finishes.

In top-loading agitator washing machines, oxygen bleaches should be added to the presoak or wash water with the detergent, before the clothes, in the amounts recommended by the manufacturer for the load size. Make sure that the bleach is thoroughly mixed and dissolved before putting the clothes in. In tumbling or high-efficiency machines, place bleach in the proper dispenser before starting the load; the machine adds it to the presoak or wash, whichever you are beginning with.

Chlorine bleach. Chlorine bleach is sold for home use either as a 5.25 percent or, in "ultra" or more concentrated versions, as a 6 percent solution of sodium hypochlorite. It is the strongest household laundry bleach. Its aesthetic and hygienic contributions to laundering are both valuable. It will whiten whites, brighten colorfast colors, remove stains, and remove mildew. It also cleans, increases the effectiveness of laundering in cooler water, sanitizes, and deodorizes. It is inexpensive. Chlorine bleach is usually safe on sturdy white and colorfast cottons and on most fabrics made of manufactured fibers other than spandex and nylon. When used at proper concentrations, it is safe for the majority of washables.

For those who dislike the unadulterated bleach odor, chlorine bleach now comes in a variety of scents. Regular-scented bleach can leave a strong bleach smell on your clothes if you use too much, and it may leave a faint one even if you use the correct amount. A faint scent is normal and harmless (and some of us like it). In fact, it mostly illustrates that we have an extraordinary ability to smell this chemical. According to the USDA, we can detect 0.01 parts per million of chlorine; our ability to smell it is more than five thousand times greater than our ability to smell ammonia.

Note: For sanitizing and disinfection, use only plain or regular-scented bleach. Do not use the thicker, nonsplashing, gel, or perfumed versions of chlorine bleach. The latter, of course, are fine for ordinary laundering and bleaching.

Improperly used, chlorine bleach can drastically weaken cloth or eat holes in it and fade clothes and linens. Proper use means diluting the bleach according to the manufacturer's instructions, using the recommended quantities, adding it to the machine in the recommended manner, and not spilling bleach on clothes. You risk damage to your clothes and linens if you use chlorine bleach in defiance of care label instructions. If you have any doubt, test the effect of diluted chlorine bleach in an inconspicuous area. (See page 21.)

Be sure always to test all components of a garment before concluding that it is safe for chlorine bleaching; facings, interfacings, linings, and trim are sometimes vulnerable when the garment-in-chief is not. In addition, read the fiber content label, and for each fiber listed on the label, determine whether any household bleach may safely be used on it.

When using chlorine bleach in your laundry, always observe these cautions:

- Chlorine bleach solutions that contain more than 200 parts per million of available chlorine (about 1 tablespoon per gallon) are toxic. Chlorine bleach solutions are corrosive and irritating to the skin. Carefully follow instructions for the safe use of chlorine bleach. Store it in a safe place, locked out of reach of children. Never store chlorine bleach in any bottle other than the one it comes in from the store, and never store any other substance in an old bleach bottle. Familiarize yourself with the safety instructions on the product label, including instructions about what to do in case of accidental ingestion. Do not mix chlorine bleach with acids, ammonia, or acid- or ammonia-containing products. Doing so will produce a toxic gas or other dangerous reaction. In fact, you should never mix chlorine bleach with anything other than water and ordinary laundry detergent unless you are specifically instructed to do so by a reliable authority. If you have questions, call a local public health authority, the poison control number in your area, or the bleach manufacturer's toll-free number printed on the bottle label.
- Frequent chlorine bleaching will usually cause fading in colored articles (essentially in all but a few vat-dyed ones), and overfrequent bleaching will harm fabrics made of some types of fibers, resulting in a weakening of the cloth and, possibly, frayed areas or holes. Using more bleach than the bleach manufacturer recommends can also create these problems.
- Chlorine bleach should never be used on silk, wool, leather, mohair, nylon, spandex, and many fabrics treated with flame retardants. It may yellow or weaken spandex and permanently damage the fibers of silk, wool, and mohair. It may yellow nylon.
- Chlorine bleach is not recommended for sheer, fine, weak, or delicate fabrics, or fabrics with trim or decoration that fit such a description.
- Too much bleach can cause yellowing.

- Spilled or splashed bleach can result in holes or discolored spots in clothes and linens, such as pale blotches on dark fabrics.
- Some permanent-press clothes and fabrics that have been given optical brightening finishes may yellow if exposed to chlorine bleach. If you are worried, test in an inconspicuous area.
- When exposed to chlorine bleach, some resin-treated fabrics may yellow or retain a chlorine odor. If you are worried, test in an inconspicuous area.
- If your water contains a great deal of iron, chlorine bleach may cause rust stains to appear on fabrics.

Use the quantity of chlorine bleach recommended on the bleach container for the load size (and choose the proper load size setting on your machine). Although you can damage your clothes if you use too much bleach, you can get poor results if you use too little. Note that you use less of "ultra" formulations than of nonconcentrated ones: ¾ cup of ultra for 1 cup of the more dilute formula.

Place liquid bleach in the proper dispenser before starting the washer, being careful not to splash or spill undiluted bleach on your laundry. If your top-loading machine has no liquid bleach dispenser, add it manually. To do this, mix the bleach with 1 to 1½ quarts of water; then, at the proper time, stir the bleach mixture into the washer with a long wooden paddle or wooden spoon to be sure that it mixes well. Always dilute chlorine bleach before adding it to wash water in which clothes are already agitating. Never add chlorine bleach to dry clothes.

And what is the appropriate time to add bleach manually? At least five or six minutes after the washing has begun and a few minutes before the washing will end. The reason for delaying, which machines with dispensers now do automatically, is that most contemporary detergents contain optical or fluorescent brighteners and enzyme cleaners, and many contain oxygen bleaches. Chlorine bleach may interfere with the action of optical brighteners and inactivate enzyme cleaners and oxygen bleaches. Adding chlorine bleach in the last few minutes of the wash period gives the brighteners and enzymes time to complete their work. (The chlorine bleach completes its action in just a few minutes—slightly faster in hot water, slightly slower in cold water.) You need not wait, of course, if your detergent does not contain these substances.

Chlorine bleach loses potency as it ages. When kept for emergency purposes as a disinfectant for water during floods or for other important functions, it should be replaced every six months. When kept for laundering or other ordinary household cleaning purposes, it should be replaced every nine to twelve months.

On environmental questions associated with the use of chlorine bleach, see page 177.

Bluing. Bluing is a colorant added to the water in which you wash white clothes. It neutralizes any yellowish tinge in the color of whites, thereby making them look whiter, although at the same time less bright or a bit duller. Or at least, we North Americans think whites look whiter and cleaner when they are more blue-white than yellow-white. To South Americans, I am told, a red-white is what looks clean.

You can usually buy bluing separately in the supermarket. It is also contained in some commercial oxygen or all-fabric bleaches and in some detergents and other laundry products. If you would like to try bluing, follow the label instructions. With top-loading agitating machines, you are generally told to add it when you add the detergent, before you put the clothes in the washer. You can add bluing in the rinse, but the clothes are already inside at this point, which increases the risk that you will cause blue spots or streaks as a result of insufficiently mixed bluing. It is important to make sure that bluing is thoroughly mixed in the wash water. But if you should end up with blue streaks on your clothes, this is a nuisance rather than a disaster; these wash out. See "Blue Spots or Streaks," pages 139–40, in chapter 9, "Common Laundry Mishaps and Problems."

Boosters and laundry aids. See "Borax," "Builders," "Trisodium phosphate," and "Washing soda."

Borax. Borax is an excellent all-around laundry aid and booster. It is gentle. It cleans, deodorizes, and helps get rid of stains. It is also a water softener and acts as a buffer, maintaining alkalinity in wash water. It makes an excellent diaper soak because it deodorizes and helps clean and whiten the diapers while rendering them more absorbent. It can be used together with chlorine bleach. Add ½ cup borax to the diaper pail with warm water. You can also add ½ cup to the wash water for diapers.

Borax will boost the cleaning ability of mild detergents. Add ¼ cup borax and 1–2 tablespoons of mild soap or detergent in a sinkful of warm water and soak the garments for ten minutes. Rinse in clear cool water and blot with a towel or roll in a towel. This preparation is not for use on silks or wools, or for any very delicate or fragile items.

Builders. Builders are substances added to detergents to improve their functioning. They soften the water, inactivate acids, buffer the washing solution in order to maintain alkalinity, and prevent the redeposit of soil.

Chlorine bleach. See "Bleaches."

Color removers. Color removers, manufactured by dye manufacturers, contain sodium hydrosulfite (Na_2S_2O—also called "sodium hyposulfite"). A color remover is a reductive bleach. (Ordinary household bleaches are oxidizing bleaches.) It does not literally remove color. It destroys many dyes on fabrics, preparing them to receive another dye. It should be used only on white clothes or on clothes that you intend to strip of color, and it should be used with great caution.

If you have yellowing of a white garment caused by a chlorine-retentive finish, such as a resin used to render cloth wrinkle-resistant, a color remover may be effective in rendering it white again. A color remover may also help when you have ruined a white or light article by washing it with another garment whose color ran. Follow the instructions on the package carefully. Be sure that the color remover is safe for the fabric. Remember that color removers will indeed destroy the color in colored garments and linens. Color removers are sold in drugstores, hardware stores, home centers, and large supermarkets. See also "Whitener/brighteners."

Detergents and soaps. Detergents contain surfactants to increase the wettability of the fabrics to be cleaned; builders and boosters of all sorts to increase cleaning power; antiredeposition agents that keep dirt suspended in the wash water and prevent it from resetting on the clothes; enzymes to attack stains, whiten, and reduce fuzz (and the worn appearance that fuzziness gives cottons) and lint; other fuzz, pilling, and lint stoppers; agents that protect color by preventing "dye transfer," act as "dye fixatives," or neutralize chlorine in tap water to reduce any fading it might cause. Bleaches, bleach activators, fabric softeners, and preservatives are also frequently added to household laundry detergents. Most laundry detergents contain optical brighteners (see pages 83–84). How many of these ingredients are likely to be listed on their labels? Fewer and fewer every year. If you want to know what you are buying, you must call the manufacturer's 800 number and beg for information. Some companies will give it, and some will not.

Detergent names that include the word "ultra" are concentrated, so you can use less of them. This "new" type of product is in fact old. When detergents were first manufactured, people were used to using laundry soaps, which had greater volume. It took less detergent than soap to get the laundry clean. But people resisted buying a small box of detergent for the same price as a bigger box of soap, even though it would last just as long and produce equally clean clothes, out of a feeling that they were being cheated. So the detergent manufacturers included fillers in their products so that the boxes would be as big as soap boxes and you would need to use about the same amount of detergent as soap to do a load. This is how things stood until the 1990s, when, finally, detergent manufacturers decided that they could sell little boxes and bottles to those of us who have little shelf space and, unlike our great-grandparents, tend to think new, different, and compact is better. This results in the problem, however, of making it more difficult to estimate how much you need. If you switch back and forth from "ultra" to "regular" detergents, you may lose your sixth sense for getting the right amount and you can forget which one you are using and accidentally add too much or too little. Follow the instructions on the package and use the measure in the box to help minimize the chances that this will happen.

Detergent names that include the word "free" contain no dyes or perfumes or fragrances. People who are prone to allergic responses to such substances and people who want to choose the most environmentally favorable products prefer these. (I sometimes wish manufacturers could be convinced to offer products with just a little environmentally favorable, pleasant fragrance, but they usually seem to offer only the extremes of chemical-smelling products "free" of perfume and those that bowl you over with their heavy odor.)

The terms "heavy-duty" and "all-purpose" are often used interchangeably to refer to detergents formulated for use on the whole family laundry—all types of soil and washable fabrics (except those that must be washed with "mild" or "gentle" soaps or detergents). These detergents are too strong—that is, alkaline—for some fibers, such as silk, wool, and many delicates. "All-purpose" sometimes means a detergent that is suitable for general household cleaning purposes as well as for laundering. All-purpose or heavy-duty detergents come in both granular and liquid form. Liquids are preferable when cold water makes it difficult to dissolve granules and for convenience in pretreating spots and stains. They are sometimes superior for washing out food and other organic stains. Granular (powdered) detergents are said to be more effective on clay, mud, and ground-in dirt.

Many all-purpose detergents and even some mild laundry detergents contain bleaching agents (oxygen bleaches) that some fabrics cannot take. The presence of bleaches in laundry detergents is not altogether a blessing. Because most laundry loads are washed at temperatures lower than 140°F, the color-safe bleaches in detergents will be relatively ineffective unless they contain activators. The only detergents containing activated bleach that I have been able to find in this country (they are common in Europe) are Tide with Bleach, Gain with Bleach, and Oxydol. Oxygen bleaches are inactivated by chlorine bleach. Their presence in detergent reduces your freedom to choose whether you will use bleach, how much you will use, and when. Detergents containing bleach may be used only on items that are safe in oxygen bleaches. You must be careful to dissolve or mix such detergents in the wash water thoroughly, too, before adding the clothes.

Many laundry detergents contain enzyme cleaners. These are more effective on organic and protein stains such as blood, eggs, grass, vomit, urine, excrement, and other body soils. Enzymes also perform a variety of other functions. See "Enzyme laundry and presoak products," below.

Detergents that contain fabric softeners are not recommended. The softener gets in the way of effective cleaning. If you want to use fabric softener, add it separately during the rinse or in the dryer.

Phosphate detergents clean better than nonphosphate detergents, but in many places the amount of phosphates permitted in home laundry detergents is strictly limited, or phosphates are prohibited by law, to protect the environment. Phosphates, such as trisodium phosphate and sodium triphosphate, are salts that form alkaline solutions in water. They are added to detergents as builders because, like borax, they inactivate acids. This prevents the formation of one kind of scum and helps soaps and detergents clean more effectively. On the environmental impact of phosphates, see page 176.

Light-duty detergents contain no or low levels of builders or boosters, but they may contain optical brighteners, oxygen bleaches, or enzymes. This group includes hand dishwashing liquids and laundry detergents designed for baby clothes and fine fabrics. Some can be used in automatic washers and some cannot. You must read the labels.

HE detergents are formulated specifically for use in high-efficiency washing machines, i.e., in front-loading and other washing machines with tumbling action. Unless the manufacturer explicitly states otherwise, they can also be used in other types of machines. They tend to be more expensive than other detergents, although the prices are said to be coming down. HE detergents are low-sudsing. Low sudsing is necessary in high-efficiency machines because their tumbling washing action produces much more suds than agitating; excessive sudsing would prevent the tumbling action from effectively cleaning the clothes. Although HE detergents are low-sudsing, not all low-sudsing detergents are HE detergents. See "Suds, soap, and detergent." Unlike regular detergents and ordinary low-sudsing detergents, HE detergents are formulated so as to dissolve readily and prevent soil redeposition and dye transfer in less water; this makes them work better in tumbling machines, which wash with reduced amounts of water.

HE detergent packages bear the HE symbol—the letters "h" and "e" in white, inside a blue oval with a white border. For a discussion of soaps and a comparison of soaps with detergents, see also chapter 12, "Science for the Laundry," pages 170–72.

Detergents and soaps, mild. When a care label tells you to use a mild detergent, it means that you should use one that contains cleaning elements safe for delicate fibers. Such detergents usually have a neutral or near-neutral (only slightly alkaline) pH of 7–8—lower than ordinary all-purpose detergents, which generally are more alkaline, with a pH of 9–11. The more alkaline detergents are, the more harsh, and—the other side of the coin—the better they tend to clean. Other things being equal, a milder detergent is going to be less effective at cleaning heavy soil or stains than products that advertise themselves as "strong," "stain-fighting," "heavy-duty," "powerful," and the like. However, some lower-pH detergents clean better than some more alkaline ones. Cleaning effectiveness and pH are related but not identical.

If a detergent states that it is safe for a certain type of fabric, in my experience it always is. But if you are worried about whether a product is mild, call the toll-free number on the product label to confirm whether it is suitable for a given fiber or fabric. If you ask, sometimes you will be told the pH or whether the product is "slightly" or more alkaline. Also, remember that detergent and soap formulations change. If the box or bottle of a product that you are used to says "new" or "improved" or "with" some new ingredient, try to confirm that the change does not alter its mildness. But keep in mind what one textile expert told me: Do not go overboard worrying about whether a detergent is mild enough. Practically all commercial laundry detergents in this country are fairly mild. One detergent manufacturer I spoke to pointed out that you can get a milder laundering effect with any detergent by simply using less of it. Even if a detergent is mild to begin with, you must follow label instructions for its use to be sure of gentle laundering, including directions as to water temperature.

Mild detergents for hand-washables. To find a good mild detergent for hand-washables, look for those that describe themselves as "mild" or "gentle for your hands" or "good for fine washables." Woolite is the best known of these products. It is quite mild, it is formulated to work in cool water, and it contains no bleaches, enzymes, or optical brighteners. Its pH is near neutral. Delicare is another mild detergent formulated for hand-washing that contains no bleaches, enzymes, or optical brighteners. For very delicate fabrics—and especially for antiques and heirlooms—textile conservators, museums, and my mother often recommend Orvus WA Paste, a mild, neutral detergent made by Procter and Gamble.

You will often find gentle but expensive detergents designed solely for hand-washing lingerie and hosiery or delicate fabrics in department store lingerie departments or linen or lingerie stores; but you need not buy an expensive product to get good results. Dishwashing liquid is much less expensive than such specialty washes and usually is quite mild, with neutral or near-neutral (only slightly alkaline) pH; otherwise it would hurt your skin when you washed the dishes. But look for those that advertise themselves as "gentle to your hands." It may be an excess of caution, but it is probably safer to pick only plain dishwashing products—those without special ingredients or additives—for use on fabrics. (Dishwashing liquids, of course, cannot be used in a washing machine.)

Mild detergents for machine-washables. As for products that can be used in the washing machine, some detergents specially formulated for wool or delicate fabrics are suitable for both the washing machine and hand-washing; carefully read the labels to see whether a particular product can be used in the machine. Woolite HE is designed for gentle, cold-water washing in high-efficiency machines. Ivory Snow Liquid and Dreft Liquid, which are only slightly alkaline, are mild detergents suitable for top-loading agitator machines.

Optical brightening agents and enzymes in mild detergents. Some mild detergents contain optical brightening agents. These do not make the detergents less mild; nor do they harm any fibers. But they can change the hue or the appearance of a few types of fabrics, including some khakis, "natural" cottons, off-whites, and creams, especially imported linens and damasks. The following detergents, which are to varying degrees mild, contain no optical brightening agents: Dreft Liquid, Ivory Snow Liquid, Liquid Cheer, Liquid CheerFree, and Delicare. None of these contains bluing, either, which makes them all well suited for natural and off-white shades of linen and cotton. Powdered Dreft and powdered Ivory Snow contain low levels of brighteners. Optical brighteners may be present in some products even though they are not listed in the ingredients. (Dishwashing liquids, too, contain no optical brighteners but, of course, cannot be used in the washing machine.)

Although a detergent that contains enzymes may be mild, in almost all instances enzyme detergents and enzyme presoak products should not be used on delicates. See "Enzyme laundry and presoak products." Detergents that contain bleaches, too, especially activated bleach, usually should not be used on delicates. The label will always tell you if a product contains bleach.

Which is milder—soap or detergent? You will encounter many recommendations to use soap and not detergent for washing fabrics as well as other materials in the home because, it is claimed, soaps are milder and clean more gently. In fact, it all depends on which soap and which detergent you are talking about. (Soap is, technically and chemically, a detergent. Some writers refer to "synthetic detergents" to distinguish them from soap itself. But I will use the terms as most people do.) As one textiles expert explained to me, soaps are always alkaline in water, and many detergents are nonalkaline. There are harsh soaps; there are neutral and very mild detergents. Ivory Bath Soap is mild; Octagon, Fels Naphtha, and similar brown soaps are strong. (For an explanation of what soaps and detergents are, see chapter 12, "Science for the Laundry," pages 170–72.)

Not only are some detergents milder than soaps, soaps are harder to work with. They may leave residues in clothes and are more difficult to rinse, which is especially problematic for delicate fabrics. The harder your water, the worse are such problems.

You can buy laundry soap bars and liquid laundry soaps from some health food stores, mail-order suppliers, and Internet-based vendors, but the last of the laundry soap flake products to be marketed in the United States, Ivory Soap Flakes, is no longer made. You can also use any bar soap, such as Ivory bath soap, for small jobs. Either rub the bar on the garment, or with a knife or cheese slicer shave fine pieces off the bar and dissolve them to get sudsy water. If you resort to bath-soap bars, choose those without moisturizers and other additives. Note that not all bath and hand bars are soaps. Some, like Dial, are detergents.

Make sure your water is soft before using soaps. If it is not, soften it with a nonprecipitating water softener. Otherwise the soap will react with the minerals in the water to form curds that stick to clothes and are hard to get off. Soaps need warm or hot water to be really effective.

Enzyme laundry and presoak products. Enzymes are found in many pretreatment or presoak products, stain removers, detergents, and some oxygen bleaches. They are safe for almost all washable fabrics. Even silk and wool can be washed with those mild enzyme detergents that explicitly state that they are safe for silk and wool. (But note that Easy Care Wool should not be washed with enzyme products.) If there is any question in your mind about the safety of enzymes for a particular article, test on an inconspicuous area before using just as you do other laundry additives. Enzymes are valuable for helping to remove organic or protein-based stains, including bodily substances (such as blood, vomit, and urine), eggs, dairy products, grass stains, chocolate, and fats and oils. Some enzymes also help whiten, prevent fuzz and lint, and reduce soil redeposition.

Several different types of enzymes are used in enzyme cleaners, and they work on different types of soil. Modern detergents may well contain a cocktail of these. Amylase works on starch soils. Lipase works on fatty and oily soils. Protease works on protein soils. Cellulase (contained, for example, in Liquid Cheer) helps to prevent cotton fabrics from developing a worn look by removing the fuzz on its surface caused by abrasion in wear and washing. It also reduces pilling and aids in removing particulate soil. To remove fuzz from wrinkle-resistant cottons, the Fabricare Institute recommends laundering with a product that contains a cellulase enzyme.

The key to the effective use of products containing enzymes is to allow them time to work. Let garments soak in an enzyme presoak, if possible, for half an hour or even longer; you will get results for up to an hour. Chlorine bleach will inactivate enzymes, so add it only when you have finished the enzyme treatment. If your laundry detergent contains enzymes, add chlorine bleach only in the last few minutes of the wash period. See also "Detergents and soaps, mild." New-model machines automatically delay adding chlorine bleach until the proper time.

Fabric softeners. Fabric softeners are supposed to make cloth fluffy, soft, and pliable, minimize wrinkles, make ironing easier, and help prevent the static electricity that commonly plagues fabrics made from synthetic fibers such as polyester and nylon. They are also said to be helpful in fluffing up the pile in pile fabrics. I never use them, and I know at least two professors of textiles who also never use them. Marketers say that people use fabric softeners because they like their nice smell.

These products achieve their effect by leaving a waxy coating on fabrics. The main problems they cause, therefore, are reduced absorbency and the tendency of the waxy coating to find its way onto other fabrics and onto your skin. Avoid using fabric softeners on towels, rags, T-shirts, cotton underwear, sheets, and pillowcases; these and any other fabrics used on and near the skin are comfortable only when absorbent. You should also avoid using fabric softeners too often, because their wax builds up, leaving garments feeling greasy and exaggerating their inabsorbency. Fabric softeners may also reduce the effectiveness of flame retardants. Wash and dry items treated with flame retardants in loads that will not receive softening treatment.

Liquid fabric softeners, if you use them, are added to the final rinse water in your washing machine. If you have a softener dispenser, you can add liquid softener at the beginning of the wash cycle and it will be added at the proper time. If you do not, be sure to dilute, mix, and dissolve softeners thoroughly in at least a quart of water before adding them to the rinse water, for if they touch clothes directly they can cause spots. If this happens, rub with a bar of pure soap and rewash them. You may need to repeat the process.

Note that fabric softener dispensing balls cannot be used in front-loading tumbling machines. The tumbling causes the softener to be released before the final rinse.

Dryer softener sheets are saturated with a waxy substance that melts in the heat of the dryer and coats the clothes as they tumble. If you like, cut one into two to four pieces and use just one of them for a lighter dose of softener that will still have a good effect. This is especially helpful when your load is not large.

There is not much difference in quality between the two types of softener. Some people think that the liquid type is slightly better at softening while the dryer sheets are slightly better at stopping static buildup, but both do both things well.

Some detergents contain fabric softeners, but the fabric softeners impede their cleaning. It is better to use a separate fabric softener.

Clothes that are line-dried, especially towels, often have a rough, stiff, boardlike feeling. Tumbling towels and other things that would dry stiff on the line is softening in and of itself, without the addition of a fabric softener. But tumbling also exaggerates static problems for synthetics because of the friction it produces.

Heavy-duty detergent. See "Detergents and soaps."

Hydrogen peroxide. See "Bleaches."

Laundry disks. You may have encountered advertisements for laundry disks, globes, balls, spheres, or doughnuts. Reliable authorities recommend you not waste your money on any such devices. These are "alternative" laundry products that purport to clean clothes without the use of laundry detergents or other ordinary laundry pretreatment and washing products. Typically, they allege that some part of the device—ceramic beads, magnets, or "activated water"—emits negative charges or far-infrared electromagnetic radiation, reducing the surface tension of water and permitting it to penetrate fabrics more readily. Studies of such products, however, indicate that water alone is just as effective at cleaning clothes as water to which laundry disks or similar devices have been added. (Indeed, it seems that reasonable people are sometimes deceived about the effectiveness of such devices because they are not aware of how effective plain water is.) Moreover, scientists say that the manufacturers' purported "scientific" explanations of how the disks function are baseless and illogical. Some states have taken legal action and levied heavy fines against companies for claims made in connection with the sale of such devices. Among the organizations that do not recommend their use are the Consumers Union, International Fabricare Institute, Maytag Corp., and the Soap and Detergent Association.

Light–duty detergent. See "Detergents and soaps."

Mild detergent. See "Detergents and soaps, mild."

Optical brighteners. Optical brighteners are now used in almost all laundry detergents, including most gentle or mild ones, and in oxygen or all-fabric bleaches. They may be present even if they are not listed in the ingredients. If they are listed, they may be referred to as "optical whiteners," "fluorescent whitening agents," "UV brighteners," or "brighteners." These are colorless dyes that absorb the energy of invisible ultraviolet rays in light and re-emit it at a lower, visible spectrum wavelength. This makes white fabrics appear whiter and colors appear brighter in the presence of ultraviolet radiation, that is, in unshielded fluorescent light or daylight. Optical brighteners will be ineffective in incandescent light, which emits very little ultraviolet radiation, so you may find that your clothes are more brilliant by day in your office than by night at home, where indoor lighting is usually incandescent.

United States manufacturers also apply optical brighteners to almost all white and pastel-colored fabrics during the manufacturing process. The brighteners in the fabrics will sometimes (infrequently, it appears) turn yellow when exposed to sunshine or to bleach. Yellowing of fabrics treated with optical brighteners may also result simply from aging, for these colorless dyes, like all dyes, fade; in fact, they have a rather low fastness to light. When this happens, not only does your fabric lose the whiteness optical brighteners supplied, but the fading by-products are themselves yellowish, which may give the fabric a yellow cast. According to the International Fabricare Institute, decomposition of optical brightening agents can also be caused by dry cleaning and steam finishing, washing with alkaline detergents and bleach, or exposure of optical brightening agents on fabrics to chlorine bleach.

The optical brighteners in detergents are intended to maintain the white or bright look that fabrics have when they are new as a result of being treated with optical brighteners during manufacture. But you can run into trouble when you use detergents (or other laundry products) that contain optical brighteners to wash fabrics that have not been treated with optical brighteners. If you use a product that contains brighteners as a pretreatment, this can lighten the color or even create an ugly dappling or spotting on untreated fabrics. I learned what optical brightening agents (OBAs) were through the sad experience of buying some imported linen towels in an off-white hue that had a label bearing these words: "OBAs will affect shade." This meant that if you used a detergent with optical brighteners, you might change the hue of the towels. Not knowing what OBAs were, I had no idea that I was actually using them. Laundering did indeed alter the hue and produced mottling of the color. Generally speaking, imported fabrics, especially linens in tan or off-white shades, are more likely to be untreated than others. Some famous-brand American manufacturers use imported fabrics that are not treated, so you cannot avoid the problem just by buying American. Watch out for khakis and "natural cottons" in particular. A manufacturer of linen damask also recommends that you not use optical brighteners on white damasks.

As of the time of writing, the following national-brand laundry detergents contained no optical brighteners: Ivory Snow Liquid, regular powdered Cheer without bleach, CheerFree, Liquid Cheer, Liquid CheerFree, powdered Dreft and Dreft Liquid, and Delicare. Powdered Dreft and powdered Ivory Snow contain low levels of brightener. In addition, dishwashing liquids, which can often be used for hand-washing delicate fabrics, contain no optical brighteners. See also "Detergents and soaps, mild" and "Bleaches: Chlorine bleach."

Oxygen bleaches. See "Bleaches."

Potassium monopersulfate. See "Bleaches: Oxygen bleaches."

Pretreatments and prewash stain removers. Pretreatments and prewash stain removers in liquid form are usually applied just before laundering. Pretreatment sticks and gels, however, may be used as much as a week in advance of laundering without danger of mildew, so they are useful when you are concerned about a stain setting if you do not immediately launder an article. (Follow package instructions and observe all package cautions when using all such products.)

These products should be tested on an inconspicuous area of the fabric just as you test other laundry products. Optical brighteners or other ingredients they contain can cause light spots or color loss in certain fabrics. This is particularly important on neon or fluorescent dyes, which such products may cause to run or fade. They may also contain enzymes. See "Enzyme laundry and presoak products."

Prewash treatments and stain removers work well on oily and greasy stains, including skin oils and perspiration, food stains, cooking oil, lotions, and cosmetics. They may be detergent-based or they may contain isopropyl alcohol, drycleaning fluids, or other petroleum-based solvents. Those containing solvents or grease- or soil-release agents are particularly likely to be effective at removing oily and greasy soil from polyester and other synthetic fibers. Sometimes you can tell by reading the ingredient list whether a pretreatment product contains solvents or grease- or soil-release agents, and sometimes you cannot. I know of one case where the manufacturer no longer lists its soil-release agent, yet still includes it in the product. Usually the pretreatment products with pump dispensers are detergent-based and those with aerosol sprays contain solvents; but this may not always be the case.

Sal soda. See "Washing soda."

Soap. See "Detergents and soaps" and "Detergents and soaps, mild."

Sodium carbonate. See "Washing soda."

Sodium perborate. See "Bleaches: Oxygen bleaches."

Sodium percarbonate. See "Bleaches: Oxygen bleaches."

Suds, soap, and detergent. When you are laundering with soap rather than detergent, the amount of suds is an indication of the cleaning power. So when you use soap, make sure you have plenty of suds. Look for soapsuds as firm as beaten egg whites.

But the suds level does not necessarily correlate with the cleaning power of detergents. Low-sudsing detergents can be stronger cleaners, and high-sudsing detergents weaker cleaners. Lack of suds with a high-sudsing detergent, however, does indeed indicate reduced cleaning power.

Suds of both soaps and detergents are decreased by heavy soil and hard water and increased by light soil and soft water. If you develop excess detergent suds, sprinkle a little rubbing alcohol on them or drop a little piece of bar soap in the water. Chlorine bleach makes suds creamier.

Low-sudsing detergents may be preferred for certain jobs, such as washing pillows and comforters. Non-HE low-suds detergents are formulated to work in top-loading agitator machines. You can use them in high-efficiency machines, but they will not work as well as HE detergents, which are low-sudsing detergents particularly formulated for the action and low water volume in high-efficiency machines. See the discussion of HE detergents in "Detergents and Soaps." Low-suds detergents currently on the market that are not HE detergents include Bold, All, Cold Power, and Dash.

Sunlight. See "Bleaches: Sunlight."

Surfactants. Surfactants are substances contained in detergents that lower the water's surface tension, making it "wetter." This enables the surface being cleaned to become wet more readily and thus enables soil to be loosened and removed more readily. Surfactants also keep soils emulsified and suspended in the water rather than resettling on the material being washed. See chapter 12, "Science for the Laundry," pages 170–71.

Trisodium phosphate. Trisodium phosphate, sometimes called TSP, is a laundry booster and a water softener. It is a strong alkali and therefore cannot be used on protein fibers such as silk or wool.

Vinegar, white. You can add white vinegar, an acid, to the second or final rinse water of your laundry as a "sour" to neutralize any residual chlorine bleach or alkalinity from the detergents and to help prevent lint. Add the white vinegar to the machine when the final rinse water has finished filling;

use 1 cup per load, a bit more for extra-large loads. Caution: Do not add vinegar to any laundry load or laundry water that contains chlorine bleach. (Use it, that is, only after you have rinsed the bleach away.)

To remove hard-water residues from clothes, soak them in 2 cups of white vinegar to 1 gallon of hot water for fifteen minutes. Use a plastic container; the vinegar may rust metal.

On removing rust and certain other stains with white vinegar, refer to chapter 11, "Removing Stains from Fabrics," and see the "Guide to Stain Removal" at the end of chapter 11.

Washing soda. Washing soda (sodium carbonate or sal soda) is a very old laundry aid, and it is still a good, very strong detergent booster or "builder" and laundry deodorizer. It is marketed under different trade names, which often contain the word "soda." Read the ingredients on labels to find out if a product is mostly washing soda. Washing soda, an alkali, helps cut grease, and it is a water softener. Follow the manufacturer's instructions, or use ½ cup per regular (normal) load or ¾ cup for an extra-large load.

Washing soda is also effective as a pretreatment for many stains, including food stains, grease, diaper stains, lipstick, and crayon. To use it as a stain pretreatment, work 4 tablespoons into a paste with water. Dampen the stain and, wearing rubber gloves, rub the paste into the stain. To use washing soda as a presoak, use 1 tablespoon per gallon of warm water or ½ cup per regular washing load. Drain the clothes before washing. If you wish, you can then add another ½ cup to the wash water as a booster.

You should exercise caution when using a strong caustic substance such as washing soda; test it first on an inconspicuous area of the garment. It should never be used on wool, silk, or other protein or animal-origin fibers. Also avoid using washing soda on any delicate cellulosic fibers. Use rubber gloves to keep it off your skin.

Water softeners. See "Borax," "Builders," "Trisodium phosphate," and "Washing soda."

Whitener/brighteners. Whitener/brighteners, unlike color removers, are not bleaches of any sort and do not remove color. Rather, they are "optical brighteners," colorless dyes that absorb invisible light (in the form of ultraviolet radiation) and re-emit it in the form of lower-energy visible light. See "Optical brighteners." Both color removers and whitener/brighteners are sold in drugstores, hardware store, home centers, and large supermarkets. See also "Color removers."

5

Drying the Laundry

*Using the automatic dryer . . . What goes in the dryer . . . Load size,
temperature, moisture sensing, cycle choices, avoiding overdrying,
sorting for drying, operating the dryer . . . Using the dryer to
unwrinkle . . . Line-drying . . . How to hang things on the line . . .
Hanging dry on hangers or hanging racks . . . Drying flat*

Most people today have no choice but to dry laundry indoors in an
automatic tumbling dryer or on a hanger, a rack, or an indoor line.
These are all fine methods, and among them they provide the best
means of drying some kinds of fabric. For those who have the option, however, outdoor line-drying gives the freshest result and would be my preference
for all those clothes and linens for which it is suitable. This chapter canvasses
how and when to use each of these options.

The Automatic Dryer

What Goes in the Dryer. Most clothes and linens can safely be dried in the
automatic dryer. The exceptions are fiberglass, rubber, and plastic; certain
especially heat-sensitive fabrics, such as olefin (polypropylene); many acetate,
acrylic, and spandex fabrics; certain knits; drip-dry clothes; and many delicate
fibers and fabrics, including viscose rayon. Drip-dry clothes should be hung
to dry. Towels, flannels, and other pile and napped fabrics, on the other hand,
need tumbling in the dryer to fluff them up. Ordinarily, they should not be
dried flat or hung to dry. Superwash and similar treated wools may be tumbled
in the dryer on a low setting (unless the care label says not to), but other wools
must be dried outside the dryer. Once wool articles have dried outside the
dryer, however, they can then be fluffed up on a setting that uses no heat, often
called "air fluff."

Load Size. A washing load is usually about the same size as a drying load. Drying loads, like washing loads, should be neither too small nor too large. A dryer with a full, wet load looks two-thirds empty. Remember that clothes will fluff up and take more space when they are dry. Too small a load will dry more slowly, as the tumbling action requires a minimum fill level to work properly. If a load is too small, add a few clean, dry items—say, two or three non-linting towels of compatible color—to bulk it up. Too large a load will wrinkle, lint excessively, and dry slowly and unevenly because air

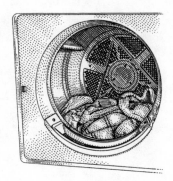

A properly loaded clothes dryer

will not be able to circulate freely around the clothes. An overlarge load can also block the vent and cause heat damage to clothes.

Temperature. Home dryers always give a choice of temperatures. Regular, or the hottest temperature, is for sturdy cottons—T-shirts, towels, cotton underwear, sheets, preshrunk blue jeans, and so on. Care labels on articles that may be dried on regular should simply say "Tumble dry." In general, the hotter the drying temperature, the greater the likelihood of shrinking, so this setting is also reserved for preshrunk or low-shrink fabrics. The medium setting is for permanent-press, wrinkle-treated clothes, many synthetics and blends, lightweight cottons and linens, some knits, and those whose care labels direct "Tumble dry medium." The low or delicate settings are for more heat-sensitive garments, including some synthetics, fine lingerie, sheer fabrics, and most cotton knits, as well as for those whose care labels direct "Tumble dry low."

Moisture Sensing and Timed Drying. All dryers let you set drying time with a timer. Many home dryers now also offer "electronic drying," in which the machine automatically senses the moisture level and turns off when it is reduced to the level you select, from "more" or "very" dry, to "less" dry. The "very dry" setting is for items you wish to get extra dry as well as hard-to-dry items like rugs, very heavy clothes, and towels. The less dry setting should be used for cottons and linens that you are going to damp-iron, although I find that they still need steam ironing or sprinkling. (See "Avoiding Overdrying; Damp Drying," below.) Everything else takes the medium or "normal dry" setting.

Cycle Choices. Many home dryers also offer a choice of cycles: regular, permanent-press, and air fluff. The regular cycle has a short cool-down period at the end for less wrinkling and easier handling when you remove the clothes. The permanent-press cycle has a long cool-down during which, on many machines, a warning buzzer sounds to let you know that you will have to remove clothes soon. This is because permanent-press and wrinkle-resistant clothes, when warm, may wrinkle if left to sit in the dryer, and they may even do so if they are only slightly warm after the cool-down. If your machine offers only temperature and time choices and no preset cycles, when drying permanent-press clothes you should generally choose a "medium" to "low" drying temperature and a wrinkle-preventing feature. The latter keeps the clothes tumbling without heat for an extended period, until you take them out and fold them, so that they do not wrinkle from sitting in the drum. With permanent-press articles the wrinkle-preventing phase is especially important, but it is helpful to reduce wrinkling in cottons, linens, and knits, too. Wrinkle-prevention options are useful features that many people fail to take advantage of. If your machine has none, try to remove the clothes from the dryer and fold them immediately.

"Air fluff" or "fluff dry" simply uses unheated air. It can be used to fluff pile fabrics or knits or to dry plastic shower curtains, diaper liners, and other items that should not be exposed to heat.

Avoiding Overdrying; Damp Drying. Success in using an automatic dryer consists in not overdoing it. Overdrying causes shrinking, wrinkling, a harsh, dry hand, and yellowing. Such yellowing is especially problematic for whites, lights, and pastels. On synthetics, elasticity may be reduced and the hand or texture may sometimes be permanently ruined by overheating.

To avoid overdrying, set the temperature and timer conservatively or, when you can, use electronic drying. The longest drying times are necessary for the largest loads and the bulkiest, thickest items, such as towels and blue jeans. Sheets and pillowcases might be dry in less than twenty minutes, but towels can take up to an hour. When you are estimating drying time, remember that a cool rinse extends the drying time. Drying in your automatic dryer also takes longer when the room in which the dryer sits is colder.

You should not aim for absolute dryness. Remove clothes while there is still a hint of dampness in thick seams or at elastic bands. Linen, especially, should never be dried bone-dry; it needs a little moisture to stay supple (and usually requires damp ironing). Blue jeans and other play and work clothes have very thick seams that dry slowly. To get the seams completely dry in the dryer, you would have to overdry the fabric in the rest of the garment, shrinking it, imposing unnecessary wear and tear, tying up the dryer when you need it for something else, and using up energy. So remove jeans and all similar articles when the flat portions are dry, and let them finish drying outside the dryer. Hang them over a clothes rack near the dryer or over a chair back that will not get used, or simply fold them loosely and set them on a table or shelf somewhere.

Sorting for Drying. When drying, you must read and follow care labels carefully. Shrinking, yellowing, linting, pilling, abrading, melting, and other problems can result from using an overhot dryer. Elastic fibers can become inelastic, and white fibers can yellow if they are machine-dried at too high a temperature. Some elasticized garments should not be machine-dried at all.

Just as you cannot wash together items that might bleed color on one another, you cannot dry them together either. Beware of mixing together wet color-sorted clothes in the dryer. Do not dry items that are not colorfast with whites or light-colored loads. All other sorting instructions for washing—instructions as to linting, avoiding damage from buckles and pins, preventing tangles with sleeves, sashes, and trims, removing decorations, keeping matched sets and pairs together, turning inside out to minimize pilling, using mesh bags for delicate and small articles—also apply equally to dryer loads.

Separate slow-drying clothes and linens from quick-drying clothes and linens or stop the dryer midway to remove items that may already be dry. Otherwise, the latter will overdry. Turkish (terry-cloth) towels, blue jeans, heavy work clothes, thicker knits, rugs, and the like dry slowly. Sheets and pillowcases, medium and lightweight woven cottons and linens, and synthetics dry more quickly. (Polyester and other synthetics tend to dry very quickly, much faster than, say, even lightweight cotton knits.)

Keep clothes and linens that are to be dried with a fabric softener sheet separate from those that are not. Softener sheets are most appropriate for synthetic fibers. Fabric softening sheets should not be used on diapers, towels, dish towels, rags, sheets, T-shirts, cotton underwear, and any other articles that must be absorbent to work well and feel good. Fabric softener gives clothes and linens a waxy coating that reduces their absorbency. You will not need fabric softener at every laundering. If you use it too often, it tends to build up and give a greasy feeling. See "Fabric softeners," in the Glossary of Laundry Products and Additives, pages 81–82.

Usually clothes that need similar washing temperatures also take similar drying temperatures. But if (as a compromise load) you have washed synthetics and wrinkle-treated clothes together with untreated cottons or linens, you may wish to dry them separately so that you can give some and not others permanent-press treatment.

One care label instruction that I sometimes ignore is commonly included on cotton knits—to dry flat. You can buy cotton knit sportswear big enough to fit after some shrinkage; dry it only on low heat, and remove it when still slightly damp. Doing this entails a risk that the garment will shrink more than you predict or that there was some other reason for the instruction besides potential shrinkage, perhaps yellowing or pilling. In the long run, however, you will save a good deal of drying time and are likely to get satisfactory results.

Operating the Dryer. Each time you dry a load, check the lint filter and empty it if necessary. Sometimes it will be necessary to do so in the middle of a large load as well. (Make sure the dryer is off before you do this.)

Choose appropriate temperatures, times, and cycles. Place a fabric softener sheet in the dryer if you intend to use fabric softener. (Try using them only every two or three washes to avoid a softener buildup.) For a small load or for a light softening effect, you can cut a sheet of fabric softener into halves or quarters and use only a piece.

Shake out each wet item to be dried. Then throw it loosely in on the others, one by one. If you throw in clothes from the washer knotted together in an impenetrable mass, they are likely to take forever to dry, or some will overdry while others remain damp because air cannot circulate around them.

If clothes have emerged sopping from the washer, put them back in for another spin if you can or, if you can't, roll any heavy or thick items in a towel before placing them in the dryer. Otherwise they will take forever to dry.

Remove all clothes from the dryer promptly when they still have a mere hint of dampness. This is especially important for thermoplastic fibers, permanent-press and wrinkle-treated clothes, and cottons that are to be ironed, to prevent or reduce their wrinkling. Remove articles that are to be damp-ironed when they are still fairly damp, roll them up, and then cover them so they stay damp until you are ready to iron. (Linen should usually be dried outside the dryer, but if you put it in and want to iron it, take it out when still very damp. Linen needs to be damper than cotton for ironing.) Many dryers have a damp-dry setting.

Hang or fold clothes promptly upon removing them from the dryer or they will take on wrinkles sitting in the basket. As you do so, shake each one out and give it a snap, as though you were cracking a whip. This helps them to return to their proper shapes. You can greatly improve their appearance and reduce the need for ironing if you finger-press them: smooth the seams, pull shapes straight, unfold edges so that they lie flat, and so on.

When you have folded or hung clothes that are still slightly damp from the dryer, let them stand on a shelf or table for a while if necessary to air and complete drying. Often they dry from their own warmth while you are folding. If they don't, avoid putting them away until they dry more thoroughly or you will get musty smells in dressers and closets.

If clothes that have dried flat or on the line, such as knits, small rugs, pile fabrics, or sheets, feel stiff or harsh or look wrinkled or flat, put them in the dryer on air fluff (cool air) for a few minutes after they dry to soften and fluff them up.

Unwrinkling with Your Dryer. You can use your dryer to unwrinkle clean, dry clothes (from, say, a suitcase or drawer) by tumbling them on reduced heat for five to ten minutes. It sometimes helps to throw in a clean, slightly damp, nonlinting towel to make a little moisture. You can also steam out wrinkles in a drying closet.

Line-Drying

Our language shows the effect of centuries of drying wet linens and clothes outdoors when we speak disapprovingly of "airing laundry in public" or "letting it all hang out." Years ago, when everyone had to hang their laundry out on the line, it was common for some people to feel ashamed at the quasi-public display of their linens and underwear, especially if they showed stains and tears. Older friends say that worst of all was hanging out the rags that all women used before the days of disposable sanitary napkins and tampons. Today, it is hard to imagine anyone being embarrassed by their underwear—now that we see billboards of celebrities in theirs. But my suburban friends tell me that you still need a private backyard to line-dry your laundry unembarrassedly because many people think that their neighbors' laundry flapping in the breeze ruins the appearance of the neighborhood and will complain when they see it.

To my mind, whether laundry on the line is unattractive depends on what kind of laundry it is and how it is hung. When I was a girl, hanging out the clothes was an art widely understood in the countryside. Familial style was given some leeway, but there were nonetheless ways you did this and ways you didn't; the rules were so clear that I remember one elderly lady stifling unseemly giggles when she saw the work of a novice. If those days ever come back, the instructions below will save you from social humiliation.

Line-drying outdoors produces appealingly fresh-smelling clothes and linens, and sunlight is a natural sanitizing and bleaching agent. See "Bleaches: Sunlight," in the Glossary of Laundry Products and Additives, page 70. (The dryer's heat also kills germs.) Line-drying is good for almost all washables. It is not good choice for fabrics that will stretch when wet, such as wool and loosely knitted articles, and for articles that need fluffing to look their best—terry-cloth, chenille, flannels, and other napped and pile fabrics. Nor should you hang filled articles such as comforters or sleeping bags over the line; the fill drops to the ends, clumps, and will not dry. Items such as towels, which take very long to dry, you may find inconvenient to hang out. Many clothes feel stiff after drying on the line, particularly if there is little wind to blow them

Outdoor clothesline

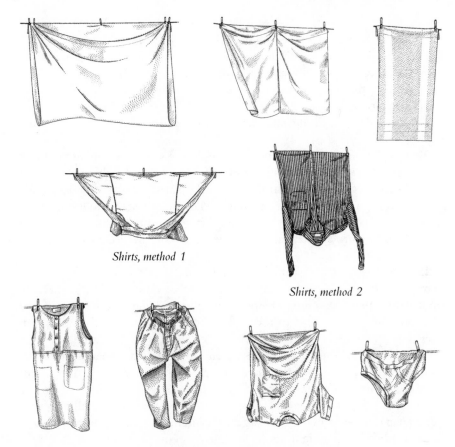

Shirts, method 1

Shirts, method 2

Hanging clothes and linens for line-drying

soft as they dry. Towels, especially, tend to get boardlike and stiff on the line and need some tumbling to make them soft. You might tumble towels until they are half-dry, then move them to the line for finishing—or vice versa. Knits, too, often need some tumbling (usually on "low" or "cool") to regain their softness, whether before or after drying flat. Delicate clothes and fabrics should be dried flat rather than line-dried. Fabrics that should not be exposed to the sun can be line-dried indoors.

If you hang things carefully, they will often look smooth when they are dry, and you can minimize or avoid ironing. The best weather for line-drying, if you have a choice, is warm, dry, and sunny with a moderate breeze. You need some wind to billow wrinkles out of the fabric and hasten drying. Line-drying can seem interminable on a humid, airless day. But avoid extremely windy days. The flapping is wearing on the clothes; the wind is hard to work in and sometimes blows clothes off the line. Avoid freezing weather also. It is painful to hang out wet things in such weather, and they will take forever to dry. Besides, water expands when it freezes; that can result in damage to fabric whose fibers have absorbed water. The idea that freezing outdoors is good for the wash is an old wives' tale, born, no doubt, out of the superstition that great suffering always produces great good.

Make sure that your line and clothespins are clean. Wash the line, if necessary, with some ordinary detergent in water or household cleaner. Make sure it is sufficiently taut, strong, and secure to prevent the clothes from dragging or dropping.

Keep a plentiful store of clothespins and do not stint on using them. (Look for sturdy ones; some are shoddily made.) You can use old-fashioned wooden push-down pins (no spring) for sheets, towels, play clothes, and other articles that will not pull out of shape or stretch. Plastic clothespins are less likely to leave marks on the clothes—but be sure they are clean. For knits and stretch wear, including underwear, panties, T-shirts, and knit dresses, use clip-on pins (with a spring).

Usually you will turn three or four inches of the fabric over the line, enough to be sure that the fold will not slip or come undone, especially important if there is a strong breeze. Heavy pieces will be more secure if you turn one-third to one-half of them over the line. On windy days, too, turn over more, for added security. Do not let clothes drag on the ground. Be sure that the pin gets a good grip. To the extent possible, hang sheets, tablecloths, and similar flatwork so that their hems are parallel to the line widthwise. This takes less room along the clothesline and puts the stress of hanging on the warp yarns (they run lengthwise), which are stronger than the filling yarns. When hanging blankets or other large, heavy items, lay them over two lines so as to distribute their weight. (See the illustration on page 125).

Hanging clothes properly reduces wrinkles and makes ironing easier. The wind smooths wrinkles and softens and dries clothes quickly, so try to hang garments so that sleeves, skirts, and legs billow out in the breeze. To accomplish this with sheets, pillowcases, skirts, and other pieces with double layers, hang them so that the fold (or the closed end of the pillowcase) hangs down and the open, hemmed edges are pinned to the line; do not pin the fabric taut on the side from which the wind is blowing but let it sag down a bit, so that there is an opening for the wind to enter. (See the illustration on page 93.) Otherwise, however, it is best to pull the pinned edges of the clothes taut to reduce wrinkles. In addition, you should finger-iron and smooth the pinned-up clothes; pull seams, collars, and pockets straight and hang items so that the lines of their construction run neatly parallel and perpendicular to the clothesline. Otherwise the clothes will dry with funny bumps and shapes.

To prevent fading, dry colored clothes in the shade or turn them inside out, or both. White linens usually benefit from drying in direct sunlight, which gives them a gentle, natural bleaching. White and light cottons may eventually yellow with prolonged exposure to sunlight, so some experts recommend that they be hung in the shade for drying. My view is that the more typical effect

HOW TO PIN LAUNDRY ON THE LINE

Sheets: Fold the sheet hem to hem, then fold 3 to 4 inches of one hem over the line and pin at both ends. Pin the corners of the other hem a few inches inside the first two. The sheet should open toward the wind so it blows out like a sail. Run your hands down the selvage edges to smooth them and make sure that the sheet is hanging square and even.

Pillowcases: Fold one side of the opening over the line, pinning at both corners, allowing one side to sag open. You want the pillowcase to fill up like a sail in the wind.

Handkerchiefs: Fold in half over the line and pin at both ends.

Towels: Fold three to four inches of one end over the line and pin at both corners. Towels will line-dry to be much softer and fluffier if you shake them energetically before you hang them on the line. Make them snap. This loosens up the pile very effectively. Shake and snap them when you take them off, too, to soften them.

Shirts and Blouses: Method 1—hang by the tail, turning under three to four inches over the line, fronts opened out to the sides. Pin at placket ends and side seams, if necessary. Method 2—hang by the tail, turning under three to four inches, but fold the fronts in.

Dresses: If the dress is straight, pin it by the shoulders. If the dress has a full or gathered skirt, pin it by the hem, shoulders hanging down. But straight dresses and the tops of many full dresses dry with fewer wrinkles and a better shape if you hang them on hangers.

Skirts: Turn over the waistband of straight skirts and pin at both ends. Hang gathered or full skirts by the hem.

Pants and Shorts: Turn the waist over and pin at both ends, or, for pants, use a trouser frame.

T-shirts and Undershirts: Fold the hem a few inches over the line and pin at both ends.

Underwear or Panties: Fold the waist over the line and pin at both sides.

Bras: Pin by the hook end.

Socks: Pin by the toe.

Hangers: If you want clothes on hangers to dry outside, make sure they will not blow off the hanger. Sometimes you can pin them on at the shoulder, but this may leave holes in fine and light fabrics, so be careful. If you hang a hanger outdoors—on the clothesline or elsewhere—watch out that it does not blow off. Try pinning the hanger to the clothesline with a clothespin, making sure that the garment is securely fastened to the hanger.

of sun on white cotton—for, say, an afternoon on the clothesline after each laundering—is to bleach it, which I like.

Where it will not make a thick lump of cloth that will take too long to dry, it is labor-saving and space-saving to pin the ends of two garments together so that you use only half as many pins. For example, you pin a pillowcase to the end of a sheet and then pin a second pillowcase to the end of the first, creating a continuous line rather than one with breaks between the items. (See the illustration on page 92.) But you cannot let two items touch if one has bleeding dyes that would be visible on the other.

Remember that clothes dry at very different rates. If you are short on line space, run out to check on the clothes periodically to see whether some are dry. Sheets dry very quickly in the breeze and take up lots of line. You'll soon be able to take them down and hang up other things. Line-dried clothes are unlikely to get overdried on the line, since they are not exposed to artificial heat, but do not leave them out on the line overnight. Articles that are to be ironed should be taken down when they are still a bit damp, rolled up, and covered with a towel or placed in a plastic bag so that they do not dry out. Iron them promptly so that they do not rot or mold.

Fold immediately all clothes that will not be ironed. As you take down clothes for folding, shake each item and snap it—that is, hold it at one end and sharply crack it like a whip. This fluffs and shapes the article. Avoid putting laundry in a basket unfolded, and especially never leave it that way for a period of time, for this will cause much wrinkling and ruin the good effects of your careful hanging.

If you are line-drying indoors, be sure to shake out the clothes vigorously before hanging them. This is necessary to reduce wrinkles and help them to dry less stiffly since you have no breezes to soften them.

Hanging Dry on Hangers or Hanging Racks

Dresses, blouses or shirts, jackets, permanent-press clothes, and pants that do not go in the dryer are usually best dried on hangers, for this preserves the shape of the garments and reduces wrinkles. Other items can be hung on clotheshorses. Wash-and-wear or drip-dry clothes should always be carefully hung to dry and finger-pressed (smoothed and straightened), particularly at seams. It is usually best to hang clothes to dry on wide hangers, for this distributes the weight of the garment better. A thin wire hanger produces strain on a very narrow band of cloth and creates unwelcome creases around the shoulder area. Jackets should be hung on hangers designed for jackets, which have wide rests for the shoulders. There are also thick-padded or inflated plastic hangers that are good for drying.

When drying dresses, blouses, and shirts, hang the garments straight and smooth. Hang slips and dresses by their straps, if they have them. Button, zip, or snap them up so that the cloth is pulled properly to shape the garment.

Jacket on hanger

*Nonrusting hangers with broad shoulders
are best for hanging clothes to dry*

Press or smooth collars, facings, seams, trim, and pockets with your fingers, especially on wash-and-wear clothes. This little step can make ironing of many garments unnecessary and reduces it considerably on all. Use a trouser frame for "hanging" pants. This pulls them taut so they do not wrinkle and creates a crease in the right places. Or hang them over a wide hanger. (If you hang them from their cuffs on a trousers hanger, the cuffs may not dry.)

Dripping garments can be hung in the bathtub or shower stall, either on a drying frame or a line. The stores are full of good gadgets for these purposes.

Underwear, hosiery, and other articles that do not need to be hung on a hanger can be hung on racks.

Indoor drying on hangers and racks can be speeded by turning an electric fan on the clothes.

Drying cabinets provide for both hanger- and shelf-drying. Be sure to choose an appropriate heat level.

Drying Flat

Clothes that must be dried flat rather than hung include fabrics that stretch when wet, such as many knits and wools, and very delicate articles that should not be pinned or blown on the line or that should not be subjected to the stress of their own weight during hanging. In addition, smaller articles, particularly knits and items made of fast-drying synthetics, such as panties, bras, or hosiery, dry so quickly on a frame or rack that there is little reason to expose them to the high temperatures and static-producing friction of a dryer. They will last longer and look better dried flat.

When drying clothes flat, keep them away from direct sources of heat, which may produce shrinking. Dry colored items out of direct sun. Pick a warm, dry room in which the air will readily take up moisture, or, if drying

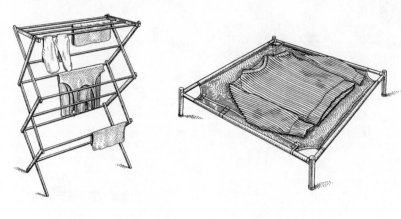

Drying rack   Flat drying rack

outdoors, a warm, dry day. Knits, especially sweaters and other garments that hold lots of moisture, should be laid on a mesh rack, which speeds drying by permitting air penetration from below as well as above, or on a thick, absorbent towel. (If the article to be dried bleeds color, choose a towel that does not matter or that is of like color. And be sure that you do not lay the drying article on something that will bleed color onto it.) Articles that do not hold a great deal of moisture, such as panty hose or panties, can be laid on a sheet. Whatever you are drying, be sure to protect wood or other surfaces that might be vulnerable to moisture if there is a chance that moisture will soak through or drip onto them.

If you turn over long-drying items, they will dry faster, but you should not disturb carefully blocked articles such as sweaters or other wool or knit clothes.

You can hasten drying of clothes laid flat by turning a fan on them.

You can also dry things flat in a drying cabinet or on a drying rack in your dryer. Choose the cycle or heat setting appropriate for the garments. When using an in-dryer rack in my machine, I have to use a time-dry setting rather than a moisture-sensing setting; the dryer does not seem to sense the moisture in a single stationary item.

6

Ironing

*What should and should not be ironed . . . Sprinkling or
dampening before ironing . . . Ironing temperatures . . . Techniques
for pressing, ironing, and steam ironing . . . Airing the ironing, and
avoiding underironing and overironing . . . Ironing clothes,
flatwork, linen, table linens, sheets . . . How to avoid ironing . . .
Starches and sizings . . . How to clean the iron*

I roning gratifies the senses. The transformation of wrinkled, shapeless
cloth into the smooth and gleaming folds of a familiar garment pleases
the eye. The good scent of ironing is the most comfortable smell in the
world. And the fingertips enjoy the changes in the fabrics from cold to warm,
wet to dry, and rough to silky. There is nothing like keeping the hands busy
with some familiar work to free the mind. You can learn Italian while you
iron, as a friend of mine did, or you can simply think.

What to Iron

Untreated cotton and linen woven fabrics almost always need ironing to look
their best. Outer clothing made of such fabrics is a top ironing priority. Tablecloths, napkins, curtains and draperies, doilies, dresser scarves, and similar decorative pieces often do not look good without ironing, and since they exist
at least half for appearance' sake, it is worthwhile to iron them.

Sheets, pillowcases, and flat-woven dish towels are a different matter. They
need not be seen, and they do not function better if ironed. If you are short
on time, you should eschew the luxury of ironed sheets and dish towels. But
they are indeed luxuries to enjoy when you can. Crisp, smooth sheets dramatically change the aesthetic appeal of your bed and heighten your sense of
repose. Pretty ironed dish towels make the kitchen look cared for when they

are hung out, and, when you change them following a morning or evening cleanup, they provide a ready symbol of freshening and renewal. Such things enlarge the vocabulary of your housekeeping, give you more attractive things to say with it. On the practical side, a newcomer to the kitchen can be sure that an ironed towel is fresh.

You need not—and should not—iron terry-cloth towels and washcloths; small rugs and mats; diapers; mattress, crib, and bumper pads; comforters or other filled articles; sweatpants and sweatshirts; spandex stretch tights and other stretch athletic wear; seersucker; or pile fabrics such as velvet and chenille. Some people like to iron men's cotton knit underwear, woven cotton boxer shorts, and women's knit and synthetic-fiber bras and panties. This is fine for those who like both the work and the result, but unnecessary.

You may be satisfied with the way permanent-press and wrinkle-resistant clothes and linens look with no ironing at all, but these articles vary in just how wrinkle-resistant they are. Wrinkle-resistance may also decrease after many launderings. Permanent-press treatments are sometimes more accurately called "durable press" because they actually last through about fifty launderings. Many permanent-press clothes and linens look better after some touch-up ironing. You must consult your own priorities and tastes as well as the appearance of the garments to determine whether and how much you wish to iron them.

Try to avoid ironing clothes after they have been worn. This sets in stains and makes dirt harder to remove.

Sprinkling Clothes and Linens

Permanent-press and synthetic fabrics sometimes iron well when dry, and, if they do not, a steam iron will supply all the moisture necessary. These fabrics usually need little or no ironing anyway. When some smoothing is desirable, their thermoplasticity makes them responsive to the warmth of the iron alone.

Untreated cottons, rayons, and silks must be slightly damp to iron out properly. They should feel as though you had left them outside overnight in summer and they became damp with dew. Linen should feel even more damp. The easiest way to get things this damp is to remove them from the dryer or line before they have gotten entirely dry. But this is not always convenient to do. When it is not, you can render them damp either by using a steam iron or by sprinkling them with water.

Sprinkling clothes is a little more trouble, but cottons and linens are far easier to iron and look far better after sprinkling than steam ironing alone. When fabrics are properly sprinkled, the moisture has a chance to penetrate the fibers and spread uniformly throughout the fabric. Steam from the iron does not penetrate so deeply or so uniformly.

The best procedure is to sprinkle clothes the night before they are to be ironed so that the moisture permeates the cloth. If you cannot do this, allow

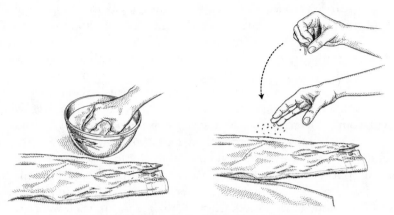

Sprinkling clothes by hand to dampen for ironing

Rolling sprinkled pillowcases for ironing

Stacking and sprinkling napkins

Rolling stacked and sprinkled napkins for ironing

at least an hour before you will iron. Clothes that will sit overnight before ironing should be placed in a tightly closed plastic bag and stored in the refrigerator or someplace else cool; otherwise there is danger of mildew. If they will not be ironed within twenty-four hours, put them in the freezer. Chilled, sprinkled fabrics make for smooth and pleasant ironing.

Some people like to spray fabrics with plain warm water from a spray bottle or to sprinkle with a sprinkle bottle. I find spray bottles to be a nuisance in dampening as they tire your hand (though they are good for dampening spots during ironing). You can make a sprinkle bottle by punching holes in the lid of a screw-top jar, testing it until it works to your satisfaction.

If you prefer sprinkling by hand, as I do, fill a basin or sink with the hottest water that is comfortable to your hand (because warmer water spreads more quickly) and dip your fingers in. Then shake them with a snap over the fabric with your palm facing you (as though you were making the familiar hand-and-finger gesture that means something like "I'm impressed"). Whether you use bottles or sprinkle by hand, you very lightly scatter water drops all over the article until it is covered with droplets as evenly spaced as you can manage. Shirts, dresses, pants, pillowcases, and other articles with fronts and backs must be sprinkled front and back, but flatwork, such as sheets, tea towels, or table-cloths, need be sprinkled only on one side. Experience, and nothing else, will finally enable you to judge with great accuracy whether you have sprinkled enough or too much. Linen should be sprinkled damper than cotton.

When the garment has been sprinkled, fold it lengthwise until it is narrow enough to make a conveniently sized roll; then roll it tightly. If the roll is not tight, the moisture will not be able to spread evenly through osmosis and the garment will dry. Store the rolls in a clean plastic bag or cover them with some-thing that will not permit the moisture to evaporate. If you have slightly damp clothes from the dryer or line that you intend to iron, you must roll and cover and store them the same way to avoid their drying prematurely or mildewing.

You can roll up a stack of sprinkled napkins or dish towels. Or if the fabric is thin, as with handkerchiefs, sprinkle only every other one and then roll up the stack. The water will spread from the sprinkled ones to the unsprin-kled, and they will not be too damp.

In deciding how damp to make your cloth, allow for the dampening effect of spray starch or sizing, if you plan to use it. If an article is too damp, simply spread it out to the air and let the moisture evaporate a bit while you iron something else.

Ironing Temperatures

The international symbols for ironing temperatures consist of one, two, and three dots.

One dot: cool (low temperature—248°F; 120°C), synthetics
Two dots: warm (medium temperature—320°F; 160°C), silk and wool
Three dots: hot (high temperature—370°F; 210°C), cotton and linen

These suggested temperatures are roughly applicable to the categories indi-cated. Consult chapters 16 and 17 with respect to particular textile fibers and

"General Ironing Strategies," below, for more specific information on proper ironing temperatures.

My unscientific impression is that many irons today do not reach particularly high temperatures, even when set for maximum heat, and that it can be hard to get heavier cottons and linens to look good. Higher wattages indicate more heating power. If you can pick up an old iron (with an intact cord and plug) at a second-hand store or tag sale, you might find it useful on clothes or linens that need a really hot iron.

Before Beginning

Your ironing board should be well padded and covered with a smooth, secure, clean, heat-resistant cover. Make sure that there are no mineral deposits inside the iron or in its steam holes and that the soleplate of your iron is clean. Mineral deposits or scorched material on the soleplate will come off on whatever you are ironing. If you have any doubts, heat and/or steam up the iron and test it on a rag. (See "Cleaning and Maintaining Your Iron," below.)

Also test the iron's heat before beginning so as to avoid scorching or melting the fabric with an overhot iron. Test on a rag of similar composition or on an inconspicuous place on the garment.

Ironing Techniques

Pressing. The terms "ironing" and "pressing" are often used interchangeably, but they are in fact different things. In ironing, you slide the iron back and forth over the cloth; in pressing, you simply press the iron in one spot and then lift it. Pressing is used on tailored and lined suits, especially men's, on wool, on some silks and rayons, on net, and on pile fabrics. Pressing is used to avoid crushing the cloth, giving it a shine, or stretching or scorching or otherwise harming it with the heat of the iron. This is done partly by not sliding the iron and partly (and usually) by using a "pressing cloth." This is simply a cloth that you lay over the fabric, pressing through it rather than touching the iron directly to the garment. Use unbleached muslin, white cheesecloth, or just a clean white dish towel for a pressing cloth. There are translucent pressing cloths that let you see what you are doing. A pressing cloth is sometimes used in ironing as well as in pressing.

Most pressing is best done professionally. At home, we usually wish to do only a little touching up by way of pressing. But it happens that one finds oneself with a wrinkled suit and an appointment when the dry cleaner is closed for the holiday, and home pressing has to be done. On these occasions, the best thing to do is to do as little as possible. First try steaming out the wrinkles, with a hand steamer if you have one or in the shower if you don't. Then try to press out intractable wrinkles. Using a dampened pressing cloth and working only on the wrinkled areas, apply the iron with a slight pressure and then lift quickly. Press on the wrong side as much as possible. Beware of creating shiny areas or seam marks on seams, lapels, and pockets by pressing too hard or too long. If you should happen to create a shine, try gently brushing with a clothes brush to remove it, or rub gently with a slightly moistened clean sponge or clean white face cloth or towel.

To Press Wool. Put a heavy, nonlinting, nonbleeding terry-cloth towel under the garment to prevent seams and folds from leaving imprints on the garment's surface. Press on the wrong side using steam or a damp pressing cloth and medium iron. Wool will develop an unpleasant shine if the iron directly touches the right side. Lift the iron after each pressing. Do not go back and forth, as this will stretch the fabric, and iron in the direction of the weave. Do not iron the garment until it is absolutely dry; stop when the fabric is smooth and almost undetectably damp.

To Press Silk Ties. Press on the wrong (back) side. Lay thick silks or ties on a terry-cloth towel. Place a dry pressing cloth over the article. If wrinkles will not come out, place a damp pressing cloth over the dry one.

General Ironing Strategies. Whether you are pressing or ironing, you lay the article on the ironing board and smooth it out. Iron as large an area as you can, then put down the iron so that you can use both hands to rotate the article around the board in preparation for ironing a new area. When you are ironing, one hand works at smoothing the garment and pulling it taut while the other works the iron. When you put down the iron, either stand it on its heel or place it on a nonflammable stand.

In real ironing, as opposed to pressing, you use moderately paced, steady back-and-forth strokes of the iron, with slight downward pressure; you usually press down more heavily on the forward strokes than on the return motion. Today's irons are very lightweight. Some people, myself included, find

Ironing a shirt collar

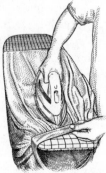

Ironing a gathered skirt

Ironing a pant leg

that ironing is easier with a heavier iron with a very smooth stroke. The weight means that you have to apply less muscle power.

- Begin ironing with those items that are to be ironed at the lowest temperatures and end with those that will be ironed at the highest temperatures—for example, polypropylene first (using a pressing cloth) and linen last.
- Keep a sprinkle or spray bottle or damp sponge at hand for spot dampening in case you accidentally iron in an unwanted crease or in case the cloth dries before you have finished ironing. You will sometimes also wish to redampen a pressing cloth.
- Spray starch and spray sizing should be kept at hand, too, if you intend to use them. Spray lightly from a distance of 6 to 10 inches with the bottle tipped at an angle. Follow instructions on the bottle. You can choose to starch only collars, cuffs, and plackets, or those areas plus fronts. The traditional way is to use more starch on these areas and less on others. Because it is easy to scorch spray starch, you may wish to turn down the heat on your iron. (For more on what to starch, see "Starches and Sizings," below.)
- To avoid unwanted creases on collars, iron from the points in, using short strokes. After ironing, the collar should be folded down and softly creased with your hand, not the iron. Iron the wrong side (the back) of the collar first, then the right side.
- French cuffs, too, should be softly creased after ironing with the hand, not with the iron.
- To avoid unwanted creases where the cloth has slack—for example, in a hem—use short strokes and stop short when you see that the slack is going to fold and crease. Try moving the iron toward the wrinkles from different directions.
- To avoid shine, iron fabric on the wrong side or use a pressing cloth. This is a particularly good idea on dark cottons, linens, rayons, and silks. (Silk should always be ironed on the wrong side with a pressing cloth; the same

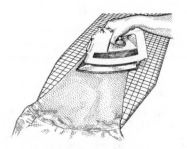

Ironing a shirt sleeve

A sleeve board

goes for any rayon that tends to develop a shine.) If shine develops on thick seams or elsewhere, wipe lightly with a barely damp cloth. When ironing double thicknesses, like collars, pockets, and cuffs, do the wrong side first and, if necessary to avoid shine, use a pressing cloth on the right side.

- Nose the iron gently around buttons, hooks, snaps, and zippers; never iron over them. Buttons will sometimes melt and will frequently crack if you iron over them. They may also scratch the soleplate of your iron.
- Close zippers, snaps, and hooks before ironing plackets. But leave button plackets unbuttoned.
- To iron gathers, begin at the edge of the cloth opposite the gathers, and wiggle the point of the iron into the gathers.
- To iron puffed sleeves or pockets, first stuff them with tissue paper or a small terry towel or washcloth.
- Some people like to use a sleeve board for shirt sleeves. (Set the sleeveboard on the ironing board and pull the sleeve over it.)
- To iron pleats, first lay or pin them in place. Some people like to pin them to the ironing board cover. Then; holding the pleats taut against the pressure of the iron, iron them in long strokes going from waist to hem.
- Lay embroidered or sequined cloth on a Turkish towel, then iron it on the wrong side with a pressing cloth. This keeps the embroidered patterns raised and prevents cracking of the sequins or scratching of the soleplate.
- Use a pressing cloth when ironing lace and cutwork. This will ensure that you do not accidentally cause a tear with the point of the iron.
- Never iron the pile of a fabric. Velvet should be steamed, not ironed, unless the manufacturer otherwise directs. Use a clothes steamer. Or, to steam a pile fabric with your steam iron, lay it on a Turkish towel; then hold your steam iron just a fraction of an inch up from the surface of the wrong side and release steam. This will refresh the pile. To get stubborn wrinkles out of corduroy, try first ironing on the wrong side of the fabric; then steam or brush up the right—pile—side if you think it needs fluffing.
- Untangle fringe while it is still wet.
- Ironing can stretch certain garments or fabrics out of shape. Iron bias-cut clothes and other stretchy fabrics, including wools and knits, in the direction of the weave—that is, in the less stretchy or nonstretchy direction. In the case of bias-cut skirts, this means that you should not iron from hem to waist, as you usually do. If the fabric is especially stretchy, use a press cloth to reduce the iron's drag.

Steam Ironing. Wait until the iron is hot enough to steam the water. When you have not sprinkled the clothes damp, steam is helpful in ironing practically any fiber. Choose a proper steam level for the fiber—most for linen, down to practically none for 100 percent thermoplastic synthetics. Use the steam button to eject a steam spray on cuffs, collars, and other thick places.

Airing the Ironing; Avoiding Under- and Overironing. It is a basic rule of ironing that you iron things until they are dry. If you leave things too damp, they will feel rough and look rumply afterward. They may also develop a faint unpleasant odor or mildew if you put them away in that state.

But there is dry, and then there's dry. Some people overiron in an effort to get the article bone-dry. This is a mistake. Scorching, yellowing, or melting of synthetics are some of the obvious effects of overironing. Shininess, brittleness, and a harsh hand can also be produced. You should stop ironing just a fraction of a degree before the flat of the cloth is perfect for use and wear, letting the last tiny increment of moisture evaporate from the heat of ironing. At this point, when the flat has a bare suggestion of dampness in it, the seams will be slightly more damp than this, but that is all right, for now you are going to air the ironing. Airing carries off the excess moisture without the dangers of overironing. One hundred years ago the ironing was aired religiously, usually overnight, often in front of the fire.

To air laundry in this day and age, fold or hang each ironed article carefully, but do not put it away until both flat and seams feel perfectly dry to the touch. Depending on the temperature and humidity of your room, this may take as little as a few minutes or as much as an hour or more. Folded articles may be aired on a table or shelf, but do not stack them on top of one another until the airing is completed. Shirts and dresses can be hung on hangers on a rack in the laundry room or in some other convenient area for airing. If you do not air them this way before replacing them in your closets, they are likely to carry dampness into your closets and create a musty smell that is very hard to get rid of.

Ironing Clothes. When ironing clothes, follow an order in which there will be minimal rewrinkling of the already ironed sections as you proceed. This means following three basic rules.

1. Iron all parts that have a double thickness—ties, bows, collars, cuffs, sleeves, pockets, and the like—because they will wrinkle less readily than larger, thinner areas like shirt backs. Collars, cuffs, plackets and facings, hems, and other parts of the garment that have two right sides should be ironed inside first. When ironing pockets, hems, or facings on the right side, use a pressing cloth to avoid ironing marks at raised places. If an article is lined, turn it inside out and iron the lining first. Iron set-in pockets from the wrong side with garments turned inside out.
2. Iron the nonflat portions, like ruffles, shoulders, and puffed sleeves, before the flat portions. Ironing these requires more turning and twisting of the garment, which could cause flat, unstructured areas to rewrinkle if they had already been ironed.
3. Iron the top parts before the bottom parts (the shirt part of a shirtwaist dress

before the skirt, the top of pants before the legs) so that you do not have to scrunch up the ironed lower section, rewrinkling it, to get at the top.

Some say you should also iron small parts before large parts. But I find that these three rules cover the ground thoroughly.

Ironing Flatwork. Much flatwork can be done extremely well and quickly on an electric rotary iron or "mangle." These machines have a heated roller that presses the cloth. They take out wrinkles but do not produce quite as fine a result as hand ironing. They are now all but unknown in the United States, but they were common equipment in middle-class homes here until the early 1960s, and they remain popular in some European countries. I am told that Americans are once again beginning to ask for them; you see them now and then in appliance stores. I acquired one several years ago because our household habits produce a great deal of flatwork to iron—sheets and pillowcases, tablecloths and napkins—since we prefer untreated cottons and linens. The rotary iron saves great amounts of ironing time and effort, but it is a fairly expensive machine and uses more electricity than a hand iron.

Rotary irons, in the hands of skilled operators, can also be used for much clothing, especially casual wear, T-shirts, and children's play clothes, that

Rotary iron or mangle

benefit from a quick smoothing but do not need fine, close ironing. Skilled users do shirts and dresses, too, perhaps with some hand finishing, but this takes practice. Cutwork and embroidery or other designs that create raised patterns will definitely need hand ironing, although on flatwork with decorated hems and edges you can often do the flat on the rotary iron and then finish the embroidery and lace with a hand iron. These areas need the point of the iron to get close to raised areas in the fabric.

When ironing or mangling sheets or tablecloths or other large items, lay an old but clean sheet or tablecloth on the floor so that items that reach the floor will not be soiled.

Ironing Linen. Some experts now sometimes recommend a warm, not hot, iron for linen. If linen or a blend containing linen has received resin treatments for wrinkle-resistance, it is true that you should avoid a hot iron and follow the care label instructions. (The permanent-press setting may be recommended.) In addition, very sheer and lightweight linens may iron well with a warm iron. Subject to this and other caveats about blends, resins, and finishes, however, linen is not harmed by the temperatures of a hot iron. Not only that, it is quite hard, if not impossible, to iron most linen free of wrinkles on a medium iron.

Even cambric or lawn, which may not need a hot iron, will not be harmed by it unless you let the iron rest upon them until they dry and burn. It is not difficult to avoid doing this. Almost any fabric would be injured if you left a hot iron standing on it.

To iron well, linen should be quite damp—damper than cotton needs to be for good results. Steam from a steam iron is adequate for sheer linens, but I find it easier to sprinkle medium-to-heavyweight linen fabric. When you dampen, allow for the additional dampening effect of spray starch if you are using it. Stretch and smooth damp linens into their proper shape before ironing. Ironing on the wrong side, or with a pressing cloth, will prevent a sheen from developing. But on damask and other light-colored linens a sheen is desirable; these you iron first on the wrong side and then on the right side. Darker linens should be ironed only on the wrong side.

Linen is rather brittle when completely dry—and the drier it is, the more brittle—so it should not be ironed bone-dry; stop while there is still a suggestion, barely detectable, of dampness. Be particularly careful not to iron creases too dry or too sharp or the cloth might be weakened along the creases and eventually crack. (This is particularly a danger with ironed linen that is stored flat. It is best to store it unironed unless you plan to use it soon.) Hang ironed linen clothes while they still retain a hint of dampness at the seams or hems, and leave them out to air-dry. Replace them in closets or drawers only when such dampness has evaporated; this will happen quickly.

Good linen tablecloths and napkins stay crisp without starch. But if your table linens or linen clothes have gone limp (even if they shouldn't have), starch will often restore the look you want. Fancy napkin-folding requires starch.

Table Linens. Ironing instructions are provided here; for folding instructions, see chapter 7.

To iron round tablecloths, begin at the center and work out, turning the cloth as you go.

Iron table napkins flat; do not iron in the creases.

Damasks, especially of linen, are supposed to look glossy or shiny after ironing. They are ironed on both sides, wrong side first. Fold square and rectangular tablecloths in half lengthwise and iron first on the wrong side until half-dry, and then refold and iron until near dry on the right side. Linen is brittle, especially when dry, so take special care to be sure that crease lines are not ironed dry and that you iron along the crease line gently. Remember to move any creases an inch or two at each ironing so that the cloth does not wear out along the crease.

Etiquette forbids creases on the cloth for formal dining or, at best, tolerates one middle crease line lengthwise. A crease across the middle offends the eye. If you are one of those who want no creases whatever on your cloth—not even down the length—after ironing on both sides and avoiding the center, softly fold the cloth into thirds and iron the small unironed strip down the center of the cloth. For informal dining, ordinary checkerboard squares caused by folding will be tolerated by everyone, and some, myself included, think they are pretty and fresh-looking. The rule against any but a lengthwise center crease is of relatively recent vintage; through the eighteenth century, tablecloths were purposely ironed in accordion pleats and checkerboard creases that were valued for their contribution to the table's beauty as much as the china or silver set upon it.

If it will be some time before they are used, it is best to store tablecloths unstarched and unironed and to iron them just before they are needed. Doing this gives you very wrinkle-free cloths on the table but also creates more work and details to keep in mind at the last minute.

Sheets. The highest traditions, which are by and large extinct, should survive at least in memory. Perhaps some people will wish to adopt them on their wedding night or similarly rare and grand occasions. These dictate that sheets, especially top sheets and more especially linen sheets, be ironed. Some actually like sheets ironed on both sides.

Ironing Flat Sheets.

Long method: Fold the sheet in half crosswise (hem to hem), wrong sides together, and iron on both (right) sides. (If you wished to iron the sheet on both sides, you would first fold it in half crosswise [hem to hem], right sides together, and iron both sides—the wrong sides. You would then go on to refold, wrong sides together, and iron the right sides.) Fold again crosswise (fold to hem), creating quarter folds, and iron both sides. Fold again crosswise (fold to hem), creating eighth folds; iron both sides. Then fold lengthwise, or selvage to selvage. Fold lengthwise again, fold to selvage, twice. The completely folded and ironed sheet is divided into thirty-two sections.

Short method: Iron only once, after the initial folding in half. Then fold as above.

Abbreviated method: Fold in half crosswise (hem to hem). Iron the bottom hem, selvage edges, and eighteen inches of the top hem (the foldover portion). Then fold as above.

Ironing Fitted Sheets.
Ironing fitted sheets is not necessary since they are pulled taut by the mattress and are further smoothed by the pressure, moisture, and warmth of bodies upon them. Moreover, they do not show. But some people like the more finished smoothness of ironed fitted sheets. If you are going to iron yours, you can do the fitted corners by stuffing them with a small terry towel. Or you can leave the fitted corners unironed and iron only the flat portions. Otherwise, iron as for a flat sheet.

Caution for those who never iron sheets: When I got married and joined my linen stores with my husband's, I was initially mystified by the dozens of small but growing holes along the selvages and hems of my husband's good-quality cotton sheets. I soon determined that the holes were caused by the creases of permanent, natural wrinkles in those places, wrinkles that did not unwrinkle even in laundering. (Cloth weakens along any permanent crease lines.) Even if you do not wish to iron your sheets, you might try ironing out just their selvages and hems now and then, to avoid getting such holes.

Starches and Sizings

Starches are plant starches, usually cornstarch nowadays, but formerly wheat or potato starch, and other substances were commonly used. Starches are used to stiffen; to add crispness, body, and glossiness; to promote soil resistance (dirt particles adhere less easily to smooth, starched surfaces); and to make ironing easier.

If you like cottons, cotton blends, and linens that have not been resin-treated for wrinkle-resistance, you may also enjoy them ironed with a bit of starch. Starch is a good idea whenever or wherever you want extra body or stiffness, or when you want a garment to continue to look ironed after you've been wearing it for hours. I like a little spray starch on cotton shirts, dresses, and skirts. Sometimes I starch just the collars, cuffs, plackets, and perhaps the shirt fronts. If you want extra body or stiffness on some or all of a garment, use heavy-duty spray starch. Heavy-duty spray starch is also desirable when you want to fold napkins into elegant or unusual shapes. True, starched napkins are not soft to the lips, but they look more formal. Starch should not be used on sheets, underwear, diapers, towels, or filled or stuffed articles. (Back in the 1940s and 1950s, starched pillowcases were de rigueur, and I know one lady who says she still cannot sleep on an unstarched pillowcase. I like the appearance of starched pillowcases and even enjoy their crisp feel. Most people do not.) Fancy handwoven hand towels for guests—lacy, embroidered, damask, etc. (not terry-cloth towels)—are sometimes starched crisply.

Spray starch is applied as you iron. You can put liquid starch in the final rinse of the wash, using the amounts recommended on the label. If you wish to use liquid starch on some but not all of the contents of a load, do the starching separately in a clean basin.

On synthetic fibers and on blends with a high percentage of synthetics, what are called "sizings" are usually preferable. Sizings are also stiffeners. (Technically, starches are sizings too, but in supermarket products the terms are used as I describe them here.) Sizings usually contain sodium carboxymethylcellulose, a derivative of cotton that dries and stiffens when exposed to heat. You spray store-bought sizing on when you iron. Sizing is softer than starch and irons at lower temperatures. That is why it is usually recommended for synthetics, which cannot be ironed at higher temperatures. You can use it on cottons and linens, too, when they do not need much stiffness. You can make an old-fashioned sizing at home using unflavored, uncolored gelatin, available at your grocery store—use one packet to two quarts of hot water. This is good for small, delicate items that need gentle stiffening. Just dip them in, and be sure to get all the parts equally wet. Let them dry, then iron with a steam iron or sprinkle to dampen.

Cleaning and Maintaining Your Iron

Irons with nonstick soleplates usually can be cleaned simply by wiping with a damp cloth when the iron is cold. If yours cannot be cleaned this way, do not resort to abrasives. This will scratch any soleplate, nonstick or not, and make your iron glide less smoothly. The best solution to cooked-on spray starch or other debris is one of the commercial cleaners made for this purpose. These are available in home centers or from iron manufacturers. One home remedy

TO REDUCE OR AVOID IRONING

- Choose low-wrinkling clothes and linens. (See chapter 13, "Fabrics That Work," page 193.)
- Use a mangle (rotary iron) on all flatwork, casual clothes and play clothes, and sportswear.
- If you like non—wrinkle-treated sheets but do not wish to iron them, dry them on the line, being sure to hang them neatly, smoothing hems and sel-vages, in such a way as to insure that the wind will billow them out. They will come very smooth. If they feel at all stiff—as can happen, particularly when there is no breeze—tumble them on cool for a few minutes in the dryer to soften them up. (But they will soften almost immediately when you sleep on them.) Yet another way to dry things smooth without ironing is to tum-ble them in the dryer; promptly remove them and fold them tautly while they are still warm and before they are bone-dry. If you let them sit in the dryer, they will wrinkle. After removing them—from the line as well as the dryer—shake them out well, pull them sharply into shape, and snap them—that is, give them a crack as one might crack a whip. Stack them neatly, place them at the bottom of the stack in your linen closet, and place something quite heavy on top of the stack. Or, rather than folding them, fold them while they are still hot into halves or quarters and then roll them tautly around a cardboard roll.
- Dry synthetics and wrinkle-treated clothes on the permanent-press cycle. Remove them from the dryer and fold them promptly.
- Use a trouser frame when drying pants. It stretches them taut so they do not wrinkle and creates creases in the right places.
- Never leave laundry sitting in the laundry basket unfolded; this causes much wrinkling. Hang and fold clothes carefully, and keep drawers and closets uncrowded.
- If you plan to wear items again, hang or fold them neatly after you take them off.

that often works, however, is a paste of baking soda and water. Dip an old, clean, soft toothbrush into the paste and brush the cool soleplate. If you do not have immediate success, let the paste stand for a few minutes and then scrub vigorously. This remedy is indeed a little abrasive, but if used rarely it should do no damage. I have also seen recommendations to use white vinegar for this purpose, but in my experience vinegar is not effective. Whatever you use, it's best to work on the problem as soon as possible. The longer you wait, the harder it becomes to remove a stuck-on substance, and scorched-on spray starch tends to come off on garments when you are ironing.

Some steam irons specify the use of tap water; others require distilled water. Be sure to use whatever your manufacturer recommends. If your iron frequently becomes clogged, perhaps you are using the wrong kind of water. Many new irons have a self-unclogging feature. If your steam iron lacks this feature and becomes clogged as a result of mineral deposits in your water, you can dissolve them—unless the manufacturer's instruction booklet says not to—by pouring some white vinegar into the water tank, turning on the iron, and letting it steam for a few minutes. Before using your iron again, iron a clean rag of some sort so that any residues are deposited on the rag. Then cool the iron, refill with cold, plain water, and drain to rinse it. There are also effective commercial products, available in home centers, for cleaning out mineral deposits from steam irons.

7

Folding Clothes and Linens

How to fold suit jackets, shirts, blouses, jackets, sweaters, T-shirts,
dresses, pants and shorts, skirts, underpants, socks, napkins,
tablecloths, blankets, sheets, pillowcases, towels, handkerchiefs . . .
How to put a duvet into a cover . . . Using tissue paper in folding

When I was a girl, every week my mother and I folded sheets together in a brisk dance, moving quickly and always turning the folds in the same direction. Periodically she would give the sheet a good sharp snap, which would jerk my end out of my hand if I didn't hang on tight. Tablecloths, sheets, and other large, unwieldy items really are folded most easily by two congenial people of roughly the same height. But when I first kept house as a single woman, I learned to lay the part that would otherwise drag on the floor on a bed or sofa. I rather liked not having to worry about the other person's suddenly giving a violent snap to her end.

Folding smaller pieces after laundering was always done by a daughter, sitting at a table. Each article was to be folded in just the right manner. Neat, separate stacks of napkins, handkerchiefs, T-shirts, towels according to their size, and piles of rolled-up sock balls, arranged according to owner, were first set on the table and left to air, if necessary, then set carefully in a basket and carried around the house to their proper storage places: linen closet, dresser drawers, or kitchen drawers.

The folding and hanging styles described in this chapter are those used in my family. Other styles might be just as good or better. But it is useful to have some habitual way of folding so as to keep things neat and wrinkle-free and to use drawer and shelf space most efficiently.

Suit Jackets. Suit jackets are hung in a closet or carried in a garment bag for traveling whenever possible. When they must be folded into a suitcase or stored flat, the following folding method works well. Put your hands into the shoulders of the unbuttoned jacket, grab the ends of the shoulder pads, and turn the shoulders inside out. Without letting go, pull the shoulders together, in the process folding the jacket inside out along the side seams. The back and sleeves now lie between the left and right front. Straighten up and align the side seams, make sure that sleeves and hems are aligned, and open the lapels. If your suitcase or drawer is large enough, you can instead simply fold the unbuttoned jacket in half lengthwise, with the lapel edges together and the side seams together.

Shirts, Blouses, Casual Jackets, Sweaters, and T-Shirts. If the shirt has buttons, button it at top, middle, and bottom. Then lay it facedown. Fold both sides of a shirt or blouse so that they meet in the back, with the sleeves aligned with the side folds. Fold the tail up to the cuffs, making a straight line at the bottom. Then fold in thirds crosswise. Casual jackets, long-sleeved sweaters, pullovers, and cardigans are folded the same way, except that there is no tail to be folded up. Do T-shirts as you do other shirts. A child's T-shirt may need only one crosswise fold, in half; but an adult's you may wish to fold into thirds, depending upon the size of the T-shirt and what fits comfortably in your drawer or on your shelf.

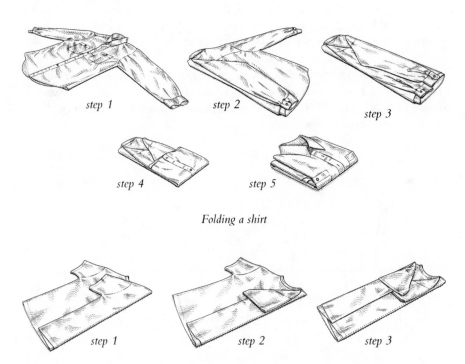

step 1   *step 2*   *step 3*

step 4   *step 5*

Folding a shirt

step 1   *step 2*   *step 3*

Folding a T-shirt (see "Folding a shirt," above, for steps 4 and 5)

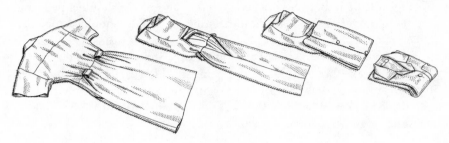

Folding a dress

Dresses. Dresses should almost always be hung rather than folded, unless they are to go in a suitcase or other type of flat storage. To fold a dress for a suitcase, lay it front down. Fold the top as though it were a shirt or blouse. Fold the bottom hem to the knees. Then fold at the waist.

Pants and Shorts. Pants are usually hung by their cuffs on trouser hangers. Or fold them over a hanger with a thick bar or a paper guard so that a crosswise crease does not form. Shorts may be folded and placed in a drawer. Whether hung or put in a suitcase or drawer, pants and shorts are folded as follows: align the inseams and outer seams of the legs and fold so that a crease forms properly at the front center of the legs. In well-made garments, the crease should run all the way to the top of the pants, joining the front waist pleats. Fold in the front placket along the pleats.

Skirts. Lay the skirt front down, with zippers and plackets closed. Fold the sides in toward the center. Then, if it is not a short skirt, fold crosswise in thirds. The idea is to avoid a vertical crease line down the front center or a horizontal crease line halfway down the front.

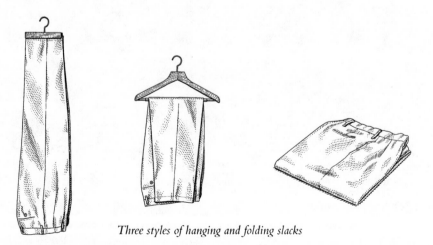

Three styles of hanging and folding slacks

Folding a skirt

Folding boxers

Folding panties

Underpants. The folding is the same for men's and women's. Fold in half crosswise, so that the crotch meets the waistband. Then fold into thirds. Underpants can also be laid flat, unfolded, in stacks, if they are not too large, or they can be rolled.

Socks. There are three ways to fold socks. Method 1, in which they are folded into balls, looks good and is space-efficient but tends to stretch out the top of the socks, especially all-cotton socks. In this method, you lay one sock on top of the other. Starting at the toe, roll them up together to the ribbing. Open the top of the outside sock and pull it over the roll. In method 2, the socks are simply rolled up together. This is neat and space-efficient, but the rolls can come undone and socks can separate. It's the best method for careful adults but not for children and those of us who sometimes rummage wildly through our drawers. In method 3, you place one sock on top of the other, then fold one top over the other. This keeps pairs together in all but the wildest rumpuses.

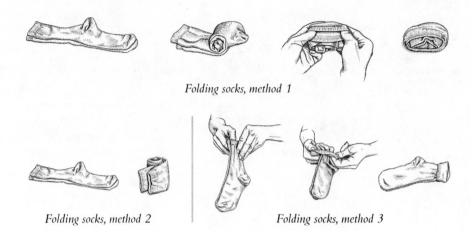

Folding socks, method 1

Folding socks, method 2   *Folding socks, method 3*

Napkins. When folding napkins, always fold loosely by hand. Do not iron creases in. A large dinner napkin is folded in a triple screen fold lengthwise, then in another triple screen fold crosswise, producing a square. You can then fold again in half, if you prefer a smaller rectangular shape to a larger square shape or just to save some room on the table. However you fold it, if there is a monogram or corner decoration, it should end up in the lower left-hand corner when the napkin is placed to the left of the forks. (The lower right-hand corner is also fine; just be consistent.)

A smaller dinner napkin is simply folded into a rectangle: in half twice, ending with the monogram or decoration in the lower left corner.

The luncheon napkin and napkins for informal occasions may be folded any way you like—for example, like a dinner napkin, in a triangle, or in a wedge formed from the triangle. To make a wedge, the two points of the tri-

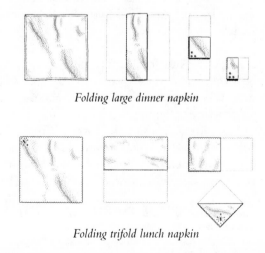

Folding large dinner napkin

Folding trifold lunch napkin

angle are folded to the back in thirds, forming a pentagon with two long sides. The monogram or decoration is in the point, which points downward.

Tablecloths. Tablecloths should be either rolled around a cardboard tube or loosely folded, so as to avoid creases as much as possible. (One lengthwise crease is acceptable.) You can also hang tablecloths if they are not too wide. Simply fold loosely in half twice, lengthwise, and fold over a hanger with a thick, round bar to avoid causing a crease.

If you wish to fold your tablecloths, large square and rectangular tablecloths may be folded in half three times lengthwise, forming eight layers (the first fold brings wrong sides together), then two or three times crosswise. The number of crosswise and lengthwise folds may be increased or decreased depending on the size of the tablecloth and your drawer space. If you wish the fold lines all to point upward to the right side of the cloth, fold the tablecloth in fourths as follows: Bring each side edge to the middle of the cloth, creating two folds along the sides of the cloth. Then fold again lengthwise along the middle line where the two side edges meet, so that the two edges are inside. Do the same with the crosswise folds.

Fold round tablecloths in half, to form a half-moon shape, with wrong sides together. Then fold in half lengthwise, bringing the arc of the half-moon to the fold. The center of the arc should be even with the center of the fold. Fold

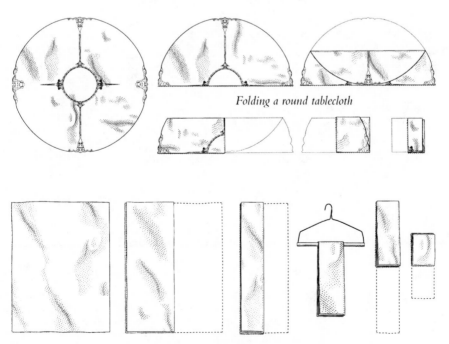

Folding a round tablecloth

Folding a rectangular tablecloth

lengthwise again if necessary—as for a large cloth. Then fold in half crosswise twice, or three times if the cloth is large. You will have a rectangle. Small round tablecloths are sometimes folded this way: Fold in half twice, forming four layers in the shape of a piece of pie. Then, bringing point to curved edge, fold in half. This makes an irregular shape.

Blankets. Fold blankets in half, head to foot, twice, then in half, side to side, twice.

Sheets. When folding a flat sheet, hold it with the side facing up that you want to face up when it is on the bed—right side up if it is a bottom sheet and wrong side up if it is a top flat. Fold in half crosswise three times, on the first time bringing right sides together—hem to hem, fold to hem, and fold to hem again, always folding in the same direction. Then fold in half lengthwise three times—selvage to selvage, fold to selvage, fold to selvage again, always folding in the same direction. ("Selvage" is defined in the Glossary of Fabric Terms, page 306. See also chapter 15, page 199.)

To fold a fitted sheet, have the wrong side of the center of the sheet and the right side of the fitted corners facing you. Fold the sheet in half crosswise, tucking the top fitted corners into the bottom fitted corners. Fold in half lengthwise, so that all the fitted corners are in a stack. Now simply fold the sheet in half three more times—once along the length and twice crosswise. This makes a neatly folded fitted sheet of approximately the same size as the folded flat sheet.

Fold two times crosswise

Folding a fitted sheet

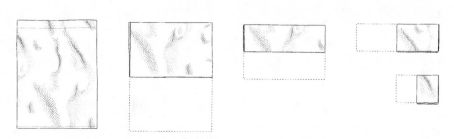

Folding a flat sheet: fold to hem two times; fold to selvage two times

HOW TO PUT A DUVET INTO A DUVET COVER

Fold both the duvet (comforter) and the duvet cover into halves and then
quarters. Insert the folded duvet into the top quarter of the folded cover so
that the duvet's end and the opening of the duvet cover are aligned. Pick up
both at the opening, hold tightly, and shake until the duvet falls to fill the
entire cover.

Pillowcases (Standard, Queen, and King). Fold in thirds lengthwise, then
in half crosswise once or twice depending upon your shelf or drawer space. Or
reverse this, folding in half crosswise twice, then three times lengthwise. Either
way will prettily display trim or lace at the opening of the pillowcase.

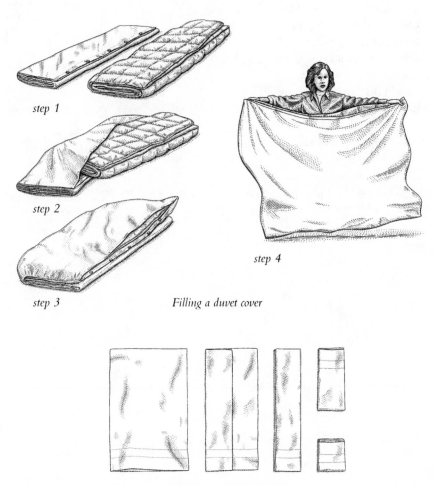

step 1

step 2

step 3   *Filling a duvet cover*

step 4

Folding a standard pillowcase

Folded articles in suitcases, on shelves, or in drawers resist wrinkling better if you cover them with tissue paper before folding so that the paper is folded up with the garments. You can also stuff puffy sleeves and hats with crumpled tissue paper—enough to gently fill them. When you are putting things into long-term storage, especially antiques, heirlooms, or other precious fabrics, use acid-free tissue paper.

Pillowcases (European). Try folding these in thirds along both dimensions.

Towels. Dish towels, tea towels, bath towels, and hand or guest towels can be folded in thirds lengthwise, then folded in half or thirds crosswise, depending upon the size of the towel and its thickness. Thinner towels are more easily folded many times. This method shows trim nicely and lets you hang the towels with their vertical folds in place; you need not refold for hanging.

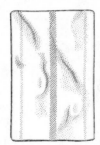

Folding a dish towel

Handkerchiefs. Fold men's handkerchiefs in half three times, forming rectangles. Fold women's handkerchiefs twice, forming squares.

8

How to Launder Tricky Items

How to launder blankets: nonwool and wool . . . Curtains and draperies . . . Shower curtains . . . Diapers . . . Gloves and mittens . . . Lace . . . Lingerie, undergarments, foundation garments . . . Down- and feather-filled clothes and furnishings . . . Polyester-filled clothes and furnishings . . . Kapok and foam fillings . . . Knits . . . Cotton knits . . . Quilts

Every home contains some clothes and furnishings that are launderable but cannot be washed in the standard ways or present unusual laundering difficulties. Suggestions are included below for the successful laundering of a number of such items: blankets; curtains and drapes; diapers; gloves and mittens; delicate lingerie, undergarments, and foundation garments; pillows, comforters, and garments filled with down, feathers, polyester, or other materials; and quilts. When the methods suggested are incompatible with care labels on any such articles, however, you should follow the care label.

Blankets, Nonwool. Be sure to look for a care label; blankets do not always have one, but, when they do, follow it. Before you decide on laundering, test for colorfastness. Nonwool blankets are almost always machine-washable and machine-dryable, assuming that your washer and dryer are large enough for them. Blankets should be washed singly, one by one. To be sure a blanket will fit, try it out in both your washer and your dryer before proceeding. If it is too large, send it to a professional laundry or take it to a laundromat that has extra-large machines. If you prefer or if your dryer is too small, blankets can be line-dried or dried flat.

To launder washable nonwool blankets in top-loading agitator machines, fill the washer with water. Use the warmest temperature safe for the fiber and construction. Warm is usually best because nonwool blankets will generally be made of a synthetic or a cotton knit or loose weave and will have a soil type that is readily removed with warm water. (But only hot water would kill germs and dust mites.) Put in sufficient detergent and thoroughly dissolve it before adding the blanket. Arrange the blanket loosely and evenly around the post. Let it soak for twenty minutes, then wash on the gentle cycle. Rinse with cold water. Spin dry on the fast (or high) setting. In tumbling machines, add detergent to the dispenser and place the blanket loosely in the tub. Set the machine for presoak. Otherwise follow the same instructions as for top-loading machines: use the gentle cycle, warm-water wash (usually), cold-water rinse, spin at high or fast speed.

Tumble dry at the temperature proper for the fiber and construction—usually low to medium. If you are line-drying, spread the blanket over two lines to distribute its weight, preventing strain and stretching. If you are drying flat, try spreading it on the lawn on an old sheet. Sometimes even though the dryer is too small for drying a blanket, it is large enough to hold it for a few minutes of air fluffing after it has dried. You can also shake, snap, or brush the blanket to fluff it.

If you are forced to dry a blanket indoors on a line or rack, you can turn an electric fan on it to hasten drying.

Blankets, Wool. If a care label on a wool blanket says "Dry-clean only," obey it. If the blanket is of Superwash wool, follow the instructions on the care label (and see chapter 21, "The Natural Fibers," pages 341, 343–45.) If there is no care label, you must use your judgment. Dry cleaning will be safe, but home laundering using proper procedures will probably be safe too—and some people feel that they can give gentler care at home. But be sure to test for color-fastness with whatever detergent you plan on using.

Measure the blanket first so that you can restore it to its original dimensions ("block it") after it is washed. As with other blankets, wash each wool blanket separately and alone.

Use a neutral, mild detergent suitable for wool (see "Detergents and soaps, mild," pages 78–80) for use in cool water and for machine-laundering. Use cool water, making sure that the detergent is thoroughly mixed and dissolved before you put in the blanket. (Cool, by the way, does not mean icy cold. See "Water Temperature," pages 65–67, in chapter 4.) And if the blanket is heavily soiled, risk-takers like myself might try lukewarm water. Years ago, if there was heavy soil, people might even have tried a regular detergent as well—but, you may wish to try an extra amount of your mild detergent instead. (We risk-takers are also probably more tolerant of less-than-ideal results than others may be.)

Be sure to use plenty of water. Soak (or presoak) the blanket for a few minutes, say five or fewer and no longer. Agitate (or tumble) on gentle very briefly—a minute or two. Or, with agitating machines, to be more cautious, do not agitate at all; just stir the blanket gently with a long wooden paddle or

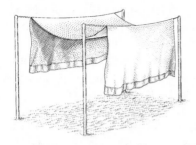

Blanket spread over two clotheslines to dry

spoon. Then manually set the machine forward to spin dry, using the fast spin speed. Then fill again with cold water to rinse, agitate or stir gently for a minute or two, and spin dry on the fast setting again. Repeat the rinse if necessary. Tumbling is gentler than agitating, so washable wool blankets receive a very safe treatment in tumbling machines if you use a short gentle cycle following the brief initial presoaking. But if you want to be more cautious, use the "hand-wash" setting (if your machine has one) rather than gentle—with cold wash and rinse water and fast spin.

Dry the blanket by laying it flat on a rack or laying it outside on an old clean sheet, stretching the blanket gently into its proper dimensions; refer to your original measurements to be sure. Or hang the blanket over two or three clotheslines to distribute its weight, pulling it gently into good shape. If you are drying a blanket indoors, you can hasten the process by turning an electric fan on it. If your dryer is large enough, air fluff the blanket after it is dry, without heat. If you cannot do this, shake the blanket and brush it gently with a clothes brush to soften and fluff it up after it is dry.

Curtains and Draperies. Read care labels on curtains and draperies carefully or consult your retailer at the time you buy as to their washability or dry-cleanability. Many curtains and draperies are not washable, whether because they are made of a nonlaunderable fabric such as silk velvet or because they have unlaunderable trim or for some other reason. In this case, they are probably dry-cleanable, but if they are quite delicate or worn, you must alert your dry cleaner to the situation.

Even when curtains and draperies are washable, they may not be machine-washable. And even when they are machine-washable, they should almost always be washed on the gentle cycle. This is so for several reasons. First, the type of soil they are likely to collect is usually easy to get out with gentle washing. Second—probably the most important consideration—they are constantly exposed to light while they are hanging, which causes deterioration of the fabric. Laundering can tear or fray them when they have been weakened by light. Third, they are often made in constructions, such as lace or extremely loose weaves, that demand gentle treatment. To choose between machine-washing on a gentle or delicate cycle and hand-washing, and to choose water temperature and detergent, use the same criteria that govern in other cases (see chapter 4). Choose lukewarm or cool water to avoid shrinkage with fibers that may shrink. Tumble dry on low if shrinkage is a problem, or line-dry if you wish to avoid any heat or abrasion.

Fiberglass curtains and draperies, which are not sold very often anymore, should be hand-laundered, not dry-cleaned, unless there is a care label stating otherwise. They should not go into your washing machine or dryer. Not only do they need a very gentle wash, but glass fibers will break off in the machines and be picked up by the next load you do. When glass fibers become embedded in fabrics they can cause severe skin irritation. (Fiberglass drapes must by law bear tags or labels saying they can cause skin irritation.) To launder fiberglass drapes and curtains, place them in a large laundry tub with water and detergent. Wearing rubber gloves, swish them around, then soak until the dirt has loosened. Swish again; then rinse thoroughly. Press water out of the curtains or drapes with your hands (still wearing rubber gloves)—do not wring—and then line-dry. Afterward, rinse the tub very thoroughly to insure that all fiberglass fibers have been removed.

Plastic Shower Curtains. Washing machine manufacturers may recommend that you not wash plastic shower curtains in the machine because they can become brittle with age and crack. I have washed mine in the machine many times without encountering this or any other problem. But if you cannot afford to have your shower curtain crack or if you are very attached to it, perhaps you had better not try to machine-wash it. Scrub it by hand with a medium-soft brush or cloth wetted with detergent and water as hot as the hand can bear. Test for safety first in an inconspicuous area; then, if you wish, add a little bleach (perhaps ¾ cup per gallon) to help with mildew. Rinse thoroughly when clean. You can also clean shower curtains by spraying them with any nonabrasive bathroom cleaner, letting the cleaner stand, and then wiping and rinsing.

Diapers. If you use cloth diapers, try to wash them at least every other day; every day is best. In the meantime, collect dirty diapers in a pail to soak. Before putting a soiled diaper in the pail, scrape off excess matter into the toilet with a tool dedicated to this function, say an old table knife or spatula. Or dip the dirty diaper in the toilet, holding one end tightly, and flush to rinse. Then place diapers in the pail with warm water and ½ cup borax per gallon of water to help remove stains and deodorize. Adding chlorine bleach to the pail also helps remove stains, deodorizes, and kills bacteria. One leading bleach manufacturer recommends using ¼ cup chlorine bleach per gallon of water and soaking for five minutes; rinse before laundering. (You may also add chlorine bleach to the wash water, as described below.) Or buy a special diaper-soaking product and use according to directions.

When you are ready to launder the diapers, which should be done separately from all other laundry, first let the machine begin filling. Add detergent; when it is fully mixed and dissolved, dump the contents of the diaper pail into the machine. Do a regular wash cycle with hot water and a mild detergent or one formulated for sensitive skin or for baby's skin; adding chlorine bleach in the quantities recommended by the manufacturer sanitizes and deodorizes.

Give at least two rinses. Dr. Spock recommends that you rinse three times if your baby has sensitive skin. Do not overcrowd the machine. About three dozen diapers are the maximum that should go in a top-loading large-capacity machine with the water level set to its maximum level.

Drying diapers in the sunshine kills germs, but they will probably not feel as soft after line-drying as after tumbling dry; and the dryer heat, too, kills germs. Do not use fabric softener, as this makes diapers less absorbent.

Diaper services will bring you clean, sterilized diapers (and sometimes training pants too) and take away the dirty ones. If you use a diaper service, you just scrape off loose matter from the diapers and place them in the pail the service provides. Do not rinse them. Do not add any chemicals or additives to the pail unless the service provides them.

Gloves and Mittens, Leather. Do not wash suede or lined leather gloves. Other leather gloves you may be able to hand-wash; machine-washing is not recommended. Consult any care instructions supplied by the manufacturer. (Usually there are none, unfortunately.)

To wash launderable leather gloves, begin by emptying the fingers of any dust or debris or lint that has accumulated inside. Then hand-wash them in warm water made sudsy with a mild soap or detergent. Squeeze water through the leather gently. Rub a little extra detergent directly on especially soiled areas. Then turn them inside out and wash the inside in the same manner. Rinse the inside thoroughly, then turn the gloves right side out and rinse the outside thoroughly. Dry flat. Work them with your hands two or three times as they dry to prevent their drying stiff. If you wait until they are dry to do this, you may cause them to crack. When they are half-dry, put them on to shape them. If they do dry stiff, wet them a little before working them to soften them up. When they are completely dry, rub them with a little leather conditioner.

I have read that you can sometimes remove light dirt and spots from leather gloves by rubbing with a clean gum eraser. This sounds plausible but potentially injurious if you are not gentle, and I have never tried it. Before you do, I recommend that you test the procedure out first by trying it on an inconspicuous area of the glove.

Gloves and Mittens, Wool. First be sure to remove any lint or dirt from the inside of the gloves. Then machine-wash on gentle or hand-wash washable wool gloves exactly as you wash wool sweaters, not forgetting to test first for colorfastness and to trace them first for blocking. See chapter 21, page 345. Roll in a towel to remove excess water, then dry flat. Brush with a fabric brush when the gloves are dry to restore fluffiness to the nap. Do not try to turn them inside out or shape them when they are wet.

Gloves, Nonwool Woven Fabric. These will usually require washing by hand separately from other clothing, as they are particularly likely to bleed or to pull apart. Use warm water made sudsy with mild soap or detergent, and squeeze it gently through the gloves. If there are especially soiled spots, work a little soap into them and let them soak for a few minutes. These gloves are usually too delicate to turn inside out for washing the inside. Rinse very thoroughly. Roll in a towel, then dry flat.

Lace. Machine-made lace is often machine-washable. Snagging, tearing, and tangling when machine-washing lace can be reduced or prevented by placing lace in a mesh bag for laundering. Use the gentle cycle and mild detergents, moderate temperatures (lukewarm for cotton and linen laces, as they may shrink), and cool-downs and gentle spins for synthetics. All-lace items are usually very lightly soiled, so you can keep the wash cycle short. They dry quickly, too. If they keep their shape well, you can just put them on a drying rack. If they need shaping or if shrinking is a danger, follow the instructions for delicate laces in the following paragraph. Cotton or linen lace may shrink if you dry it in the dryer, but this is not a problem for polyester. You might even let polyester lace curtains or draperies finish drying on the curtain rod, but, of course, if they need some touching up with an iron this is not feasible.

Very delicate laces, especially handmade ones, should be hand-washed. Place in a basin, let soak for a few minutes in a solution of lukewarm to warm water with mild soap or detergent, then gently pat—this presses water through the fibers—until clean. Rinse very thoroughly. Press with a towel to remove excess water, then dry flat on a flat mesh rack or on a dry towel, arranging the lace in its proper shape. You can use a gentle tug to do this. You will sometimes read that you should pin lace down to dry it. If you are careful (and use nonrusting pins), this will do no harm and may obviate the need for ironing by keeping the lace from rolling or getting out of shape.

Lingerie, Undergarments, and Foundation Garments. A clerk at one of New York City's fine department stores once told me that the expected life span of a good bra is six months. After that you can expect limpness, discoloration or dinginess, and loss of elasticity. What she said is true unless you follow my mother's advice, in which case you can do considerably better than this.

How Good Girls Wash Their Underclothes. My mother taught me that you were supposed to hand-wash panty hose, bras, panties, slips, camisoles, girdles (which are making a comeback), and all other fine lingerie immediately after use. Many women still follow this policy, and their bathrooms are moist with dripping silks and hosiery almost every night. To wash fine lingerie, use plain, mild detergent in lukewarm water. Ivory bath soap was what Mother used, and it is still a good choice; but mild detergents are easier to rinse out and work better in hard water than soaps. The specialty cleaners made for lingerie are always good, too, in my experience, and they have nice perfumes. But they are almost always terribly overpriced. Plain, mild dishwashing detergent works just as well. Never rub and scrub; simply soak for a couple of minutes, then press and squeeze suds through the fabric. Rinse thoroughly in lukewarm water and roll in a clean, colorfast towel to remove excess water. Dry small items flat or on a drying rack. You can hang slips by their straps. Do not use clothespins on stretchy parts—it will harm their elasticity. Do not put fine lingerie in the dryer, except on a no-heat setting. (See the discussion below in "How Most Women Wash Their Underclothes.")

The reason for washing intimate garments immediately after wear is that they are worn next to the skin, where they absorb perspiration, skin oils, antiperspirants, perfumes and their oils, and lotions and moisturizers, as well as ordinary dust and dirt from the environment. Perspiration will cause natural fibers to deteriorate. Dust and dirt affect all fibers negatively. Many chemicals contained in antiperspirants, perfumes, and other substances used on the body will also discolor, stain, or cause deterioration in fine fabrics. In each case, the longer the substance stays on the fiber, the greater the damage or the more permanent the stain or discoloration. These causes can also produce loss of elasticity over time. If you wash the garments immediately, thoroughly, and very gently, they may stay fine and fresh-looking for years, not months.

How Most Women Wash Their Underclothes. Since few of us have time to care so nicely for nice things, what many of us do is buy less delicate, machine-washable fabrics and fibers for everyday use and take out the elegant, delicate ones only on weekends and special occasions. Check care labels to be certain that what you buy for everyday use is indeed machine-washable. Practically all less delicate foundation garments and lingerie are machine-washable nowadays, including most stretch undergarments. If for hygienic reasons you wish to be able to use hot water and bleach on panties or other undergarments, avoid silk and buy white or colorfast cottons or polyester with cotton crotches. The cottons are likely to shrink, so get them large enough to fit after shrinking.

Wash soon after wear. Turn panties inside out for laundering. Panty hose, articles with delicate lace, or articles that tangle up (such as bras) can be placed in mesh bags for laundering (and drying items that go in the dryer) when you want to avoid hand-washing. Fasten the bras so that they cannot catch in other garments; this also reduces tangling.

Use the gentle cycle and wash for five minutes or so, using warm water, cool rinse, and mild detergent on those garments that require it—otherwise use a regular detergent. Or you might use regular detergent every now and then to do a very thorough cleaning, and mild detergent in the meantime. Be particularly careful not to overheat stretch fabrics, which will lose elasticity, and avoid using chlorine bleach on spandex, nylon, and silk.

Dry underclothes on a drying rack or simply lay them on a towel or sheet on the floor. Much of women's lingerie and underwear dries so quickly that the dryer is really unnecessary. (Cotton underpants can take longer.) The heat of the dryer ages such garments greatly, often discolors them, causes their elasticity to decline far more rapidly, and offers no real convenience. If you let them air-dry, moreover, you avoid static cling. Of course, fabric softener would remedy this problem too, but it also reduces the absorbency of the fabrics, and when fabrics go next to the skin you want them to be absorbent.

On removing yellow perspiration stains from lingerie, see chapter 9, "Common Laundry Mishaps and Problems: Yellowing," pages 142–43.

Down- and Feather-Filled Articles. Down-filled and feather-filled pillows, comforters, jackets, sleeping bags, and other filled articles can be difficult to clean: they are unwieldy to launder at home and expensive to send out. This makes it important to keep them clean as long as you can so that they need laundering or dry cleaning less frequently.

According to contemporary manufacturers, the trick in cleaning these filled articles is to avoid stripping the down and feathers of their natural oils in the process. These oils sustain the loft and resilience of down and feather, which in turn are the source of the articles' warmth and soft comfort. Although both dry cleaning and laundering will to some extent remove oils, most manufacturers today seem to regard laundering as the cleaning method of choice for down- and feather-filled clothes and furnishings. You occasionally run into a care label that prescribes dry cleaning, however, and when this happens you should obey it. Only the manufacturer knows what finishes (for example, water repellancy) or other features of the article might be vulnerable to damage from a given cleaning method. You also occasionally run into a care label that tells you to hand-wash or to have dry-cleaned only by an experienced dry cleaner (using only certain solvents, and clean solvents)—a clear indication that some people have not had the best luck when sending these sorts of things out for dry cleaning.

Instructions for laundering down- and feather-filled articles today are much more cautious than they were fifteen or twenty years ago. Then (and in many instances now) the standard advice was to wash washable pillows on the machine's regular cycle for eight to ten minutes with ordinary detergents, and to dry them at "regular"—that is, hot—temperatures. This certainly would produce cleaner, faster-drying pillows than the more conservative instructions you find now, but manufacturers of such articles say they now understand better than they once did the harm that rough laundering can cause.

Many manufacturers—perhaps a majority—now recommend that you use only a soap to launder their filled products, on the grounds that soap will be more neutral and milder than a detergent and less likely to strip oils. When pressed, one told me that a really mild, neutral, powdered detergent would be acceptable, although not as good as soap. However, the idea that soaps necessarily are milder than detergents is mistaken, and until someone informs me of any other reason for choosing soap for laundering down- and feather-filled objects, I will continue to use a mild detergent. (See "Detergents and soaps, mild," pages 78–80.) Whatever you choose, rinse thoroughly; the residues of soap or detergent left in the filled items can eventually cause deterioration. A low-sudsing product is very helpful.

Although some manufacturers still provide instructions for washing their filled products in a regular top-loading machine, many now recommend that you either hand-launder their filled products or machine-wash them only in a front-loading tumbling machine. The idea here is that the rough, jerking agitation in a regular top-loading machine can pack the down or push it out of its proper place (so that it becomes poorly distributed throughout the article), or it can rip out delicate seams or baffling. Whatever type of machine you have, first make sure that it is really large enough to wash, thoroughly rinse, and spin dry bulky filled articles. (I know someone whose machine's spin mechanism was ruined when she washed a heavy comforter in it.) When you think about drying your comforter in your home dryer, remember that the dryer has to accommodate its much larger dry size as well as its wet size.

The risks of not following care labels are extremely hard to calculate with filled articles, and the potential damage is great. There is not only the launderability of the down filling and ticking to consider, but also that of linings, outer fabrics, trims, zippers, and finishes. So follow care labels. If you have none or have to fill in for care labels that leave too much to your imagination, you might use one of the following laundering recipes. (Test for colorfastness or other qualities as necessary.)

Three Methods of Washing Down- and Feather-Filled Clothes and Furnishings

Hand-Washing. Hand-washing a large filled object takes some physical vigor. It also takes a large laundry tub. Make sure yours is large enough before proceeding. If not, use the bathtub. Fill the tub with warm or lukewarm water and add a mild powdered detergent (preferably a low-sudsing one) or soap. Make sure the soap or detergent is thoroughly dissolved and mixed before adding the article to be washed. Place the article in the sudsy water and let it soak for a few minutes, pressing out air bubbles with your hands. Then wash by gently pressing the sudsy water through it (and pressing out air bubbles); continue this for a few minutes to be sure you are getting the article clean. Drain the wash water. Fill with fresh cool water and rinse by the same pressing technique. Repeat until all traces of suds are gone. Do not wring. Squeeze out excess water. As the squeezing part of the hand-laundering tends to be onerous and as drying takes so very long, you might wish to spin the article in your washing machine to get out some excess moisture. Spinning it does not jerk or beat or twist the article as do agitating or wringing—front-loading tumbling machines spin too—and it can help you get the filled article dry much more quickly. Just set your washing machine control forward to the spin, skipping the fill and the agitation or tumble portion of the cycle.

Machine-Washing, Front-Loading. If you have a tumbling front-loading machine that is large enough, simply wash with warm or lukewarm water and a mild powdered HE or low-sudsing detergent or soap. Rinse thoroughly with cool water. If need be, do an extra rinse.

Machine-Washing, Top-Loading. Make sure that your machine is large enough. When washing in an agitating top-loading machine, use gentle agitation and fast spin with warm or lukewarm water and mild powdered detergent (preferably a low-sudsing one) or soap. First partially fill the machine and dissolve the detergent and then add two pillows or other filled items for balance, pressing them down to expel the air. Let the machine continue to fill and wash. As the objects wash, open the lid now and then to press out air. (Because air pockets often form inside filled articles, it sometimes helps to wet down the article thoroughly and spin it in the machine first; then wash it as prescribed.) Rinse thoroughly with cold water. Do an extra rinse if necessary.

Be careful when you lift the wet filled object. Do not pick it up by one end or all the wet filling will fall to the other and be packed down. For similar reasons, never hand filled articles to dry; the filling will fall to the ends, clump, and fail to dry quickly enough, and the article can be ruined.

Whatever washing method you use, you can tumble dry on low. This takes a very long time—several hours, perhaps, for a comforter or other large or thick object. You can speed drying by putting a couple of clean, dry, color-fast towels in the dryer to take up moisture. It also helps to put in two or three tennis balls or clean tennis shoes to knock any clumps apart. Or you can half-dry the article in the dryer, then continue the drying in the air. Whatever you do, it is important to get down- and feather-filled articles completely dry. If you leave them damp, they will smell and mildew. Note, however, that feathers and down always have a strong, rather unpleasant smell when they are wet. Do not be alarmed; this will go away after they are dry.

Polyester-Filled Clothes and Bedding. Polyester-filled pillows, comforters, jackets, and other articles are highly washable. You can wash polyester-filled articles by hand or machine. Use lukewarm or warm water with the regular cycle. Dry on regular (hot), making sure that thick items are thoroughly dry. Use low-sudsing detergents.

Kapok and Foam Rubber. Do not wash kapok pillows. Do not dry foam rubber pillows in the dryer. Foam rubber poses a fire hazard in the dryer.

Knits. Knits vary greatly according to fiber content. Cotton and linen knits that are not preshrunk will shrink less if they are washed in cold or warm rather than hot water and if they are dried on the low to medium setting. (In general, the hotter the water, the greater the danger of shrinking.) Some knits will require blocking (see page 345) and should not be machine-dried. Wool knits often should be dry-cleaned because of their propensity for shrinking and felting. Knits of Superwash wools can readily be machine-washed and machine-dried. Polyester, acrylic, and other synthetic knits are far more resistant to shrinking and can almost always be successfully machine-washed. See the recommendations in chapter 22.

Knits, cotton. Fine cotton knits, especially all-cotton lingerie, nightgowns, and fine sportswear, will lose their silky hand or lustrous appearance if subjected to hot washing or drying temperatures. Hot temperatures will make them shrink and grow rough, less soft, and thick or feltlike. To preserve their fine look and feel, use the gentle cycle, cool to lukewarm wash water, and dry on a rack. When they are dry, tumble them in a cold dryer to soften them up. Such gentle laundering will usually get these articles clean and fresh.

But children's cotton knit play clothes that are covered with ketchup or chocolate milk are another matter. Gentle laundering with cool water will not remove these stains. Ordinary T-shirts and cotton underwear, which are subjected to heavy wear and perspiration and body oils, also need more vigorous laundering. First treat stains, remembering that hot water sets protein stains. Then give these a regular wash with warm to hot water and tumble them in a low to warm dryer (but buy them large enough to shrink). If you keep them long enough, they will grow thin and supple with repeated laundering and wearing; some people like them best this way.

Quilts. You should carefully read care label instructions to see what cycle, water temperature, and detergent are recommended for washing quilts. Very often, however, you end up with a quilt that has no care label. In that case be alert to three main potential difficulties if you wish to wash it.

First, the quilt must be neither too old nor too delicate to endure laundering. Fragile, faded, worn cloth is all too likely to break, tear, and pull apart even in the gentlest laundering procedures. If you own heirloom, aged, or antique quilts that are very valuable, you had better consult a conservator about cleaning. Very old and delicate quilts should probably not be laundered or dry-cleaned at all but would ordinarily benefit from careful vacuuming through a screen. (See chapter 16, "Textile Furnishings," pages 228–29.) Quilts that are not excessively delicate, old, or valuable, however, can ordinarily be cleaned either by dry-cleaning or laundering.

But—and this is the second problem to be alert for—many quilts are either not made entirely of launderable materials or contain at least some materials that are not colorfast. The two main types of filling used in quilts are cotton and polyester batting. In principle, both are washable, but you also have the shell and lining to keep in mind. You must make sure that all the fibers in the shell of a crazy-patch quilt are launderable and that all the different patches are colorfast to at least lukewarm water and mild detergent. Test as best you can in inconspicuous areas, and try not to let the test water run through to another piece or part of the quilt. (You can stop as soon as you find one patch that bleeds.) Remember to test all types of cloth or thread used, including the lining, trims, and embroidery threads. A patchwork quilt of silk velvet squares, lined with silk, will clearly not be washable at all, but other quilts may mislead you. I have seen a quilt of cotton patchwork in which just a few of the squares were made of fabric whose dyes ran. This quilt had to be dry-cleaned, as the silk velvet one would.

The third problem can arise even with quilts whose fibers and dyes are fit for laundering. To survive laundering well, quilts must be firmly stitched, and the filling, in particular, must be firmly stitched down. Otherwise, it moves around during laundering and forms lumps inside—a state of affairs that generally cannot be cured without taking the quilt apart.

Once you have determined that it is safe to proceed with washing, you must choose between hand-washing and machine-washing (choosing a cycle appropriate to the fiber and delicacy of the quilt). If you choose to hand-wash, you may in certain cases still wish to spin dry in the machine.

New, store-bought quilts can usually be washed and dried in the machine; these tend to have a highly launderable polyester shell and polyester filling. Such quilts can be laundered in the same way as ordinary washable blankets. Water temperature, type of detergent, and choice of regular, permanent-press, or delicate cycle depend on the same criteria as in other cases—fibers, finishes, type of filling, type and quality of construction, trim, and likelihood of shrinkage. When in doubt, the safest choices are always lukewarm or cool water, mild detergent, and the gentle cycle.

Tumble dry, dry flat, or line-dry, then air fluff, based on the same type of determinations. More delicate quilts should be dried flat. If you line-dry, spread the quilt over two lines so that its weight is distributed more broadly. Or lay it on a sheet on the grass, turning the quilt over when it is half-dry. If you are an apartment dweller, lay your quilt gently over a drying rack and turn a fan on it.

9

Common Laundry Mishaps and Problems

Fading and bleeding dyes . . . What to do if a colored garment's bleeding dye tints a load of wash . . . Fading of acid, indigo, and fluorescent dyes . . . Fading caused by light . . . Loss of color from abrasion . . . What to do about fading . . . Grayness or dinginess . . . Holes and tears . . . Lint . . . Mildew . . . Perspiration . . . Pilling . . . Spots or streaks—blue, brown, or light spots . . . Spots from uneven cleaning or soiling . . . Miscellaneous causes of spots . . . Streaks, residue, stiffness due to hard water . . . Yellowing due to perspiration, skin oils, antiperspirants, hard water, chlorine bleach, inadequate rinsing, sunlight, or heat and age

L aundering problems have solutions in most but not all instances. This chapter can help in diagnosing a variety of common laundering difficulties and, where possible, it suggests remedies when things have gone wrong. In laundering, however, as in so many things, prevention is always better than cure. Good basic laundering techniques can usually prevent the misfortunes catalogued below.

Fading and Bleeding

Some dyes bleed slightly every time you wash a garment, even though the color of the garment does not seem to change. Other dyes, such as indigo, "wash down," or fade, a little every time you wash them; these dyes are more likely to be used on natural fibers. Dyes may also fade as a result of exposure to water, hot water, prolonged soaking, detergents, and bleaches of all types.

Abrasion, exposure to drycleaning fluids, light, ozone, and many other factors can cause fading.

Clothes and linens whose colors run should be washed separately from others or, if the loss of color is slight, washed with articles of like color. If a print has dyes that run, unless it is a madras print in which the effect is desired, it cannot be laundered and must be dry-cleaned.

People used to add salt or vinegar to the wash water in an effort to "set" dyes that run, and you still see this suggested in various "tips and hints" books and columns. Doing so might help reduce dye loss by reducing the alkalinity—and the cleaning power—of the wash water. It does not actually cause any color to "set," however. The amount of salt or vinegar needed to do that would be very large (10 percent of the weight of cotton goods in salt, or 3 to 5 percent of the weight of wool or silk goods in vinegar). Moreover, salt or vinegar will not, in any event, set many classes of textile dyes.

What to Do If a Dye Runs and Tints Other Clothes. If a garment bleeds color that ruins the appearance of other articles in your laundry, do not dry them. Remove the offending piece and rewash the entire load using the strongest detergent, the hottest water, and the strongest type of bleach safe for the fabric. If this does not work, on white articles you might try a color remover. (See "Color removers," pages 75–76.) Follow instructions and cautions on the package to the letter.

Fading of Acid Dyes. Silk, wool, cashmere, and nylon may be colored with acid dyes that discolor when exposed to underarm perspiration or prolonged exposure to soap or detergent and water. I know of no remedies for this problem in colored garments. For whites that have yellowed, see "Yellowing," below.

Fading of Indigo Dyes. Indigo dyes produce various shades of blue that bleed and fade, particularly when exposed to bleach. Most people like their blue denims faded. Still, such garments should be washed with like colors or with darker colors that will not be tinted. However, if something is tinted by an accidental washing with blue denim, simply rewash before you dry it; the color will come out.

Fading of Fluorescent Dyes. Many fluorescent dyes are much less colorfast than other dyes, so wash fluorescent-dyed articles separately unless they pass a colorfastness test. Do not use stain removers or pretreatments on them without first testing in an inconspicuous area.

Fading Caused by Light. Light fading has no cure.

Loss of Color from Abrasion. Some types of dyes will rub right off fabrics. This is a phenomenon everyone is familiar with in blue jeans. The white areas at the knees and the seat of the pants develop because these are the points of highest abrasion. To forestall some of this—assuming that you want to—wash garments inside out.

The color on fiberglass curtains can also rub off against contact points, for example, the windowsill or furniture that touches the curtain.

What to Do About Fading. Usually there is no good solution to faded fabrics. Sometimes redyeing is possible, but my only notable successes with redyeing have been with blacks, which can really look like new. Before attempting redyeing, carefully study the home dye instructions. Some fibers, such as acrylics and polyesters, will not take home dyes. If the fading is irregular, redyeing may not produce uniform color, and you may find you preferred the faded look.

Grayness or Dinginess

If your laundry or some piece of it appears gray or dingy, rewash. Begin with a presoak, using the strongest detergent (and plenty of it), the hottest water, and the strongest type of bleach that are safe for the fabric. You might also try a double wash or the addition of a laundry booster such as borax. Be sure to rinse thoroughly after any such effort; one or more extra rinses are advisable. Detergent residues themselves will cause a dingy appearance. On whites, if all else, including bleach and strenuous laundering, fails, you might try a whitener/brightener. (See "Whitener/brighteners," page 86.)

Holes and Tears

The common causes of holes and tears in fabrics, when these are not caused by long wear and use, are excessive bleaching, failure to rinse out bleach and detergent thoroughly, bleach spills, failure to dilute bleach properly before adding it to wash water, prolonged exposure to sunlight, or exposure to any of a wide variety of destructive household chemicals, such as acid toilet bowl cleaners and depilatories. Occasionally tears result if a fabric is washed with a pin in it, or when one garment gets caught on the open zipper, buckle, or hook of another.

Overloading the washer produces faster wear, which eventually results in fraying, holes, or tearing. Sometimes clothes catch on a rough, broken place inside the dryer or washer. It is imperative to locate such damage and have it repaired before you use the machine again.

Mice, insects, moths, or other pests can eat holes in fabric, too.

Lint

Lint consists of fuzz or bits of thread and fiber that rub off fabrics during laundering, drying, and wearing. Lint rubbed off one article in a load can cling stubbornly to all the others in the load, making them look unattractive. When the lint is of a different color from the article it clings to, it looks especially unpleasant. Fabrics with a pile and those made with fuzzy fibers—such as terry-cloth towels or chenille bathrobes—usually lint more than others because it is easier to rub fibers off them. But almost all fabrics will produce at least a little lint. Tissues left in the pockets of articles thrown into the wash load, however, are the most common cause of lint problems.

If your clothes frequently come out of the laundry covered with lint, be sure that you are sorting properly and preparing garments adequately for the wash. Separate the lint-giving articles (such as chenille) from the lint-taking ones (such as polyester) in the washer and the dryer; avoid washing or drying polyester or other synthetics with towels. Empty pockets of all contents, especially tissues and other debris. (See chapter 1, "Gathering, Storing, and Sorting Laundry.")

Besides improper sorting, lint may be caused by overloading of the washer or dryer, which causes increased abrasion. Another possible cause is overdrying; by creating excess static electricity, it can cause lint to stick to clothes more stubbornly instead of being deposited in the lint filter. Or you may simply need to empty the lint filter more often in either washer or dryer or both. Most washing machines nowadays have automatic lint removal.

Rather surprisingly to us lay launderers, using too little detergent can cause excess lint. Just like dirt, lint is held in suspension in the water by chemicals in detergents that prevent soil redeposition. When you use too little detergent, not only dirt but lint gets redeposited on the clothes.

Mildew

Fabrics made of natural fibers will mildew if they are left damp or even if they are stored in a place with high atmospheric humidity and little air circulation. For recommendations on removing mildew, see "Mildew," page 166.

Perspiration

Perspiration is usually mildly acidic as it emerges from your pores, but tends to turn alkaline when exposed to the environment. The pH of individuals' perspiration, however, does not always fit the rule and may be acidic or alkaline, depending upon variations in metabolism. Dyes and some textile fibers are affected by perspiration, and, depending upon whether the pH of the perspiration is acidic or alkaline, different effects are likely. Fading, yellowing, discoloring, or weakening of cloth after prolonged exposure is quite common.

The most important thing to do to protect fabrics from such damage is simply to clean or wash frequently clothes and other fabrics that have skin contact. In the case of silk, it is advisable to wash or clean the garment as soon after wearing as possible. For other preventive measures and cures for problems caused by perspiration in clothes, see "Yellowing: Perspiration," pages 142–43, and "Perspiration," page 167.

Pilling

If pilling—the rubbing up of little balls of fiber on the surface of the cloth—is or may be a problem, try turning garments inside out for laundering and drying. Or you can put them in a mesh bag, making certain that it is securely closed. A shorter or slower agitation or tumbling period is also helpful. When the type of soil and kind of article permit, hand-wash without rubbing or scrubbing and either line-dry or dry flat. It is said that using fabric softeners helps too. Note that strong fibers may actually pill worse than weaker ones because the fibers that are rubbed into little balls do not break off but cling tenaciously to the surface.

The foregoing techniques are designed simply to reduce the amount of rubbing on the fibers. But because the fabric unavoidably gets rubbed in use and wear, there is not much that can be done to prevent entirely the pilling that develops on fabrics like sheeting or shirt material that are made of polyester blends or polyester and some other synthetic fibers.

There is a downside to turning garments inside out to prevent pilling: sometimes pills then develop on the inside of the garment rather than the outside. If the garment is worn next to the skin, this can feel rather uncomfortable. Turning a garment inside out also makes it more difficult to get the outside clean.

You can buy pill-removing gadgets at houseware stores. These are safer than shaving them with a razor.

Spots or Streaks

Blue Spots or Streaks. Blue spots or streaks usually consist of undiluted or undissolved detergent or fabric softener. They might once have been due to unmixed bluing, too. Few people use straight bluing anymore, but it is an ingredient in many detergents and all-fabric bleaches. To prevent detergent spots, dissolve and mix detergent in the water before adding clothes. To prevent softener spots, add softener to the dispenser at the start of the load or, if you add it during the final rinse, first mix it with water to dilute it before adding to the rinse water. To prevent bluing spots, see "Bluing," page 75.

To remove undissolved detergent that is adhering to clothes, one detergent manufacturer suggests that you soak the article for one hour in a vinegar/water solution—1 cup white vinegar to 1 quart water—and then rinse thoroughly. My own method (so far 100 percent successful) is to soak the article in water as hot as it will bear until the detergent dissolves, and then rewash.

To remove fabric softener spots, rub with bar soap and rewash. You may need to repeat the process.

To remove bluing streaks, rewash.

Brown Spots. Brown or yellow spots on fabrics can be caused by iron in the water or iron that is deposited on fabrics by a steam iron. If your water contains too much iron, chlorine bleach may result in further discoloration. (The water on our family farm, for example, is so iron-rich that if we use chlorine bleach the clothes all turn tan.) To cure iron spots, see "Yellowing: Hard Water," page 143. Do not use chlorine bleach to cure rust or iron-caused spots; this will only make the problem worse.

Brown spots may also be caused by a failure to rinse chlorine bleach out completely; by soil or soap or detergent or other residues left in the cloth that oxidize over time; by fabric softeners, when liquid softener is not fully mixed with the water or is not completely dissolved or when softener sheets in the dryer do not move around freely. (The softener spots may also be blue. See "Blue Spots or Streaks," above.)

To prevent brown spots, always rinse laundry thoroughly. Brown spots caused by oxidized residues often may be cured by soaking and laundering with the strongest detergent, the strongest bleach, and the hottest water that the type, age, and condition of the fabric warrant. Follow by normal laundering with one or two extra-thorough rinses. On more delicate fabrics of cotton or linen that cannot take strong detergents or bleaches, the spots may remain. If they persist, try pouring on a solution of lemon juice or white vinegar mixed in equal parts with water. If you get partial results, repeat until the mark is gone. Or try a paste of salt and vinegar. This treatment is not for very old or very delicate fibers, however. On such items, if you very much want to get rid of the spots, you had better consult a specialist.

Storing linens and clothes in acid-free paper will prevent those brown spots that are caused by chemicals in woods and other materials that the fabrics may rest against in storage.

Light Spots. Pretreatments—the direct application of liquid detergent or a detergent paste to some areas of a fabric and not others—can cause light spots on some fabrics. Such light spots on unbleached, off-white, tan, or natural cottons and pastel cottons are sometimes due to optical brighteners in the products. (See "Optical brighteners," pages 83–84.) Over time, the rest of the garment may become similarly lightened and the spots may disappear. If this doesn't happen or you do not wish to wait, one detergent manufacturer advises that you can usually at least accelerate the process of evening out the color in the following way: Make a solution of 1 part heavy-duty detergent to 2 parts warm water in an amount sufficient to submerge the article. When you are sure that the detergent is thoroughly mixed or dissolved, soak the article for two hours. If you have to, weigh it down (with something that will not bleed colors or do any other harm) to keep it entirely submerged, or the part that sticks out of the solution will be a different color from the rest. Wring the article out. Then rewash without adding more detergent, and rinse very thoroughly. Repeat the entire process if necessary until uniform coloring is achieved. If you are dealing with one piece of a set, remember that it will be a different color from the others unless you subject the entire set to this procedure.

Spills of bleach or other chemicals can sometimes produce light spots too. Undiluted chlorine bleach splashed on dry cloth can completely strip most dyes. Some colored cottons will spot as a result of direct contact with non-chlorine bleaches. This will not occur if the bleach or bleach-containing detergent is first dissolved in water before you add the clothes. There is generally no remedy when color has been stripped or spotted by a bleach accident. Even redyeing will not remedy the problem because the cloth will not dye evenly.

Uneven Cleaning or Soiling. Polyester and polyester blends have an affinity for oily soil and a tendency to hold oily soil even when laundered. Particularly troublesome areas of clothes are any that contact skin and hair, around the chest and shoulders, and where the face and hair rub on pillowcases made of blends or polyester. Soak the problematic article in a solution of 1 cup heavy-duty liquid laundry detergent to 2 cups warm water for a couple of hours, then rewash in warm water without additional detergent. Rinse thoroughly. An extra rinse or two may be necessary to remove all the detergent. To keep this problem from arising, do not treat polyester and other synthetics more gently than is necessary. Launder frequently, pretreat (especially with solvent-containing pretreatment products), presoak, and use plenty of detergent and the hottest water that the fabric can bear.

Miscellaneous. Household chemicals often contain strong acids, bases, alcohol, or other strong chemicals that can affect the dyes on clothes or eat right through fabrics. Be careful to keep all of these away from fabrics: hair permanents, hair dyes, toilet bowl cleaners, scouring powders, pool chemicals, acids (including battery acids), bleaches, antiseptics, astringents, and any other strong household chemicals.

Benzoyl peroxide, which is used in acne medications and cosmetics, selectively removes many dyes, especially blue ones. If a susceptible color, say a blue, is mixed with other dyes, benzoyl peroxide might remove the blue and leave the rest, making a red spot on a purple dress, for example, or leaving a yellow spot on a green carpet. Problems resulting from this chemical may appear in places that contact the face or neck, such as collars, sheets or pillowcases, and towels.

Fiberglass curtains and drapes may be colored by pigments held in acrylic binder resins that can dissolve in solvent cleaners. Thus they cannot be dry-cleaned. They should be washed by hand unless care instructions specify some other method.

Streaks, Residue, Stiffness, Harshness, or Premature Wear from Abrasion Caused by Hard Water

Some nonphosphate detergents used in hard water can cause a buildup of residues that can make fabric appear streaky, render it stiff or harsh to the touch, and even contribute to its premature wearing out as a result of increased abrasion. Clean out such residues by soaking the article in a solution of 1 cup white vinegar per gallon of plain water in a plastic container. (Do not use a container that will rust or react with the acid vinegar.) Rinse thoroughly. To prevent the problem, use a nonprecipitating water softener with the detergent, or change to a liquid detergent.

Yellowing

There are many reasons why fabrics develop yellowed areas or become yellow overall. The chief ones are covered in this section. See also "Yellowing of White Cottons and Linens" and "Yellowing of White Nylon," page 168.

Perspiration, Skin Oils, and Antiperspirant Stains. Any buildup of perspiration, skin oils, or antiperspirants on fabrics can result in yellowing. Everybody's shirts tend to turn yellow under the arms, men's shirts to a greater degree than women's because men perspire more than women. Polyester fabrics in particular may turn yellowish in areas with the greatest skin contact as they age because they tend to hold any oil, including skin oil. There are both preventive and curative measures for this problem that are very effective.

To prevent perspiration yellowing on the underarm area of garments, men might wear undershirts and women might wear dress shields, especially when they are wearing silk. For your information, if you have never used them, dress shields are little padded wedges of cloth that attach to your blouse, slip, or bra or come sewn on a bralike garment. There are also disposable ones. (You can sometimes buy them where lingerie is sold. I have also found them in variety stores that carry sewing materials and in sewing and piece goods stores.) Undershirts or dress shields will absorb perspiration, oil, and antiperspirants, and you can wash them with brutal effectiveness. Unfortunately, many men feel as enthusiastic about undershirts as most women feel about dress shields. A second preventive measure, effective on any area of a garment, is to wash it (or dry-clean it) frequently and as soon after wearing as you can, because the longer perspiration stands on the cloth, especially silk, the more damage it does.

Once the problem has developed, the solution for hardier fibers (not silk or wool) is to do one or two exceedingly vigorous launderings. Try pretreating the affected areas, and then presoak for up to thirty minutes using an enzyme-containing presoak. Launder with the hottest water the fiber will bear, using plenty of detergent—more than normal or with a detergent booster added.

Use the strongest bleach the fabric will bear as well. Rinse very thoroughly (synthetics in cool water).

Even when silks can be washed, they cannot take prolonged soaking, strong bleaches and detergents, or high water temperatures. Thus you must wash washable silk promptly and frequently. Try sodium perborate bleach on washable white silks, but only after testing.

If yellow perspiration stains have appeared in the underarm areas of hand-washable lingerie such as bras, slips, or camisoles, try pretreating by rubbing the affected area with a pure bar soap or a mild detergent formulated for fine and delicate washables. Let it soak in sudsy water for up to thirty minutes. Then wash the article normally, rubbing together the wrong sides of the fabric in the stain area if you can. See also "Perspiration," page 167.

Hard Water. Certain types of minerals (iron and manganese salts) in the water will cause clothes to yellow or to acquire yellow or brownish spots. Use a nonprecipitating water softener to keep this from happening. (See Chapter 4, pages 67–68.) Iron spots may also be deposited on fabric by a steam iron. To remove yellow or brown streaks or overall discoloring caused by minerals in the water, use a rust remover advertised as safe for fabrics. These are available in hardware stores, in houseware stores, and from washing machine dealers. Or you can work on spots by spreading the fabric over a pan of boiling water and squeezing lemon juice on it, or by immersing it in a solution of equal parts lemon juice and water or white vinegar and water. (Lemon juice is more effective in my experience.) Do not use chlorine bleach on clothes suffering from this problem. It will only make the stain worse.

Chlorine Bleach. Chlorine bleach will produce yellow discoloration of silk, wool, nylon, and spandex. This discoloration is permanent.

Chlorine bleach may also produce a yellow discoloration on some white or light-colored, resin-treated cotton, linen, or resin-treated blends containing these fibers. I have never experienced this, and it seems to be quite unusual today. Chlorine bleach can cause yellowing of fabrics that have been treated with optical brighteners. This problem, too, appears to be quite uncommon. Sometimes interfacings have been resin-treated, even when the fabric of the garment has not. When bleached, the interfacing yellows and shows through the shirt, making it look unattractively two-toned. This possibility illustrates the risks of ignoring care label instructions and of failing to test bleach on all components of a garment. You can use a color remover on whites to try to remove the yellow coloration.

If you fail to rinse chlorine bleach completely out of clothes and then put them in the dryer, the heat can turn the chlorine left in the clothes yellow. Wash the clothes again and rinse them very well.

Overheating in the dryer can also cause yellowing of white or light fabrics.

Inadequate Rinsing. Alkaline salts from laundry products may remain in the fabric after washing and rinsing are completed. These residues can cause yellowing, discolor dyes, and irritate skin. The solution is to use less detergent, use more rinse water, or do one or more additional deep rinses. Institutional laundries add a "sour"—that is, an acidic compound—to neutralize alkalies. You can make your own sour by adding a cup of white vinegar (more for extra-large loads) to your rinse water.

Sunlight. Sunlight can produce yellowing in two circumstances. First, prolonged exposure to sunlight will turn white or very light cotton yellow. (This will not happen with rayon or linen.) The short-term consequence of putting cotton in the sun, however, is that it bleaches. If you line-dry white cottons, you can try to take care not to leave them out too long, or else hang them in the shade. Yellowing caused by sunshine can be diminished by chemical bleaching.

You may read that sunlight can also produce yellowing in some fabrics that have been treated with optical brighteners. (See "Optical brighteners," pages 83–84.) It is true that when some optical brighteners are exposed to sunlight, they break down, causing clothes to appear yellowish and duller or to have a gray cast. They are particularly vulnerable to breaking down when they are wet, so this problem might happen as a result of line-drying. I am told, however, that laundering removes these degradation by-products, and because we generally launder frequently, they are gone before we start to see them.

Heat and Age. Aging is in large part a slow oxidation of the cloth, a process that naturally produces yellowing in many types of fabric. Heat speeds up the natural aging process. If you store clothes in hot places, such as in unventilated attics or near radiators, or if you overdry clothes in the dryer, yellowing is likely to result. Always store clothes in cool, dry places, and be careful to use proper dryer settings and to remove clothes from the dryer when they are just one degree less dry than you want them.

Sometimes laundering with bleach, where possible, will cure this type of yellowing. The optical brighteners in laundry detergents can sometimes help too. Or try using a whitener/brightener. (See "Whitener/brighteners," page 86.)

White wools that yellow can sometimes be brightened by bleaching with hydrogen peroxide. Or you can try a whitener/brightener, although this will produce a bluish white that makes wool look like something else, such as an acrylic, an effect that many people dislike.

An overhot iron can scorch or yellow fabrics.

Polyethylene Bags. Plasticizers in the plastic bags used by dry cleaners may migrate to clothes and cause yellow places. I know of no cure, but this is easy to prevent by removing the bags when you bring the garments home. This is better for them in any case. (See chapter 18, "Closets for Clothes and Linens.")

10

Sanitizing the Laundry

Killing germs on cloth . . . Germicidal effects of ordinary laundering and dry cleaning . . . Chlorine bleach and other disinfectants for the laundry . . . Laundering away dust mites and mite allergens . . . Importance of hot water . . . Lice and nits, fleas . . . Textile dermatitis . . . Poison ivy and other plant allergens

The home laundry sometimes has to deal with clothing or bedding that has been contaminated by more than ordinary soil. When microorganisms, dust mites, vermin, or allergic substances adhere to fabrics, the best solution is almost always a trip to the washing machine. Home laundering is usually your most effective means of sanitizing textile goods.

This chapter describes the ways in which ordinary laundering has sanitizing effects and the ordinary means by which we can heighten these effects in our home laundries. None of the methods discussed guarantees germ-free fabrics. They are merely ways of reducing the numbers of pathogens that may adhere to fabrics as part of ordinary good housekeeping. Those who wish to target specific pathogens and those who are dealing with situations that pose serious health threats should seek medical advice or the advice of public health authorities in their own communities.

Infectious Microorganisms

Germs and Cloth. Long before anyone had ever heard of bacteria, it was discovered that cloth could transmit infection from the sick to the well, a fact that was used for both good and ill. The pox was sent to enemies on infected fabrics. The spread of infectious disease was restrained by avoiding contact with contaminated cloth and burning the clothes and linens of victims. The eponymous *Velveteen Rabbit* has to be saved by magic because it is to be burned, along with all the other fabrics that touched the skin of the child who has just survived scarlet fever.

Scientific research confirms that microorganisms—bacteria, viruses, yeasts—may survive on fabrics for significant periods of time and may survive transfer from one cloth to another. One study, in fact, has found that some fibers are more hospitable than others to certain viruses. In the age of antibiotics, advanced indoor plumbing, and vaccinations, however, sickroom routines that were once familiar in every household through the early twentieth century are now forgotten. No smelly disinfectants are used to wipe down every surface and utensil near the sick one. No linens are burned or boiled, and handkerchiefs, "body linen," and bed linens of the sick are not laundered separately. By and large, this is as it should be.

In every household, however, there are times when it is valuable to exercise a degree of special caution—for example, in the case of dangerous infectious illness, dirty diapers, or flood-contaminated textiles. It is helpful for all of us to understand how ordinary laundering procedures include physical, thermal, and chemical elements, each of which has profound sanitizing effects. Of course, in the event of a natural disaster or serious illness, you must seek expert advice on what safety measures you need to take. Your local extension service will have valuable information on disinfecting after a flood or other disaster. Your medical advisors will have guidance on household disinfection when there is infection in the home. You may also wish to contact your local public health agency.

Germicidal Aspects of Ordinary Laundering and Dry Cleaning. If you did nothing more than wash cloth goods in plain water in your washing machine, this would to some degree be sanitizing. Plain water physically removes vast numbers of microorganisms and sends them down the drain— alive and well, perhaps, but gone from your clothes and linens. When the water is hot, the sanitizing effect of agitating in plain water is greatly increased, for water that is hot enough kills germs. More water, hotter water, and longer exposure to heat increase the sanitizing effects of laundering. Ordinary detergents inactivate great numbers of microorganisms. Many studies have shown that sodium hypochlorite (household chlorine bleach) is a highly effective germicide in the laundry, and adding chlorine bleach to your wash also increases the sanitizing effect of cooler-water washes. The heat of the dryer kills off still more microorganisms, and so does dryness per se. If you hang your clothes to dry in the sun, the ultraviolet radiation from the sun kills many microorganisms. Hot irons are also highly germicidal. Thus germs are killed very effectively by the procedures of ordinary laundering in hot water with detergent and bleach, tumbling dry in heat or sunning, and ironing.

But plain laundering, while sufficiently germ-killing for normal household purposes, should not be overestimated. It does not permit you to be confident that you have killed any particular microorganism that you may be targeting, or that the fabrics have been completely disinfected. Home laundries are not set up to permit you to monitor or maintain the water temperature; few home washing machines even deliver water initially hot enough to kill many microorganisms. The amount of bleach used may not be sufficient. The duration of the germicidal action may not be long enough to be effective. For example, the polio virus would be inactivated within ten minutes if exposed to temperatures exceeding 122°F (50°C), but hepatitis B would require higher temperatures. *Candida albicans,* a yeastlike pathogen that causes one type of vaginal infection and is thought to be transmittable on underwear, survives in ordinary laundering with a water temperature of 120°F. You would have to launder articles at 158°F or higher to kill it, or iron them with a hot iron. Keep in mind that today's home washers, even set on hot, often give water cooler than 120°F. See chapter 4, "Laundering," pages 65–67.

If clothes or furnishings are not washable but must be dry-cleaned, the solvents and heat of the steam used in professional dry cleaning, too, will have a germ-killing effect. But the sort of dry cleaning you do yourself at coin-operated machines does not use steam and is not recommended, for example, as a way of cleaning flood-soiled clothes.

Laundering and Sanitizing Kitchen Cloth. I much prefer cloth for kitchen cleanups and dishwashing to sponges. This is a personal preference, but it is a fact that sponges are harder to keep sanitary. Sponges are havens for bacteria; food particles get deep inside them and they stay wet longer. Studies show that sponges typically hold large numbers of potentially hazardous microorganisms. But dishcloths and towels, too, will breed huge numbers of bacteria if left wet and soiled. Odors in sponges, dishcloths, or other kitchen cleaning implements indicate that bacteria are growing, but if a cloth or sponge lacks odors, this is no guarantee of safety. If you do not want to give up sponges, wash them thoroughly after use in hot sudsy water, sanitize them occasionally (see below), and do not keep them long. Launder dishcloths frequently too; use one or more fresh ones each time you do a kitchen cleanup or wash the dishes.

When you have finished a kitchen cleanup, hang any still-usable rags, cloths, and towels to dry on a rack kept for that purpose. Remove soiled ones for laundering (you can hang them to dry on the side of a laundry basket so that they do not make odors in the laundry room) and put out fresh ones, ready for the next round of cooking. Do not leave anything to dry in the kitchen that you would not want to be used. Someone will surely come along and use it.

Ordinary laundering in hot water and all-purpose detergent of dish towels, hand towels, dishcloths, aprons, potholders, cheesecloths, pastry cloths, rags, and other kitchen cloths will generally make them safely clean. For extra insurance, when you feel it is necessary, you can use chlorine bleach to sanitize them; chlorine bleach is effective in warm or cool water although it is best to avoid washing kitchen cloths in cool. (Sanitizing instructions for kitchen cloths are given below.) Some people do not like to use chlorine bleach, but they might wish to do so when they have some particular reason to be concerned or when the kitchen linens are beginning to look dingy. To give yourself the option of using bleach on kitchen cloths, never buy cloth for the kitchen that you cannot bleach.

Note that the trend to elevate looks over function has infiltrated even the manufacture of these utilitarian articles. Many manufacturers try to sell cloth for the kitchen that not only cannot be bleached but that bleeds dye, shrinks, is inabsorbent, and is heat-sensitive. Read the care label and resist such items no matter how attractive they look in the store. You will hate them in your kitchen.

Disinfecting in the Laundry with Chlorine Bleach. Chlorine bleach is highly effective against a wide range of bacteria, viruses, molds, and mildew and serves as an excellent sanitizer and deodorant in the laundry for all chlorine bleach–safe fabrics. (See chapter 4, "Laundering," page 59 and "Bleaches" in the Glossary of Laundry Products and Additives, pages 72–74, on the effective use of chlorine bleach in the laundry. Refer to pages 73–74 for information on which fabrics chlorine bleach is safe for.) Nonetheless, if you are targeting some particular microorganism rather than aiming for a general sanitizing effect in your laundry, seek expert advice. The suggestions given below are not suitable for such specific purposes.

After six months or so, household bleach may no longer be fresh and should not be used for sanitizing or disinfection. (After nine to twelve months, bleach kept for laundering purposes should also be replaced.) Note: For sanitizing and disinfection use only plain or regular-scented chlorine bleach, not the perfumed types. In addition, do not use the thicker, nonsplashing or gel versions of chlorine bleach for sanitizing or disinfection.

For instructions on safety in using chlorine bleach, refer to pages 73–74, and read the bottle label. Do not mix chlorine bleach with acids, ammonia, or acid- or ammonia-containing products. Doing so will produce a toxic gas or other dangerous reaction. In fact, you should never mix chlorine bleach with anything other than water and ordinary detergent unless you are specifically instructed to do so by a reliable authority. Be careful not to splash chlorine bleach on clothes, furniture, or other furnishings. Also, never pour undiluted bleach directly on clothes and linens and never use it on dry clothes or clothes that are not immersed in water. Either use your machine's automatic dispenser or mix bleach with a quart or two of water before pouring it into a washer or laundry tub containing water and clothes.

Disinfect chlorine bleach–safe laundry as follows:

In top-loading agitator-type washing machines: ¾ cup chlorine bleach per load. For extra-large washers, use 1¼ cups. Use with detergent. In

HE and front-loading machines use the maximum amount of bleach your dispenser permits. (The low volume of water these machines use makes it possible for the lesser amount of bleach to offer a similar sanitizing effect.)

For tub sanitizing, first rinse out any heavy soil. Then soak garments for five minutes in a solution of ¼ cup chlorine bleach to 1 gallon water.

For disinfecting and deodorizing diapers in pails, soak in a solution of ¼ cup chlorine bleach per 1 gallon water for five minutes.

To sanitize dishcloths, dish towels, and rags, first wash soiled items thoroughly in hot sudsy water; be sure to remove all food particles. Then make a chlorine bleach solution using ¾ cup chlorine bleach per gallon of water. Let items soak in the solution for five minutes or more. (This also works for sponges, kitchen brushes, and pot scratchers, but do these implements separately from cloth.)

Hydrogen Peroxide/Oxygen Bleaches. Hydrogen peroxide (H_2O_2) is effective against molds and many bacteria and viruses. It is the active element, directly or indirectly, in oxygen bleaches. Ordinary, nonactivated oxygen bleaches, or all-fabric or colorsafe bleaches, however, are not nearly as effective as chlorine bleach and are not effective sanitizers in the laundry. Activated oxygen bleaches such as Biz, however, are considerably more germicidal than nonactivated ones.[1] See the Glossary of Laundry Products and Additives, pages 71–72. At this time, unfortunately, I am unable to find a scientific comparison of activated oxygen bleach with chlorine bleach for laundry sanitizing purposes. I note, however, that government extension services and agencies suggest using chlorine bleach for decontaminating flood-damaged fabrics and do not list activated oxygen bleach among other disinfectants recommended for this purpose.

A 3 to 5 percent solution of hydrogen peroxide that you buy in the drugstore in a brown bottle is commonly used in the home as an antiseptic and gentle, all-fabric bleach. (See pages 70–71 in the Glossary of Laundry Products and Additives.) It becomes inactive in nine months to a year.[2]

Other Disinfectants. To disinfect clothes and linens that cannot tolerate chlorine bleach, the use of quaternary compounds or pine oil or other phenolic disinfectants is sometimes suggested. These products will say "disinfectant" on the label and will bear an EPA registration number, as chlorine bleach does, but, unlike chlorine bleach, they are not laundry products, are not especially formulated for use as laundry disinfectants, and usually bear no instructions, or very limited instructions, on how to use them on fabrics. You can find these products in drugstores, janitorial supply stores, home centers, or in supermarkets on the cleaning product shelves—not in the laundry section.

Quaternary Ammonium Compounds. Quaternary ammonium compounds (sometimes called "quats") are found in a variety of household products—for example, in kitchen and bathroom cleaning products, mouthwashes, and skin washes. There are exceptions, but if a product contains quats you are likely to find in its active ingredients list the names of chemicals ending in "-ium chloride" or "-ium bromide"—for example, cetylmethylbenzyl-ammonium chloride or cetylpyridinium chloride. An exception is alkyl dimethyl benzyl ammonium saccharinate, a type of quat. Some quaternary disinfectants that might be used for sanitizing laundry are Roccal, Zephrin, or End-Bac. They are said to be very effective.

You would have to add quaternaries at the beginning of the rinse cycle, as they are inactivated by detergents (unlike chlorine bleach). They are said to be safe for all fibers but not for some dyes; they sometimes cause color change. So be sure to test for safety in an inconspicuous area. Set your washer for its hottest and longest wash cycle. Follow the instructions on the label. If you find no instructions, try using 4 tablespoons of Roccal or 2 tablespoons of Zephrin in top-loading agitator machines; or 2 tablespoons of Roccal or 1 tablespoon of Zephrin in front-loading machines.

Phenolics; Pine Oil. Phenolics are disinfectants that include phenol (C_6H_5OH) and analogous compounds. Pine oil is a phenol. Be sure to read labels. If pine oil is the only active ingredient, you need 80 percent pine oil to be sure you are getting a disinfectant effect. For this reason, pine oil is sometimes combined with quats or other phenolics. You can sometimes tell that a product contains phenols or phenolic derivatives by looking on the label for chemical names that include the term "phenol"—for example, ortho-phenylphenol. Phenolics and pine oil disinfectants will reduce bacterial counts on clothes but are not considered as effective in this as chlorine bleach or quaternaries.

Note: Phenols should not be used near a baby, in a baby's room, or on a baby's things, especially beds and bedding. Phenolics are also toxic to cats.

Phenols and pine oil products cannot be used on wool and silk. Their odors will cling strongly to these fabrics.

To sanitize in your washing machine with pine oil and phenolic disinfectants, dilute them with water before adding them to the wash or mix them well in the water before adding the clothes. They can be added either in the wash or the rinse cycle, as you wish. Again, use the hottest water and the longest cycles you have. Follow instructions on the label.

Pine oil disinfectants that might be used to disinfect laundry include Fyne Pine, King Pine, Pine-o-Pine, or Texize-O-Pine. If you find no instructions on the label, try using ½ cup in top-loading (agitator) machines, or ¼ cup in front-loaders.

Phenolic disinfectants include Pine-Sol, Al-Pine, or Sea-Air. If you find no instructions on the label, try using 1 cup in top-loading (agitator) machines, or ½ plus 2 tablespoons in front-loaders.

For further information on how to use these or other disinfectants effectively in situations where this is important for health or safety, contact your local public health authority, your local extension service, or your doctor.

Dust Mites

Dust mites are actually arachnids—bugs, not germs—that are so tiny that you cannot see them without magnification. They do not cause infection. The presence of dust mites does not imply dirtiness, and they are a normal part of environments that offer favorable physical conditions for their survival. However, they are strongly associated with allergic rhinitis and dermatitis and are thought to be one of the most common triggers of asthma attacks. They can be controlled by a variety of housekeeping measures, including informed laundering. For the most part, this is an issue on which you may choose your level of caution—higher if there are allergies in the house or children you want to avoid sensitizing. Many people happily ignore them and suffer no health effects at all.

Dust mites are killed by laundering at high enough temperatures. One study finds that wash water temperatures of 131°F kill dust mites after ten minutes and notes that at cooler temperatures the acaricidal (mite-killing) effect is not increased by detergents or other chemicals tested. Some authorities, however, recommend higher wash temperatures, 140°F or 150°F. One study determined that water below 113°F killed no mites at all and that water at 122°F killed 49.7 percent of them. Unfortunately, today's home washers rarely reach even the lower recommended temperature of 131°F. See chapter 4, pages 65–67. Thus there is speculation that the increase in low-temperature and cold-water home laundering in recent decades is among the many factors that may have caused an increase in the incidence of allergic asthma, as it has inadvertently rendered bedding more mite-ridden than it was in the good old days of hot-washed or boiled bedding.[3]

Because water cools during agitation in home washers, those who can get wash temperatures of 130°F to 140°F or higher might begin with water hotter than necessary just to be sure the water stays in the proper range for ten minutes. Those whose wash water is not very hot might try De-Mite, a popular acaricidal laundry additive that works in cold water. Its active ingredient is benzyl benzoate, and it is advertised as safe for all washable, colorfast fabrics.

Laundering is perhaps most important, however, in removing the allergens produced by dust mites. Wash water of any temperature removes more than 90 percent of dust mite allergens, even when it leaves the mites alive and well (and clean, presumably). Dry cleaning, by comparison, kills all the mites but does not remove the allergens, which may cling for very long periods of time. This is a strong reason to buy only launderable bedding and blankets. Weekly launderings at 140°F or higher of all bedding—sheets, pillowcases, blankets, and mattress pads—is best to keep dust mites and dust mite allergens at low levels. As stored clothing can also harbor large numbers of mites, you might wash it before wearing, especially if you notice any allergic symptoms when you put such an article on.

Dryer heat probably also helps kill mites, but there is far less research on the effects of hot drying on mites than there is on the effects of washing (and drying does not remove allergens). One study suggests that mites on blankets were killed after several hours in a dryer, a time period too lengthy to encourage anyone to look hopefully to this method. Also, keep in mind that new dryers may not get as hot as old ones. At least until we have more research that might let us know how to use the heat of the dryer to kill mites, we should probably continue to rely on hot washing; dryer heat is a good backup. Ironing would undoubtedly kill mites, but I wonder whether many would not survive tucked into flat-felled seams and similarly protected places. Ironing would not, of course, remove allergens.

Lice and Nits; Fleas

Water temperatures of 150°F will kill lice and nits (leave laundry in the hot water for ten minutes to be sure), so hot laundering is effective to rid fabrics of these miserable pests. Some say you need only a temperature of 140°F or even 130°F, but since the water in your machine cools during the wash, the hotter you begin the wash the better.

Wash all sheets, pillowcases, blankets, comforters (duvets), and clothes, including hats and coats, that the afflicted person has been in contact with, and if it is not head lice but body lice of some sort, you must be sure to do a good job washing underwear. Then dry all items in a hot dryer for twenty minutes too, just for good measure. If you cannot wash certain items, dry cleaning is also effective. Or place things in airtight plastic bags, tightly sealed, and leave them for thirty days, which is longer than nits can survive at room temperature. Away from the human body, the lice themselves die much sooner— within three days. The plastic-bag option is an especially good idea for headsets, helmets, and similar items.

Fleas and their eggs will also be killed by hot-water laundering.

Textile Dermatitis

Many people are allergic to residue left on cloth by detergents and other laundry products. The solution to such problems is using no more detergent than you need, rinsing carefully (doing extra rinses if necessary), using products that contain as few inessential additives (such as perfumes) as possible, and trying to use hypoallergenic products. If these measures fail, change products until you find one that does not irritate or consult your doctor.

There are also allergic reactions to certain textile fabrics. Allergic reactions have been associated with cloth made of nylon, fiberglass, rubber, and wool fibers. When nylon fabric first appeared, many people reported that it made them itch. It turned out that nylon fabric required more rinsing than people were used to doing and that soap was the cause of the itching, which ended with adequate rinsing. In the past, spandex, too, was sometimes associated with allergic problems, but it is apparently no longer made with the problematic substance. And it is not clear that all discomfort described as "allergic" by sufferers is really that. Dermatologists find that many people report "allergies" to polyester or nylon fabric that may reflect experiences of ordinary skin irritation, perhaps the result of these fabrics being unabsorbent.

Whatever the nature of the difficulties, the solution is to stop wearing what itches you, to stop wearing it next to the skin, or, in the case of fiberglass, to stay away from it. If it is synthetics that bother you, switch to natural fibers. If it is wool, substitute acrylics. Acrylic functions and looks like wool and is nonirritating and nonallergenic. Wearing a thin cotton or silk liner or T-shirt under a wool sweater may be enough for many people.

Poison Ivy, Oak, or Sumac

Poison ivy, poison oak, and poison sumac are forms of allergic dermatitis caused by substances contained in these plants. The allergenic substances can be transferred from the plants to clothing or other fabric, or from someone's skin to fabric. Either way, the next person to touch the fabric can come down with a case of poison ivy, oak, or sumac. Many people have caused themselves a renewed outbreak by rewearing a contaminated garment without first cleaning it. Both ordinary good laundering and dry cleaning will remove the offending substance and render fabric safe.

11

Removing Stains
from Fabrics

Tolerating stains . . . Recognizing a potential stain . . . Common staining substances . . . What removes what . . . Stain-removing substances to stock in your home . . . Chemical vulnerabilities of certain fibers . . . Uses of detergent and water, bleaches, acids, alkalies or ammonia, solvents, enzymes . . . Common stains that respond to solvent-based removers . . . Common household solvents . . . Commercial stain removers and pretreatment products . . . Removing printer toner powder . . . Stain-removing techniques . . . Stain removal mistakes to avoid . . . Removing unknown stains . . . Guide to Stain Removal

I f a beautiful object has a tiny flaw, some people do not notice it and others notice nothing else. In dealing with stains, the most important skill you can acquire is the ability not to be bothered by small imperfections that you cannot fix. Many fabrics are ruined by overzealous and unrealistic attempts to make them perfect. If you find that your pleasure in a favorite textile object is spoiled by a minor flaw, consider whether this is because you equate stains with dirt. Stains are not dirt; they are inadvertent dyeings. While dirt should continue to arouse your fighting spirit, it is perfectly all right to surrender to insignificant stains. But when stains threaten to pass your tolerance threshold, you should be prepared to act quickly.

Sometimes acting quickly means running for help. When a stain afflicts a very valuable or obscure material, the wisest course, usually, is not to tackle it yourself but to seek the help of an appropriate expert. Where clothing and household fabrics are at stake, that is usually a dry cleaner; if the care label on the article advises dry cleaning, in fact, going to the dry cleaner is usually the only thing you can do other than apply drycleaning fluids or solvent spot removers yourself. Take the article to the dry cleaner as fast as you possibly can. Point out the area of the stain and explain what caused it. Do not leave it to the dry cleaner to notice the stain and guess what it is. If the object is an antique, an heirloom, or a work of art, consult a conservator. Check the yellow pages of your telephone directory or the directory of the nearest city, or call a local reputable antique dealer. Dealers often know of a good conservator who can deal with your problem.

For times when you decide to deal with stains yourself, you will want a compact chart, like the Guide to Stain Removal at the end of this chapter, that tells you what substances and techniques are likely to be effective for removing common types of stains. Tape a copy of it to the wall in your laundry room. This chapter describes the basic materials you should keep in the house for fabric stain removal purposes and explains the basic ideas and techniques that will help you deal with most household stains successfully.

COMMON STAINING SUBSTANCES

Red wine

Purple grape juice

Berries, cranberries, and their juices

Chocolate

Grease or oil from food, cars, machines, tools, cosmetics

Blood

Tar

Crayon

Paint, latex or enamel

Ink, including felt marker ink

Rust

Wax, candle or other

Dyes

Nail polish

Shoe polish

Lipstick and other makeup

Perspiration (sometimes)

Mud (sometimes)

Grass

Recognize a Potential Stain When You See One

Whether a substance will actually stain depends on the fiber and the fabric and what sorts of stains they are particularly vulnerable to. It also depends on what cleaning procedures the fabric in question can tolerate. Delicate antique lace that will not take bleaching or rubbing is a far more difficult case for stain removal than sturdy cloth, carpets, or upholstery that you can subject to vigorous cleaning measures.

What Removes What

There is more than one way to remove a stain. You will read widely different remedies for the same kind of problem, all of which may work. But there are some stains that you have to give up on. Some stains will respond gradually, so that you will have to apply your remedy a half dozen or more times before you are completely successful. You may need all your patience. Test the effect of any substance you choose to use on an inconspicuous area of the fabric. Many substances that will remove stains sometimes cause fabrics to deteriorate or affect dyes or finishes.

The following collection of home stain-removing agents will serve for most purposes. The majority of the items included are also used in other ways in the home.

All-purpose detergent

White vinegar

Lemons

Bleaches
　　Hydrogen peroxide (3 percent solution)
　　Commercial oxygen (all-fabric) bleach
　　Household chlorine bleach

Ammonia

Rubbing alcohol

Fingernail-polish remover (acetone type)

Solvent-type cleaning fluids, drycleaning fluids, or spot removers (for use on items that require dry cleaning)

Nonsolvent stain or spot remover (these contain detergents and water and cannot be used on items that require dry cleaning)

Enzyme pretreatment product or detergent

Laundry stain pretreatment product (some contain solvents)

1. Detergents. The best stain remover for practically all types of textile "stains" is plain detergent and water. I follow common usage in referring to just about any soil as a "stain," but in my family we used that word to refer only to marks that would not come out at all after ordinary efforts. When you read ads for substances that remove food and grease "stains," don't be deceived. Rarely should extraordinary efforts be necessary to remove spaghetti sauce or butter smears from your child's clothes. Usually, if you simply scrape off the excess, rub in a little liquid detergent, and throw the article into the washer with hot water and more detergent, the "stain" disappears. Generally speaking, granular detergents are better at stains that respond to builders, such as mud and clay, because these detergents rely more on builders for their cleaning power. Liquid detergents are better at organic stains such as gravy, blood, and grass because they rely more on surfactants for their cleaning power. But most detergents of either type will remove food stains and oils and grease effectively.

Most stubborn food soils respond readily to pretreatment, whether with a pretreatment product or a little liquid detergent rubbed into the spot. Oil stains on synthetic fibers such as polyester and nylon are the most resistant. For these, a solvent-containing prewash stain remover is particularly helpful. See chapter 22, pages 369–70. In general, when fabrics are prone to staining or just to be sure, you should pretreat spots. Presoaking laundry is also highly effective. Enzyme presoak products help with food soils.

If, after washing, you find a spot, do not dry the article and certainly do not iron it. Heat sets many stains. Instead, try to treat the stain again while the article is still wet, and pretreat, presoak, and launder again.

2. Bleaches. Bleaches are used in stain removal to render the staining material colorless and invisible, as well as to help actually remove it. A mild bleach such as hydrogen peroxide will be safe for almost every white fabric. It will remove most fruit stains. Test it before using on any colored fabrics. Chlorine bleaches can be tried on chlorine bleach–safe fabrics (most whites, some colorfast colors) to lighten or remove a wide variety of stains, among them those caused by coffee, tea, soft drinks, Popsicles and fruit ices, children's medications, grass, mustard, fruits or fruit juices, ink, or blood. But chlorine bleaches will not work on rust.

3. Acids. Acids are used on rust, oxides, and mineral deposits. If a clothes hanger leaves rusty marks on a shirt, you might apply a solution of lemon juice with water or white vinegar mixed with water, then rinse thoroughly and launder (or see "Rust," page 167, in the Guide to Stain Removal). You could try the same solution on brown or yellow spots in stored linens, as these tend to be caused by oxidized residues of soil or detergent. (In each case, half-and-half proportions are usually good enough, but you might sometimes try full strength for more effect. Some people add salt to the lemon juice solution. You must test a vinegar or lemon juice solution on an out-of-sight area of the article, just as you test detergents and spot removers, as such a solution can adversely affect some fibers and some dyes.) Refer to chapter 12 for a discussion of common household acids and bases and related subjects. There are also commercial rust-removing preparations, such as RoVer or Whink, that you can buy at home centers, houseware and hardware stores, or stores where washing machines are sold. These commercial preparations contain acids (hydrofluoric acid or oxalic acid); read their labels and follow all cautions carefully.

Warning! Do not mix acids or acid-containing substances with chlorine bleach or substances containing chlorine bleach. This will produce hazardous fumes.

4. Ammonia. Ammonia, which is alkaline, is sometimes used to neutralize acid substances. For example, you are sometimes advised to apply ammonia to fresh perspiration stains or stains from antiperspirants, which tend to be acidic. With old perspiration stains, you are advised to apply white vinegar because they will have oxidized. You are also advised to try ammonia on fresh urine stains and white vinegar on old, for the same reasons. Then rinse and wash the garment.

Warning! Do not mix ammonia or preparations containing ammonia with chlorine bleach or substances containing chlorine bleach. This will produce hazardous fumes.

5. Solvents. Use appropriate solvent-based cleaners to remove nonwater-soluble substances. You can remove enamel paint or varnish with turpentine but not with plain soap and water. (See the Guide to Stain Removal at the end of this chapter.) Although some stains, such as oily or greasy soils, can be removed both by solvents and by water-and-detergent solutions, others can be removed only with some sort of solvent. Solvents, which are nonpolar liquids, remove stains caused by substances that are not water soluble. (See chapter 12 for an explanation of polarity.) Water is very highly polar. Polar substances remove stains caused by water-soluble substances. The more nonpolar a substance is, the more nonpolar a solvent you need to dissolve it. Drycleaning fluids are nonpolar solvents. Below is a list of substances that may require or respond to solvent-based removers. Note, however, that stains from these substances—especially ink—may be permanent no matter what you do. (They may also respond to other methods of removal than the application of some solvent. Check the Guide to Stain Removal at the end of this chapter.)

Chewing gum

Lipstick

Eye makeup and other makeup

Shoe polish

Fingernail polish

Tar/asphalt

Enamel paints

Grease

Ballpoint pen ink

Felt-tip marker ink (unless labeled "washable")

Wax

Crayon

Glue (some types)

When you are dealing with an unknown stain, begin working on it with water, which is highly polar, or a water-and-detergent solution. If this does not work, try solvents in order of decreasing polarity—rubbing alcohol, then a commercial solvent-containing spot cleaner, and so forth. The following list of common household solvents gives them in order of decreasing polarity.

Rubbing alcohol (30 percent water and 70 percent isopropyl alcohol) (polar)

Fingernail-polish remover (ethyl acetate) (slightly polar)

Commercial stain removers containing ethylene dichloride (very slightly polar) or other solvents

Hydrocarbons (nonpolar)—extremely flammable and volatile
 Drycleaning fluids (perchloroethylene, trichloroethylene petroleum distillates, Varsol)
 Turpentine

Hydrocarbons are dangerous. Keep tightly sealed. Use only with plenty of ventilation and always far from potential sparks or flames. Fabrics treated with hydrocarbons should always be rinsed before washing. Less volatile solvents may also pose risks. Always read label cautions carefully and follow them to the letter.

6. Enzymes. Enzymes help to remove organic and protein-based stains. Such stains include bodily substances (blood, mucus, feces, urine, vomit), most food stains (egg, ketchup, gravy and meat, grease, milk and milk products), grass, mud, and some glue. Because not all enzymes work on all such stains, enzyme-containing products for the laundry usually contain more than one enzyme. Heat may set some protein-containing stains. Thus you are advised to soak many of them in cold water. This is standard advice for stains of blood, egg, meat or gravy, milk or ice cream, urine, or feces. As food stains are likely to contain more than one staining substance—say, both ketchup and grease—you usually work on the protein part first so as to avoid setting it.

CHEMICAL VULNERABILITIES OF CERTAIN FIBERS

Even when diluted, chlorine bleach damages wool, silk, mohair, leather, and other protein-based fibers. It also harms nylon and spandex.

Acetone (contained in nail-polish remover and paint thinner) harms acetate, triacetate, and modacrylic.

Cellulosic fabrics are more vulnerable to acids, and protein fibers are more vulnerable to alkalies.

Polypropylene (olefin) is damaged by perchloroethylene, the drycleaning solvent most commonly used by dry cleaners. (Polypropylene can be dry-cleaned with other solvents.)

COMMERCIAL SPOT REMOVERS AND PRETREATMENT STAIN REMOVAL PRODUCTS

Commercial spot removers may contain solvents or surfactants or both. Among the solvents that may be present in spot removers are ethylene dichloride and isopropyl alcohol. Some laundry pretreatment soil and stain removal products contain drycleaning fluids.

7. Color Removers. Color removers may be used on certain white fabrics. (See "Color removers," pages 75–76.) These contain sodium hydrosulfite, a strong bleaching agent. Make sure it is safe for the fabric you intend to use it on.

Stain-Removing Techniques

1. Act quickly before stains have a chance to penetrate too deeply or to set. On the other hand, do not use any new substance, including laundry pretreatment products and "safe" stain removers, on any fabric without first testing it on an out-of-sight place to see if it damages the fabric or color. Always follow instructions on labels and packages. If a fabric's care label prescribes dry cleaning, spot and stain removal, too, must be done with drycleaning fluids. Practice triage when you mop up spills. To save the heirloom tablecloth from what promises to be permanent damage, sacrifice your cotton shirttail, if that happens to be the only absorbent material you have at hand. (Rational triage presupposes that you know which spills are likely to be highly staining and which are likely to be easy to remove.)

    When you have more than one potential remedy, always begin with the gentlest and end with the strongest.

    In order for your efforts to be successful, a stain remover must penetrate as deeply into the material as the stain. It must be of a type able to dissolve the particular kind of stain. It must be applied in sufficient quantity to dissolve all of it.

2. Gently blot up liquids with a clean, absorbent white cloth or paper towels or sponges. In theory, you could use colorfast cloth, but it is best not to take a chance that the wiping cloth would compound the problem. Do not let your blotting material get so wet that you cannot carry it off without causing new drips to fall in new places. Scrape off solid material with a knife or spatula. Do nothing that

TONER POWDER

Heat will set spots on fabrics caused by toner powder from your computer's printer. If you should soil your clothes with toner powder, wipe it off with a clean dry cloth and wash it out with cold water.

could spread the stain: wipe, pat, blot, or scrape from the outer edge to the center of the spot. (If you are using a solvent-based cleaner, be sure to provide plenty of ventilation. If your cleaner is flammable, keep it far from sources of sparks or flames.)

3. When removing stains from clothes and linens, work from the wrong side of the cloth to the right side to ensure that you do not simply force the stain in deeper when you apply a cleaning agent. One way to do this is by draping the article wrong side up over a basin and pouring the stain-removing substance through it. Another is to make an absorbent pad under the fabric of clean white paper towels or other absorbent material, and lay the fabric, wrong side up, upon it. In the latter case, you then apply a small amount of your cleaning solvent or agent on a clean white cloth and begin to pat the stain (from the wrong side), working from the outside toward its center so as not to spread it. When the absorbent material underneath begins to absorb the staining material, change it for fresh. Continue in this fashion until the entire stain is removed.

4. When there is no danger of spreading the stain farther, and only on sturdy fabrics—such as denim, muslin, or gabardine—that can stand the abrasion without pilling or tearing, you might try rubbing or scrubbing with your cleaning agent. Mechanical action helps the cleaner to penetrate and act effectively.

5. Once you have removed the stain, you must rinse thoroughly and then launder the fabric to remove entirely any last traces of your cleaning agent or soil. You must wash out drycleaning fluids (and spot removers containing drycleaning fluids) before placing an article that has been cleaned with them in the dryer. Otherwise you create a fire hazard.

6. Do not mix different stain removal products together. Not only is there no guarantee that the mixture will be effective, but you may inadvertently mix a chlorine bleach with ammonia or some other substance that will react and produce dangerous reactions or hazardous fumes.

7. In stain removing, there are a number of common mistakes to take care to avoid:
   - Avoid soaking protein stains in hot water. The heat will cook the stain into the fabric.
   - Avoid ironing any kind of stain or using heat to tumble dry the article, as this may make the stain more resistant to removal.
   - Use detergents, not soap, when removing stains, as stains that contain tannins may become permanent when exposed to soap. There are tannins in alcoholic beverages, beer, berries (cranberries, raspberries, and strawberries), coffee, cologne, felt-tip pen or washable ink, fruit juice (apple, grape, and orange), soft drinks, tea, and tomato juice. (This list is from the Ohio State Cooperative Extension Service.) Detergents will not have this effect.
   - Do not try to remove rust with a chlorine bleach; it will worsen the stain.

- Do not use automatic dishwasher detergents, which are very alkaline and may irritate your skin or harm wool, silk, nylon, or other fabrics.
- Shampoos, which are sometimes recommended, are no more effective than detergents and cost more. Those that are colored, opaque, or milky may contain staining ingredients or prove difficult to rinse out because they foam so much.
- Do not iron candle wax. This drives the wax deeper into the fabric, making it hard for a solvent or detergent to reach it. It will also more permanently set into the fabric any color in the wax. See "Candle Wax" on page 164 and "Wax" on page 247.
- Do not use hair spray as a remover of, for instance, ballpoint pen ink. It is the alcohol in hair spray that seems to help. But the gums and lacquers in hair spray get in the way of the solvent's action and must then be removed themselves.

Removing Unknown Stains

The following procedures for attempting to remove stains of unknown origins are provided by the University Extension, University of Missouri.* Follow each step until the stain is removed. Then wash the garment according to instructions on the care label.

- Soak the stain in cold water for twenty minutes. Work liquid laundry detergent into the area and allow to stand for thirty minutes. Rinse. If you suspect that it might be rust, treat with rust remover before using bleach. Bleach will make rust stains worse. Launder in the washer using the regular cycle with hot or warm water. Silk and wool cannot take chlorine bleach and should be soaked in warm water and agitated very briefly, if at all. Air dry.
- Soak the stain overnight in an enzyme presoak. Launder.
- Sponge the stain with drycleaning fluid. Let stand for twenty minutes. Rub with detergent. Rinse thoroughly.
- If the fabric can be bleached, mix equal parts liquid chlorine bleach and water and apply with an eyedropper. Do not use on wool, silk, spandex, or noncolorfast items. For these fabrics, sprinkle oxygen bleach on the stain and dip briefly in very hot or boiling water. Launder immediately.

If the stain remains after all these steps have been completed, nothing can be done to remove it.

---

*Reprinted with minor alterations from "Stain Removal from Washable Fabrics," by Sharon Stevens, Department of Textile and Apparel Management, University of Missouri—Columbia (1993).

GUIDE TO STAIN REMOVAL FROM CLOTHES, LINENS, AND OTHER HOUSEHOLD FABRICS*

General Rules

[See also the Guide to Carpet and Upholstery Stain Removal at the end of chapter 16, page 241.]

- Read care labels to see if the article is dry-clean only or wash only.
- Treat stains promptly. Fresh stains are easier to remove than old ones. If the stain is on a nonwashable fabric, take it to the dry cleaner as soon as possible. Tell the stain and the fiber content of the garment.
- Read and follow package directions when using any stain removal product.
- Always test stain removers on an inside seam or other hidden part of garment for color fastness. To test, apply product and let stand 2–5 minutes, then rinse. If color changes, do not use product on garment.
- When using a bleach, do not try to bleach just one area of garment; bleach the entire garment to prevent uneven color removal.
- When treating, place stained area face down on a clean paper towel or white cloth. Apply stain remover to the underside of the stain, forcing stain off the fabric surface instead of through it.
- Never put chemical dry-cleaning solvents directly into washer.
- Thoroughly rinse and air dry areas treated with dry-cleaning solvents before placing in washer, to avoid a fire.
- Do not mix stain removal products together. Some mixtures, such as ammonia and chlorine bleach, produce hazardous fumes.
- Always launder washable items after treating to remove residues of the stain and the stain remover.
- Have patience; it takes a little extra time and effort to remove some stains.
- Remember, some stains cannot be removed.

Adhesive Tape, Chewing Gum, Rubber Cement. Harden surface with ice; scrape with a dull knife. Saturate with a prewash stain remover or cleaning fluid. Rinse, then launder.

Baby Formula. Pretreat or soak stain using a product containing enzymes; soak for at least thirty minutes or several hours for aged stains. Launder.

---

*Excerpted from "Stain Removal Guide," prepared by Dr. Everlyn S. Johnson, Extension Apparel and Textiles Specialist, Mississippi State University Extension Service, and published on the Service's Web site, http://msucares.com.

Beverages (coffee, tea, soft drinks, wine, alcoholic drinks). Soak stain in cool water. Pretreat with prewash stain remover, liquid laundry detergent, or a paste of powder detergent and water. Launder with the bleach safe for that fabric. Note: Older stains might respond to treatment with an enzyme product, then laundering.

Blood. Soak freshly stained garment in cold water for thirty minutes. Rub detergent into any remaining stain. Rinse, then launder. Dried stains should be pretreated or soaked in tepid water with a product containing enzymes, then laundered. Note: If stain remains, rewash, using a bleach that is safe for that fabric.

Candle Wax. Harden with ice, then remove surface wax with a dull knife. Place wax stain between clean paper towels and press with a warm iron. Replace paper towels regularly to absorb more wax and to prevent transferring the stain. Place stain face down on clean paper towels. Sponge remaining stain with a prewash stain remover or dry-cleaning fluid; blot with paper towels. Let dry, then launder. Note: If any color remains, relaunder with a bleach that is safe for that fabric.

Catsup/Tomato Sauce. Rinse in cold water, then soak in cool water with ¼ cup detergent per gallon of water. Spray with a prewash product; launder with a bleach that is safe for that fabric.

Chocolate. Treat the stain with a prewash spray or pretreat with a product containing enzymes. If stain remains, relaunder with bleach that is safe for that fabric.

Coffee, Tea (plain or with sugar/sweetener). Flush stain immediately with cool water if possible; or soak for 30 minutes in cool water. Rub the stain with detergent and launder with bleach that is safe for that fabric.

Coffee, Tea (with cream only). Sponge stain with a dry-cleaning solvent. Air dry. Rub with detergent, then launder in hottest water safe for that fabric (with bleach that is safe for that fabric). Pretreat or soak older stains with an enzyme product, then launder.

Collar/Cuff Soils. Rub area with a stain stick product and let remain for 30 minutes, or longer for heavy stains; launder.

Cosmetics. Pretreat with stain stick, prewash stain remover, liquid detergent, or a paste of granular detergent or laundry additive and water, or rub with bar soap. Work into dampened stain until outline of stain is gone; rinse. If greasy stain remains, soak in an enzyme product. Rinse and launder.

Crayon (few spots). Treat the same as for candle wax, or rub dampened stain with bar soap. Launder with hottest water safe for that fabric. Washer load of clothes can be washed in hot water, using a laundry soap (not detergent) plus

1 cup baking soda. If colored stain remains, launder again, using chlorine bleach, if safe for the fabrics. Otherwise, pretreat or soak in a product containing enzyme or an oxygen bleach using hottest water safe for fabric, then launder.

Dairy Products (milk, cream, ice cream, yogurt, sour cream, cheese, cream soup). Pretreat with stain stick or soak in an enzyme presoak product for thirty minutes if stain is new, or several hours for aged stains; launder.

Deodorants, Antiperspirants. Treat light stains with a liquid detergent and then launder. Pretreat heavy stains with a prewash stain remover. Allow to stand 5 to 10 minutes. Launder, using an all-fabric bleach.

Dye Transfer (white garment that has picked up bleeding dye from other garment). Remove stains with a commercial color remover; launder. If stain remains, launder again with chlorine bleach, if safe for that fabric. For colored fabrics and whites that cannot be chlorine bleached, soak in oxygen bleach or an enzyme presoak product, then launder. Note: Proper sorting before laundering and not allowing wet clothing to stay in washer after cycle is completed helps prevent this type of stain.

Egg. Pretreat with an enzyme product for 30 minutes for new stain, or several hours for aged stains; launder.

Fabric Softener. Moisten stain and rub with bar soap. Rinse, then launder. If stain remains, sponge area with rubbing alcohol or dry-cleaning solvent. Rinse thoroughly and relaunder.

Fingernail Polish. Try nail-polish remover, but do not use on acetate or triacetate fabrics. Place stain face down on paper towels and flush with remover. Replace paper towels regularly. Repeat until stain disappears; rinse and launder. Some polishes may be impossible to remove.

Fruit Juices. Soak garment in cool water. Wash with bleach that is safe for that fabric.

Grass Stains. Pretreat with stain stick or soak with an enzyme product. If stain remains, and if safe for dye, sponge stain with alcohol (dilute alcohol with 2 parts water for use on acetate). If stain still remains, launder in hottest water safe for fabrics, with bleach that is safe for that fabric.

Grease (motor oil, animal fat, mayonnaise, salad dressing, butter, cooking oil and car grease). Light stains can be pretreated with a spray stain remover, liquid laundry detergent, or a detergent booster. Launder in hottest water safe for fabric. Place heavy stains face down on clean paper towels. Apply cleaning fluid to the back of stain. Replace towels frequently. Let air dry; rinse. Launder in hottest water safe for that fabric.

Ink. Test stain with water or dry-cleaning solvent by placing a drop of each on stain. Use method that removes more of the ink. Ballpoint ink stains can be placed stain face down on white paper towels. Sponge with rubbing or denatured alcohol or dry-cleaning solvent, or rub detergent into stained area. Repeat if some stain remains. Rinse; launder. Drawing ink usually cannot be removed. Try flushing with cold water until pigments are removed; rub liquid detergent into stain; rinse. Repeat process. Soak in warm sudsy water to which 1 to 4 tablespoons of household ammonia per quart of water have been added. Rinse thoroughly. Launder in hottest water safe for that fabric, with bleach safe for the fabric. Felt tip or India ink—Usually cannot be removed. Try pouring water through the stain before it dries, until pigments are removed. Allow to dry. If you notice some reduction in stain, sponge with dry-cleaning solvent. Allow to dry. Rub liquid household cleaner into stain. Rinse. Soak stain (possible overnight) in warm water to which 1 to 4 tablespoons of household ammonia have been added. Rinse and repeat treatment if necessary; launder.

Iodine. Rinse from back side of stain under cool, running water. Soak in solution of color remover, or sponge with a solution of sodium thiosulfate crystals (available at drug store). Rinse and launder.

Lipstick. Place face down on paper towels. Sponge area with dry-cleaning solvent, or use a prewash soil and stain remover. Replace towels frequently; rinse. Rub light-duty liquid detergent into stain until outline is removed; launder. Repeat treatment if needed.

Liquid Paper. Sponge the stain with amyl acetate (banana oil). Air dry. Repeat treatment if necessary. Rub gently with detergent, then launder.

Mercurochrome or Merthiolate. Rinse out as much of the stain as possible under cool, running water. Soak for 30 minutes in a solution of ½ teaspoon ammonia per quart of water. Rinse; if stain remains, soak in a solution of 1 quart warm water and 1 tablespoon vinegar for one hour. Rinse thoroughly and allow to dry. Launder with detergent and bleach. For delicate fabrics, apply alcohol and cover with pad moistened with alcohol. Change pads frequently until stain is removed. Rinse; launder.

Mildew. Launder stained items using chlorine bleach, if safe for that fabric. Otherwise, soak in an all-fabric bleach and hot water, then launder. If some stain remains, sponge with hydrogen peroxide. Rinse and relaunder. Dry in sunlight. Badly mildewed fabrics may be damaged beyond repair.

Mud. Let dry, then brush off as much mud as possible; or rinse under running water and let soak overnight. For light stains, pretreat with a paste of dry detergent and water, liquid detergent, or a liquid detergent booster; launder. Pretreat heavy stains by presoaking with a laundry detergent, a product containing enzymes, or a container of water with ¼ cup each of ammonia and liquid detergent; launder. Red clay can be rubbed with a paste of vinegar and table salt. Leave for 30 minutes. Launder with hottest water safe for that fabric and bleach. Repeat if needed.

Mustard. Treat with a prewash stain remover, or dampen with water and rub with bar soap. Launder with chlorine bleach, if safe for that fabric, or use an all-fabric bleach.

Paint. Water-based paint, such as latex acrylic stains, should be rinsed in warm water while stain is still wet; launder. This stain usually cannot be removed after it dries. For oil-based paints, including varnish, use the solvent listed on the label as a thinner. If label information is unavailable, use turpentine. Rinse. Pretreat with prewash stain remover, bar soap, or detergent. Rinse and launder.

Perfume. Treat with prewash stain remover or liquid laundry detergent; rinse and launder.

Perspiration. Treat with prewash stain remover, or dampen stain and rub with bar soap. If the color of the fabric has changed slightly, apply ammonia to fresh stain or white vinegar to old stain; rinse. Launder in hottest water safe for that fabric. Stubborn stains may respond to pretreating with a product containing enzymes, then launder using an all-fabric bleach.

Pine Resin. Sponge the stain with cleaning fluid; let air dry. Rub with detergent and launder as usual. If stains persist, apply a few drops of household ammonia. Air dry. Launder, using liquid laundry detergent.

Pollen (tree or flower). Sponge, then flush with dry-cleaning solvent. Let air dry. Rub gently with detergent. Launder as usual, using bleach that is safe for that fabric.

Rust. Apply a commercial rust remover. Follow manufacturer's instructions. Do not use chlorine bleach on rust.

Scorch. Launder with chlorine bleach, if safe for that fabric. Otherwise, soak in an all-fabric bleach and hot water, then launder. Note: Badly scorched stains cannot be removed.

Shoe Polish. Pretreat liquid shoe polish with a paste of dry detergent and water; launder. Use a dull knife to scrape residue of paste shoe polish from the fabric. Pretreat with a prewash stain remover or cleaning fluid; rinse. Rub detergent into dampened area. Launder with chlorine bleach, if safe for fabric, or an all-fabric bleach.

Tar. Act quickly before stain dries. Use a dull knife to scrape excess tar from the fabric. Place stain face down on paper towels. Sponge with cleaning fluid. Replace towels frequently for better absorption. Launder, using hottest water safe for that fabric.

Tobacco. Moisten stain and rub with bar soap; rinse. Pretreat with stain stick or soak in an enzyme solution; launder. Note: If stain remains, launder again using chlorine bleach, if safe for fabric, or use oxygen bleach.

Urine, Vomit, Mucus, or Feces. Treat with prewash spray or pretreat with a product containing enzymes. Launder with chlorine bleach that is safe for fabric, or use an all-fabric bleach.

Yellowing of White Cottons or Linens. Fill washer with hot water. Add twice the detergent as normal. Place items in washer and agitate four minutes on regular cycle. Stop washer and soak clothes for 15 minutes. Restart washer and agitate 15 minutes. Complete the wash cycle. Repeat process if needed.

Yellowing of White Nylon. Soak garment overnight in an enzyme presoak or oxygen bleach. Launder, using hot water and twice as much detergent as usual with an oxygen bleach.

Science for the Laundry

Cleaning grease and oil; suds vs. solvent . . . Why water and oil do not mix: ionic, polar, and nonpolar substances . . . Why soap and detergent work on oil and grease . . . Acids and alkalies, what pH means, list of pHs of common household substances . . . Green laundering

Readers who dislike anything technical should skip this chapter. But for those who can tolerate a short excursion into grade school science, it offers much traditional household lore. If you are the sort of housekeeping beginner who has always wondered why white vinegar and baking soda are supposed to be useful in the laundry, you can find here brief explanations of these and other snippets of household chemistry.

Laundering and stain removal make use of four basic types of chemical cleaning agents: soaps or detergents in water, solvents (such as drycleaning fluids), acids, and alkalies. (These categories can overlap.) A few simple chemical concepts explain why these are used for certain standard household purposes.

Cleaning Grease and Oil; Suds

You cannot clean anything greasy or oily with plain water. Grease and oil are not soluble in water. Most of the dirt on our bodies and clothes and much of the dirt in our homes—especially in kitchens—is combined with grease or oil. To clean grease and oil, you can use either soaps and detergents, mixed in water to make a sudsy solution, or a solvent-based cleaner. Because solvents are usually more toxic, more expensive, more odorous, less versatile, and flammable, soaps and detergents are what we try to use whenever possible on clothes, linens, draperies, carpets, and other fabrics in the home. We turn to solvents for cleaning fabrics that cannot withstand water, hot water, or soaps and detergents.

Why Water and Oil Do Not Mix: Ionic, Polar, and Nonpolar Substances. Dirt, foods, cleaners, and other substances in the home can be divided into three chemical categories: ionic, polar, and nonpolar. Ionic compounds are those whose smallest units are charged particles called "ions," such as ordinary salt and hydrogen peroxide (H_2O_2). When salt (sodium chloride, NaCl) dissolves in water, its chemical units dissociate into one positively charged sodium ion ($Na+$) and one negatively charged chloride ion (Cl_2). Polar substances are composed of molecules that have different charges at each end. For example, water molecules, which are polar, have different charges, negative and positive, at their sides or ends. Nonpolar molecules, such as those that make up olive oil, do not. Because they are polar, water molecules bond tightly to one another: the positively charged hydrogen atoms of one molecule are attracted to the negatively charged oxygen atoms of another. This is why water, unlike olive oil, beads on flat surfaces and has a high surface tension (as though a skin on its surface holds the drop of water together). Some other examples of familiar substances made of ionic, polar, and nonpolar molecules include:

Ionic: salt, baking soda ($NaHCO_3$), hydrogen peroxide

Polar: water, alcohol (wine, spirits, rubbing alcohol), lemon juice, vinegar, chlorine bleach

Nonpolar: grease, oils such as cooking oils, fat from meats, furniture oils, drycleaning fluids, mineral spirits (paint thinners), floor waxes

As a rule, substances made of polar molecules do not mix with substances made of nonpolar molecules. And generally speaking, the more polar a substance is, the more soluble it is in water; the more nonpolar it is, the less soluble in water. When grease or oil is mixed with water (for example, when olive oil is mixed with vinegar, which is mostly water), the water bonds so tightly to itself that it forces the grease or oil molecules to form separate globules; they don't mix. Nonpolar substances are also considerably less effective at dissolving ionic compounds such as salt, because they do not attract the charged $Na+$ and $Cl-$ ions away from one another. Salt, for example, will not dissolve in olive oil—one more reason to put a little vinegar on the salad.

But nonpolar substances are effective solvents for one another. To put it in simple terms, nonpolar substances dissolve in other nonpolar substances. So drycleaning fluids are good for removing body oils and grease splatters from clothes, and you can remove wax with mineral spirits.

Why Soap and Detergents Work on Oil and Grease. Soap and detergents are surfactants. Surfactants reduce the surface tension of water. This causes the water to spread and to wet objects rather than bead up on them; when surfactants are mixed with water, oil and grease in the water are emulsified—they stay mixed or spread throughout the water in tiny droplets. The explanation for this is that surfactants' molecules have long, complicated hydrocarbon chains, one end of which is polar and the other end of which is nonpolar. The polar end is attracted to water: it is water-loving or hydrophilic. The nonpolar end is soluble in oil and grease and repelled by water: it is water-hating or hydrophobic. The nonpolar ends of these surfactant molecules form a kind of circle-barrier around a droplet of oil in water, with their water-insoluble ends next to the oil and the water-soluble ends away from it. When the oil is emulsified, the polar ends of the surfactant molecules keep the droplet suspended in the water and keep it from joining other oil droplets and separating into large globules. Thus it can be rinsed out of fabrics or off countertops with water.

Both soaps and detergents are, or contain, surfactants. Chemically, soaps and detergents are similar, but detergents—also called "synthetic detergents"—are made from petrochemicals. Soaps are produced by mixing animal or vegetable fats and oils with some strong alkali such as sodium hydroxide (caustic soda, NaOH) or potassium hydroxide (caustic potash, KOH). Hard soaps, such as bar soaps, are generally made with sodium hydroxide, and liquid soaps are usually made with potassium hydroxide. Soaps often contain many other ingredients—from moisturizers, abrasives, deodorants, and bactericides to perfumes. Soaps are now rarely used for laundry in the United States, although cleaning soaps such as Murphy's Oil Soap remain in use. Laundry soaps are still widely used in other parts of the world.

Soap has been supplanted as queen of the laundry by synthetic detergents because soap causes a scum to form when used in hard water. Hard water contains calcium or magnesium ions that combine with the soap to form insoluble salts, or scum, which then is deposited on clothes in the washing machine or on bathroom tiles and bathtubs. It looks ugly, and it can be hard to dislodge. Soap also is problematic when it is used in the presence of acids, for they will render the soap inactive and create a different kind of scum. Skin and clothing often contain acids from the decomposition of perspiration or food spills. Thus, the average load of laundry contains some acids, and these cause problems for laundry soap.

There are four types of detergents: anionic, nonionic, cationic, and amphoteric. Anionic detergents are the ordinary high-sudsing types generally used in laundry and all-purpose detergent products. Anionic detergents do essentially the same chemical job that soaps do, without causing hard-water scum to form. They are more powerful and less expensive than cationic or nonionic detergents. Unlike cationic and nonionic detergents, however, they can be partly deactivated by too-hard water. For this reason, alkaline substances such as phosphates or borax are sometimes added to anionic detergents (and to soaps, which are also anionic). The alkalies react with acids in the hard water and help the anionic detergents clean better, and, in the case of soap, also reduce scum formation. The first truly effective detergents contained phosphates, and it is still true, alas, that phosphate detergents clean better. But for good environmental reasons their use is widely restricted. See page 176.

Nonionic detergents are used for low-sudsing laundry detergents and dishwasher detergents. They are effective in hard water and work well on most types of dirt, especially oily dirt. Some cationic surfactants are used in fabric softeners and fabric-softening detergents. All soaps and detergents are antibacterial to some extent. But certain cationic detergents—quaternary ammonium compounds, or "quats"—have a stronger antibacterial effect and, therefore, are used as sanitizers or disinfectants. Amphoteric detergents are mild and are widely used in shampoos, personal-care products, and some household detergents.

Both soaps and detergents work better in warmer water and with the aid of mechanical action, whether muscle power applied in scrubbing or rubbing on a washboard or the agitation of a washing machine. Despite the advantages of detergents, some people prefer soaps because detergents are made from petroleum products, a nonrenewable resource, unlike the fats and alkalies from which soaps are made. But see "Green Laundering," below. Others choose soaps when they want a mild product even though soaps are not necessarily "milder" than detergents. Some soaps are harsh, and some detergents quite mild. See "Detergents and soaps, mild," on pages 78–80.

Laundry detergents marked "heavy-duty" or "all-purpose" are perfectly good all-purpose cleaners for the household. These are detergents that contain various "builders"—substances that enhance the detergent solution's alkalinity and ability to emulsify grease and oil or inactivate water hardness. Phosphates are the builders that have most commonly been used, but they are now banned in many states—a decision the soap and detergent industry is still protesting.* See "Green Laundering," page 176. Light-duty detergents, such as dishwashing liquids, are those that contain no builders. They are milder. Mild, generally, means neutral or near-neutral in pH. Strongly alkaline solutions burn the eyes and are harsh on the skin and on many household materials as well. Shampoos that do not burn the eyes have a pH between 6.0 and 7.0.

Acids and Alkalies

The efficacy of a household cleaner for any given purpose is in great part a function of its pH, the number that expresses how acidic or alkaline it is.

---

*Automatic dishwashing detergents are exempted from the ban on phosphates because of the difficulty the industry has had in attempting to formulate an effective nonphosphate product. However, some "ultra" versions of automatic dishwashing detergents do not contain phosphates.

Which substances clean which kinds of dirt and what cleaners are safe for what materials are strongly affected by pH. The pH scale runs from 0 to 14, with 7 being neutral. The higher the number over 7, the more alkaline the solution is. The lower the number under 7, the more acidic the solution is. Pure water is neutral, with a pH of about 7, but rainwater is slightly acidic, with a pH of about 6. (Pure water, by the way, should not be confused with potable water or plain tap water. Drinkable tap water and bottled water—unless the bottled water is distilled—contain many minerals and other substances in addition to H_2O.)

A water-soluble substance is alkaline if a solution of the substance in water contains a greater concentration of hydroxyl ions (OH_2) than of hydrogen ions ($H+$). It is acidic if, when mixed with water, the resulting solution contains more hydrogen ions than hydroxyl ions. Because most dirt and body soils are slightly acidic, most good cleaners are at least slightly alkaline. The term "base" is a synonym for "alkali," and "basic" is a synonym for "alkaline." (I use "alkali" and "alkaline," however, to avoid confusion.)

Alkalies make it possible to clean without too much rubbing. Soap and soap-containing products and detergents are alkaline and perform well only in an alkaline solution. Automatic dishwashing detergents, all-purpose laundry soaps and detergents, and hard-surface cleaners (liquid or granules) are usually alkaline to one degree or another, but hand dishwashing detergents and "mild" detergents are neutral or close to neutral because more alkaline solutions are too harsh on the skin. (Some hand dishwashing liquids advertised as good for "sensitive skin" are actually slightly acidic.) These milder alkalies nonetheless work well sometimes because you add a little muscle power to the chemical power they provide. Because soaps and detergents form alkaline solutions, acids are sometimes added to shampoos to lower the pH to prevent them from burning your eyes. You sometimes see such products advertised as "pH balanced."

Alkalies, such as ammonia, help in cleaning acidic, fatty, and oily dirt, which is why laundry products (and kitchen cleaners) tend to be alkaline. Baking soda (sodium bicarbonate or $NaHCO_3$), a much weaker alkali than ammonia, has correspondingly gentle cleaning and deodorizing abilities. As a deodorizer, it works neither by perfuming nor masking odors, but by chemically neutralizing them. Pleasant odors are neutral in pH. Most unpleasant odors are caused by strong acids (e.g., sour milk) or strong alkalies (e.g., rotten fish). Baking soda reacts with the odor molecules to bring them to a more neutral pH. On the use of baking soda in the laundry as a deodorizer and mild detergent booster, see pages 69–70.

Acids can remove soap scum and hard-water deposits (calcium carbonate). Many bathroom cleaners, therefore, are mildly acidic. Acids—such as lemon juice or white vinegar—will also remove rust stains. Strong acids can damage clothing, leather, and other materials in the home. Although we enjoy eating many foods that are weakly acidic, such as tomato sauces and salad dressings containing vinegar, strong acids are extremely toxic if ingested.

Both alkalies and acids are found in the household in different degrees of weakness and strength. Strong alkalies and acids can cause serious injury to skin and eyes, and if swallowed can cause serious injury or death. Do not induce vomiting after accidental ingestion of such substances, as they can cause grave damage in the process of being ejected from the body. Instead, immediately call your local poison control center and follow the instructions you are given.

Here is a list of various foods and substances commonly found in the home, arranged according to pH, beginning with the strongest alkalies and ending with the strongest acids:

Very Strong Alkalies

13   Lye, caustic soda (sodium hydroxide—$NaOH$) (found in some oven cleaners and drain cleaners, e.g., Drano), caustic potash (potassium hydroxide—KOH)

11.8 Washing soda, sal soda, or sodium carbonate (Na_2CO_3) (added to detergents as a builder and to cleaners and presoaks to increase alkalinity; used in some drain cleaners)

Moderate Alkalies

11   Household ammonia (ammonia gas [NH_3] in a 5 to 10 percent water solution) (a grease cutter, wax stripper, and general soil remover)

9–11 All-purpose detergents, soaps, window cleaners, mildew cleaners, most bathroom scouring powders, liquid cleaners, builders

9.28 Borax (a white crystalline powder)

Mild Alkalies

8.35 1 percent solution of baking soda (sodium bicarbonate—$NaHCO_3$) and water

8.3   Seawater

8.1   Soap

9 percent solution of baking soda and water

Gentle liquid detergent

7.8   Eggs

7.5   Blood

Neutrals

7+   Woolite

7   Pure water, milk, sugar water, saltwater

Fabuloso All-Purpose Cleaner

Orvus WA Paste

Ultra Palmolive for Pots and Pans

Ultra Palmolive Antibacterial

Dawn and Ultra Dawn

Very Mild Acids

6+   Some dishwashing liquids for "sensitive skin"

5–6   Rain in unpolluted environments

5.1   Seltzer water or carbonated water (contains carbonic acid [H_2CO_3], which breaks down and gives off carbon dioxide as fizz)

Cream of tartar in water

5   Boric acid solution (H_3BO_3) (used in eyewash)

4.2   Tomatoes

4   Rain in polluted environments (can be as low as 2)

4   Orange juice

Moderately Strong Acids

3.1   White vinegar (5 percent acetic acid)

3   Carbonated beverages, apples

2.3   Lemon juice, lime juice (contain citric acid)

2.1   Citric acid

Very Strong Acids

1.1   Sulfuric acid ($NaHSO_4$) (found in many dry toilet-bowl cleaners)

0.8   Hydrochloric acid, or muriatic acid (HCl) (found in many liquid toilet-bowl cleaners)

Oxalic acid ($H_2C_2O_2$) (effective as a rust remover, but toxic; contained in some scouring powders recommended for rust removal, such as Zud and Barkeeper's Friend)

Green Laundering

Making Environmentally Sound Choices. There are many important ways to make environmentally favorable choices in laundering. One of the most valuable things you can do is to use as little detergent as necessary to get a good laundering result. This is true even if you use allegedly "natural" or "green" types. The same goes for all other laundry products. Tablets or other premeasured forms of delivery might help you to control quantities by preventing you from heaping the measure or throwing in a little more just for insurance. You can also use much less detergent simply by not overwashing your clothes and washing only with a full load. If you wash smaller loads, use less detergent.

Avoid detergents that contain phosphates. Phosphates that get into the waterways cause eutrophication. That is, they cause algae and other water plants to grow excessively, reducing and, finally, depleting the water of dissolved oxygen. Without oxygen, the water cannot support life. Eventually the pond, lake, or stream itself is destroyed.

Choose laundry products that come in biodegradable or recyclable packages, and choose those that omit unnecessary ingredients such as optical brighteners, dyes, and perfumes. Remember that "natural" dyes and perfumes are not necessarily harmless, and "synthetic" ones are not necessarily harmful; I am aware of no scientific evidence that environmentally condemns "artificial" scents and absolves "natural" or plant-derived scents. Avoid detergents that contain fabric softeners and bleaches (which may also have bleach stabilizers and bleach activators). Instead, buy bleach and softeners separately and use them sparingly. Fabric softener is much overused. See pages 81–82. Or try to use detergents with extra additives only occasionally instead of regularly. Choosing concentrated or "ultra" products is beneficial, as these contain fewer fillers and use less packaging. It is good to wash and rinse your clothes in water as cool as will work, but if you use water that is too cold, you are likely to end up using more chemicals to make up for the reduced cleaning and sanitizing power.

Questionable Advice? Some well-intentioned recommendations for environmentally aware laundering that you may encounter raise more questions than those just reviewed. Stores and websites offer dozens of laundry products advertised as "natural" and environmentally superior to common supermarket brands. It is often difficult to be sure their claims are warranted.

Do not assume that a product calling itself "natural" or "green" or "enviro-" anything is necessarily environmentally better. Look for specific claims about ingredients and choose the products of "green" companies with a good business reputation and a scientific orientation. Do not assume that the list of ingredients on the label includes all the ingredients in the box (unless the manufacturer is reputable and explicitly tells you that this is the case). In a frustrating trend, detergent manufacturers are listing fewer ingredients each year—many fewer than are actually used. This makes it impossible for people to make informed choices from any point of view, whether as to function, environmental favorability, or economy.

How Bad Is Household Chlorine Bleach for the Environment? Chlorine bleach is a powerful chemical. No one should store or use it in the home who does not understand how to do so safely. See page 73. Check manufacturers' websites or the websites of the FDA, CDC, or USDA for information on the safe use of bleach as a general household disinfectant. But is it environmentally incorrect? Almost certainly, it is not nearly the profound environmental hazard that some people seem to think it is. The Internet is full of misinformation on this subject, much of it purveyed by vendors of allegedly "green" products who urge you not to pour dangerous chlorine into our streams and lakes. "Chlorine," a gas in its pure form, is certainly dangerous to the environment, but household "chlorine" bleach (a 5.25 percent or 6 percent solution of sodium hypochlorite) neither contains chlorine gas nor releases chlorine gas into the environment as a result of laundering. (It contains chloride ions, just as table salt does.) Although certain uses of certain types of chlorine products in manufacturing and industry can result in the formation of dioxin, household bleaching does not.

In household use, sodium hypochlorite rapidly—before it leaves your home—breaks down, almost entirely, into table salt and water. Although no dioxins form, a small amount of other chemicals, including a very small amount of adsorbable organic halides (AOX) are formed. The term AOX is a measure of total halogens—fluorine, chlorine, bromine, and iodine—that encompasses naturally formed substances as well as pollutants. The amount of these created by domestic use of chlorine bleach is small not only in absolute terms but also relative to what is created by other human activities and relative to what comes from natural sources. Some say that the majority of the small fraction of AOX attributable to household bleach readily biodegrade, are water-soluble, and do not bioaccumulate. Moreover, chlorine bleach is remarkably cheap, effective, and versatile. Accordingly, they conclude that household bleach should be fairly low on the rational environmentalist's list of household substances to worry about. Others say that because we do not really know what else might be included in these residues, we should either not use bleach or keep use to a minimum.[1]

In deciding whether or not you will use household chlorine bleach, keep in mind this question: If you are going to use an alternative in place of chlorine bleach, are you sure that it is better for the environment than chlorine bleach?[2]

Green Detergents? Many so-called green products contain surfactants made from plant oils and fats—oleochemicals, that is, rather than petrochemicals.

(Most green products exclude animal fats on vegetarian or other principles.) Surfactants made from plant sources, including soaps, are chemically very similar to those made from petrochemicals, and in sewage plants and in the environment they act similarly to surfactants made from petrochemicals. Although surfactants differ in the rates at which they biodegrade, faster degradation is a function of the surfactants' chemical structure; it is not a function of the type of raw materials from which they are made.

Nonetheless, many people argue that because plants are a sustainable resource and petrochemicals a finite one, we should use in our detergents only surfactants manufactured from oleochemicals. Of course, we need to husband our limited petrochemical resources. But it is not so obvious to what extent using oleochemical surfactants helps to do so when one takes into account the environmental effects and overall energy consumption (including energy derived from petrochemicals) involved in making oleochemical surfactants. This involves growing the plant (and, occasionally, animal) sources, which conceivably could involve pesticides, fertilizers, long transports, or other petrochemical uses, extracting the necessary substances from the plants, and engaging in the other complex chemical manufacturing processes required to create surfactants out of them.

Comparative studies of the environmental pros and cons of oleochemical versus petrochemical surfactants show that each type has certain environmental advantages over the other; oleochemical surfactants may, on balance, have more, but, if so, their advantages are not startlingly or conclusively better. Moreover, in evaluating such studies, we should keep this in mind: The amount of petrochemicals that it takes to supply the world with detergent is small compared with the amounts used for farming, airplanes, ships, trains, cars and other forms of transportation, industrial and manufacturing uses, heating, lighting, etc.

PART II

LIVING WITH CLOTH

13

Fabrics That Work

*General guidelines for choosing fabrics for clothes or
furnishings . . . Choosing ultraviolet light—resistant fibers . . .
Dish towels and dishcloths . . . Bath towels and hand towels . . .
Bath rugs and mats . . . Table linens, sizes of tablecloths and
napkins . . . Upholstery . . . Rugs and carpets . . . Carpet
padding or underlay . . . Clothes that are cool, warm,
low- or no-iron, UV protective*

A beautiful cotton print tablecloth I once bought turned out to be colored with bleeding dyes, a fact I discovered only when I brought it
home and read all its labels. Such dyes are unsuitable for a tablecloth,
which requires frequent, vigorous laundering. Because this madras cloth had
to be washed in cold water, separately from the rest of the laundry, I could
not get oily food spots out of it. Even with cold-water washing, its lovely colors turned muddy after only two or three trips through the washer, and it
became downright ugly. If I had read its labels before I bought it, instead of
letting my eyes make the decision, I could have had an equally pretty cloth that
would have stayed pretty.

The lesson here is that you cannot assume that an article sold for a particular function is well designed to perform that function. The store shelves all
too often contain eye-catching textile goods that do not make sense when you
try to use them. Suggestions for finding fabrics that work in household jobs,
from towels to upholstery, and for avoiding the frustration, expense, and
inconvenience of poor choices, are set forth in the material below. For guidance on how to choose bed linens and blankets, see chapter 15, "Beds and
Bedding."

General Guidelines on Choosing Fabrics for Clothes or Furnishings

Before buying fabric goods, read all the information provided on hang tags, packages, and fiber content and other labels, including, of course, care labels. Look for logos that convey information about the nature or origin of a fabric. Look for evidence of finishing treatments or types of dye used, for example, a tag that says an article is vat-dyed or yarn-dyed, or is a madras print. Does it require separate washing and hand-washing? Is it wrinkle-resistant? Water-resistant? Stain-resistant? Avoid inexpensive goods that are expensive or impossible to clean.

Carefully examine clothes and furnishings inside and out before buying. Evaluate them in terms of probable comfort, durability, and functioning: examine their construction, finishes, fiber content, and workmanship.

Buy preshrunk goods whenever possible.

To reduce your risks from unknowable factors, choose reputable retailers and manufacturers. A company whose major business for many years has been manufacturing towels is more likely to sell you a towel that performs well than a company whose major asset is a fashion logo. Of course, every rule has its exceptions, except perhaps the rule of caveat emptor.

Seams should hold together tightly and not pull apart. Look at the kinds of seams that are used. Although a plain running stitch is the right type of seam on many articles, flat-felled or other reinforced seams have much more strength and are desirable in play or sports clothes. Better quality sweaters and other knits often provide a length of matching yarn attached to a hang tag for use in case you ever need to make repairs.

Stitching should be small, smooth, straight, even, and tight. Look at the hems on sheets and towels, and at the quilting stitches on mattress pads and comforters. Mitered corners are often a sign of quality in bed and table linens.

Buttons should be securely attached, with a shank or thread shank, so that

Flat-felled seams on denims

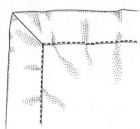

Mitered corner

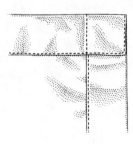

Nonmitered corner

they fit readily into the buttonholes. On heavy garments such as winter coats, buttons should be attached with heavy-duty thread or by some other extra-strong means. Extra buttons should be provided. Buttonholes should be neatly and closely stitched all around.

Look for linings in blazers, jackets, skirts, and other garments. These improve the wear, hang, comfort, and appearance of many kinds of clothes and are usually a sign of better quality.

Although we all sometimes like clothes of a rough cut for fashion reasons, better kinds of clothing are usually shaped to the body, sometimes so subtly that you can barely detect how it is done. Look to see whether a dress or shirt is simply square or shows shaping through the cut of the cloth or darts, tucks, pleats, or other types of construction.

Weave should be even, close or tight, and uniform, with no crooked threads, knots, protruding threads, broken threads, or slubs (unless slubs are put there intentionally, for example, for fashion reasons). You should not see thick or thin spots except where this is done purposely for effect. You should not see crooked lines in the weave. The yarns should be of uniform size, and the individual yarns should show uniform diameter.

Goods should be cut straight. Unfold napkins and other flat goods (handkerchiefs, blankets, sheets) and hold them up to the light. You should be able to see that the threads are parallel and perpendicular to the edge of the cloth. The shape should be even and square at the corners.

Color should be even and uniform and penetrate well. Check for color penetration at the seams and darts especially.

Avoid overstarched goods—those whose appearance, body, or firmness is actually a function of starches that will launder out. If you rub the fabric between your hands, sometimes you can actually see excess starch powder fall out.

Choosing Ultraviolet Light–Resistant Fibers

The chart below gives a rough ranking of the various textile fibers in accordance with their ability to resist degradation—loss of strength, deterioration, yellowing, and other ill effects—caused by exposure to the ultraviolet radiation in sunlight and other types of light. Resistance to degradation as a result of exposure to light is obviously crucial in furnishings, especially draperies but also carpeting and upholstery. Treatments are sometimes available that increase a fiber's resistance to UV radiation, however, and other factors are also relevant. For example, southern light causes more damage than other light; higher humidity increases the rate of damage. Most importantly, the dyes used on the fabrics may have low resistance to light and thus fade, even though the fibers themselves have good light resistance. Thus the chart gives only some of the relevant facts you need to consider when assessing probable light resistance.

Excellent Ultraviolet Light–Resistance

Acrylic

Modacrylic

Polyester

Good Resistance

Linen

Cotton

Rayon

Acetate

Triacetate

Poor Resistance

Nylon

Wool

Silk

Olefin/Polypropylene

Choosing Dish Towels and Dishcloths

Functional Properties to Look For

Highly absorbent

Soft, flexible

Nonlinting, especially for drying china and glass

Durable

Care Characteristics. Dish towels and dishcloths must be launderable and colorfast, and they should be able to take hot washing and drying temperatures, ordinary laundry detergents, and chlorine bleaches. When you launder kitchen toweling, you want to be able to remove food stains and sanitize. Avoid buying towels with care labels that say "Wash separately" or "Wash with like colors" or "No bleach."

Good Choices. There are stalwart defenders of cotton dish towels, but in my opinion linen are best. For drying glass and china they are particularly desirable because they do not lint. Huckaback or huck toweling makes a fine towel. Crash towels are also good. They are cheaper and rougher than another, finer, type of plain-weave towel called a "glass towel" or "dish towel." ("Huck towel," "huckaback," "crash," and other fabric terms used in this chapter are defined in the Glossary of Fabric Terms, page 298, at the end of chapter 19, "The Fabric

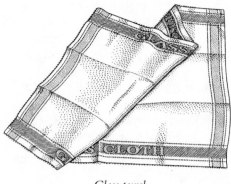

Glass towel

of Your Home.") The words "glass towel" or "dish towel" may be woven into such towels. They are indeed good for drying glass and china because they have smooth, hard-twisted yarns to prevent linting. Glass towels often come in white with blue or red checks or stripes, but some are in prints as well. Damask dish towels look beautiful but may be less absorbent because of the tightness of their weave.

Cotton towels, too, come in crash or huckaback weaves and various plain weaves, especially basket weaves. They are a bit less absorbent and more likely than linen to yellow or gray with age and to lint. But cotton still makes an excellent towel and is less expensive than linen. Good-quality cotton towels do not lint. Cotton terry-cloth dish towels are widely available in a range of styles and quality.

Waffle or similar spongy weaves, terry-cloth, and basket weaves will be naturally wrinkle-resistant, so these are for you if you can bear neither to iron dish towels nor to look at wrinkles. Crash and glass towels work fine in their wrinkled state, but you might roll them tightly around a tube while they are warm from the dryer to smooth them out. Or fold them neatly and set a weight on the stack while they are still warm. (See chapter 6, "Ironing.")

Choose dishcloths for washing dishes in any spongy, bumpy, soft weave of cotton, such as a waffle weave. The raised portions of the weave provide good friction for rubbing dishes clean, and a good, spongy weave will hold plenty of water. Thickest is not necessarily best, however, as you will be unable to get into small places with very thick fabrics and you will be less able to feel bumps through such fabrics with your fingers.

Choosing Bath and Hand Towels

Functional Properties to Look For

Soft

Highly absorbent

Durable

Thick or thin, according to preference

Care Characteristics. Traditional housekeepers sought bath and hand towels and washcloths able to take hot water and dryer temperatures, ordinary detergents, and—if needed—chlorine bleach. This is because you want to be able to sanitize them if necessary and to be able to remove stains and soils wiped off the skin. You will search long and hard before you find any today that have care labels permitting such vigorous laundering. But I find that towels can quite often be laundered vigorously despite care label instructions to the contrary. (See chapter 2, "Carefully Disregarding Care Labels.") Towels should always be colorfast. Avoid buying towels with care labels that say "Wash separately" or "Wash with like colors." This is a care instruction that makes no sense for towels. But care instructions to wash separately for the first two or three launderings are not objectionable, as this indicates that the towels are really colorfast but may hold some excess dye that will readily and permanently wash out.

Although colored towels are lovely, it is not a bad idea to stock some plain white towels as well. White towels, usually, can take the most vigorous laundering with hot water, strong detergents, and bleaches; thus they are not hard to keep looking good. Not only are they attractive in the bath, you will find many uses for them outside the bath, such as laying wet clothes on them or rolling wet clothes in them to dry, and for hot and cold compresses; everyone finds further uses special to their own homes.

Most people prefer thick towels, and, other things being equal, thicker towels will be more durable. But there are those who like thinner towels. Some members of my family hate thick towels, insisting that they make it hard to get behind the ears or between toes. They like old towels worn to thinness or inexpensive thin, new towels. The others prefer the luxurious softness and greater absorbency of thick towels.

Most towels will shrink a little; towels of lower quality may shrink greatly, often becoming misshapen in the process.

Good Choices. Turkish towels or cotton terry-cloth towels, which were introduced in the late nineteenth century, are wonderfully soft and absorbent for the bath. And nothing beats cotton terry-cloth washcloths, which mildly abrade the skin to remove soil, oil, and dead cells. Although cotton is less absorbent than linen and, when dry, initially resists moisture, the loops on the face of terry towels help them to pick up more moisture and to hold more of it than other towels, including linen ones. The most absorbent towels have the most pile loops, which should be long and not too tightly twisted. When the loops are cropped to form velour terry, the cloth feels velvety and shows prints well but is much less absorbent. Terry towels with cotton pile and a polyester back will still be fairly absorbent, since most of the drying that your towels do is with the pile. (Polyester in the back adds strength and durability.) A tight, balanced weave, preferably a twill, is desirable. But the thread count of the towel is less important in determining absorbency than the weight of the towel: heavier towels are more absorbent.

Look for dense, thick, firm towels with high pile, even selvage edges, and small, even hem stitches. Hold terry-cloth towels up to the light to check

TOWEL SIZES

Towel sizes are not uniform from manu-facturer to manufacturer. The sizes below are common, but do not be surprised to encounter different dimensions. Store three sets of towels per person plus one or more sets for guests.

Finger or guest: 12 × 18; 11 × 16; 14 × 22

Hand: 18 × 30; 16 × 30; 20 × 32

Bath: 24 × 46; 28 × 52

Bath sheet: 38 × 72; 36 × 70; 40 × 70

Bath mat: 19 × 27; 22 × 36

Washcloth: 12 × 12; 13 × 13

the quality of the underlying weave. Feel it for softness and resilience. Avoid towels that lack that cottony, dry, terry-cloth feeling and instead have a certain (seductively pleasant) silky or smooth feel. In my experience, the latter are not very absorbent until they have received long wear and grown more cottony.

Although you see extra-long-staple Egyptian and pima cotton towels praised, I prefer terry-cloth towels made of upland cotton, which seem to me more absorbent and softer. Towels of extralong-staple cotton, however, grow softer and more absorbent as they age.

Most people in this country would never exchange the great comfort, absorbency, and reasonable prices of terry-cloth towels for old-fashioned linen bath towels. The latter lacked a pile and were made in a variety of weaves, such as huck, honeycomb, or waffle weave. Linen bath towels vied with terry-cloth through the opening decades of the twentieth century and are still favored in some places in Europe. They are often quite large but quickly grow damp and soaked and can chill you in cold bathrooms; they wrinkle readily. They can be quite beautiful, especially those with long, silky fringes. But although people look more elegant wrapped in the folds of fine, fringed linen fabric after a bath, people wrapped in terry towels are warmer and more comfy. If you would like to try linen bath towels, the most sensi-ble (and the warmest) have thick, spongy weaves such as waffle weave and natural colors—cream, tan, and off-white. The most beautiful are in jacquard or dobby weaves. You may be able to find such nonterry bath towels in cot-tons as well.

Some companies make linen terry-cloth towels, often marketing them espe-cially to men. These towels are invigoratingly scratchy and quite absorbent, especially after a couple of washes, but the ones I have seen are not nearly as pretty as cotton terry-cloth.

Hand towels of linen are traditional. They come in beautiful damask weaves or huck, crash, honeycomb, or waffle weaves. Linen towels are absorbent and durable, do not yellow or turn gray, and can take strong laundering. Cotton terry is more absorbent than other types of cotton hand towels, but all are good. Guest hand towels often are delicate and elegant, with fringe, embroi-dery, cutwork, or lace. These require careful ironing to look good.

Bath Rugs and Mats

Functional Properties to Look For

Absorbent

Slip-resistant

Care Characteristics. Bath rugs and mats should be easily launderable and colorfast. Although bleaching is not so important for bath mats and rugs as for towels and sheets, it is always easier to get out stains using a chlorine bleach. Nonslip backings on bathroom rugs are indispensable. (Usually you can machine-launder these; if the care label says not to, do not buy the rug.) Bath mats, which are often made simply of thick, absorbent woven cotton, have no nonslip backings. Be careful using them! Laying them on a bathroom rug that has a nonslip back sometimes solves the slippage problem and keeps the rug drier as well.

Table Linen

Functional Properties to Look For

Absorbent

Smooth hand

Crisp, drapable

Durable

Care Characteristics. Tablecloths and napkins, ideally, should be able to take hot-water laundering, ordinary commercial detergents, and chlorine bleach, for they will be exposed to food, drink, and lipstick stains, among others. In practice, few care labels prescribe vigorous laundering for table linens. Yet unless you can at least sometimes use your strongest laundry weapons, you may not be able to keep them looking good. Although you might take risks with everyday table linens to get out stains, you can face agonizing choices when it is your beloved damasks or lace, hand-embroidered, or cutwork cloths that have become spotted. Therefore consider whether you should choose table linens that minimize such risks: whites and colorfast table linens in heavier weights, for example, are better able to endure the occasional stain-removal trauma. Linen gives up stains and soil more readily than cotton but, on the other hand, is more readily damaged by bleach.

Table linens of untreated cotton or linen will require ironing. If natural fibers receive wrinkle-resistance treatments, you may find you are satisfied with their appearance with little or no ironing. When natural fibers are blended with synthetics, too, you can often get by with little or no ironing. But both resin-treated cloth and cloth containing hydrophobic synthetic fibers tend to oil-stain. If you buy these, therefore, look for labels that say the cloth has received soil-repelling and soil-releasing treatments to make laundering them easier. (See chapter 20, "Transformations," pages 323-24, on soil-resistance treatments.

Sizes. Breakfast or lunch cloths should hang over the edge of the table 6 to 8 inches. The dinner cloth should hang over the edge 8 to 12 inches. The more formal the occasion, the longer the desirable overhang—from 12 to 18 inches for formal dinners. There are those, however, who object to the table-cloth hitting the chair seat. More than 12 inches of overhang will cause the cloth to begin folding up on the chair. The suggestions below, therefore, are rough and must be adapted to the occasion. Allow for shrinkage in laundering when you choose your table linens. As with sheets, expect most of the shrinkage to occur in the length—up to 10 percent.

Shape	Table Size (in inches)	Cloth Size (in inches)	Persons Seated
Square	28 × 28 to 40 × 40	52 × 52	4
Round	30 to 42 diameter	52 round	4
	42 to 44 diameter	60 to 68	4 to 6
	42 to 46 diameter	68 with fringe	4 to 6
	42 to 54 diameter	68 with fringe	6
	42 to 60 diameter	72 round	6
	64 to 76 diameter	90 round	6 to 8
Oblong	28 × 46 to 36 × 64	52 × 70	4 to 6
	36 × 56 to 42 × 62	60 × 80	6 to 8
	42 × 60 to 48 × 72	72 × 90	6 to 8
	42 × 72 to 48 × 90	72 × 108	8 to 10
Oval	28 × 46 to 36 × 54	52 × 70	4 to 6
	36 × 56 to 42 × 62	60 × 80	6 to 8
	42 × 60 to 48 × 72	72 × 90	6 to 8
	42 × 72 to 48 × 90	72 × 108	8 to 10

Napkin sizes have grown smaller over time, and they are not particularly standardized. Hundreds of years ago, they were truly blanketlike—in the eighteenth century, perhaps a square yard or even larger—but more petite napkins are now the rule, as the expectation is that you will not soil your hands, face, or clothes while eating, or at least not much. In general, the more formal the occasion, the more ample the napkin should be. Luncheon napkins may be from 12 × 12 to 18 × 18 inches. Cocktail napkins will be even smaller. Dinner napkins vary from 18 × 18 to 24 × 24 inches. Banquet napkins may be from 24 × 24 to 32 × 32 inches.

Good Choices. Linen, cotton, rayon, and blends of these with synthetic fibers are all sensible choices for tablecloths and napkins, depending on your goals. To avoid or reduce ironing, choose tablecloths and napkins in permanent-press fabrics or fabrics made of synthetic fibers and their blends. For best launderability, choose untreated white cotton and linen, but plan to iron. Less absorbent fabrics, such as synthetics, blends, and resin-treated cloth, do not make ideal napkins. For formal and elegant tables, choose damask in linen or cotton. Generally speaking, you get greater durability in linens with greater weight. Those of us with a budget usually aim to have one or two elegant tablecloths for special occasions and some relatively casual ones for ordinary uses.

Extra work in laundering and ironing will usually be required if you choose tablecloths that are embroidered, have cutwork, or are lace or trimmed with lace. Although handmade lace of natural fibers is expensive and requires thoughtful laundering and ironing, machine-made lace is often easy to care for—machine-washable or no-iron—and affordable.

Choosing Upholstery

Functional properties to look for

Durable

Abrasion-resistant

Strong

Ultraviolet light–resistant

Nonfading

Nonshrinking or preshrunk

Colorfast

Nonpilling

Nonshedding

Nonstatic

Good hand (not harsh, slick, or scratchy)

Flame-resistant

Care Characteristics. The most important care consideration is to make sure that the fabric of your upholstery is cleanable by the method you prefer to use: home or professional wet cleaning (a new professional cleaning technique that can often replace dry cleaning) or shampooing, or professional dry cleaning. If you plan on wet cleaning, you must inquire carefully about colorfastness and shrinking. Soil-repellant and soil-release treatments are always a good idea for upholstery fabrics.

Good Choices. Almost all fibers have been adapted for use in upholstering, and well-designed blends and synthetics are often good choices. When you choose a synthetic or blend, inquire about whether it is prone to the problems that synthetics often face, such as pilling and static. People most often go wrong when they buy a fabric for upholstering that is intended for draperies, apparel, or some other use, and thus lacks the strength and abrasion-resistance that upholstery fabrics need for enduring the hard wear they will receive. Silk is elegant and beautiful, but it stains readily and cannot take much abrasion; thus it is not a practical choice for places that will get hard use or in places where children and pets will play.

Choosing Rugs and Carpets

Functional Properties to Look For

Durable

Abrasion-resistant

Resilient

Nonpilling

Nonshedding

Nonstatic

Ultraviolet light–resistant

Nonfading

Colorfast

Flame-resistant

Care Characteristics. As with upholstery, the most important consideration is to make sure that a rug or carpet you are buying can be cleaned by the method you would plan to use on it: Can it be cleaned by home shampooing using a machine or professional cleaning, or must it receive gentle hand cleaning? Soil-repellancy or soil-release treatments are a good idea, and some carpets are more naturally stain-resistant than others.

Good Choices. See chapter 16, "Textile Furnishings."

Choosing Carpet Padding, Cushion, or Underlay

Functional Properties to Look For

Level of cushioning

Proportional to carpet

Thickness proper for comfort

Insulating effect

Noise

Heat and cold

Nonmildewing

Care Characteristics. This is not usually an issue. Carpet padding is generally cared for by vacuuming now and then.

Good Choices. Other things being equal, choose thinner padding for thinner carpets and thicker padding for thicker carpets, but the Carpet and Rug Institute recommends a maximum thickness of ⁷⁄₁₆ of an inch. For high-traffic areas, choose less cushiony, harder types. It is tiring to walk a great deal on a highly cushioned surface, and also difficult when you are wearing high-heeled shoes. For low traffic, softer types of padding will work. A thicker padding is good where you want noise insulation.

Have the pad cut to the correct size by the vendor. If you have a carpet pad that does not extend to the edge of the carpet, over the years this can cause premature wear; an unattractive line can develop at the place in the carpet where the pad stops. The thicker the pad, the worse this problem can be. A carpet pad that is larger than the carpet is unsightly.

When evaluating durability, remember that jute will mildew if it gets damp and a synthetic will not. Fiberglass-based pads are recommended for high-traffic areas and for rugs on which office chairs or other rolling or frequently moved furniture are placed; they last longer and are less likely to disintegrate under such pressure than other types of padding. Sponge rubber is available in various thicknesses and degrees of firmness, but only thinner, firmer types will be sufficiently durable for high-traffic areas. Polyurethane foam is also available; the type I have experience with was best suited for lighter uses, as in a small child's room. Felted padding made of hair is sold in many thicknesses and degrees of firmness, but it is not very durable and should not be used in heavy traffic areas.

Clothing

To Stay Cool, Look For

Fabrics of linen, cotton, rayon

Absorbent fibers

Smooth fibers and fabrics (avoid spun fibers, or napped, pile, or fuzzy fabrics)

Open, smoother, looser weaves or knits such as mesh or seersucker

Lightweight fabrics

Light colors

To Stay Warm, Choose

Wool and acrylic

Fuzzy fibers, crimped fibers

Fabrics with pile or nap

Tight weaves, thick weaves, thick knits, satin weaves, especially in heavier weights

Heavyweight fabrics

Dark colors

To Reduce Ironing, Choose

Wool, silk, permanent-press and wash-and-wear clothes, any woven synthetic other than rayon

Seersucker

Waffle weaves and similar weaves

Napped or pile fabrics such as flannel, corduroy, or velvet

Knits of all sorts

Corduroy

To Gain Protection from the Sun's Ultraviolet Rays, Choose

Tightly woven fabrics (avoid loose or open weaves such as basket weaves or gauze)

Blue denim

Satin weaves and other smooth-surface weaves

Fabrics treated to render them UV blocking

Dark colors

Dry clothes—wet ones transmit more UV radiation

See also chapter 20, pages 322–23.

14

Aprons, Dish Towels, and Rags

Dressing for the occasion, clothes for cleaning . . . Rags,
cloth rags vs. paper towels . . . The art of rag making, ragbags

Although many of us wear aprons when we cook, I know hardly anyone who puts one on to do housework, even though this is a useful, clothes-friendly, and laundry-reducing habit. Instead we wear old clothes to perform potentially dirty chores. A friend keeps an assortment of oversized T-shirts in her cleaning closet, and uses them as smocks over her clothes when she cleans. But nothing beats a real apron or smock with several pockets for carrying coins, paper clips, screws, and other small objects back and forth, for wiping your hands on without remorse, for keeping your midriff free of oily stains and grime, for sticking pins in, and the like. When you take it off, you can sit down to lunch or a tea break in a clean shirt without changing.

Pictures of 1950s housewives vacuuming in pearls, high heels, and an apron seem funny now, but probably only because we have forgotten the context. My grandmothers always insisted on doing housework nicely dressed (although not in pearls and high heels). Whatever their differences, they each donned and doffed the same kinds of aprons according to the same housekeeping and social patterns. They wore plain white muslin ones for everyday. The apron went on first thing in the morning and came off when they ate and when the day's housework was done. These work aprons, however, were for the eyes of the family only. Fancy, frilled, and embroidered aprons came out when there was cooking to be done in the presence of company, but even these would be removed for answering the door. Thus, in addition to their more obvious functions, the aprons were also used to enforce a distinction between the private and public part of home life.

You may wish to tie a scarf around your hair or wear a cap, as everyone would have done in the days before showers and detangling hair conditioners, when women's hair might be a couple of feet long and washing it was a once-weekly ordeal.

Rags

Cloth Versus Paper. For most purposes, rags are better than sponges or paper towels. Cloth cleans better than disposable materials and is far easier to work with. It is hard to know whether cloth or disposables offer the more environmentally correct solution, but I vote in favor of cloth. Worn-out bath towels are better than anything else for big spills, and small towels of thin terry, cotton knit, or other soft, absorbent cloth are good for small spills. Paper towels are inconvenient (and expensive) for big spills, which might absorb entire rolls. A sponge or mop will have you wiping and squeezing a few dozen times and will be harder to clean or launder than old towels or rags. But you can just cover a spill with an old towel or two that you have reserved for dirty jobs, and the spill is soaked up. Then launder the towels. Usually you can launder a lot of rags and cleaning materials together.

Rags are much preferable to paper towels for hard jobs because they do not disintegrate when you scrub with them, they make handy dirt-loosening ridges when you scrunch them up, and they hold much more liquid. They are also superior to sponges for difficult jobs. You cannot feel through sponges with your fingers well enough to know whether a surface is free of bumps of hardened food or other matter. You cannot apply finger and nail pressure through a sponge so easily; trying to would poke holes in paper towels. Rags are also more sanitary than sponges.

The Art of Rag Making; Ragbags. Make distinctions among your towels, cloths, and rags. A fundamental rule of housekeeping is that separate cloths are used for cleaning or wiping dishes, kitchen sinks, counters and tabletops, floors, bathroom tubs and sinks, and people. Except for those to be used on the kitchen floor, moreover, cloths and rags to be used in the kitchen should generally be stored in the kitchen, not in the ragbag in the general cleaning closet. Keep different sets of rags for dirty jobs and lighter, cleaner jobs—for example, old, thin terry-cloth for washing floors and soft, white flannel for dusting wood and china. Old bath and kitchen towels, flannel sheets and pajamas, T-shirts, and soft knits of all sorts make good rags. Any nonlinting, absorbent, soft, white or colorfast cloth will do.

Cut rags to convenient sizes for your hand and purposes. Keep some big towels for big spills, and some soft white squares for dusting. If you cut the rags with pinking shears, they are less likely to fray at the edges.

Store your different types of rags in different ragbags or boxes, and keep plentiful supplies for all purposes. When you dirty one while cleaning or dusting, you want to be able to reach for the next without hesitation. When choosing materials to make rags, avoid or remove buttons, studs, zippers, and even thick and lumpy seams, such as the flat-felled seams on denims. These can harm surfaces and are hard to work with. After housecleaning, throw all your dirty rags into the washing machine—separately, not with your regular laundry—and launder them with hot water, detergent, and chlorine bleach; tumble them dry in a hot dryer. They are now sanitized and ready to be returned to the ragbag for the next cleaning day. (If you cannot launder them immediately, hang them on a rack or line until you can—but do not use them.)

Kitchen Cloth

Cloths, Towels, and Rags; Their Division of Labor. Use towels, cloths, and rags prodigally in your kitchen. Keep plenty on hand so that you can replace them readily. When they are only slightly soiled and damp, they will grow microbial armies. If you wipe down the countertop with a bacteria-laden towel or cloth, you spread bacteria everywhere. So don't hesitate to go through several of each every day. They are easy to launder.

Use separate cloths, rags, and towels for different kitchen purposes. Dishcloths are used for dishes, sinks, counters, and tabletops. Rags are used to wash the floors and clean up spills. Hand towels are used for drying people's hands. Dish towels are for drying dishes. In addition, it is convenient to set aside some cloths, towels, or rags within each category to be used for very dirty jobs of that sort. For example, you can have some dishcloths that you use for very dirty pot-washing jobs or for mopping up nasty countertop spills; you can permit these to become stained. Give them vigorous laundering, but you need not take special measures if stains do not come out. Save other cloths or rags for lighter or cleaner jobs. To the extent possible, most people try to keep their fine linen towels free of stains; these are reserved for drying and polishing glassware, crystal, and silver.

For drying your hands in the kitchen after cutting up raw chicken or meat or doing other chores that might leave dangerous pathogens on your hands, use paper towels rather than run the risk of leaving dangerous microorganisms on a hand towel that someone else might use before preparing the salad greens.

For sanitizing kitchen cloths, see pages 147–48.

15

Beds and Bedding

How much linen to stock . . . Standard mattress, sheet, and pillowcase sizes . . . Calculating desirable sizes for sheets . . . Blanket cover, coverlet, and bedspread sizes . . . Blanket, comforter, and comforter cover sizes . . . Durability of sheets; thread counts, weave and weight, fiber, effect of decorative stitching on durability, whites vs. colors and prints . . . Choosing comfortable sheets . . . Hand, absorbency, warmth, decorative stitching . . . Launderability of sheets; no-iron sheets; wrinkly sheets . . . Blankets and comforters . . . Changing and laundering linens . . . Dressing and making the bed

A good bedroom requires good bedding. To be satisfied with your bedroom linens and your bed, you need to know more about bedding than merchandisers today give you credit for. Linen stores once expected their patrons to be knowledgeable, penny-wise women who would pore over merchandise with sharp eyes. Today they seem to expect us to make decisions based purely on the looks of the linens and our supposed love of luxury. I have made more than one foolish purchase of sheets and other bedding, acting just like the naïve spender whom advertisers target. Poorer but wiser after these experiences, I describe for you in this chapter many things I wish I had kept in mind during a few shopping trips in the past. We should always try to buy linens we regard as beautiful. But when you think through the ways in which sheets and other bedding are used and laundered, you may revise your ideas about what a beautiful sheet looks like.

About Bed Linens

How Much Linen to Stock. For each bed in your home, you will probably find it convenient to stock the following:

3 sets of sheets, top and bottom (including, if you wish, 1 guest set)

3 sets of pillowcases (including, if you wish, 1 guest set)

2 pillow protectors (sometimes called pillow "covers")

1 or 2 allergen-proof undercovers

2 mattress pads

1 or 2 allergen-proof mattress covers

This gives, for each bed, one set of sheets on the bed, one set in the wash, and one in reserve for accidents or extra changes of the bed for guests. People who keep a set of guest sheets for one or more beds usually choose especially fine or attractive sheets for this purpose and may also use them for a variety of special occasions like anniversaries or special holidays. Because you change protectors, undercovers, and mattress pads less frequently, you will need only one extra set of each of these. Crib sheets and blankets must be changed daily or more often if they become wet or soiled, so stock at least a half dozen of each.

It does not pay to overstock bed linens, for they will simply age on the shelf. An overstocked linen closet also makes more work for you. It is prey to odors and dust. Linens that have sat unused for long periods have had more opportunities to become damp and to develop mold, yellowing, weakness along crease lines, and other problems, so you will have to go in and wash and refold them periodically.

Types of Sheets. What to choose, as opposed to how many, is a more complicated question than it used to be. It pays to understand fibers, fabrics, and their characteristics in making these choices; so the reader is referred generally to chapter 19, "The Fabric of Your Home," and chapter 21, "The Natural Fibers." The desiderata in sheets are good fit, resistance to shrinking, durability, resistance to pilling, comfort (a complicated thing in itself), launderability, economy, and beauty. Comfort in a sheet depends greatly on a good hand or feeling, warmth or coolness, absorbency, and absence of pilling.

Getting the Right Size:
Standard Measurements of Bed Linens

Standard Mattress, Sheet, and Pillowcase Sizes. Sheet sizes used to be highly standardized and still are fairly uniform, but you now encounter more variations—reflecting, no doubt, more variation in mattress sizes. Be especially alert for different measurements in European-made sheets and pillowcases, and for differences between linen and cotton sheets and pillowcases. The sizes set out in this section, however, are still considered fairly "standard." They fit the following standard mattress widths and lengths (but see the discussion of extra-deep mattresses below):

Mattress Sizes

Twin	39 × 75
Full/double	54 × 75
Queen	60 × 80
King	78 × 80
California king	72 × 84

The length and width of sheets will be stated on the package when you buy them. Flat sheets of all sizes are given a 2- to 4-inch hem at top and ½- to 1-inch hem at bottom. Although almost all sheets have selvage edges at the sides, very fine sheets (and the occasional inferior sheet) may have hems of an inch or so at the sides too. The dimensions of a sheet stated on the package nowadays are the finished sizes, not the "torn" sizes. (The torn size is the size before hemming. When hemmed, sheets are up to 5 inches shorter in length and 2 inches shorter in width. Until the 1970s, sheet packages gave the torn size, not the hemmed size.)

Dimensions of Standard Sheets

Crib flat	42 × 72
Crib fitted	28 × 52
Twin flat	66 × 96
Twin fitted	39 × 75
Double or full flat	81 × 96; 81 × 100
Double or full fitted	54 × 75
Queen flat	90 × 102; 90 × 106
Queen fitted	60 × 80
King flat	108 × 102; 108 × 106
King fitted	78 × 80
California king flat	102 × 110
California king fitted	72 × 84

A pillowcase should be 4 inches longer than the pillow and 2 inches greater in circumference.

Dimensions of Pillowcases

Standard	20 × 26
Queen	20 × 30
King	20 × 40; 20 × 36
European	26 × 26
Boudoir (baby)	12 × 16
Neck roll	6 × 14

All new sheets will shrink a little when laundered, but the shrinkage is almost entirely in the length, with very little change in the width. The long-term shrinkage in the average cotton sheet will be about 5 percent, which works out to about 5 inches in a 108-inch sheet. Flannel sheets will shrink more but are cut longer to allow for this. Thus, even if you have standard-length mattresses, it can pay to buy extra-long sheets (these are often 108 inches long) to assure plenty of overhang for tucking after the shrinking. Once upon a time, you would have planned on providing flat sheets large enough to give 10 to 12 inches to tuck on each edge and top sheets that extended 6 to 10 inches past the head of the mattress (so that you could have a generous fold over the top of the blanket). To do this even twenty years ago, you had to buy the next size larger sheet (for example, a queen flat for a double bed) because standard sheet sizes on a standard mattress gave you only 6 or 7 inches for tucking. (Many people regard 6 or 7 inches as quite adequate, by the way, and the 10 to 12 inches I like is a rather old-fashioned standard. But it still works best.)

It is crucial to measure the depth of your mattress before purchasing sheets because of all the extra-deep mattresses being sold today. Not uncommonly these have a 14-inch depth, and some are even deeper—up to 20 inches. The mattress most commonly sold today is 8 to 10 inches deep. The old "standard" mattress was 6 to 8 inches deep. With a mattress 14 to 20 inches deep, to get the same allowance for tucking that the standard top sheet gives for a standard 8-inch mattress, you need a sheet that is 6 to 12 inches longer, depending on how deep your mattress is, and 12 to 24 inches wider. (A flat bottom sheet would need as much extra length as width.) If you have a deep mattress, therefore, you must buy the next size larger flat sheet, preferably in an extra-long length, to provide a decent allowance for tucking under and turning down. When purchasing fitted sheets, however, you cannot safely get the next larger size, as they probably will not fit. Instead, if you have a deep mattress, make sure you purchase fitted sheets with "universal" or deep corners. Sometimes the package specifies the corner depth, so check labels. Linen stores will often undertake to make custom-size sheets for you, and these are often necessary for beds with unusual shapes or unusually deep mattresses.

Common Sizes for Blanket Covers or Coverlets and Bedspreads. Keep two covers or spreads for each bed. People today tend to leave their pillows uncovered, use dust ruffles, and cover the bed with blanket covers or coverlets that expose the dust ruffle, pillowcases, and sheet tops. Unlike sheet sizes, the sizes of blanket covers and coverlets are not highly standardized. If the exact size matters, measure before you go shopping! Remember to make allowances for extra-deep mattresses. Some common sizes of blanket covers or coverlets are as follows:

Blanket Covers

Twin	69 × 90
Full/double	84 × 90
Queen	95 × 95
King	102 × 95

It has become hard to find old-fashioned bedspreads that cover the pillows and the sides of the bed down to the floor. Here are bedspread sizes that would work for standard mattresses, but, again, you might need to make allowances if you have an extra-deep mattress:

Bedspreads

Twin	74 × 108
Full/double	88 × 108
Queen/king	99 × 114

Sizes of Blankets and Comforters. Blankets are sized so as to fit under a coverlet. If you want sufficient overhang for a comforter or blanket to serve also as a bed cover, you must be sure to select a size large enough. Blanket sizes are highly variable, as the following list of sizes I have found in stores and catalogues shows. If the exact size matters, measure and calculate, before buying, just how much overhang or tuck you will need.

Blankets

Crib	36 × 50
Twin	68 × 86; 68 × 90; 66 × 96
Full	81 × 83; 80 × 96
Queen	91 × 91; 90 × 96
King	108 × 96
California king	102 × 102

Comforters (duvets) are variable in size. The sizes of comforter covers are the same as the sizes of the comforters themselves, and they also vary considerably. Measuring is needed if you are concerned about exact fit. The following examples of sizes are typical:

Comforters and Comforter Covers

Twin	68 × 88; 68 × 86; 66 × 88
Full	81 × 88
Full/queen	86 × 86; 88 × 88
Queen	88 × 96
King	107 × 96; 102 × 86; 102 × 88

CALCULATING DESIRABLE SIZES FOR BED LINENS

Example 1: Calculating top sheet length for standard double (full) mattress. Suppose you have a double (full) mattress, 54 × 75, that is 8 inches deep. If you wanted to tuck in 12 inches of your top sheet at the bottom of the mattress and have 10 extra inches at the top, you would have to buy a sheet that is no less than 105 inches in length.

Extra at top + mattress length + mattress depth + tuck

10 + 75 + 8 + 12 = 105 inches

Example 2: Calculating sheet size for an extra-deep queen-size mattress. Suppose that you have a queen-size pillow-top mattress, 60 × 80, that is 14 inches deep. You find some linen sheets that come only in flat sizes, and you would like to buy some for your bed. Here is how you would calculate the size of the flat sheet you would need as a bottom sheet, if you were to insist on tucking in 10 inches on all sides. As the calculation shows, you will not be able to buy any standard sheet to fit because no sheet is manufactured in so large a size. In length, it would have to be as follows:

Top tuck + mattress depth + mattress length + mattress depth + bottom tuck

10 + 14 + 80 + 14 + 10 = 128 inches

The width would have to be as follows:

Side tuck + mattress depth + mattress width + mattress depth + side tuck

10 + 14 + 60 + 14 + 10 = 108 inches

Durability in Sheets

Thread Counts. Do not be deceived into thinking that the higher the thread count, the better the sheet. This is an oversimplified and mistaken idea that is frequently purveyed by merchandisers and fashion writers. It may lead you into paying too much money for a sheet that will not last as long, feel as good, or launder as well as one with a lower thread count. (For an explanation of thread counts, see chapter 19, "The Fabric of Your Home," pages 276–77.)

Until recent decades, most sheets sold were muslin, a cotton plain-weave cloth with a thread count of about 140. Hospitals and other institutions used muslin sheets exclusively because they were inexpensive, comfortable, and very long-lasting. Most people used them at home, too, especially on children's beds. The next grade of sheet was percale, with a thread count of 180. It felt finer and was also quite durable. In all middle-class homes until recent decades, there were no aspirations to any sheets better than 180 thread count percale. But in the 1980s increasingly higher thread counts in cotton sheets began to appear—200, 220, 250, 300, and upward—and these typically had ever-finer, softer, smoother hand and were made of ever-better cotton— Egyptian cotton or pima cotton. Some of these, therefore, were and are good buys. Using fine yarns, high thread counts, and high-quality fiber, they achieve a good balance of durability, launderability, and improved hand. My favorite type of sheet for ordinary home use is a resin-free all-combed-cotton percale with a thread count of 200 to 250 and a care label that says merely "Machine-wash."

But superfine, supersoft, high thread count cotton sheets that are somewhat delicate now dominate the market. On a recent trip to Bloomingdale's I found for sale only one type of plain-weave sheet and one type of twill sheet, both with thread counts of 300; all the other sheets were sateen with thread counts higher than 300. Sateen sheets (cotton sheets in satin weaves), which have more or less replaced hardy plain-weave and twill in upscale stores, have high thread counts of 400 and up—to 1000 or more. Yet they are less durable than plain or twill weaves because they use looser twists and floats in the weave, and they are very light and thin. (The terms "twist" and "float" are explained in chapter 19.) They cannot be bleached; they soon acquire the grayish or yellowish tinge of aging cotton. They wear holes faster. They are costly. Of course, if they suit your fancy and your pocketbook, you should have them; and if you are on a budget, you can reserve them for special occasions, guests' beds, and the like. Just be sure you are not under the impression that you are necessarily getting a long-wearing (or highly launderable) sheet fitted for hard, everyday use. This will depend on many more factors than high thread count.

Weave and Weight. Both twill, the most durable type of weave, and plain-weave sheets tend to be more durable than satin weaves, because the latter contain threads with floats and low twist, which are vulnerable to abrasion and tearing. Cotton knit sheets tend to be less durable than woven ones. Heavier-weight fabrics tend to be more durable than lighter.

Some high thread count cotton sheets in plain weave are very sheer and light. They are, therefore, quite lovely and cool, but they are not likely to wear as well as heavier sheeting, particularly if subjected to vigorous laundering and heavy use. You may wish to keep them for special occasions or for hot summer nights. Very sheer linen sheets (of lawn, say, or a similar weave) are equally delicate. For some people, these, not sateen, are the height of luxury.

Fiber. The best cotton fabric used for sheets is combed pima or Egyptian cotton. (Sea Island cotton is rarely seen in sheets.) Wrinkle-treated cotton sheets generally do not last as long as untreated cotton or cotton/polyester sheets, but the latter may pill and all-cotton will not. High-quality cotton is extremely durable, even when subjected to frequent vigorous laundering. So is unbleached linen; bleached and dyed linen is less durable. You can, unfortunately, all too easily pay premium prices for linen sheets that are not of the highest quality and will wear poorly. (See chapter 21, "The Natural Fibers," pages 327–31, on how to evaluate the quality of linen.) Even high-quality linen, moreover, will not be able to take hard wear if it is very finely woven or lacy or bears other delicate decorative needlework.

Decorative Stitching, Cutwork, Lace, and the Like. Decorative stitching on any sheets can make them less durable. Cutwork and lace are highly susceptible to tearing. Embroidery can fray or fade. Even simple hem stitching at the pillow and sheet hem will wear through far, far sooner than the rest of the sheet. If you have bought expensive sheets for special occasions only, you will be using them infrequently and you can launder them gently; thus they will last. But when you are buying sheets for hard everyday use and are trying to make economical decisions, your best bet is to choose sheets without these features.

Whites Versus Colors and Prints. The colored and print sheets in linen stores are often as hard-wearing as they are beautiful. In fact, they are so widely appreciated and so reliably used to advantage that I feel I need to add only a word of praise for the now-overlooked plain white ones. White sheets do not fade. If they are made of a fiber that can take hot water and bleach, you can also keep them white and spotless for many years. Most colored and print cotton sheets tend to fade; polyester and polyester blends tend to be more resistant to fading. Some prints and colors are bleachable, but the bleaching will hasten the fading; unless you wash all pieces of a set at the same time in the same loads, some will fade at different rates from others and they will no longer look good together. Off-white and unbleached muslin and other cotton and linen sheets present similar problems. They may come to look dingy over time or begin to lighten with continued laundering. Unbleached linen inevitably whitens over time. You can brighten off-whites and unbleached sets with bleaching, but then you must be sure to do all pieces of the set together or they will turn different shades of off-white. Eventually you will end up with either white or dingy sheets.

The colored, satin-stitched scalloped edging on some cotton sheets has never faded perceptibly in my experience, even with chlorine bleaching. (But you should follow care labels or test the fabric for bleach-fastness before resorting to bleach.) I also find that if you pick your prints carefully and take care to launder sets together, fading may not look bad or may not be noticeable. The bright blue stripes on a blue-and-white-striped sheet, for example, my objectively become less bright blue but do not look washed out. The real problem is dealing with stains: strong stain removers and chlorine bleach may create uneven lightened areas in the print.

There is no denying that white cotton, without wrinkle treatments, is easiest to use and to keep looking good. It is also convenient not to have to worry about matching bottom sheets with top sheets and pillowcases, or with spreads, comforters, and other aspects of the bedroom. White is the color of choice for those who have no time. In fact, because of its launderability I prefer it even for children's bedding. The idea that prints "hide" stains and dirty marks has never really been convincing to me; I find that I see them quite well and that the need to protect the color of the print often interferes with removing marks effectively. Thus, although I find prints hard to resist, I have moved gradually during a very busy period of my life to white and bleachable mostly white bedding of all sorts. If you decide to go with white, you can compensate with plenty of colors and prints in area rugs, spreads or quilts, artwork, wallpaper or wall paint, and the like.

Comfortable Sheets

It is more important to choose comfort in your sheets than in any other fabric you buy, except, possibly, your underwear. A number of factors affect the comfort of a sheet, and some of them are highly subjective. Do not be unduly swayed in your choices by the fads of the day.

Hand: Silky Soft or Crisp? My best friend dearly loves sleeping in silky smooth, softly draping, lustrous sheets; sateen sheets answering to this taste are available in ever-greater variety and in several types of fiber. In some stores offering high-end goods, it is hard to find sheets that are not sateen. Still, I prefer crisp, plain-weave sheets. My friend's luxurious sheets caress the skin, but they also cling closer to the body, which means that they prevent air from circulating in the little tunnels and valleys that form between your skin and a crisper sheet. The silky feeling can transform into a clammy one, especially if you are the sort of person who perspires a great deal. Satiny sheets also tend to slide all over you. Sometimes this produces a hot feeling, perhaps because of the airless friction of skin against moving, clinging cloth. Satin-weave sheets, moreover, do not let air in or out well, which aggravates the problem.

Still, if you are one of those to whom a silky hand and a soft, light drape appeal, some of the beautiful all-cotton, high thread count sateen sheets are just what you want. Although you can often find some good buys in these, I wore holes in a costly set of them in three years—a short life for a costly sheet—and they grayed early but could not be chlorine-bleached (presumably because the fine exposed threads in the floats would have been damaged, the luster would have been lost, or, perhaps, the holes would have come even sooner).

Real silk satin sheets, which are extremely costly, are highly absorbent and skin-friendly in many ways. However, they are quite warm, and their care labels sometimes call for dry cleaning; they cannot be bleached or subjected to the vigorous laundering you may need to give to sheets. If this type of sheet is your ideal, perhaps you could have a set for "good" or for special occasions, just as once upon a time the real linen sheets were kept for important days and people. Avoid "satin" sheets made of polyester. Polyester, which is unabsorbent, is not a desirable fiber for sheeting.

Those who prefer a crisper or cottony smoothness in sheets will always love, as I do, good combed all-cotton percale with a thread count between 180 and 250—the standard luxury sheet of the prior generation. (At higher thread counts, you lose crispness.) It provides superior comfort, durability, and launderability at lower prices. All-cotton sheets with lower thread counts are no longer sold, which is a shame because fine muslin sheets (thread count 140) also excel in crisp comfort and durability.* Cotton/polyester blends, which have replaced muslin in the low end of the market, are wrinkle-resistant but have a slightly scratchy or harsh hand that is less pleasant than that of all-cotton sheets. Wrinkle-resistant, all-cotton percale sheets with moderate thread counts have a better hand than cotton/polyester sheets, although there is a faint rubbery quality to them.

Cotton flannel and knit sheets offer you more softness without crispness, which is just what some people want. Consider lightweight cotton knits for summer and flannels for winter. (But cotton knits sometimes have inconvenient laundering instructions. See "Launderability of Sheets," below.) Even if you generally prefer a crisp sheet, you might find you enjoy the warmth of flannel in winter. If aged percale is what you love best, you can even buy prewashed percale, which has lost its initial crispness. I find it annoying, how-

---

*When I discovered, to my amazement, that you could no longer buy a plain, all-cotton muslin sheet, I happened to mention this to my aunt, a chronic overstocker. Stored on her shelf were several high-quality muslin sheets that she had bought some thirty years earlier in Macy's and A & S in Brooklyn, and she sent them to me, still in their original packages, unopened. I have been using them for a few years now, laundering them with the strongest methods. They are extremely comfortable, snowy white, and appear to be indestructible. White muslin sheets, if you could get hold of any, would be an excellent bet for children's beds.

ever, to pay more for sheets that are slightly worn and would rather wear them soft myself.

The queen of fibers when it comes to sheets is real linen (flax), the fiber that gave bed "linens" their name. If real linen sheets sound or look dreamy to you but you have not tried them, do not expect satiny smoothness or silky softness. Linen is very crisp and, until much laundered, rather stiff. If cotton sateen appeals to you, linen probably will not. It is highly absorbent, and although good linen fabric is exceedingly smooth and lustrous, its greater body and crispness gives it something of the quality of good muslin. Like muslin, it softens with age, wears like iron (if of good quality), and wrinkles easily. Many people, including me, like it best of all sheeting. Much of the appeal of linen and muslin to their fans is that because they are crisp they let air in and out, do not cling, and do not slide all over you, as satiny sheets do.

Absorbency. Absorbency is one of the chief factors affecting the comfort of sheets. Linen (flax) sheets are most absorbent, but all-cotton sheets that have received no resin treatments are also highly absorbent. Polyester is unabsorbent and thus uncomfortable in sheets, which are going to have your perspiring bare skin and body weight pressed against them for hours and hours. One hundred percent polyester sheets are rarely marketed for adults, but I have often seen all-polyester crib sheets. All-cotton knit crib sheets, which do not need ironing either, are a much better choice.

Cotton/polyester blend sheets are superior to all-polyester sheets—the hand is better, and they are more absorbent. They come in both expensive and inexpensive styles. I know many people who find them indistinguishable from cotton, but I believe that those who perspire heavily can tell the difference readily and are likely to find them uncomfortable. Trading wrinkles for comfort is a bad bargain—better just to let the sheets wrinkle and feel comfortable.

Generally speaking, very light, fine, or flimsy sheets are less absorbent than those with more body simply because there is less fiber present to absorb moisture.

Warmth. Cold sheets are less of a problem in today's warmer houses and apartments. You can always add warmth to the bed by means of blankets or comforters or nightclothes and need not rely on your sheets. If your bedroom gets very cold, however, cotton flannel sheets are best. Flannel and knit sheets do not have that initial icy feeling that is so unpleasant in a cold bedroom. Nor do polyester, polyester-blend, and silk sheets, which are all generally less cool than cotton. The coolest sheets of all are lightweight linen (flax). All-combed-cotton percale sheets are also very cool. In general, finer, lighter sheets are cooler than those of heavier weights. Cotton sheets that feel icy in winter when you first get in bed will quickly feel warm again, but you can put a hot water bottle in the bed to take off the initial chill, especially at the feet. A heating pad will do the same thing, but you have to remember to turn it off.

Decorative Stitching. Decorative stitching can be scratchy or make uncomfortable ridges on your pillowcase or sheet. When buying pillowcases, look to see that embroidery, lace, or cutwork is positioned on the pillowcase in places where your face will not rest upon it. You can also choose to use plain pillowcases on your sleeping pillow and save fancy work for decorative pillows. Simple hem stitching will not affect your comfort, but the stitching will wear out and tear long before the rest of the pillowcase.

Launderability and Ironing

Launderability of Sheets. Irresponsible merchandising seems to have bred a generation of people who expend time and money on sheets that are much more trouble than they need to be. In the time-pressed household, this can matter. Everyone needs everyday sheets that can take vigorous laundering (the particulars of which are described below). No one should buy everyday bedding that must be dry-cleaned. Dry cleaning is expensive, inconvenient, and does not remove mite allergens. Moreover, you press your face into your bedding, and this might expose you to drycleaning fluid fumes that are not healthy to breathe.

Sheets must be changed and washed vigorously once a week or more often if they stop smelling or feeling fresh. It is not a bad idea to change pillowcases twice a week or sometimes more often, as they soil faster than the sheets, particularly in hot weather or when you are perspiring from illness or other causes. Crib sheets for infants should be changed daily or more often if they become soiled. Do not forget that sheets lie next to your skin hour after hour, night after night. They receive saliva, perspiration, body oils and more intimate fluids, skin flakes, and any soil on your body. Sometimes you bleed on them. You sometimes get sick in your bed, and sick people and the very young may be incontinent. Children's beds are subject to a miscellany of stains and spills, including cough syrup and colored medicines. Therefore, your everyday sheets, especially those on infants' and children's beds, should be easy to launder vigorously and should never require gentle or complicated treatment. Sheets should be colorfast. You should not have to wash sheets separately. Nor should you have to try to clean them with gentle soaps or detergents. For reasons of health (to decrease the risks of allergies and infections), to remove stains, and to keep the sheets really clean and bright or snowy white, you should be able to wash them in hot water with strong detergent and, in my opinion, chlorine or other strong bleach—even on print or colored sheets—as necessary to sanitize and to remove stains and dirt.

Your sheets should shrink only minimally with hot-water washing and drying on the regular setting. You should be able to dry them in the dryer or on the line, as you wish. If sheets are not preshrunk, insist on knowing how much they will shrink and buy them big enough to fit after shrinkage.

The care label you want on sheets will either say all this or may say simply

"Machine-washable," which implies most of it. Whatever the care label says, plain white cotton percale sheets (preshrunk and not subjected to wrinkle-resistance treatments or other resin treatments) can be laundered in the way you need to launder them. Wrinkle-treated sheets, cotton/polyester sheets, and colored and print sheets sometimes have care labels saying "No bleach" or "No chlorine bleach" or "Wash warm." Check care labels, decide if you believe them (see chapter 2), and decide if the sheets are worth it to you, given these limitations. My white cotton knit twin-size sheets, which I am sorry I bought, had a care label that specified cold water, gentle detergent, no bleach of any sort, and tumbling dry on the low setting—everything that a care label on a sheet should not say. (And even with cold-water washing the sheets shrank, so if you are considering buying any, you might try getting them a size too large.) On the other hand, I ignored the care label on white cotton knit crib sheets and laundered them with regular detergent and chlorine bleach, and encountered no mishap other than shrinking. By the time my son had outgrown the crib, the crib mattress had so outgrown the sheets that it took both my husband and me to stretch them on. But I would buy them again anyway; these crib sheets feel so warm and soft that they are perfect for a baby's skin.

Cotton/polyester sheets launder less well than all-cotton. They tend to hold body oils and as a result sometimes yellow or develop a stale odor. They may pill as well. (For curing or preventing such problems, refer to chapter 22, "The Man-Made Fibers and Blends," pages 369–70.)

My impression is that when you are buying sheets and towels it is often safest to buy them from manufacturers that specialize in making linens and towels rather than from "designer" companies. Designer sheets and towels, more often than those from specialized manufacturers, have poor durability, fade, and have care labels calling for inappropriate laundering procedures. In everyday linens, beauty, practicality, and quality go together. Do not trust a maker who forces you to choose between them.

No-Iron Sheets; Wrinkly Sheets. Cotton/polyester blend sheets have the highest wrinkle-resistance. Resin-treated all-cotton sheets have varying degrees of resistance to wrinkling, some a lot and some a little; their wrinkle-resistance diminishes as they age. Knit and flannel sheets are naturally wrinkle-resistant.

Untreated all-cotton and linen woven sheets wrinkle considerably. Traditionally, therefore, they were always ironed. Sleeping on fresh, ironed sheets is one of life's treats, but ironed sheets are not necessary to health or comfort. If you are hard-pressed for time or have better things to do, feel free to laugh loudly at the thought. Certainly, it is gracious to give a guest ironed sheets. Giving them to yourself for special nights, or anytime you particularly need rest or simply feel like making your room look especially good, is pleasant too. But if you do not want to iron sheets—and this does take time unless you have a mangle—don't conclude that you must buy wrinkle-resistant sheets. Wrinkled cotton or linen sheets look fine. Cover them with a day spread if they do not look fine to you. When you are sleeping in the dark, you'll like the way they feel and you won't be able to see them, and wrinkled cotton tends to smooth out as you sleep on it. (To reduce wrinkles without ironing, see chapter 6, "Ironing," page 112, and chapter 13, "Fabrics That Work," page 193.)

Blankets and Comforters

In blankets, you look for functional qualities such as warmth, comfortable weight, a pleasant hand, durability, and static and pilling resistance. Assuming you do not use the blanket next to your skin, absorbency is less important in a blanket than a sheet.

Blankets that are used in the traditional way—layered between sheet and cover—need laundering or cleaning less frequently than sheets, but if you sleep with the blanket next to the skin, you will need launderable blankets that can be washed and changed in the same manner and on the same schedule as your sheets. If you want to avoid breathing drycleaning fumes, avoid blankets that need dry cleaning. If you are worried about allergies, choose only blankets that can be frequently laundered in hot water. Read care labels carefully. When high launderability is your main concern, especially if you want to use hot water, cotton blankets in colorfast colors or white are superior to wool, acrylic, nylon, or comforters. Some wool blankets are washable, but do not purchase a wool blanket expecting to wash it frequently. A polyester blanket will probably be fine with frequent laundering, but you may be forced to second-guess the care labels—it may tell you to use warm or cool wash water.

Some people sleep better with a blanket that has some weight, but those who want a lightweight warm blanket should try acrylic, polyester, or nylon. Acrylic and polyester sometimes pill, which looks and feels unpleasant, but they will keep you warm even if they do pill. The synthetics also tend to develop static electricity, which can start you off in the morning with flyaway hair. Wool, properly cared for, will look good and function well without pilling for a very long time. It drapes to the body better than synthetics. When the atmosphere is very dry, it will develop a little static but less than synthetics. Some wool blankets are soft, smooth, or even fairly silky; others are thick and scratchy. Synthetics tend to feel soft and smooth and fluffier, never scratchy.

When you want only a little warmth, a thin cotton blanket or cotton "thermal" blanket is best. The latter are made in a knit or waffle or honeycomb weave. Such weaves are also available in wool, acrylic, polyester, and blends. All are machine-washable (except, perhaps, the wool), but the synthetics may not take hotter water temperatures. Be sure cotton is preshrunk.

Conventional blankets of both natural and synthetic fibers are usually, but not always, napped to produce the comfortable, fuzzy, warmth-holding surface. In cold weather, wool blankets are quite warm, as are quilts. Acrylic blankets are warm, sometimes even warmer than wool. Use two or three blankets for greater warmth, or a down-filled comforter. Or use a blanket plus a comforter for frigid quarters. You may read in newspaper articles or advertisements that a comforter will keep you warm in the winter and cool in the summer. Remember, however, that a comforter is a sack filled with down or some other insulating filler and that covering yourself with it will always make you warm. If you do not find a down-filled jacket comfortable in August, a down-filled comforter will not seem so either. I would not recommend creating a bedroom routine and decor overly dependent upon a comforter that will not be comfortable for half the year. If you are using a comforter or duvet, choose its weight carefully. In any city apartment I have ever lived, a lightweight down comforter was too warm even in winter, but in a cold Midwestern house the same comforter was delightful.

Electric blankets can be a godsend in very cold bedrooms. They are not for children, however, and even adults must use them with care.

Changing and Laundering Linens: When and Why

Long tradition dictates changing sheets and laundering them once a week. This should be considered a minimum. And if you or your mate perspires heavily or if ill-health causes you to spend extra time in bed, twice a week, or even more often, makes more sense. When you are spending all day in bed recuperating, you can change the sheets daily (or ask someone else to do it). Likewise, if you make extra use of your bed for any reason—you like to work there on your laptop, you read or watch television there, or you snack there—you may need to change the sheets more often than once a week.

Because your pillowcase becomes soiled faster than your sheets, you might want to consider changing only your pillowcases twice a week rather than once. If you use no top sheet, it is probably best that you wash whatever bedding is next to your skin on the same schedule that you follow for sheets.

Launder pillow covers (the zip-up ones under the pillowcases), mattress covers and pads, blankets, and comforter covers once a month or more often (once a week, or as frequently as the doctor orders, for asthmatics or other allergy sufferers).

Once or twice a year or more often if they become soiled, launder and change the allergen-proof undercovers, if any, on the mattress and on the pillows. (See "Bedclothes: Making the Bed," below.)

Assuming that allergens are not a problem (you have no allergies or you use allergen-proof undercovers), you need to wash pillows and comforters when they smell stale or unpleasant, when they look dirty, or when you have reason to know that they are not clean—typically about once a year or even less often.

From time to time, turn the mattress and flip it over. Traditionally, mattresses were aired and sunned twice a year, in spring and fall. This kills mites and dis-

> ## WHY YOU WASH YOUR UNDERBEDDING AND PILLOWS
>
> Sheets help keep mattress pads and covers and blankets clean, but the protection is not absolute. The oils and perspiration to some extent get through the sheets; the mattress cover or pad and blanket eventually get soiled, and over the years so does the mattress. The more frequently you wash the sheets, the better your chance of keeping the next layer clean, and the more often you wash that layer, the longer the mattress remains clean.
>
> Pillows get even dirtier than other parts of the bed and bedding. Your eyes tear on the case; your mouth drools on it; your face, which is sweatier and oilier than the rest of you, rubs against it; your hair, which is often dirtier than your face, also rubs against it. And since your nose is pushed into the pillow all night long, you have to make sure you wash your pillow when it is soiled and wash its cases and covers frequently.

courages molds and funguses. Pillows need to be aired and sunned more often. Urban dwellers can try to make up for the impossibility of sunning and airing bedding by careful use and laundering of mattress and pillow undercovers and by diligent vacuuming of pillows, mattress pads, and mattresses.

If you dress the bed properly, you should never need to wash the ticking on your mattress. But if it is soiled by a spill or accident, you would clean it as you would any upholstery. The main thing is not to soak it and to be extremely careful not to get the interior wet; otherwise you might get molding or rotting inside.

If you have throw rugs or small carpets in your bedroom, take them out for sunning and airing now and then if that is possible.

Keep Bedding Mite- and Allergen-Free. The most important precaution you can take in the battle against dust mites and their allergens is to use mite- and allergen-proof covers for pillows, mattresses, box springs, and comforters. These can be ordered from companies that specialize in allergy-control products, and they can be found in many stores that sell household linens. Vinyl and plastic were once used for this purpose, but they are uncomfortable. Newer materials prevent mites and allergens from passing through yet are water-vapor permeable, soft, and comfortable, with a luxurious hand; they are available in a range of prices. It seems wise to use them on all beds, whether or not anyone in your family is now mite-sensitive.

In addition, it is advisable to wash sheets, pillowcases, blankets, and mattress covers with hot water—over 130°F; higher is better. Wash bedroom curtains the same way. Even cool wash temperatures will remove dust-mite allergens, but only hot water will kill the mites. Dry cleaning will also kill the mites, but it will not remove the allergens. See chapter 10, "Sanitizing the Laundry," pages 151–52.

If you use allergen-impermeable pillow covers, it probably does not matter whether you use synthetic, feather, or down pillows, but we all should follow our doctors' advice. It is worth noting, because allergic people are often advised to use polyester pillows rather than feather or down ones, that two studies raise questions about the superiority of polyester pillows when it comes to allergens and allergic reactions. One found that there was a substantially lower risk of serious asthmatic attacks among children using feather pillows than among children using polyester ones.[1] The other found that after six months of use, new polyester pillows contained about eight times as many dust-mite allergens as new feather pillows—a significant difference.[2] Do not use foam rubber pillows, which can support the growth of mold, further aggravating allergies.

Dressing and Making the Bed

A friend of mine remembers being counseled by her elderly aunt long ago that even if she found herself in poverty or sickness she should always make a good bed for herself. Not only is this advice as good today as it was then, the bed that was good then is still good today, too, since people discovered the secrets of good bed-making many centuries ago.

The minimum well-dressed contemporary bed has a mattress for softness (and box springs or some other undermattress to make the bed less hard), which is encased in a cover for cleanliness and comfort. The sleeper lies on a sheet, which serves the dual function of protecting the skin from the scratchiness of the mattress or mattress cover and preventing the deposit of skin oils and perspiration on the mattress. There is also a sheet above the sleeper, and this, too, serves a double function, protecting the skin from the scratchy blanket and protecting the blanket from the skin oils and perspiration of the skin. The sleeper's head rests on a pillow covered in a case, which does the same two jobs as the sheets. On top of the sheets there is a blanket or two—or a quilt or comforter—to keep the sleeper warm. During the day, when no one is sleeping, a decorative cloth covers the whole arrangement, keeping it clean and making it look beautiful while not in use. All this was also true of the bed of any person of means in twelfth-century France. Museums have Renaissance paintings of beds made up just like yours.

Bedclothes: Making the Bed. To dress a modern bed, you need the following items:

Protectors and covers for mattresses and pillows
　　Allergen-impermeable undercovers for mattresses, pillows, and duvets
　　　or comforters (optional)
　　Mattress pad or cover
　　Pillow protector or cover (zip-up type that goes under the pillowcase)

Skin-contact linens
  Bottom sheet
  Top sheet
  Pillowcase

Warmth-providing covers
  Blankets and quilts, comforter, or duvet
  Day cover for dust
  Blanket cover, coverlet, or bedspread (counterpane)

You may wish to enclose your pillows, comforters, and mattresses in allergen-impermeable undercovers. These are made of fabrics coated with a polymer membrane that is permeable only to water vapor and heat and prevents dust mites, allergens, and other fine particles from passing through. Such undercovers are indispensable for the bed of anyone who suffers from asthma or other allergies as well as on the beds of all children as a preventive measure.

Next, on the beds of the incontinent or ill or of children still of an age to wet the bed, place a rubberized cotton waterproof sheet or some other type of waterproof shield. This prevents the mattress from getting soaked. (If the mattress does become soaked, you can never really get it clean again. You can try the upholstery shampooing machine that injects and then extracts moisture, but this may not be entirely successful.) The all-plastic waterproof shields are less comfortable than the rubberized cotton.

Over the waterproof sheet, or, if there is none, directly on top of the allergenic undercover, or, if there is none, directly on the mattress, you place a mattress cover, a mattress pad plus a cover, or a padded mattress cover. This is to keep the mattress clean and places an additional layer of absorbent, skin-friendly material between you and the mattress, which is likely to be made of a less comfortable synthetic fiber. All-cotton mattress pads with cotton stuffing are sometimes hard to find, but they are preferable. You may think that only the princess in the fairy tale could detect through her sheet whether the mattress pad, or its stuffing, was made of polyester. It is true that many people cannot, or don't mind even if they can. But do not conclude that you cannot unless you give it an all-night test. What feels comfortable for a minute or two might not after a few hours.

On each pillow, place a zippered muslin cover—also called a "pillow protector"—directly next to the ticking if you are not using an allergen-proof undercover, or over the allergen-proof undercover if you are using one. (Yes, this means two covers and you haven't even gotten to the pillowcase yet.) Place the zipper of the muslin pillow protector at the opposite end from the zipper of the allergenic undercover. Then pull the pillowcase over the pillow protector, placing the open or buttoning end of the case opposite the zippered end of the pillow protector. This helps keep the pillow and its contents clean longer.

Then, in the manner described below, put on the bottom sheet, the top sheet, a blanket or comforter or other warm cover, and finally the bedspread (also called a counterpane), quilt, or other day cover. Tuck in all sheets and blankets snugly and smoothly. Wrinkles and folds are uncomfortable to sleep on and look unsightly. Use sheets with a generous allowance for tucking to anchor them securely so they do not pull out when you are sleeping; this helps you sleep better and saves you labor making up the bed when you get up. (For recommended tucking allowances and information on sheet sizes, see pages 199, 202.)

How to Make the Bed

Fitted Bottom Sheet. Lay the sheet right side up. For a fitted sheet the only trick is to use enough muscle power. Walk from one corner of the bed to the next, pulling the elasticized corner of the sheet over the corner of the mattress. If the sheet has shrunk, try doing diagonally opposite corners first, as this will hold the sheet in place better while you struggle with the other two. Let the weight of the mattress work for you to stretch the sheet by lifting the mattress corner enough to get the sheet corner on, then letting go. Be sure to purchase preshrunk fitted sheets; if you have deep mattresses, buy sheets that have "deep pockets" or "universal" or "high-contour" corners.

Flat Bottom Sheet. A flat bottom sheet is tucked under with mitered or "hospital" corners on all four corners. (See instructions for mitered corners below.) The selvages on the long sides of the sheet go along the sides of the bed, the wider hem goes at the head of the bed, and the narrower hem goes at the bottom. (Because sheets wear more at the top of the bed, my Italian grandmother sometimes put the sheets on with the foot at the head and vice versa, for more even wear.)

Top Sheet. Assuming that you have folded the top sheet according to the directions in chapter 7, "Folding Clothes and Linens," you now unfold the folds parallel to the selvage ends and lay the sheet, with the crosswise folds still folded, across the width of the bed, in its center. Then grasp the two loose corners of the hem nearest you and give the sheet a flick; it will unfurl, with the wide hem at the top and the narrow hem at the bottom. If the sheet is a print, it should be placed wrong side up so that when the top hem is folded down over the blanket, the print shows its right side. Fold under and miter the two corners at the foot of the bed.

Mitered or "Hospital" Corners. A properly mitered sheet corner will both look neater and stay securely tucked while you sleep, keeping you comfortable and making the job of making the bed the next day much easier. First, tuck in the bottom edge of the sheet. Then pick up the corner of the sheet (the place on

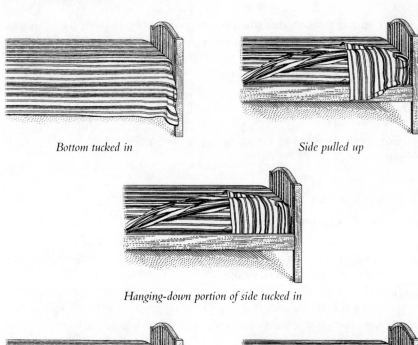

Bottom tucked in   *Side pulled up*

Hanging-down portion of side tucked in

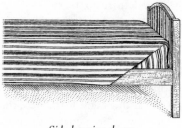

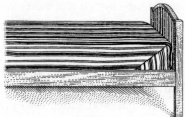

Side hanging down   *Tuck-in of entire side of sheet
(optional on top sheet)*

How to make "mitered" or "hospital" corners

the side edge of the sheet directly opposite the top corner of the mattress) between the thumb and forefinger of one hand, and bring the corner around to the side of the bed. Put the side of the sheet up on the bed, out of your way, for a moment. Tuck in the part of the sheet that is left hanging down while you hold the corner taut at the side of the bed. Let the corner fall and tuck under the side of the sheet near the foot of the bed. The corner is now mitered. (Some people prefer to leave the side of the top sheet untucked.)

Blankets, Quilts, and Comforters or Duvets. If you intend to use one or more blankets, you put them on now. Put on the blanket, right side up, over the top sheet so that the top of the blanket comes to a point about 6 to 10 inches from the head of the bed. Tuck the blanket in at the foot and make corners at the bottom, as for sheets. Then fold down the top sheet over the blanket. You should have a generous portion of the sheet turned down so as to protect the blanket from body soils and odors. If you like, you can tuck the blanket and top sheet under at the sides of the mattress; but this is a matter of taste. You may, if you wish, add a second top sheet or some other thin, light spread on top of the blanket. This adds a modest degree of weight and warmth and helps keep the blanket clean. Or, in summer, you can use a second sheet in place of a blanket.

Comforters (duvets) are usually left untucked because they are too thick (and sometimes too narrow or too short) for tucking. Some people use no cover over the comforter. Quilts, too, may be used like blankets, under a spread or coverlet, or may be used decoratively as the final cover on the bed.

Day Cover. Finally, place the day cover—a blanket cover, coverlet, or bed-spread—on the bed to protect the bedclothes from dust and soil and to look good. A bedspread, which used to be used in most homes but is now much less common, may or may not come all the way to the floor. (If it does, it is not used with a dust ruffle.) Although some people sleep under a bedspread for warmth, you may wish to remove it when you sleep, folding it over a rack or placing it over a chair or chest; some people simply fold it neatly at the foot of the bed. If you use a dust ruffle on your bed frame, you usually use a blanket cover or a coverlet over the blanket (or over the comforter or quilt) instead of a bedspread. A blanket cover or coverlet comes down only to the edge of the bed frame, leaving the dust ruffle showing.

Finishing the Bed. Once the day cover is spread evenly and smoothly over the bed, you put the pillows in their cases and finish the bed in any style you like. A very common contemporary style is to fold the top sheet over the comforter or blanket cover, leaving two, four, or more pillows showing at the top of the bed. Any pillows that are not for sleeping are often covered with decorative cases.

Some old-fashioned ways of finishing the bed, which give more daytime protection to the pillows, are these:

- Fold the spread over the top sheet fold line, allowing about three feet of it to be turned down. Put the pillows in place, then fold the cover back over the pillows.
- Fold the pillows in half, then push the open-edge sides against the headboard snugly so that they do not unroll. Then cover the pillows with the spread, tucking them in behind.

Variations. In temperate weather, sometimes you are most comfortable using two top sheets and no blanket. In cooler weather, when you are using a blanket it may still be useful to use two top sheets, as described above. The extra sheet adds less warmth and weight than a second blanket but may keep you

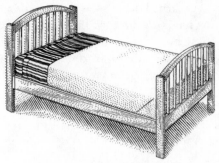

*Blanket on bed with sheet folded
over top edge of blanket*

Bed with bedspread

*Blanket cover with pillows exposed and sheet
turned down over blanket cover*

just warm enough. If you use the second sheet, you may put it on top of the blanket to keep the blanket clean longer.

I do not favor the new style of using no top sheet. People who do this simply spread a comforter or duvet, with or without a removable cover, over the bottom sheet. Or even if they make a more traditional bed for themselves, this simpler bed is what they provide for their children. The main attraction of this ascetic habit is that in the morning the bed can be fixed in an instant simply by pulling the comforter up, or even leaving it attractively rumpled— a system quick enough for the busiest parent and easy enough even for very young children.

The habit of voluntarily forgoing a top sheet to avoid the trouble of pulling up a second one in the morning would have been unfathomable to countless poor people who, over long centuries, could only dream of the luxury of two sheets. I admit that it is unfathomable to me too. This is one of those shortcuts that actually cost a lot in time and trouble and gain you very little. There are concrete reasons to use a top sheet: it is more comfortable, cleaner, and more convenient.

Sheets are designed to be comfortable next to your skin, and there are many different types of sheets to suit many different tastes. (See pages 205–8.) Blankets and quilts and comforter covers are not; they are less skin-friendly, not really being intended for this. Not only are sheets—good ones—meant to feel good on your skin, they are meant to save you the trouble of having to launder your blankets or other warm covers every week or more often.

You can wash sheets—good ones—often and vigorously and easily, but many blankets and comforters are hard to launder or must be sent out to be laundered in commercial-size machines. (See chapter 8, "How to Launder Tricky Items.") Laundering also makes comforters and blankets age quickly—they fade, bunch up, grow thin and spindly, pill, or even pull apart; and they are expensive. Cotton and synthetic blankets are fairly easy to wash, but even they do not hold up to laundering nearly as well as sheets do, and they cost more than sheets. You might think that your comforter is protected by its cover and thus will stay cleaner, but the fewer protective layers between you and your comforter, the more often you are going to have to wash it. Comforter covers, too, often do not launder easily or well, and are nearly always bizarrely costly for what they are. (You can easily make one by stitching together a couple of sheets of the right size, and putting on snaps or ties to close the opening.) If you are going to use a comforter or duvet cover and you do not use a top sheet, keep three covers for each comforter, and change and launder the cover once a week or more often. (If you do not use a comforter cover, the comforter itself will need frequent washing.)

Although doing without a top sheet may save you a few seconds straightening the bed in the morning, it costs you time washing duvet covers, comforters, blankets, or quilts, for these will definitely become soiled and odorous quickly. In my view, the long-term savings in bed-making time is not worth the cost in laundering, bedding replacement costs (when the appearance or function is damaged by frequent laundering), or loss of comfort. It would be far better to have a more traditional bed and simply not worry about getting it perfectly smooth on rushed mornings: pull up the bedding, throw on the cover, and go.

Dust Ruffles. Dust ruffles (or valances) for beds are ruffles or pleated cloth sewn onto a rectangle of cloth. You lay the rectangle between the mattress and the box springs, and the ruffles or pleats hang down to the floor, covering the box springs and bed frame. They are there to make the bed look attractive, and they are entirely optional. If you find them difficult to take off and replace for laundering, just do without. If you need to cover the sides of your bed entirely, get a spread or other cover that reaches nearly to the floor. Vacuuming dust ruffles regularly will make laundering necessary less often.

Turning Down the Bed at Night. When you turn down the bed at night, you first fold down or remove the day cover; fold it over a rack or the footboard of the bed, or lay it neatly somewhere. Then turn back the corner of the top sheet and blanket in a diagonal fold deep enough to permit someone to insert herself or himself, as into a pocket, without untucking the bedding. This makes the bed feel more welcoming. You can turn down the bed for children or yourself, say before your bath, so that it looks inviting when you come back ready to turn in. Or if you are first in bed, you can turn down the other side for your mate.

Miscellaneous Bed Manners. For both physical and psychological reasons, a bed treated with respect will be fresher and will more readily induce sleep. Old-fashioned bed manners forbade sitting on a bed in street clothes, especially someone else's bed and most especially a sick person's bed. If you lie down on a made-up bed for your afternoon nap, cover the bedspread with something you can readily launder. Otherwise, wash your face, undress, and crawl between the sheets. Don't put bags, purses, briefcases, shoes, and similar things on the bed. They have been on too many floors, sidewalks, and other questionable places.

16

Textile Furnishings: Carpets, Rugs, and Upholstery

About rugs and carpets . . . Fiber qualities . . . Effect of structure: tufted and woven carpets . . . Pests . . . Chemical emissions . . . Preserving carpets and rugs with good household habits . . . Shampooing carpets . . . Stains and spills . . . Cleaning valuable antiques, Oriental rugs, and delicate carpets . . . Safeguards for delicate carpets . . . Shampooing delicate carpets . . . Spills and stains on delicate carpets . . . Caring for rugs made of rushes, grasses, sisal, and similar materials . . . Upholstery . . . Preventing soiling of and damage to upholstery . . . Shampooing upholstery . . . Leather upholstery . . . Draperies . . . Lampshades, dusting lampshades, cleaning fabric shades by immersion and parchment and plastic shades by nonimmersion methods . . . Glossary of Rugs and Carpets . . . Guide to Carpet and Upholstery Stain Removal

All furnishings made of textiles require the same basic care. They must be vacuumed at frequent intervals and washed or dry-cleaned at less frequent ones. The frequency with which you vacuum and clean them will vary according to the type of fabric and the level of use they receive. By vacuuming regularly you not only extend the life of your furnishings, but also increase the intervals between the times when you will need to subject them to the laborious, and sometimes expensive, ordeal of shampooing or dry cleaning.

About Rugs and Carpets

The purpose of fabric floor coverings is to provide a softer, more beautiful, more comfortable surface for walking, standing, and, sometimes, sitting, and to act as an insulator for noise and warmth. They are also used to protect a hard surface such as wood or marble from wear. How a carpet looks, feels, and wears, and how easy or hard it is to maintain, are determined both by the fiber from which it is made and the construction of the fabric. (The terms "rugs" and "carpets" are for the most part used interchangeably, but there is some tendency to use "rugs" to refer to smaller floor coverings.)

Fiber Qualities. Ninety-nine percent of all carpets today are made of synthetic materials. Silk and cotton are rarely used for floor coverings because they lack resilience and, for this purpose, sufficient durability. Wool, which is the most expensive carpet fiber commonly in use, accounts for only 0.6 percent of domestic carpet manufacture—a dramatic change from 1950, when wool accounted for 97 percent. Nonetheless, the finest rugs are still made of wool, and all carpeting still strives to match the appearance and qualities of wool carpeting. Wool is durable and does not attract static, dyes beautifully and subtly, feels soft and pleasant, has a natural luster, and is wonderfully resilient—it springs back when stepped on. In appearance, none of the synthetics can match wool. Wool's appearance and its good functional qualities are a combination that has so far proved unbeatable, despite the many excellences of synthetics and the many flaws of wool. Wool weakens and bleaches with prolonged exposure to light. Although it is not particularly prone to mildew, it will mildew if left damp. It can be attacked by the larvae of moths and carpet beetles. Wool holds dirt, is less stain-resistant than synthetics, retains odors, and is not easy to clean.

All of the major synthetic fibers used for carpets—nylon, polyester, polypropylene, and acrylic—are more stain-resistant than wool because they are relatively unabsorbent. A water-based spill can often be wiped off carpets made of synthetic fibers, although they are prone to being stained by oils. None of them will be attacked by moths or beetles. They also resist abrasion better. Nylon is extremely durable and can take a great deal of bending and twisting without breaking. Polyester is less durable than nylon. Some types of polyester, nylon, and acrylic tend to pill when abraded. Unless they receive an antistatic treatment, many types of nylon, acrylic, and polyester will develop a static-electricity charge; this is annoying and uncomfortable and attracts lint and dirt. Polypropylene has good resistance to pilling and static, but it is less resilient than nylon.

The ability of carpets to withstand exposure to light is an important factor in their durability. Synthetics that have been solution dyed will have excellent colorfastness to light. Natural fibers have varying degrees of colorfastness. As for the fibers themselves, polyester and acrylic are most resistant to ultraviolet rays. Nylon and wool fibers—the one the most common and the other the most beautiful and expensive of carpet fibers—both have poor resistance to light. Silk and polypropylene fibers have the lowest resistance of all. See chapter 13, "Fabrics That Work," pages 183–84.

Effect of Structure. Both tufted and woven carpets can give good wear, but, other things being equal, woven rugs are generally considered more desirable than nonwoven or tufted carpets, and they are more expensive. (See "Tufted carpets" and "Woven carpets" in the Glossary of Rugs and Carpets, pages 239 and 240.) The design of woven carpets is often preferred. With a woven rug in high-traffic areas, you needn't worry about yarns getting pulled out, as you must with tufted carpets. And woven rugs, unlike tufted carpets, do not need a secondary backing, which can present wear problems of its own. (The layers can separate, for example. See the illustration on page 239.) But other things may not be equal: a well-made tufted carpet of good design and material will be superior to a poorly made woven one.

The denser the carpet, the better it wears—that is, the more closely the tufts occur to one another or the more yarn in the pile weave, the more durable the carpet. Carpets with a thicker pile wear better than those with a thinner pile. Carpets whose surface yarns have a harder twist are more durable than those with a softer twist. Carpets made of thicker yarn are more durable than those made of thinner yarn.

With tufted carpets, the more securely the tufts are fastened to the backing, the better the carpet will hold up and the better resistance the carpet will have to runs. The material most commonly used for the backings of tufted carpets is polypropylene, which does not mold, mildew, rot, or shrink. Jute is also used, but woven rugs with jute as a backing are subject to all those ills and must be protected from dampness. Polyurethane and polyvinyl chloride (PVC), like polypropylene, are used as synthetic carpet backing that will not mold, mildew, rot, or shrink. (But according to the EPA, in the manufacture of PVC, dioxin and other chlorinated by-products are formed.)

Level types of pile wear better than multilevel pile because pressures get distributed more widely on the former. With a multilevel carpet, the yarns that stick up highest take a disproportionate amount of wear and give out faster. Carpets with deeper pile are harder to vacuum; shag carpets are particularly hard to keep clean. But a thick, deep pile feels softer and more luxurious than a thin, hard pile, and a carpet with soft-twisted surface yarns feels softer than one with hard-twisted yarns. A thicker, softer pile insulates against noise and holds in heat better.

See the Glossary of Rugs and Carpets at the end of this chapter for more information on structures and types of rugs and carpets.

Pests. Unfortunately, rugs and carpets, whether of natural or synthetic fibers, can host various pests. Such floor coverings offer favorable environments to dust mites, which cling deep in the pile and thrive on the skin scales and other edibles that collect there. Moths and carpet beetles in their larval phase eat wool.

Carpets in use will not be damaged by carpet beetles and moths so long as the carpets are frequently vacuumed; and vacuuming with a low-emission vacuum will substantially reduce the level of dust-mite allergens. Because mites, beetles, and moths all like damp, dark conditions, keeping the humidity down, supplying good ventilation, and letting in some sunshine, along with frequent, thorough vacuuming, will usually suffice to keep pest problems at bay. Carpets in storage, however, are highly vulnerable to damage from beetles and moths.

If you must store carpets and you can store them in an area apart from your living space, use mothballs or other moth repellants, as described in chapter 21, "The Natural Fibers," pages 351–52. Some carpets are treated to resist moths and beetles. According to manufacturers, these treatments pose no danger to children or pets.

Chemical Emissions from Carpets. New carpeting made of synthetic fiber often emits volatile organic compounds into the air. The emissions may be from the backing or the adhesive used to lay wall-to-wall carpet. The odor of such emissions is often surprisingly strong and unpleasant. There are disputes about how harmful such fumes are. Some people seem to get headaches, allergic reactions, or flulike symptoms from the fumes. There is no hard evidence that worse harm results. However, there is little reason to think that breathing such compounds does you any good.

Usually, emissions from new carpets subside greatly within a few days, but they can continue at a lower level for a much longer period. The remedy is to open doors and windows and use fans to bring fresh air in. The Carpet and Rug Institute (CRI), an industry organization, recommends you do this for forty-eight to seventy-two hours and that you call your retailer if the problem persists. (And if the problem persists, so should your ventilation efforts.) The Carpet and Rug Institute suggests that you might consider scheduling installation of new carpeting at a time when most family members will be out of the house. Having had a taste of this problem, I strongly endorse that suggestion, especially for families with infants, young children, or members with allergic tendencies, and further suggest that you try to find a way to be absent for a few days, if possible, leaving your home to ventilate, particularly after installation of a large amount of carpeting. If you are allergic or sensitive to dust, you should also try to avoid being around when your old carpet is lifted and new carpet is laid. This process can create a great deal of temporary air pollution. Vacuum and clean carefully after the removal.

When buying new carpets and carpet cushioning or mats, look for the green-and-white label of the Carpet and Rug Institute. This indicates that the item has met CRI low-emission standards as part of a voluntary testing program carried out by the CRI; insist that the installer use adhesives with the

CRI label too. Although some observers express doubt about whether the CRI standards are stringent enough, this is clearly a step in the right direction and for some time will probably be the only way you have of assessing the potential emissions of any new American-manufactured carpeting you buy. It is also a good idea to ask your retailer to roll out and air your new carpeting before delivering it to you.

Preserving Carpets and Rugs. Regular, proper vacuuming is the most important action you can take to preserve the good looks and quality of your carpets and rugs. Dirt and dust not only ruin the appearance of carpeting; they are ground deep into the carpet where they cut and destroy the fibers of the pile and the carpet's backing. This will eventually cause worn areas to appear. A thorough vacuuming on cleaning day and a partial vacuuming once or twice a week between cleaning days will keep your carpets in good condition and the dust and allergen levels down.

The second most important part of carpet care is having good cushioning or matting. Carpet cushioning adds to comfort by increasing softness and providing insulation. Functionally, the extra cushion prevents dirt from being ground into the carpet and saves wear by absorbing some of the impact of footsteps as well. It also creates a suction layer, or air pocket, between the floor and the carpet, which improves the effectiveness of vacuuming.

A third major means of preservation is to use doormats at each entrance to your home, preferably one immediately inside and one immediately outside each door that opens to the outdoors. (You may need just one of these if you live in an apartment building with carpeted hallways that are frequently vacuumed.) The mats will absorb great quantities of dust and dirt that would otherwise be tracked onto your carpets and floors. You can also do wonders for your carpets by carefully wiping shoes and boots at the door or, even better, taking them off at the door. These steps will save much labor in vacuuming and shampooing. They will also save the additional wear on the carpet that these cleaning measures extract. Unfortunately, cleaning the carpet also contributes to its aging in direct proportion to the vigor of the cleaning procedure. The goal, therefore, is not only to clean the carpet but insofar as possible to keep it from getting dirty in the first place.

You can help preserve your carpets through some simple habits and practices. Use casters and protectors under furniture legs to prevent the pile from being crushed or broken. You can get these with pointed legs or prongs so that they themselves do not crush or mat the pile. (If your synthetic carpets develop impressions, place an ice cube on them and the fibers will regain their loft. Do not do this with natural-fiber carpets or rugs.) Never walk on any carpets when they are wet, but be especially careful not to walk on wet wool carpets. Wool is less resilient when wet, and you may damage the fibers. Turn the carpet periodically so that light and traffic wear and age it uniformly. Move the furniture now and then so that the pile is not permanently crushed or matted. Clip stray pile yarns that are too long. Whenever you move furniture, always lift it; never push it across the carpet. Pushing and sliding are hard on both rugs and furniture. Do not use delicate and valuable rugs in high-traffic spots, such as entries and hallways, or in high-abrasion spots, such as stairs and turns or corners. If a carpet develops an edge that rolls or turns up, iron it flat on both sides using a damp pressing cloth. This condition usually is a result of walkers' pushing the edge up with their feet as they pass. It is not only unsightly but will also damage the fibers of the carpet over time.

Improper storage can result in damage to carpets. Wool carpets are far more likely to be attacked by pests in storage than when they are left on the floor, because pests like dark, damp, undisturbed areas. If you must store a carpet, never fold but roll it, right side out (so as not to crush the pile), fringe to fringe, if it has any. Antiques or delicate heirlooms should be lined with acid-free paper and placed in acid-free boxes. (This protects them from contact with environmental hazards without creating any new ones.) Roll larger carpets on a roller. Do not roll them so loosely that wrinkles will form or so tightly that the carpets cannot breathe and the pile is crushed. Stored wool carpets should be aired periodically to reduce any moisture that may have accumulated and to allow you to check for insect infestation.

Carpets, like people, flourish in temperatures of about 70°F and relative humidity of about 50 percent.

Shampooing. Old-fashioned housewives shampooed the carpets at every spring cleaning, and this is still the most hygienic schedule. If no one in the household is troubled by allergies, you can preserve appearances with less-frequent shampooing. The schedule depends on the amount of traffic and dirt and the number of children to which your carpets are exposed. If you give your carpets thorough, regular vacuuming and traffic is light to moderate, shampooing every two or three years can suffice to keep them looking good. Whether sooner or later, there inevitably comes a day when dirt and spots have accumulated and vacuuming no longer restores a good appearance. Then you must shampoo.*

There are four methods of carpet shampooing: with commercial rug-cleaning products and a vacuum cleaner; with a rented or purchased cleaning

---

*There is some evidence that some episodes of Kawasaki syndrome, a dangerous illness of children, were associated with exposure to rug shampooing. Kawasaki syndrome, which is the main cause of acquired heart disease in children in this country, predominantly affects children under five. Although the connection between Kawasaki syndrome and rug shampooing is not regarded as proved, you may wish, if there are crawling babies, toddlers, or preschoolers in the home, either to avoid shampooing or spot-cleaning rugs or to have the carpets sent out for cleaning and thorough drying before they are returned. Whenever you shampoo carpets, you should ventilate the room well, so do not attempt to shampoo carpets or upholstery in cold, damp weather. Choose a time when drying is likely to be quickest and when you can leave doors and windows open.

machine; by professional cleaners in the home; or by professional cleaners out of the home at a cleaning company. Each of these methods has strengths and weaknesses, and it is wise to choose on a case-by-case basis. None of them, however, should be used on valuable antique rugs, which should be cleaned only by professionals who specialize in such work. Also, send silk rugs to an expert.

Thoroughly vacuum the carpet before using any method of shampooing.

The first shampooing method, using commercial rug shampoos and cleaning products and a vacuum, may not be the most pleasant, but it is the cheapest. Effective foam sprays, liquid shampoos, and powders are available in supermarkets, hardware stores, and home centers. Dry shampooing, however, should probably be reserved for small areas. Follow the directions on the product. Never overwet the carpet. Mildew can result unless both pile and backing are of synthetic fiber. Even when mildew is not a worry, an overwet carpet of any fiber takes a long time to dry and cannot be walked on until it is because it is more vulnerable to soil and stain. (Also, in some instances its fibers are weaker and more easily damaged when it is wet.) Always vacuum or rinse out all chemical cleaners thoroughly; their residue can damage the carpet and hasten resoiling, and they may be toxic. When scrubbing these products into carpets, a brush is recommended because it does not flatten the pile so much as a sponge does. A sponge is good for blotting; a natural sponge is more absorbent and creates no risk of transferring color onto the carpet.

Steam- or drycleaning equipment can be either rented or bought if you wish to try the second method. Drycleaning compounds need a much shorter drying time (approximately one hour), and they are good for spot-cleaning and high-traffic areas. Do not overwet the carpet with them. Drycleaning fluids pose a fire hazard. Use them only with plenty of ventilation. It can be difficult to remove all of the cleaning chemicals in the carpet, and it may take a second procedure. A steam-cleaned carpet can take many hours to dry. Steam cleaning does a more thorough job, but the quality of the work depends on the skill of the operator. In general, rented equipment is cumbersome, the cleaning chemicals are expensive, and the results vary.

Often the increased cost of hiring a professional carpet-cleaning service to come into your home is worth it. Many services pick up, clean, and return your carpets to you in a thoroughly dried state, and also do competent repairs. (This is not feasible, of course, for wall-to-wall carpeting.) As with all professional services in the home, you should research the best companies in your area.

Stains and Spills. With spills, time is of the essence; once set, many carpet stains are nearly impossible to remove completely. Act swiftly, and remove as much of the spill as you can. Blot, do not rub, spills with an absorbent white towel or paper towel. Sometimes you can spoon them up too. The main consideration is not to make matters worse by spreading the spill more widely. For a liquid spill, sparingly pour soda water or seltzer over the area; the bubbles will cause more of the spilled substance to rise to the surface, which should then be blotted quickly.

Once the spill is contained, try to remove any remaining stain with carpet shampoo or commercial stain removers, following product instructions. Most spills, once contained, can also be dealt with effectively using the foam from the suds of a solution of water and a mild detergent. Brush lightly, then wipe off the excess foam with a clean cloth. Rinse with a half-and-half solution of white vinegar and water to remove any alkalinity left by the cleaner. Finally, rinse with plain warm water, taking care to blot thoroughly. Carry out both rinses either by spraying the liquid onto the carpet, taking care not to get it too wet, or by patting it on with a clean white cloth or paper towel. Then blot it with a dry white cloth or paper towel.

Consult the Guide to Carpet and Upholstery Stain Removal at the end of this chapter for stains that do not respond to this treatment.

Cleaning Valuable Antiques, Oriental Rugs, and Delicate Carpets. Your goal with rugs that are old, delicate, or valuable should be to lift dirt while avoiding damage to the delicate fibers of the pile caused by bending, pulling, and crushing them during cleaning. There is a troublesome trade-off here because dirt will harm carpets too. For less-delicate but valuable rugs, the trade-off between damage caused by dirt and damage caused by the vacuuming itself tilts toward removing the dirt more effectively: the best guarantee of long life for such a carpet is a high level of cleanliness. For a very delicate, very old carpet, the balance tilts the other way: use every possible caution. There are many in-between cases for which you must simply consult your own wishes and intentions. If you have irresolvable doubts, ask a specialist.

Safeguards. A number of safety measures should be taken when caring for old, delicate, and valuable carpets. First, and most important, never use a power brush. Vacuum only with reduced suction. If you cannot turn down the power of the vacuum, reduce its suction by placing a screen of nylon or plastic over the nozzle of the vacuum or by laying a screen over the carpet. This is especially desirable on carpets with fringe, particularly if it is hand-knotted. The screen reduces suction and prevents the vacuum from sucking fringe or fiber into the hose. Vacuum old and delicate carpets and rugs in the following way: using the "universal" floor attachment, slowly vacuum in the direction of the pile, getting off as much dirt as possible; then go over the carpet one more

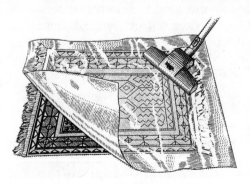

Vacuuming carpet with screen over it

time (with a hand brush, gently, if you have vacuumed through a screen) against the direction of the pile to stand the fibers up and restore their natural sheen. Once a year or so, give it a deeper vacuuming by hanging it vertically over the back of a chair or two chairs, for example, and going over it slowly with a hand-held vacuum of no more than one horsepower.

Cleaning an older or delicate carpet with any sort of liquid will result in a loss of fiber (or in a disastrous case, a large loss of fiber), and therefore is inadvisable. Wet cleaning or shampooing and dry cleaning should be done only by specialists and on the recommendation of specialists.

With old and delicate carpets, observe somewhat more rigorously the cautions you observe for ordinary carpeting. For example, place carpets needing special protection out of high-traffic areas, such as entryways and hallways, and high-abrasion areas, such as stairs, turns, and corners. Extremely delicate and valuable rugs do not belong on the floor at all; hang these on walls, or lay them on tables. Others may go on the floor in places where no one will be tempted to walk on them. If a valuable, somewhat vulnerable carpet has been placed where it generally needs vacuuming more than once a week, it should be moved. Frequent cleaning as well as frequent soiling will cause it to wear more quickly. Keep antique and other valuable rugs out of all light, natural and artificial, as much as possible, especially direct sunlight; make sure that any light striking them strikes uniformly. Keep the humidity moderate. Do not let furniture stand where it will crush the pile.

For the most valuable and most delicate carpets, you should take all of the foregoing safety measures. For others, choose the level of caution that makes a comfortable compromise between the importance of the rug and your time and willingness to take trouble.

Shampooing Delicate Carpets. Generally speaking, do not attempt to shampoo valuable carpets yourself. Too much can go wrong. However, with those troublesome carpets that fall in the gray area of "somewhat old but not really a valuable antique" or "delicate but not really irreplaceable," you might trust yourself to give them a gentle moist cleaning in the manner described below. Be certain that you believe the benefits of doing so outweigh the possible costs.

The mildest wet cleaning you can perform is simply to sponge the rug gently with a natural sponge or clean white cloth dipped in spring water and wrung dry. (Tap water is too heavy with chemicals, and distilled water will remove too many natural oils.) First, however, carefully test a few fibers at an edge for colorfastness by wetting them with your cloth or sponge, then wiping them with a clean, dry white cloth and observing whether dye comes off. If not, then proceed with your sponging. Afterward, dry the carpet quickly and thoroughly. Wipe it with a clean white towel to take up as much moisture as possible. Then air the carpet. Open the windows and use fans, if necessary, to increase the ventilation. Carry out such an operation only in warm, dry weather.

For a slightly less mild cleaning, brush the carpet gently with the foam of a solution of mild detergent and water. Orvus WA Paste, manufactured by Procter & Gamble, is an excellent choice. See "Detergents and soaps, mild," pages 78–80. Do not use commercial rug shampoos or strong cleaners. You will need a bucket of mild detergent and water, a second bucket of plain water, a soft brush, and a clean white cloth. First, in a small, inconspicuous area at the edge, test to be sure the colors in the carpet will not run. Make a good foam in your solution of detergent and water. Then dip the soft brush in the foam only—not in the water—and gently brush the carpet with the foam. Start on the back side of the carpet and work from the middle out in a circular motion, cleaning a small section at a time. Rinse by wiping off the foam with a well-wrung cloth that has been dipped in plain water, being careful not to soak the carpet. Once finished with the back side, flip the carpet and proceed in the same manner on the right side. Dry the carpet thoroughly, as described above, by first wiping it with a clean white towel and then airing it. Finally, brush the top side of the carpet gently with a soft, dry brush to raise the pile.

Spills and Stains on Delicate Carpets. Accidents involving valuable and delicate rugs require fast action. But do not attempt to deal with such stains yourself.

Immediately try to isolate the substance, blotting or gently scraping up what you can. Then wrap the carpet tightly in plastic so as to avoid the drying of the stain—if this happens it is likely to set forever—and make haste to the nearest professional cleaner or conservator.

Caring for Rugs Made of Rushes, Grasses, Sisal, and Similar Natural Materials.

Use rugs of rushes and grasses only in dry areas of your home. They will rot or mold if they are left damp. Stronger, more coarsely woven types can be used on the floor like any other rug. Fine and delicate ones will quickly break down and tear if you walk on them.

Vacuum such rugs front and back. Then lift them and vacuum the floor under them. I have never attempted to wash such a rug, but I have read that it can be done. I would be wary, however. Especially if the rug has colors or is painted or decorated, I would attempt to wash it only if the manufacturer or retailer assured me that washing would do no harm. Test the effect of water and mild detergent in an inconspicuous area before beginning.

The trick is to try to avoid soaking the rug and to dry it quickly so that it does not mildew or deteriorate. Use a solution of mild detergent and water and a soft brush or cloth. A stiff brush, or even a not-so-stiff brush, may damage the fibers or designs or decorations on some weaves. Wash the rug quickly. Rinse it thoroughly. Then dry it fast. Hang it on a clothesline in the sun, over a drying frame, or in any other fashion that lets air go through. Do this outside if you can. (You may see suggestions to hose the rug down, if you are outside, but I would hesitate to soak such a rug.) Apartment dwellers can resort to a terrace, bathroom, or kitchen.

Upholstery

Vacuum upholstery once a week.

Shampoo upholstery as needed. Once every year or two is usually enough unless you have a large family or an unusually active household. You can hire professionals to come into your home to do this modestly onerous task. You can also purchase or rent equipment and do the job yourself. Or you can do the job without machines, using hand brushes. (It takes a bit of muscle, though, and can raise a little anxiety or frustration because you may fail to remove the soil.) If you have antique upholstery that you wish to preserve, however, you should have the job done by a trained professional.

Preventing Soiling and Damage to Upholstery. Because upholstery cleaning is often only moderately successful, it is important to concentrate on preventive measures: vacuuming, using soil repellants and cloth protectors of various sorts, and using care and caution. When preventives fail, you must keep in mind that upholstery is generally not intended to last for anywhere near a lifetime.

Soil-resistance treatments and guards work well. Soil repellants help by causing spills to bead up rather than to soak in and by creating a barrier against dirt. You can apply these yourself with spray or have the job done by professionals. If you apply a soil repellant yourself, be sure the product you choose is recommended for the fiber you have and apply it as evenly as possible. Note that some soil repellants work on both oil- and water-based soil, but others do not. Read labels, or if you hire professionals to do this job, be sure to ask what you are getting before you commit yourself.

Crocheted antimacassars—the small lace and cloth circles, rectangles, and squares that used to adorn the backs and arms of chairs and sofas—are quite out of fashion, but if hair oil ever becomes popular again, pull them out of the attic immediately. The young will deduce that these are launderable materials used as soil guards on the high-soil areas of upholstery. They will not remember how, in the days before daily shampoos, oil spots on walls and furniture from people's heads were a major cleaning problem. (There is a mild, morose character in Dickens's *Bleak House*—Mr. Jellyby—whose custom of sitting in a certain spot to indulge in despair is indicated by a greasy spot on the wall where his head habitually lolls.) Hair and skin, even with our frenzied bathing and shampooing, continue to have natural oil and a bit of soil on them that is transferred to upholstery. Some people still preserve the backs and arms of upholstered furniture by acquiring arm guards and back guards made out of the upholstery material. Others take advantage of a bit of a vogue in slip-covers. These are all good ideas. You could also design up-to-date anti-macassars in some washable fiber.

Light will cause most fabrics and wood to fade and deteriorate, but there is a vast difference in the susceptibility of different fibers and dyes to light.

Choose the more light-resistant types for your upholstery. Place antiques where direct light will not strike them. Place all furniture in such a way that light strikes it uniformly. It is remarkable how quickly bleaching can occur.

Shampooing Upholstery. Begin with a thorough vacuuming. If you have slipcovers, simply remove them and launder or dry-clean as appropriate. Follow the care label instructions. If you plan to wash them, you must ensure that they are preshrunk when you buy them or that the initial fit is loose enough to tolerate whatever degree of shrinkage you are told you can expect. When you are worried that launderable slipcovers may shrink, wash them in cold water and either line-dry or tumble on low/gentle until they are three-quarters dry, then replace them on the furniture while they are still slightly damp.

The best way to shampoo upholstery yourself is almost always to use a home steam extraction machine. (This is also the method professional cleaners use.) If you do not own one, you can rent one. This machine shoots cleaning solution into the upholstery, then sucks the dirty water back out with tremendous force, so you are not left with soggy cushions that will mold before they dry. At the same time, your cleaning solution is able to penetrate the fabric, which is the only way to get it really clean. Proceed according to the manufacturers' instructions. Use any commercial upholstery shampoo that works in the machine. Always test a patch first in a hidden area. Do not use the furniture until it has dried thoroughly, and do everything in your power to ensure that it dries quickly. Good ventilation and low relative humidity will help. (Dirt adheres more readily to damp surfaces, and dampness can leach colors from clothing, paper, and other materials.)

It is best to shampoo upholstery by hand when the soiled upholstery is too delicate to tolerate machine cleaning and not worth the expense of professional cleaning. Hand-shampooing works well on light, even soil and on fabrics without nap, and it is the method to use on occasional small pieces of furniture. Most of us, however, would find the job of cleaning several large pieces in this manner quite tiring, and, considering the labor expended, the results obtained can be disappointing when this gentle method of cleaning is applied to heavy soil or stubborn stains.

There are many methods of hand-shampooing. One popular method is to spray a commercial upholstery cleaner onto the fabric; rub it as vigorously as the cloth will tolerate with a brush or sponge; then vacuum. Some methods are wet; some use solvents. Just be sure to follow whatever specific instructions are on the product you buy. To shampoo upholstery in the traditional way, you will need a clean cloth, a soft brush, a bucket of clean water, and a second bucket of a very sudsy solution of upholstery shampoo and water. Make sure the upholstery shampoo is safe for your upholstery fabric. (Orvus WA Paste is excellent for this.) Dip the brush into the foam or suds only. Do not actually get the brush wet. Using only the suds, brush a small section of the upholstery as vigorously as the fabric will tolerate. Rinse by wiping the foam off with a well-wrung cloth dipped in the clean water. Continue in this manner until the entire piece is finished. The main object is to avoid soaking the upholstery. If it gets soaked, it may rot inside or smell unpleasant forever after. Do not remove covers from pillows; clean them in place. Let the upholstery dry thoroughly; then vacuum it. Never use upholstery when it is damp.

Leather. You need not clean leather-upholstered furniture or desktops more than once a year under ordinary circumstances. First dust; then use saddle soap or another leather cleaner according to the product directions. (Waxes and polishes formulated for woods and other surfaces contain solvents that may harm leather; don't use them.) After cleaning leather, let it dry before using it again. If the leather seems too dry or is beginning to crack, use a conditioner after cleaning. Be sure to select products that will not darken light leathers. If you are in doubt, test in an inconspicuous place.

You can wipe leather with water to clean off an occasional spot so long as you do not let it get damp through. Never let water stand on leather. Sun will bleach and cause deterioration of leather, and heat will make it crack and dry.

Draperies

Launder or dry-clean draperies as necessary—that is, when vacuuming does not make the draperies look good or when you know that they are quite dirty even if they look all right. For suggestions on laundering draperies, refer to chapter 8, "How to Launder Tricky Items." Obey the care labels, particularly when they forbid either laundering or dry cleaning.

To vacuum, use the upholstery nozzle, and set the suction level on low. Begin at the top and go to the bottom, using short, repeated strokes. In bedrooms, vacuum draperies weekly. In other areas, if weekly vacuuming is not feasible, try for a once-monthly vacuuming, or simply do it as often as you can get to it. It is a quick job.

Lampshades

Nothing much has changed for fifty or more years when it comes to taking care of lampshades. The newer synthetic fibers of which some lampshades are made are perhaps less expensive than silk or linen, but not much easier to clean once they are fastened to the frame.

Dusting Lampshades. Because most lampshades are either difficult or impossible to wash or dry-clean, dusting them frequently and carefully is all the more important. By doing so you can put off the vile necessity of cleaning them for a long time. You can also preserve the life of the shades.

Remove dust from lampshades by vacuuming with the dust brush and low

suction. Hold the shade steady with your hand, but be careful not to leave fin-
gerprints. You can also use a clothes brush or a dry sponge effectively. Some
people use a feather duster, but I think this leaves too much dust within the
fabric and seams that other means would remove. Dust gently, because lampshades are breakable and can easily be bent permanently out of shape under
pressure.

Long ago, to get the dust out from between the threads of fabric lampshades, the housekeeper would "snap" the shade with a piece of cheesecloth
or linen towel, rather as boys snap one another with towels in the locker room.
(She duly removed the shades from the lamps before doing this, and stabilized
them, or she might have sent the lamp bases flying.) When I was told of snap-
ping, I decided that it would actually be a useful adjunct to vacuuming
because it would loosen dust so that it could be sucked up, but I can't say that
I noticed any increased cleaning effect when I tried it.

Choosing a Cleaning Method. After years of being dusted and vacuumed,
a lampshade may finally reach a point where it needs a more ambitious kind
of cleaning. Then you must decide whether you can wash it or whether you
must replace it. Not long ago you would also have had the option of sending
it to a laundry or dry cleaner, but today it is all but impossible to find a business willing to take on this chore, so home washing is the only option.

Some shades cannot be washed. These include hand-painted lampshades,
fabric lampshades with paper interiors, and lampshades whose fabric is glued
rather than sewn to the frame. The paint and paper will be ruined and glued
places will come unglued if you wet such lampshades. (Some people recommend washing otherwise washable glued shades with detergent-suds foam,
then rinsing with a well-wrung, clean cloth. This is worth a try when you
have nothing to lose. If trim comes unglued, you can sometimes glue it back
on.) I have never had a colored-fabric lampshade, but I have heard that bleeding or running dyes can be a problem. If you have a colored one you had
better test the effect of your washing solution first in an inconspicuous area.

Washable-fabric lampshades sewn to the frame can be washed by immersion in a washing solution. Parchment, plastic, and laminated or plastic-coated
lampshades need not and should not be washed by immersion. The parchment
and plastic are not harmed by water but, because they do not hold dust the
way fabrics do, they can be thoroughly cleaned by dusting and washed by
damp wiping. This is also the safest thing to do, as they may be constructed
with glues or other materials that might not survive immersion in water.
Instructions for both immersion and nonimmersion cleaning are set forth
below.

Note that it would be inadvisable to immerse any antique or old fabric
shade in water. These are usually exceedingly fragile after long exposure to
light and other harmful elements of the environment. I would gently brush
such a shade with a soft brush or gently vacuum it with reduced suction

power. For any other cleaning, if the shade were valuable or valued, I would consult a professional.

Glass, wood, and bamboo shades should be washed pursuant to the special instructions given elsewhere in this book for those materials. Shades that might shrink a great deal and those made of noncolorfast materials should not be washed. You can regard silk, rayon, synthetic fibers, and preshrunk, color-fast cotton and linen shades—those sewn to the frame—as washable unless the manufacturers' labels state otherwise. If a label states that you cannot wash or dry-clean a shade, I would believe it. Some experts recommend that you not try to wash even "washable" shades because you are so likely to get poor results. I do not think such pessimism is called for, but because I have gotten poor results in at least one attempt at washing a cloth lampshade, I will second the opinion that it is a tricky business. Consider the following suggestions with this caveat in mind: Even faint streaks and spots are terribly noticeable in a lampshade with a light shining behind it.

Fabric Shades: Immersion Method. The hazards to be avoided in home washing are rusting frames (towel-dry and then quickly finish air-drying) and streaking or uneven color tone in the end product. The immersion method is best for washable, all-fabric, nonplastic shades because it is the most likely to produce a uniform result. Be as quick as you can through the entire procedure. First remove the shade from the lamp and dust or vacuum the shade thoroughly. Then fill a bathtub with enough lukewarm water to cover the lampshade when it is immersed. Mix in a small amount of a gentle detergent that is safe for the fabric. Immerse the shade. Using a soft brush, cloth, or sponge, start washing at a side seam, working gently in an up-and-down, overlapping motion. Go over the top material first, then the lining. Rinse twice by immersion in clear, lukewarm water. Use white or colorfast terry-cloth towels to dry the shade thoroughly, outside and inside. Blot all excess water with the towels. Then set the shade to dry outdoors on a clean towel or other cloth. Because it is important that the shade dry as quickly as possible, do this only on a sunny, breezy day. If you are an apartment dweller, choose a day when you have a warm, dry room to set the shades in and turn a fan on them while they dry.

Plastic, Plastic-Coated, Laminated Paper, Parchment, and Vellum Shades: No Immersion. Again, begin by removing the shade from the lamp and dusting or vacuuming it thoroughly. Then, to use the nonimmersion method, fill two pails or basins with lukewarm water and add a small amount of mild detergent to one of them. Working quickly on a small area at a time, wash the shade using a well-wrung cloth dampened in the detergent solution, being careful not to soak the shade. Thoroughly rinse each small area with a cloth dampened with clear water and wrung before going on to the next. Wash and rinse both outside and inside and blot with towels as in the immersion method, and finish drying as for the immersion method.

Stains. Stain-removal efforts will be more successful if the shade is first rendered as clean and dust-free as possible. Otherwise, your efforts may simply make a smeary, dark place on the shade.

Try gently erasing marks from the shade with a clean eraser. Be sure to supply some backing as you work: Hold a clean towel behind the shade as you gently erase the marks. If this does not work, try some solvent-based stain remover or drycleaning fluid safe for the fabric. Try to test it first on an inconspicuous area, for discoloration is a big danger, and discoloration on a shade always shows clearly when the lamp is turned on.

GLOSSARY OF RUGS AND CARPETS

American or "sheen-type" Oriental rugs. Reproductions of Oriental rug patterns in Wilton, Axminster, or velvet weave. (The sheen is produced by a chlorine wash or the use of synthetic fibers and is intended to imitate the luster of Oriental rugs.) They may be of good quality and may be woven through to the back, as real Oriental rugs are.

Axminster. A type of cut-pile woven carpet, known for the great variety of colors and designs it can accommodate. It often looks like a hand-knotted carpet.

Backing. The base material into which the pile yarn of tufted carpets is inserted. It may be made of a woven material such as jute or polypropylene or a nonwoven material such as plastic, urethane, vinyl, or latex.

Berber. See "Tufted carpets: Level-loop pile."

Braided rugs. Rugs made of rags, often of a variety of fibers, braided into long chains, then sewn together, usually in a circle, to form a mat. See "Hooked and rag rugs."

Broadloom. A one-piece carpet in various weaves about twelve to fifteen feet wide. It must be made on a loom broad enough to accommodate this width. Also, a name used for wall-to-wall carpeting.

Brussels. A Jacquard-woven carpet with hard-twisted loops (instead of cut pile like Axminster and Wilton carpets). It is quite durable and of slightly lower quality than Wilton carpets.

Chenille. A type of Axminster rug with a high, dense pile made by weaving together narrow cut strips of woven material with a high pile. It is soft, resilient, luxurious, durable, and expensive. It can be made in a great variety of colors and designs.

Grass rugs. Rugs made of prairie grass harvested in the United States or Canada. The grass is tied into ropes, which are woven into rugs. Sometimes, grass rugs are stenciled or printed with designs, or designs may be woven in. They are usually varnished.

Hooked and rag rugs. Rugs usually used as throw rugs and usually handmade, although some are produced commercially. Loops of fabric or heavy yarn form a pile by being drawn with a hook through some coarse backing—for example, canvas or burlap—that has been stretched on a frame. Hooked rugs can be of wool, cotton, or man-made fibers. Rag rugs are made of pieces of cloth—rags—that are braided, sewn, or crocheted together. Like hooked rugs, rag rugs are available in both machine- and handmade versions. Hand-made rag rugs typically are made from rag strips that are braided together into a long rope, which is then coiled and sewn together into an oval or circular shape. Usually the rags are of many different colors and patterns, giving the rugs an irregular design.

Both hooked and rag rugs come in small and large sizes, but are most often used as small scatter rugs. Antiques are likely to be made of fabrics with bleeding dyes, and they should not be shampooed.

Oriental rugs. Handmade woven rugs that come from the East, usually Asia, especially Iran, Turkey, the Bukhara region of Uzbekistan, Afghanistan, India, and China. They are woven in a knotted-pile weave using one of two kinds of knots: the Ghiordes or Turkish knot and the Senna or Persian knot. The knot secures the pile yarn to the warp yarn, and the ends of its strands stand up as tufts. The Ghiordes knot is actually a twist of the pile yarn. The Senna knot is a real knot. The quality of the rug is in great part determined by the number of knots it has per square inch—the more, the better. Other factors affecting quality are coloring, design, the depth of the pile, the quality of the yarn, and the age and condition of the rug. Oriental rugs are almost always made of wool. A few very fine rugs have a silk pile.

A real Oriental rug can sometimes be identified by two or three characteristics. You should be able to see the entire pattern of the rug in detail on the reverse side. The fringe is produced as an extension of the warp threads; it is never sewn on. The natural dyes used in Oriental rugs fade differently from the aniline dyes used in domestic carpets. The latter fade to different shades; natural dyes fade to paler shades of the original color. To examine the dye, look at the pile closest to the knot. Domestic carpets are lighter in weight in proportion to their size than Orientals. These methods are far from foolproof, however. When in doubt you must ask a reliable expert, who will examine many additional factors such as the knots, the design, and the colors.

Pile. The raised loops, tufts, or yarns on the surface of a rug. A pile is not the same as a nap. Naps are formed by shredding the surface of woven material. Napped materials do not have stand-up loops and tufts. Pile carpets may be produced by many techniques, including weaving, tufting, and gluing.

Rugs and carpets. Sometimes interchangeable terms. Some use the term "carpeting" to refer only to floor covering that is sold by the yard. "Rug" usually refers to smaller, less substantial floor coverings than carpets. Rugs are usually woven.

Rya rugs. Scandinavian wool rugs with a long pile of one to three inches, often in one-of-a-kind abstract patterns of colors in one family. May be hand-knotted with Ghiordes knots (see "Oriental rugs") or machine-made.

Saxony Wiltons. See "Wiltons."

Shag rugs. Rugs with extra-long pile yarns of an inch or two or even more. The pile yarns flop over in all different directions because they are so long, and this makes the rug look more densely woven than it is. Shag rugs are hard to clean.

Sisal rugs. Rugs made from the leaf of the sisal plant, grown in Indonesia and Africa. Sisal, a strong and durable fiber, is twisted into strands and woven into rugs.

Tufted carpets. Carpets made by inserting pile yarn into a base fabric or backing, which is usually a woven fabric such as jute or polypropylene. Tufted carpets usually use a secondary backing for added strength and stability. Unlike woven carpets, tufted carpets can develop runs: a row of tufts gets pulled out. The chief types of tufted carpets are Saxony, velvet or plush, shag, level-loop, cut-and-loop, and sculptured. Variations on tufting, which glue the tufts to the backing or increase the color and pattern versatility of this type of carpeting, are numerous.

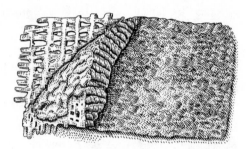

Tufted carpet

Cut pile

> Cut-and-loop pile. A pile with some loops and some cut yarns. It can be either level or multilevel.

> Level-loop pile. A pile formed of loops of all the same length. (Multilevel-loop pile has loops of different heights.) What is now called a Berber rug is a level-loop carpet with low, fat loops and a pebbly texture.

> Multilevel-loop pile. A pile that has two to three different loop heights, creating patterns.

> Saxony tufted carpet. A carpet that uses twisted, plied yarns (but not yarns with a hard

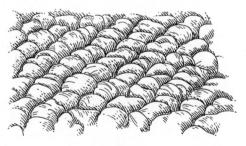

Berber rug

twist). It has more twist than velvet rugs, but not much. It has a level-cut pile.

Sculptured carpet. A carpet with a pile surface cut in different lengths to form patterns.

Shag. See "Shag rugs."

Velvet or plush tufted carpet. A carpet with little twist in the surface yarns, in which the cut ends meet closely, giving a smooth, velvety effect. (Plush looks like velvet, but with a longer pile.)

Velvet. A woven rug that, unlike Wiltons and Brussels, is woven on ordinary, not Jacquard, looms, so its color design is limited. The pile is woven over wires that are pulled out, cutting the loops and leaving standing tufts. Because the pile yarn is all brought to the surface, it is quite a durable carpet. It is the least expensive and most common type of woven rug sold in this country.

Wiltons. Cut-pile rugs considered to be among the best of all machine-made woven rugs. Wiltons are expensive. They used to be made only of wool (with pile of either worsted or woolen yarns), but now are made in a number of synthetic fibers as well. Unlike Axminsters, they use only three to six colors and are woven on a Jacquard loom using a method that produces a thick cushion of fibers. Worsted Wiltons, considered the best wool carpets made, are extremely durable and tightly woven, with a fine texture, delicate design, and short pile. A woolen Wilton, which has yarns that are less tightly twisted, is both soft and durable but less resilient than a worsted Wilton. A Saxony is a Wilton made of heavily twisted woolen (rather than worsted) yarns, with a medium-high pile; despite its softness it is quite durable.

Woven carpets. Carpets whose pile yarn is woven in, perpendicular to the warp and backing yarn. They were once the dominant type of carpet but now form a small percentage of all carpets made. The chief types of woven carpets are Axminster, chenille, Wilton, Saxony (a type of Wilton), Brussels, velvet, tapestry rugs, and American Orientals.

GUIDE TO CARPET AND UPHOLSTERY STAIN REMOVAL*

See also chapter 11, "Removing Stains from Fabrics," and the Guide to Stain Removal from Clothes, Linens, and Other Household Fabrics at the end of chapter 11.

Basic Directions for Carpet Stain Removal
Use these steps for all the stains listed.

For Synthetic Fibers Only
When anything is spilled on carpet surface, removal results are best when stain is treated immediately, before it dries. Water sponging over area will dilute stain, but be careful not to spread stain farther.

For All Carpets
1. Remove excess soil promptly by blotting or scraping with a dull edge first.
2. Apply cleaning materials directly to stain in order listed under numbered steps. Test for ten seconds and blot in an inconspicuous spot before using a solvent or cleaning materials.
3. Do not rub stain, always blot with clean absorbent white cloth.
4. Avoid getting carpet too wet.
5. When dry, gently brush to restore pile.
6. Some stains are very hard to remove. May need to repeat process two or more times. Some stains are permanent and cannot be removed.

Basic Directions for Upholstery Stain Removal
Use for all the stains listed.

Remove excess soil promptly, by scraping off residue with dull knife or spoon, and/or blotting up spills with absorbent materials.

Be sure to pretest in an inconspicuous spot. Basically fabrics are cleanable if they don't fade or shrink. See "Testing Cleanability."

---

*All material in this guide was written by Anne Field, Michigan State University Extension Specialist, Emeritus, with reference to the Georgia Extension bulletins, "How to Care for Carpets and Rugs" and "How to Care for Your Furnishings," the Hoover Company, Nebraska Extension bulletin "Carpet Care—Cleaning and Stain Removal," the Carpet and Rug Institute, Allied Fibers and Plastics Inc. and DuPont "Clean Up Carpeting" bulletin. All this material is available on the Web site of the Michigan State University Extension (http://web1.msue.msu.edu) under "Home Maintenance and Repair"; a vast amount of further excellent advice on carpets, upholstery, and cleaning throughout the home may also be found on this site.

Do not remove cushion from the cover.

No harsh rubbing—use soft white cloth or a sponge.

Rinse with a damp sponge.

Rapid drying is essential.

Symbols and their meanings—found on upholstery labels or tags, read tag on furniture.

W—Spot-clean with the foam only of a water-based cleaning agent such as mild detergent or upholstery shampoo.

S—Spot-clean using solvent only. Use sparingly in a well-ventilated room. Use of water-based solvent cleaners may cause spotting and/or excessive shrinkage. Water stains may become permanent.

S-W—Spot-clean with solvent or water-based foam.

X—Vacuum only.

Blood
Cleaning ingredients must be cold.
1. Mix one teaspoon of a neutral detergent (a mild detergent containing no alkalies or bleaches) to a cup of lukewarm water. Blot.
2. Mix one tablespoon of household ammonia with a half cup of water. Blot.
3. Sponge with clean water. Blot.

Beer
1. Mix one teaspoon of a neutral detergent (a mild detergent containing no alkalies or bleaches) with a cup of lukewarm water. Blot.
2. Mix one-third cup of white household vinegar with two-thirds cup of water. Blot.
3. Sponge with clean water. Blot.

Butter
1. Sponge with a small amount of dry-cleaning solvent. Blot. (Use small amounts to prevent any possible damage to sizings, backings, or stuffing materials. Do not use gasoline, lighter fluid, or carbon tetrachloride.)
2. Mix one teaspoon of a neutral detergent (a mild detergent containing no alkalies or bleaches) with a cup of lukewarm water. Blot.

Chewing Gum
1. Sponge with a small amount of dry-cleaning solvent. Blot. (Use small amounts to prevent any possible damage to sizings, backings, or stuffing materials. Do not use gasoline, lighter fluid, or carbon tetrachloride.)
2. Mix one teaspoon of a neutral detergent (a mild detergent containing no alkalies or bleaches) with a cup of lukewarm water. Blot.

Chocolate

1. Mix one teaspoon of a neutral detergent (a mild detergent containing no alkalies or bleaches) with a cup of lukewarm water. Blot.
2. Mix one tablespoon of household ammonia with a half-cup of water. Blot.
3. Repeat step one.
4. Sponge with clean water. Blot.

Coffee

1. Mix one teaspoon of a neutral detergent (a mild detergent containing no alkalies or bleaches) with a cup of lukewarm water. Blot.
2. Mix one-third cup of white household vinegar with two-thirds cup of water. Blot.
3. Sponge with clean water. Blot.

Cola Drinks

1. Mix one teaspoon of a neutral detergent (a mild detergent containing no alkalies or bleaches) with a cup of lukewarm water. Blot.
2. Mix one-third cup of white household vinegar with two-thirds cup of water. Blot.

Crayons

1. Sponge with a small amount of dry-cleaning solvent. Blot. (Use small amounts to prevent any possible damage to sizings, backings, or stuffing materials. Do not use gasoline, lighter fluid, or carbon tetrachloride.)
2. Mix one teaspoon of a neutral detergent (a mild detergent containing no alkalies or bleaches) with a cup of lukewarm water. Blot.
3. Sponge with clean water. Blot.

Earth (Dirt)

1. Mix one teaspoon of a neutral detergent (a mild detergent containing no alkalies or bleaches) with a cup of lukewarm water. Blot.
2. Mix one tablespoon of household ammonia with a half-cup of water. Blot.
3. Repeat step one with the detergent.
4. Sponge with clean water. Blot.

Egg (Raw)

1. Mix one teaspoon of a neutral detergent (a mild detergent containing no alkalies or bleaches) with a cup of lukewarm water. Blot.
2. Mix one tablespoon of household ammonia with a half-cup of water. Blot.
3. Repeat step one.
4. Sponge with clean water. Blot

Food Coloring or Dye

1. Seek the help of a professional carpet cleaner.

Fruit and Juices

1. Mix one teaspoon of a neutral detergent (a mild detergent containing no alkalies or bleaches) with a cup of lukewarm water. Blot.
2. Rinse with white household vinegar. Blot.
3. Repeat step one.
4. Sponge with clean water. Blot.

Furniture Polish

1. Sponge with a small amount of dry-cleaning solvent. Blot. (Use small amounts to prevent any possible damage to sizings, backings, or stuffing materials. Do not use gasoline, lighter fluid, or carbon tetrachloride.)
2. Mix one teaspoon of a neutral detergent (a mild detergent containing no alkalies or bleaches) with a cup of lukewarm water. Blot.
3. Sponge with clear water. Blot.

Glue (School, White)

1. Mix one teaspoon of a neutral detergent (a mild detergent containing no alkalies or bleaches) with a cup of lukewarm water. Blot.
2. Mix one tablespoon of household ammonia with a half-cup of water. Blot.
3. Repeat step one.
4. Sponge with clean water. Blot.

Gravy

1. Sponge with a small amount of dry-cleaning solvent. Blot. (Use small amounts to prevent any possible damage to sizings, backings, or stuffing materials. Do not use gasoline, lighter fluid, or carbon tetrachloride.)
2. Mix one teaspoon of a neutral detergent (a mild detergent containing no alkalies or bleaches) with a cup of lukewarm water. Blot.
3. Sponge with clear water. Blot.

Hand Lotion

1. Sponge with a small amount of dry-cleaning solvent. Blot. (Use small amounts to prevent any possible damage to sizings, backings, or stuffing materials. Do not use gasoline, lighter fluid, or carbon tetrachloride.)
2. Mix one teaspoon of a neutral detergent (a mild detergent containing no alkalies or bleaches) with a cup of lukewarm water. Blot.
3. Sponge with clean water. Blot.

Ice Cream

1. Mix one teaspoon of a neutral detergent (a mild detergent containing no alkalies or bleaches) with a cup of lukewarm water. Blot.
2. Mix one tablespoon of household ammonia with a half-cup of water. Blot.
3. Repeat step one.
4. Sponge with clean water. Blot.

Ink (Ballpoint)

1. Sponge with a small amount of dry-cleaning solvent. Blot. (Use small amounts to prevent any possible damage to sizings, backings, or stuffing materials. Do not use gasoline, lighter fluid, or tetrachloride.)
2. Mix one teaspoon of a neutral detergent (a mild detergent containing no alkalies or bleaches) with a cup of lukewarm water. Blot.
3. Sponge with clean water. Blot.

Iodine, Merthiolate

1. Mix one teaspoon of a neutral detergent (a mild detergent containing no alkalies or bleaches) with a cup of lukewarm water. Blot.
2. Mix one tablespoon of household ammonia with a half-cup of water. Blot.
3. Mix one-third cup of white household vinegar with two-thirds cup of water. Blot.
4. Repeat step one. Blot.
5. Sponge with clean water. Blot.

Marking Ink Pen

1. Sponge with a small amount of dry-cleaning solvent. Blot. (Use small amounts to prevent any possible damage to sizings, backings, or stuffing materials. Do not use gasoline, lighter fluid, or carbon tetrachloride.)
2. Mix one teaspoon of a neutral detergent (a mild detergent containing no alkalies or bleaches) with a cup of lukewarm water. Blot.
3. Sponge with clean water. Blot.

Milk

1. Mix one teaspoon of a neutral detergent (a mild detergent containing no alkalies or bleaches) with a cup of lukewarm water. Blot.
2. Mix one tablespoon of household ammonia with a half-cup of water. Blot.
3. Repeat step one. Blot.
4. Sponge with clean water. Blot.

Nail Polish

1. Apply nail-polish remover (acetone). Blot.
2. Mix one teaspoon of a neutral detergent (a mild detergent containing no alkalies or bleaches) with a cup of lukewarm water. Blot.
3. Sponge with clean water. Blot.

Paint (Latex)

1. Mix one teaspoon of a neutral detergent (a mild detergent containing no alkalies or bleaches) with a cup of lukewarm water. Blot.
2. Sponge with clean water. Blot.

Paint (Oil-Base)

1. Sponge with a small amount of dry-cleaning solvent. Blot. (Use small amounts to prevent any possible damage to sizings, backings, or stuffing materials. Do not use gasoline, lighter fluid, or carbon tetrachloride.)
2. Mix one teaspoon of a neutral detergent (a mild detergent containing no alkalies or bleaches) with a cup of lukewarm water. Blot.
3. Sponge with clean water. Blot.

Rubber Cement

1. Sponge with a small amount of dry-cleaning solvent. Blot. (Use small amounts to prevent any possible damage to sizings, backings, or stuffing materials. Do not use gasoline, lighter fluid, or carbon tetrachloride.)
2. Mix one teaspoon of a neutral detergent (a mild detergent containing no alkalies or bleaches) with a cup of lukewarm water. Blot.
3. Sponge with clean water. Blot.

Rust

1. Use Whink or Zud or other rust remover. Follow directions on package.

Shoe Polish

1. Sponge with a small amount of dry-cleaning solvent. Blot. (Use small amounts to prevent any possible damage to sizings, backings, or stuffing materials. Do not use gasoline, lighter fluid, or carbon tetrachloride.)
2. Mix one teaspoon of a neutral detergent (a mild detergent containing no alkalies or bleaches) with a cup of lukewarm water. Blot.
3. Sponge with clean water. Blot.
4. Or seek the help of a professional carpet cleaner.

Soft Drinks

1. Mix one teaspoon of a neutral detergent (a mild detergent containing no alkalies or bleaches) with a cup of lukewarm water. Blot.
2. Mix one-third cup of white household vinegar with two-thirds cup of water. Blot.
3. Repeat step one.
4. Sponge with clean water. Blot.

Soy Sauce

1. Mix one teaspoon of a neutral detergent (a mild detergent containing no alkalies or bleaches) with a cup of lukewarm water. Blot.
2. Mix one tablespoon of household ammonia with a half-cup of water. Blot.
3. Repeat step one.
4. Sponge with clean water. Blot.

Tea

1. Mix one teaspoon of a neutral detergent (a mild detergent containing no alkalies or bleaches) with a cup of lukewarm water. Blot.
2. Mix one-third cup of white household vinegar with two-thirds cup of water. Blot.
3. Repeat step one.
4. Sponge with clean water. Blot.

Urine (Dry)

1. Mix one teaspoon of a neutral detergent (a mild detergent containing no alkalies or bleaches) with a cup of lukewarm water. Blot.
2. Mix one-third cup of white household vinegar with two-thirds cup of water. Blot.
3. Mix one tablespoon of household ammonia with a half-cup of water. Blot.
4. Mix one teaspoon of a neutral detergent (a mild detergent containing no alkalies or bleaches) with a cup of lukewarm water. Blot.
5. Sponge with clean water. Blot again.

Urine (Fresh)

1. Blot.
2. Sponge with clean water. Blot again.
3. Mix one tablespoon of household ammonia with a half-cup of water. Blot.
4. Mix one teaspoon of a neutral detergent (a mild detergent containing no alkalies or bleaches) with a cup of lukewarm water. Blot.
5. Sponge with clean water. Blot again.

Vaseline

1. Sponge with a small amount of dry-cleaning solvent. Blot. (Use small amounts to prevent any possible damage to sizings, backings, or stuffing materials. Do not use gasoline, lighter fluid, or carbon tetrachloride.)
2. Mix one teaspoon of a neutral detergent (a mild detergent containing no alkalies or bleaches) with a cup of lukewarm water. Blot.
3. Sponge with clean water. Blot.

Wax (Paste)

1. Sponge with a small amount of dry-cleaning solvent. Blot. (Use small amounts to prevent any possible damage to sizings, backings, or stuffing materials. Do not use gasoline, lighter fluid, or carbon tetrachloride.)
2. Mix one teaspoon of a neutral detergent (a mild detergent containing no alkalies or bleaches) with a cup of lukewarm water. Blot.
3. Sponge with clean water. Blot.

Wine

1. Mix one teaspoon of a neutral detergent (a mild detergent containing no alkalies or bleaches) with a cup of lukewarm water. Blot.
2. Mix one-third cup of white household vinegar with two-thirds cup of water. Blot.
3. Repeat step one.
4. Sponge with clean water. Blot.

17

Sewing

Basic home sewing equipment and skills . . . Sewing basket contents . . . Threading your needle . . . Basic hand stitches: running stitch, basting stitch, back stitch, hem stitch, slip stitch, overhand or whipping stitch, overcast stitch, blanket stitch . . . Four basic machine stitches: regular, basting, backward, zigzag . . . Basic sewing techniques . . . Hemming skirts and uncuffed pants . . . Patching . . . Repairing ripped or torn seams and reinforcing seams . . . Sewing on buttons, two- and four-hole, shank, widening and narrowing buttonholes . . . Snaps and hooks and eyes . . . Broken zippers

H ome sewing is enjoying a renaissance. There is no economic justification for this. In many cases, the sewers spend so much money on high-tech sewing machines and aids, not to mention hours of their time buying materials, cutting, stitching, and fitting, that their sewing is not cost-effective compared with store-bought items. On the other hand, if what you want is not out there to be bought, and you want it badly enough, it makes sense to make it; and only by sewing at home or hiring a tailor can you get clothes made to fit, in precisely the styles, colors, and fabrics you choose, with high-quality workmanship and attention to detail. Now there is even computer software that prints out patterns according to measurements you type in, which makes personalized fit even easier to attain. Most people have never worn well-made, well-fitting clothes, made to taste, in their lives. It is a heady experience. You can also easily make a variety of home furnishings to your exact taste—napkins, curtains, comforter covers, and many other articles.

Sewing itself is more fun, more satisfying, and more challenging than many people would believe without trying it. If you do not know how, there are classes everywhere, and friends are almost always willing to help. Sewing is something that you can do alone or with someone else, a friend or family member.

You need not invest in a lot of expensive equipment if you wish to sew at home. Even advanced sewers can stitch pretty much anything they want on a sturdy portable that does nothing more than go forward and backward. A few "zigzag" stitch patterns and a buttonhole capacity are quite useful but will not get a great deal of use by the casual or beginning sewer. If you hope to go at sewing seriously, however, you want both a good machine with the latest bells and whistles and, probably, a serger, a machine that is credited with having revolutionized home sewing in the past decade. Without exaggeration, you can say that sergers have certainly contributed enormously to its revitalization. Sergers simultaneously trim, stitch, and finish seams with an overcast stitch. They save great amounts of labor and give articles made at home a professional, finished look that until recently very few could achieve. Some sergers are much more versatile and easier to use than others, and the fanciest ones can be very costly. Check consumer information sources before making a choice.

Basic Home Sewing: Equipment and Skills

Some basic skills in sewing are perennially useful; if you have them, you will use them many times in the course of a year. Not being able to sew on a button, hem a skirt or pants, patch a hole or tear, or repair a seam can be terribly inconvenient, as it is far more trouble to track down a seamstress or tailor to do these little jobs than to take a couple of minutes to do them yourself. With limited skill, you can do these jobs or even make a curtain, napkins, comforter covers, and so forth.

Sewing Baskets. A sewing basket or box in every home is indispensable. Either is preferable to a sewing drawer because you want something that you can carry around with you. If you plan on sewing nothing more than a ripped hem or a loose button, your sewing box need not be elaborate. A sewing basket that includes the following items will see you through all the ordinary sewing chores:

Sewing shears and scissors. You may find it useful to have both a pair of larger shears (6 to 8 inches) and a pair of smaller scissors (3 to 6 inches). The handles of sewing shears angle upward so that you can cut fabric easily holding the bottom blade against your cutting surface. They have a small hole for your thumb and a large one for a couple of fingers. Scissors have equal-size handle holes and are straight. (Reserve your sewing scissors for sewing; other jobs, such as cutting paper, will blunt them.)

Pinking shears. These cut zigzag edges on cloth. Pinked edges are sufficient finishing for the edges of cloth that does not unravel badly.

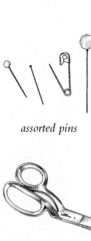

assorted pins

needle threader

pinking shears

dressmaker shears

embroidery scissors

all-purpose scissors

assorted threads

assorted buttons

assorted snaps, hooks and eyes

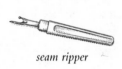

seam ripper

sharps (hand needles)
assorted sizes

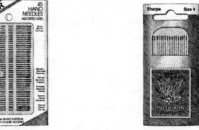

sharps (hand needles)
size 4

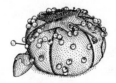

pincushion

thimble

tape measure

Sewing basket contents

(Seam edges should always be finished somehow, with pinking, stitching or serging, or seam binding.)

Seam ripper. The seam ripper is a small cutter with a tiny curved cutting blade used for ripping out seams.

Sewing needles ("sharps"). Buy a package of assorted sizes and lengths. The sizes range from 1 (the thickest) to 12 (the finest), but you will rarely use the very low or high numbers for ordinary household chores. Embroidery needles have long eyes to accommodate several threads. Darning needles have even bigger holes. A variety of lengths is useful.

Straight pins. Medium gauge is the most useful, but use only fine gauge for silks and sheer fabrics. Heavy gauge are necessary for coating, carpeting, and upholstery; lighter ones will break off in the cloth. Those with colored heads are easier to see. You might like Japanese-made straight pins that have larger, colored heads and longer, finer shafts. (I have heard them called "flowerhead pins.")

Pincushion

Snaps or hooks and eyes

Tape measure

Dressmaker's chalk

Thimble. Wear the thimble on the middle finger of the hand with which you hold the needle. When it is hard to push the needle through the cloth, do so with the thimble to avoid hurting your finger.

Needle threader. For those who are farsighted or have shaky hands, there are completely automatic ones or simple guides—whatever you need.

Thread
   —Heavy-duty cotton or cotton-bound polyester in white and black.
   —Fine cotton thread, mercerized, in white and black, size 80. (The higher the number, the finer the thread.)
   —Mercerized cotton or cotton-bound polyester, size 50, in an assortment of colors: white, black, gray, brown, off-white, red, pink, purple, light blue, royal blue, dark or navy blue, yellow, dark and light green, orange.

Wool threads or fine yarns. Get an assortment in various colors for mending sweaters and socks. Choose either the same colors as you select in threads, or start with black and white and add colors as is convenient.

Buttons. It is useful to have an assortment of sizes, shapes, colors, and styles: two-hole, four-hole, and shank buttons. When you throw shirts, coats, or dresses away or turn them into rags, cut off the buttons and save them, either in a pocket in your sewing basket or in a button box. They'll come in handy. Likewise, when new clothing comes with small packages containing thread, yarn, or buttons, save the little packages in your sewing basket so you will have them for repairs.

Rag bag. Save swatches of cloth from old clothes and linens to be used for rags or patches, odd chores, crafts, and so on.

Threading Your Needle. Choose a fine, medium, or heavy thread and needle in proportion to your cloth—very fine needles and thread for organdy, medium for percale, heavy-duty for thick denims. The size numbers for needles and threads are in inverse relation to the thickness of the needle and thread—that is, the finest needles and threads have the highest number. Choose thread color slightly darker than the fabric, as thread appears a bit lighter off the spool.

If you keep a variety of size 50 threads (mercerized if they are cotton) plus a few spools of fine and heavy-duty, you should be able to handle most household chores with what you have on hand. Medium thread will do when medium-heavy or medium-light would be better. But size 50 cotton thread will look bad and create holes and tears in very sheer fabric. If your garment has a satiny or shiny appearance, you will be dissatisfied with the look of mending done in cotton. You can use silk thread on silk, wool, and synthetics with a sheen. Use wool thread to darn wool. There are a variety of threads designed to suit special purposes, too, which you might have occasion to acquire—quilting thread, buttonhole twist, and so forth.

Use a needle threader if you have shaky hands or are farsighted. It makes things easy.

Basic Hand Stitches. Thread your needle and then secure the thread to the fabric so that it does not pull out. The easiest way to secure the thread is to make a tiny knot at its end. A more attractive way is to take two or three tiny stitches at the beginning of your sewing (you will do so again at the end), as experienced sewers do.

For greater strength, double your sewing thread. When you use a double thread, knot the loose ends together or secure both loose ends by taking a couple of inconspicuous stitches. However, for less visible stitching, desirable in hemming, for example, sew with a single strand of thread. To do this, you

Needle threader

Knotted thread ready for sewing

knot or secure only one of the loose ends of thread, and leave the other hanging 2 or 3 inches down from the eye of the needle. When you are sewing with a single thread, watch out that you do not accidentally catch the loose end in your stitching and begin sewing with a double thread. Do not use a longer thread than you need—the length of your arm extended is the maximum you can comfortably sew with; you sew faster with a shorter thread, and shorter thread is not so prone to tangle and knot. On the other hand, when you are sewing long seams or a hem with a wide circumference, it is annoying to have to keep rethreading your needle, so most of us choose to use a longer thread. Just before you run out of thread, secure it again with tiny stitches or a tiny knot, then snip the thread. (If you let the thread get too short, you will not have enough left to make a knot or a couple of stitches.)

The most common and useful hand stitches are described below.

Running Stitch. Used for most basic sewing, mending, seams, and quilting. You use a long, thin needle. Push the needle in and out of one or more layers of cloth every ¹⁄₁₆ to ¼ inch in a straight line, keeping all the stitches even (the same size) and small. The smaller the stitch, the stronger the seam.

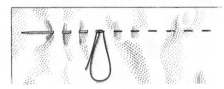

Running stitch

Basting Stitch. This is just a longer running stitch, from ¼ to ½ inch, used to hold things together temporarily until you do a more permanent stitch. Remove basting when the permanent stitches are in.

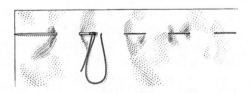

Basting stitch

Back Stitch. This is a strong stitch, a variation on the running stitch, used for repairing ripped seams and reinforcing vulnerable ones. It looks like machine stitching on the right side, but you see overlapping on the wrong side. You use a shorter needle than for the

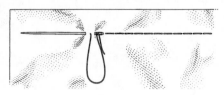

Back stitch

running stitch. After securing the thread, take a small (say ⅛ inch) running stitch, pushing the needle from the right side of the cloth through to the underside and then bringing it back up to the right side. Now reinsert your needle in the first hole of this first stitch and take a running stitch twice as long (say ¼ inch) and from now on, all the stitches will be the longer length. (Your needle will emerge ¼ inch ahead of the beginning of the first stitch.) Go back and reinsert the needle at the middle hole—halfway through the second stitch—and take another stitch. Repeat until the seam is completed. Basically, you simply repeatedly reinsert your needle in the hole from which it last emerged.

Hem Stitch. This is not a strong stitch, so it is not used where it would be subjected to strain. Begin with your needle coming through the edge of the fold of the hem. (See "Hemming Skirts and Uncuffed Casual Pants," below.) Pick up one or two threads of the fabric, then one of the fold of the

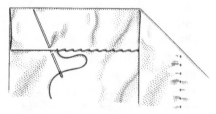

Hem stitch

hem, then one of the fabric, and so forth, creating small slanted stitches. (My grandmother would let me take only one thread of the fabric, but I will approve if you take two.) Do not pull too tight or the hem will pucker. If your stitches are too loose or too far apart, the hem will sag or catch on things and pull out.

Slip Stitch. This invisible stitch, similar to a hem stitch and likewise not strong, is used to secure hems, facings, and so on. Turn back the edge of the hem or fold about ¼ of an inch. Secure the thread. Then proceed by taking a small stitch in the fold, then picking up a thread of the fabric, then taking a small stitch in the fold, then picking up a thread of the fabric, and so forth, until it is all hemmed. For heavy fabrics or skirt hems, stitches should be close together, but in other places you can space them widely—up to ½ inch apart.

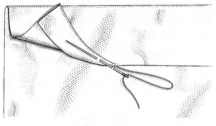

Slip stitch

Overhand or Whipping Stitch. These are basically the same stitch, called overhand if it is perpendicular and whipping if it is slanted. It is used for less visible, strong seams. With a whipping stitch, you usually stitch from the right side of the cloth. Hold the folded edges of the seam allowances together.

Secure the thread. Then pick up one or two threads from each fold in turn, always beginning with the edge of the cloth in the back and proceeding to the front. Keep the stitches close together.

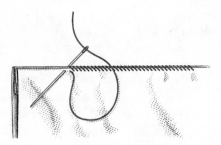

Whipping stitch

Overcast Stitch. Overcast stitching is used to finish the raw edges of hems and seams. It is similar to the whipping stitch, except that it is done on raw edges of cloth and is about ¼ inch deep, so it is more visible. Secure the thread. Holding together the two raw edges of the cloth, take slanting stitches over the two together. Proceed from the back of the cloth to the front.

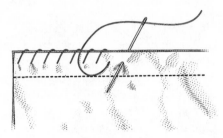

Overcast stitch

Blanket Stitch. This is another stitch for finishing raw edges. Turn under the edge of whatever you are sewing. Secure the thread on the wrong side and push the needle through to the right side. Working from left to right and facing the right side of the article, insert the needle on the right side—at about ¼ inch from the edge of the fold, at the right of the thread—and

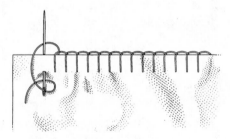

Blanket stitch

push it through to the wrong side, holding the thread to the needle's left. You will catch the thread right at the edge of the fold. As you repeat the stitch, a row of stitches forms along the edge of the fold of the cloth.

Four Basic Machine Stitches. Follow your machine's instructions on threading the needle, filling the bobbin, setting the tension, and adjusting the stitch size.

Regular. This is a running stitch. Standard or "regulation" stitching gets 12 stitches per inch. Use 16 per inch on fine and sheer cloth, and 8 to 10 for heavy cloth. Remember to use fine, medium, and heavy-

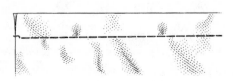

Running machine stitch

duty needles for cloth of different weights.

Basting. This is a long running stitch. Use 6 to 8 stitches per inch.

Basting machine stitch

Backward. This is a running stitch in reverse.

Zigzag. You set the machine to sew in a pattern instead of in a straight line. You can make the stitches narrower or wider, longer or shorter. See your instruction

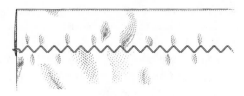

Zigzag machine stitch

manual for using the zigzag feature on your machine. Zigzag patterns are used for decoration and reinforcing and finishing seams.

Basic Sewing Techniques

Hemming Skirts and Uncuffed Casual Pants. Besides looking good and preventing unraveling, hemming gives weight and shape at the bottom of a garment to make it hang properly. To lengthen or shorten a hemmed garment, remove the stitching in its hem, iron out the old hem fold-line, and refold the hem to the desired length. When lengthening, especially when the garment is not new, keep in mind that sometimes the original hem fold-line shows as an unattractive line that laundering and ironing fail to remove.

There is no law stating how wide a hem should be. Generally, dresses hang better with a generous hem, say two inches, and the stitch that almost always looks best on dresses is a hem stitch. But on blouses, the legs of casual pants without cuffs, and some other articles, narrow machine-stitched hems are often preferable. If the hem is to be on a skirt or dress or uncuffed pants, you must try

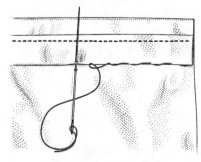

Hem using seam binding

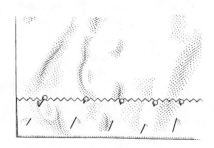

Hem using pinked edge

the garment on and measure how much hem should be turned up to create a good length. With some garments, this can lead to intricacies that are beyond the scope of this book. For example, if the finished hem would be too wide, you will have to cut off some cloth; getting the hem to hang an even distance from the ground can present difficulties; garments that widen toward the bottom, like flared skirts and bellbottoms, must be tucked, gathered, or otherwise narrowed when you turn them up. When such difficulties are all settled to your satisfaction, there are several ways to go ahead and put in the hem.

One standard way of hemming a garment that would be the desired length with, say, a 1½-inch finished hem, is this. (Note that making this 1½-inch finished hem will shorten the garment by 1¾ inches.) First, to finish the raw edge of the cloth, turn under to the wrong side ¼ inch of the raw edge and baste it down using either a machine or hand-basting stitch. Then turn the ironed or basted edge under (to the wrong side), making a fold about 1½ inches wide and, to hold the fold in place while you hem-stitch it to the fabric, pin it or baste it near the fold-line so that it stays in place. (You can sometimes avoid basting or pinning these folds and simply iron them in.) Then stitch the hem by hand, using the hem stitch. Some machines will do a hem stitch. Remove the basting stitches. Press or iron.

There are other ways of hemming than simply turning under the raw edge and stitching it down. You might sew seam binding to the raw edge, using a machine (or by hand, if you have no machine). (Seam binding is a narrow, ribbonlike strip of cloth.) Then hem by hand, stitching the outside edge of the seam binding to the cloth, again using the hem stitch. Or you could, for very casual purposes, simply pink the raw edge, assuming that the cloth does not unravel, turn it under, and hem as before. This would be good for a child's Halloween costume, for example.

Patching. You can patch almost any kind of tear, but patches do not look good on everything. There are many ways of patching. You can put patches on the right or wrong side of the garment, and you can make them of the same fabric as the garment or of a different fabric. If you want to make them of the same fabric as a purchased garment, you have to find a place on the garment where you can snip enough off to make a patch without its being noticeable. Usually this is impossible, but sometimes you can find enough in a hem or facing where the cut-out will be invisible to mend a small tear or hole. (But you may need to know how to repair the place from which you took your patch as well.) Make the patch extend at least an inch beyond the hole or tear in all directions.

First, to make sure that the raw edge of the patch will not unravel, pink it, overcast it, do a running stitch around the border, zigzag it on your machine, or hem it. If you are putting the patch on the wrong side of the garment, you should make sure that the edges of the hole or tear do not fray: turn under the raw edges of the hole or do a zigzag stitch around them with your

Whipping stitch patch   *Zigzag stitch patch*   *Running stitch patch*

machine. If you are making a patch of the same fabric, be sure to align it with any pattern, weave, or grain in the fabric. Pin the patch to the garment. If there is to be no strain on the place where the patch is, sew the fabric to the patch with a tiny slip stitch (invisible but weak), with a running stitch (hand or machine), or any other stitch you like. Where strength is not an issue, it is only a question of whether you like the look of the stitch. But if you need a tough patch, as for the knees on children's pants, you should use a generous-size patch and secure it with an overhand or whipping stitch, a back stitch, or a zigzag machine stitch.

There are also iron-on patches, but they often come off and you have few choices of color and fabric when you use these. Follow the instructions for their use on their labels.

Repairing Ripped or Torn Seams; Reinforcing Seams. Garments are most likely to tear at their seams. Shirts and blouses tear at the point where the sleeve is sewn to the body; trousers tear at the seat of the pants or the crotch; skirts split at the side seam; gloves split along the finger seams. You can resew the seam by machine unless the article is too tiny or the tear is in too awkward a spot. Gloves will often have to be sewn by hand; turn them inside out to work.

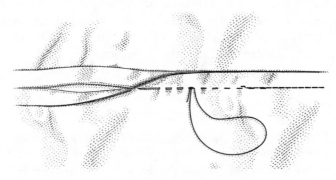

Seam repair

To repair by hand the portion of a seam that has come undone, use a small running stitch. If the seam must be very strong, use a back stitch. Work on the wrong side of the garment. Begin an inch or so before the rip, stitching right over the old stitches, and continue an inch or so beyond the rip, securing the thread carefully at both ends by making a few tiny stitches. On a machine, you do this with a regular stitch, securing at both ends by stitching backward for a few stitches. Be sure to use the sturdiest thread consistent with the weight of the fabric. Press the seam open after you have finished so that the fabric does not pucker where you have mended.

If you know that you tend to tear your shirts or blouses under the arm or at the shoulder back, or that you often split the seams of your trousers, you can reinforce the seam and prevent the damage from happening. This is a particularly good idea when the garment is made of something sheer that might tear along the seam, or whenever you notice that a garment's stitching does not appear strong. Simply sew along the vulnerable seam, using a small running stitch (or a back stitch when you need a particularly strong seam) in the same way that you would repair a seam.

Sewing on Buttons. I learned about sewing on buttons in 4-H. We were given small, square, pale blue swatches along with what seemed an infinite variety of buttons and arbitrary rules about fastening them to the little blue swatches. The rules were not so arbitrary in retrospect, but we were not told much about what they were for.

Be sure to use strong thread—heavy-duty if the fabric is not delicate. On very delicate fabrics, it is often necessary to put some kind of fabric reinforcement under the button or else the fabric will tear when the button gets pulled.

If you are missing a button on a shirt or a dress in a place where it shows and cannot find a button that matches, remove one from the bottom edge or tail (or some other place where it doesn't show) and put it in the place that does show. Then sew an unmatched button of the right size in the less conspicuous place where you removed the button. Try to make the unmatched button as similar to the others as you can manage.

When you notice that a button is coming loose, reinforce its stitching before it actually falls off and you lose a pretty or unusual button or have to pass half your day half-buttoned. Observe new garments carefully. Often even expensive clothes that should have been made with every attention to detail will have buttons secured by only a couple of threads.

Two- and Four-Hole Buttons. To be sure that you get the button in the right place, close up the garment, buttoning it above and below the missing button so that its buttonhole is at the proper place for buttoning. Mark this place with dressmaker's chalk. Then secure the thread to the right side of the material at that spot by taking several tiny stitches, until the thread feels tight and

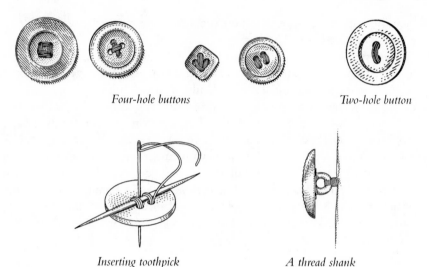

Four-hole buttons   Two-hole button

Inserting toothpick   A thread shank

does not pull out. Place the button so that it is centered at the spot and so that its holes or pattern are parallel to those of all the other buttons. Now insert the needle into one hole of the button from its wrong side. Then insert the needle into the other (or another) hole on the button's right side, passing it through to the wrong side of the cloth. To ensure that the button is not sewn so tight that it cannot be buttoned, you can insert a pin or a matchstick under the thread, between the button and the fabric, as you work.

Repeat the in-and-out stitching five or six times, following the same pattern each time. Try to make the stitches very close together so that the stitching looks neat on the right and wrong sides of the cloth. Never sew a stitch over the edge of the button.

When the button has been well secured, remove the pin or matchstick and check to see that the button is just loose enough to button easily. (For a heavy item such as a coat, you would need a longer set of threads connecting the button to the fabric, and a good sewer would make a thread shank of the slack. See "Shank Buttons," below.) Then draw the needle through to the wrong side of the cloth and again secure the thread with several tiny stitches. Cut the thread.

Shank Buttons. A shank button has a shank, or a projection on its back that has a hole in it, through which the attaching threads are drawn. Mark the spot where the shank button is to go in the same way as for two- and four-hole buttons. Secure the thread to the right side of the fabric at that spot by taking several tiny stitches. Then pass the needle and thread five or six times from the wrong side of the cloth through the shank hole and back to the wrong side of the cloth again. Try to make the stitches very close to one another.

When the button is firmly sewed on, secure the thread on the wrong side of the cloth with a few tiny stitches.

Sometimes with a stiff or thick shank, or when the button and shank form one piece, the button will not lie easily and attractively in the buttonhole unless you make an additional thread shank. (You will not need to do this for the thin metal or plastic shanks that are so often used.) To do this, insert a matchstick between the button and the cloth as before, if this is feasible; if the shank is not properly shaped to allow this, hold the button taut at a slight distance from the cloth, or put the tip of your finger between the button and the cloth, as you stitch in and out of the shank. Then, after the button is sewn on, do not yet cut the thread. Holding the button away from the cloth so that the slack is pulled taut, wrap the sewing thread around it several times, forming the thread shank. Then secure the thread on the underside, as before, with a few tiny stitches.

Widening and Narrowing Buttonholes. Without learning to make buttonholes or to do the buttonhole stitch, on casual and informal clothes you can often satisfactorily widen a tight buttonhole or tighten one that is so loose that the button keeps slipping out. Those with limited sewing experience should not try this on elegant, formal, or "good" clothes.

To widen a buttonhole, take small, sharp scissors and snip the corner of the buttonhole a tiny bit, no more than 1/16 inch. (If you oversnip, stop; find a sewing friend to help you repair the damage.) Try to fit in the button now. If it is still too tight, take another tiny snip. When the button fits perfectly, choose a thread color that will look satisfactory and close your snipped edge with several overhand stitches perpendicular to the buttonhole to prevent the hole from tearing farther. Secure the thread very firmly before clipping, as buttonholes take a great deal of strain.

To narrow a buttonhole, sew together one corner of it with several overhand stitches perpendicular to the buttonhole. Before clipping your thread, try the button to see if the hole fits with proper snugness. If it is still loose, take a few more stitches. Secure the thread very firmly before clipping.

Snaps. Choose smaller ones for sheer fabrics; larger ones for heavy. The part with the ball goes on the top of the closure, on the hidden side, and the part with the hole goes on the other side of the closure (the one that gets covered), on the right side of the cloth. Mark the places where each should go with dressmaker's chalk. To sew on the ball portion, secure the thread with a few tiny stitches. Then, using an overhand stitch, go through the cloth and then up to and through first one hole of the snap

Snaps sewn on

and then another. The thread will lap over the outer rim. Sew on the hole portion of the snap in the same manner.

Hooks and Eyes. Hooks and eyes have to be very precisely placed and aligned to work properly. This takes patience, but the actual stitching is simple. Choose smaller ones for sheers and larger ones for heavy fabrics. You use the kind with a straight catch (or eye) when the sides of the opening will overlap when closed. You use the kind with a round eye when the edges meet without overlapping. A hook is often used with just a loop made out of thread.

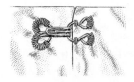

Hook and eye—closed

With dressmaker's chalk, mark the positions the hook and eye will take. Say you are putting the hook and eye on a neck closure that will overlap. Put the hook on the side of the closure that will cover the other, on the underside of the garment and with the hook

Hook and eye—open

facing down, placed so that the end of the hook is recessed ⅛ inch in from the edge. Put the eye—the straight type—on the right side of the covered closure, set back to the seam, or about ⅜ inch in from the edge. For a closure that will not overlap, place the round eye so that it extends about ⅛ inch past the edge of the cloth. Using the overhand stitch, attach the hook and eye to the spots you have marked.

If you are making a thread loop, just secure the thread at one end of where the loop should be and then insert the needle at the place where the other end should be, leaving the stitch loose. Bring the needle up through the first end and then again down through the second, again leaving the stitch loose. Secure and cut off the thread. You now have a two-stranded loop. To complete the loop, work the entire edge of the loop with a blanket stitch (described above).

Broken Zippers. It is rarely possible to repair a zipper, and it takes some practice to learn to remove an old zipper and sew in a new one neatly. But with metal zippers you can sometimes make a rough repair that at least lets you continue to use the garment. One common problem on metal zippers is that the metal teeth at the bottom of the zipper become bent or pulled and the lead cannot be pulled past them. You can repair this sometimes by getting a pair of pliers and straightening the teeth. If the zipper is closed at the bottom (that is, if it is not the kind used on a coat with two unattached sides), you can sometimes fix it in a way that involves limiting how far down you can pull the zipper. What you do, when there is a bump or broken tooth past which the zipper lead will not proceed, is cut the zipper there and reinsert the lead just past the cut. Then sew up the cut with a whipping or overhand stitch, intentionally making a thick block past which the zipper will not go. From now on you'll just zip down to this point. This works on many skirt and trouser zippers, and these often do break at the bottom. You will not, however, be able to use this technique with tight garments, as you probably could not pull them on with the zipper only partially opened.

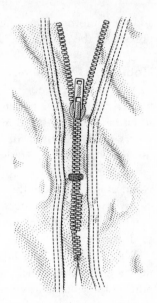

Mended zipper

18

Closets for
Clothes and Linens

*Storing clothes and linens . . . Moths, mites, and other
creatures . . . Putting away linens . . . Putting away clothes . . .
Caring for your clothes . . . Hats . . . Gloves . . . Shoes*

Clothes and linens stay fresher, safer, and cleaner in well-managed closets. Here is a summary of what good management of linen and clothes closets consists of.

In General: Storing Clothes and Linens

Closets should be cool, dry, and airy. Mildew grows in warm, humid conditions, and it can infect cottons, linens, and other materials in your closets, including the very wood the closet is made of. Beware of hot pipes running through closets. Heat can age and discolor fabrics.

Closets need to undergo a major cleaning periodically. During spring or fall cleaning or whenever the mood hits you, empty the closets and chests; dust or wash down shelves, floors, walls, and ceilings. Let closets and chests dry and air thoroughly before you replace things; and wash or clean as many of their contents as feasible, even if they have not been used. Things that are stored for a long time tend to develop a musty smell that will, if not removed, infect the other things stored with them.

To keep clothing and linens fresh-smelling, give them air. Do not overcrowd your drawers and closets. Laying things on slatted shelves that permit air circulation is beneficial. For linens particularly, but for all stored fabrics, narrow shelves are preferable to deep ones both because things are easier to find and because air circulates better. You can also leave the door to the closet ajar now and then so that the closet gets frequent changes of air. (Do this, however, only at times when the air likely to circulate is fresh and sweet.) Air all clothes and linens after laundering and ironing and before replacing them in the closet to be sure that any hint of dampness is entirely dissipated. If you put even slightly damp linens or clothes in your closet, you can produce a musty smell that is impossible to obliterate without totally emptying the closet and cleaning or washing all its contents. (You can try using silica gel, activated alumina, anhydrous calcium sulfate, and other desiccants to remove moisture from damp closets and cabinets.)

If odors afflict your closets, you might try a chemical deodorizer. Calcium carbonate and activated charcoal absorb odors; baking soda effectively neutralizes them. Home centers sell a variety of deodorizers. You put one of these substances in an open container and set it in the chest or closet or follow package directions. (Potpourris and perfumes cannot remove odors, and the attempt to mask them usually just makes things worse.) But once the contents of the closet have absorbed the odors, in my miserably experienced opinion, none of these remedies is going to remove the odors from fabrics that have absorbed them. Curing closet mustiness takes so much labor, and fresh closets provide such continual benefits, that it is worthwhile being vigilant.

Although potpourris are not much good for removing odors, many of us enjoy their pleasant scents on our clothes or linens. Potpourris are perfumes. Commercial ones are often too strong. If you have one that is too strong, take just a portion of it, wrap it in cheesecloth, and tie it with a ribbon. Store the rest in an airtight container in a cool, dark place until you want more. My grandmother always used lavender (which she grew and dried herself)—and so sparingly that you could not detect the odor unless your face was pressed against the pillow. She would sometimes put a quince apple into the chest in which she stored linens to make a good scent. (Watch out for rotten quince apple stains.) Overuse of potpourris can contribute to stale closet odors. It is best if, when you open the closet door, you smell nothing at all, or perhaps if you can just catch the faint, reassuring scent of laundered cloth, one of the best smells in the world.

Wash or dry-clean all clothes and linens before seasonal or long-term storage. Insects and pests of all sorts will be attracted to dirt left on clothes and linens, and in the process of eating the dirt will harm the fibers. It is important to store them unstarched, too, since insects like silverfish will eat the starch and the fabric with it. Soil encourages mildew as well.

Store linen (flax fiber) unironed and loosely folded, since it is brittle and may otherwise crack at creases. Or you can roll linen. When it is stored for long periods, refold it with any creases in new places so that weakness or cracks do not develop along a crease line.

Acid causes deterioration of cellulosic fibers. When doing long-term storage, and storage of antique, delicate, or heirloom linens, you should wrap the articles in acid-free paper and store them in acid- and lignin-free boxes. Acid-free storage materials are now widely available at home centers, photographic supply stores, and archival supply companies.

Do not store cotton or linen in plastic bags from the dry cleaner or in garment bags made of synthetic fibers that do not breathe. These can trap moisture inside. Dry-cleaner plastic bags contain plasticizers that can produce yellow streaks on fabrics. Besides causing yellowing and trapping moisture, these prevent the drycleaning fluids and fumes from evaporating. Muslin or canvas garment bags are a good choice. You can also wrap things in clean and well-rinsed sheets or similar articles of white or undyed cotton or linen.

Cedar chests are not recommended for long-term storage or for storage of antique, heirloom, or delicate linens and cottons. The cedar gives off fumes and acids that can yellow and damage cellulosic fibers.

Moths, Mites, and Other Creatures

Cleaning wool and silk before storing them is the most important thing you can do to keep them moth-free, for moths, like other pests, are attracted to soils. Moth larvae will attack silk, but silk is not as vulnerable as wool and other hair fibers. Carpet beetles will damage wool and other hair fibers as well. In rare instances, silverfish will attack cotton or linen; this is more likely with starched cloth. Never put away fabrics made of cellulosic fibers that have been starched unless you plan to use them within a few weeks. No synthetic fibers are vulnerable to pests; however, pests may attack fabrics made of blends containing man-made fibers. (On mothproofing and the vulnerabilities of natural fibers to pests, refer to chapter 21.)

Clothing. Dust mites can live in clothes. A wool sweater or pair of slacks that is put away without having been cleaned retains perspiration and skin scales sufficient to support armies of mites. Research has found that during a month of storage, mites and allergens greatly increase. The best solution for clothes that can take it is laundering in hot water often, and always before putting them away for any long period of time. Wool garments and others that must be dry-cleaned or laundered at temperatures too low to kill mites should be thoroughly aired and sunned before replacing them in closets or drawers; try to wash or dry-clean them frequently, especially before storing them.

Putting Away Linens

The time-honored method of stacking linens is to place the freshly laundered pieces on the bottom of the stack. The purpose of this is to make sure that one set of sheets or towels is not used again and again and worn to pieces while others are untouched; it also ensures that unused linens do not grow stale or musty-smelling. Stack sets together so that they are used together and age evenly. Fold as described in chapter 7, "Folding Clothes and Linens."

Putting Away Clothes

Airing and brushing clothes is effective. Air thoroughly garments that you have worn and brush them to remove any superficial dirt or dust before returning them to the closet. Airing and brushing is particularly crucial for wool clothes. This removes dust and perspiration and reduces the number of times you will have to clean or launder them, which helps them last longer. Periodically take out and air wool garments that are infrequently worn.

Let wool garments rest for a day or two after wearing. Through the natural elasticity of the wool, they will regain their proper shape.

Review the contents of clothes closets yearly. Garments that have hung a year without use should be washed or cleaned and then removed to long-term storage. They will begin to smell musty if left month after month or, worse, year after year, and their smell will taint the other clothes. After two years without wearing, give them away to someone who can use them.

Hang clothes with the top, middle, and bottom buttons buttoned and zippers closed. Empty pockets before hanging garments, especially those of wool garments that are easily stretched, to preserve shape and prevent sagging and bulging. Woven wool, suits, dresses, blazers, and the like should be hung on wide, shaped hangers—padded ones are good—to reduce stress on the fabric at the point of hanging and to preserve proper shape.

Do not hang clothes too close together or they will wrinkle and there will be insufficient air in the closet to keep odors at bay. Clothes that shed will leave fibers on other clothes.

Traditionally, one hung only the clothes of the season in the closet, and the others were stored. This left plenty of room. But now people have far more clothes than they used to, and many city apartment dwellers have little closet space and even less storage space. As a result, closet design companies have sprung up, and they will renovate your closets, making astonishingly efficient use of their space. If you cannot afford this service, you can do much the same thing on your own by taking advantage of all the gadgetry available at the stores specializing in closet and storage widgets.

Even if you create highly efficient closets, however, seasonal storage of clothes is best. It causes a regular turnover of your closet contents that reduces the possibility of staleness (and chaos) developing. If storage is proper, it results in slower aging of your clothes. The traditional changeover times are Memorial Day and Labor Day, but it depends upon your local climate; March or April and October or November might be more sensible for you. Some people like to do this at spring and fall cleaning.

When putting away clothes in dressers and on shelves, follow the folding instructions in chapter 7.

Caring for Your Clothes

Do not wash or clean clothes more frequently than necessary. These processes visit wear and tear on garments, contributing over time to fading, pilling, fraying, holes, and the like. If you have worn a shirt for an hour and did not soil it or perspire heavily, hang it, button the neck, middle, and bottom buttons, and air it. Then put it back in your closet. If you have been wearing a garment for a short time and spill a drop of coffee or food on it, try to remove the spot without laundering or cleaning the whole garment.

But if clothes have received a real perspiration bath or heavy soil, wash them sooner rather than later, and wash them frequently. Dirt and sweat will cause fabrics to deteriorate faster than washing.

Use smocks and aprons when cooking, painting, or doing anything else liable to spot or soil your clothes. In the nineteenth century, the world was hard on people but kind to clothes. The poor clerks who, for miserly wages, drudged from early morning to nine o'clock in the evening had sleeve guards to keep their shirts and coats free of ink and other soil. Desk workers today have the same problem with sleeves after leaning all day long on penciled paper, papers from a copier, and newsprint. Although they would be laughed out of the office if they took to wearing sleeve guards, at least they get to go home after eight hours to wash their clothes.

Use scarves to protect the necks and collars of coats (especially leather ones) and other outerwear, because hair and skin oils tend to cause oil-staining and soiling in these areas. Such soil is hard to remove and is especially unsightly.

Hats

Store hats on shelves in separate hat boxes to keep off dust and prevent crushing and denting. Or wrap them in clean muslin cloth. If a hat has a crown, stuff it with tissue.

Gloves

Put away gloves flat, in a drawer or box. Keep colored gloves separate by placing a piece of cloth or tissue paper around them, for occasionally they can transfer color to other gloves.

Shoes

Shoes are safer on shelves than on the floor. Place shoe trees inside them to ensure that they stay straight, and keep them in individual shoe sacks or wrap them in tissue paper, especially if you do not wear them often.

PART III

ABOUT CLOTH

19

The Fabric of Your Home

Modern fabrics . . . Fiber content labels, care labels, low labeling . . . Warp and filling yarns . . . Thread count and its effect on durability . . . Plain weave, twill weave, satin weave, and other common weaves . . . Weft and warp knits . . . Jersey, garter, rib, cable, tricot, and other knits . . . Carded and combed yarns, staple and filament yarns . . . Twist . . . Natural vs. synthetic fibers and the environment . . . Effect of fiber content and other factors on fabric comfort . . . Absorbency and permeability of fibers . . . Hydrophilic natural fibers and hydrophobic man-made fibers . . . Effect of fiber content and other factors on look, feel, resilience, durability, cleanliness, and launderability . . . Glossary of Fabric Terms

Most parents have had the experience of observing their child's intense attachment to a beloved rag of a blanket or a disintegrating bit of cloth diaper. As many of them know, professional psychologists give the child's lovey the cold-sounding name "transitional object" and explain it as an attempt to evoke maternal comfort by creating a symbol of Mother. Cloth, or something similarly soft and fuzzy, is the all but inevitable infantile symbol of a mother whose touch comes through blankets and diapers from within moments of birth. In fact, the child's first work of art, motivated by the longing for security and affection, is this transformation of a grubby bit of cloth into something invested with the power to satisfy that longing.

In our adult lives, cloth continues to play intertwined aesthetic and functional roles. Textiles—from Oriental rugs to gleaming damasks—are the single most powerful source of domestic beauty. At the same time, they provide protection and comfort of a kind nothing else in the home can offer, shielding us and objects around us from cold, heat, dirt, damp, air, and light and from hard and rough surfaces that might bruise or scratch. The emotional warmth and security of a home, in our world, depend to a remarkable extent on the resonance of the sensations aroused by cool sheets, soft carpets, fabric-filtered light, nubby upholstery, thick towels, and so forth. By intricate chains of memory and association, these link up eventually to the primordial feelings of comfort, safety, love, and warmth that were first experienced through the medium of cloth in infancy.

All of us inevitably become textile connoisseurs. Nowadays, however, our taste is usually unconscious and inarticulate because, for a variety of historical reasons, most of us know far less about textiles than ordinary people once did. We may know what we like when we see or touch it, but we do not know what to look or ask for or how to use and care for fabrics. This diminished understanding of what so intimately concerns all of us is partly due to our increasing distance from the manufacturing, production, and care processes. But there is also far more to know than there used to be.

Until the late nineteenth century, Western people were familiar with the domestic use of four or five of the so-called natural fibers. Even in 1940, a housekeeper had to understand, by and large, the use and care of fabrics made of only six fibers: silk, linen (flax), cotton, wool, rayon (a generic name for a group of cellulosic fibers drawn from natural sources such as wood pulp), and acetate (a generic name for a group of fibers composed of cellulose acetate). By 1960 this number had more than doubled, swelled by the addition of several completely synthetic fibers. These included nylon, acrylic and modacrylic, olefin (polypropylene), and polyester. In the past few decades there has been an explosive increase in the number of processes and treatments, mechanical and chemical, to which fibers and fabrics are subjected, as manufacturers have sought not only to develop new "miracle" fabrics but to improve the appearance and function of the old ones. Endless modifications, combinations, and blends of each of the fibers are possible—for whiter whites, enhanced flame resistance, water repellancy, resistance to shrinking or pilling or static electricity buildup, environmental friendliness, and a hundred other purposes. The result is fabrics, fabric care, and cleaning requirements the identity and nature of which not even professionals can always discern by mere visual or tactile examination.

The government mandates labels that identify fiber content and provide care instructions as the solution to the problem of figuring out safe and effective care procedures. It also requires fiber content labels that specify which different fibers are contained in a garment and their percentages by weight—for example, "100% cotton" or "50% cotton, 40% polyester, 10% nylon." (Explanations of care labels and lists of terms and symbols commonly employed on them are provided in the Glossary of Care Label Terms and Symbols on page 34.) Valuable as they are, care labels are not a perfect solution. The information given on them is exceedingly limited, even when correct, which it sometimes is not as a result of mistakes, negligence, or, occasionally, intention. "Low labeling" (when manufacturers recommend a more conservative treatment than is necessary) is common. But even when the instructions are valid, they do not tell you what rationale lies behind them, so you do not know what consequences, great or small, you risk if you use procedures different from those recommended. And many people do not really know how to read and interpret care labels. For these reasons, relying on care labels is often a frustrating business. But it is not nearly as frustrating as not having any care labels at all—a situation you will sometimes encounter with household furnishings such as tablecloths, sheets, blankets, or draperies, for which the law does not currently require care labels.

The fiber content label fills in some of the blanks that the care label leaves open. Once you learn the fiber content of the article, in theory you learn much about the nature of the fabric—whether it is durable, wrinkle-prone, stain-resistant, hot or cool, absorbent, and so forth. In practice, however, people today are so little familiar with the properties of different fibers that to learn that a piece of upholstery or a garment is made of a cotton/synthetic blend or of acrylic in fact tells them little. And even if you understand the properties of the fiber or fibers used in the fabric, you also need to know something about the way the fabric is made and the quality of its manufacture to be sure you know how it will feel and function, how durable it will be, and how best to care for it. This chapter and the next explain the basics about fabrics. Familiarity with textile fundamentals gives you a foundation on which you can continue to increase your understanding of fibers and fabrics with each casual encounter.

The appearance, potential uses, and safe care of fabrics are determined by five factors: fiber content, yarn construction, weave or knit, dyes, and finishing and other treatments. In this chapter, I take up the first three factors in the reverse manufacturing order, first considering the weave, then unraveling the weave to consider the yarns it is composed of, and finally examining the fibers used to make the yarns. Dyes and finishing treatments, which may be applied at practically any step in the manufacturing process—on raw fiber, yarn, fabric, or even finished garments—are taken up in chapter 20.

Weaves and Knits

In woven fabrics, the yarns interlace; in knits, the yarns interloop. Woven fabrics are made on looms. The lengthwise threads on a loom are called the "warp" yarns, and the crosswise yarns are called "filling"—or "weft" or "woof"—yarns. (See the illustration below.) When weaving is done well with good-quality yarns, a pleasing, smooth, regular pattern is formed from the interlacing of the warp yarns and the filling yarns. The pattern of the weaving largely determines what type of cloth is being made—batiste, damask, oxford cloth, or corduroy. (These and many other useful terms relating to fabrics are explained in the Glossary of Fabric Terms, which begins on page 298.)

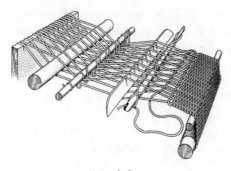

A simple loom

To determine the quality of the weave, hold the fabric up to the light. It should have no knots, weak spots, protruding yarns, crooked or broken yarns, or overthick yarns (slubs). The weave should be firm, close, uniform, and even.

Thread Count (Fabric Count). A fabric's thread count, now called the fabric count by textile professionals, tells you just how closely woven it is. (I will use the old term because it is still widely used on packages of sheets and other household goods.) The stated thread count on packages or in catalogues helps you evaluate the nature and quality of the goods offered for sale.

A fabric may be manufactured with a tight or a loose weave. In a tight or compact weave, the yarns lie more closely together than in a loose weave. The thread count tells you just how many warp and filling yarns per square inch there are in the fabric. A thread count of 64 × 60 means that the fabric has 64 warp yarns and 60 filling yarns per square inch. The finer the yarns, the more of them can be compressed into the space of an inch; the coarser the yarns, the fewer of them go into an inch. Thus muslin sheeting made of a coarser yarn may be quite closely woven even though its thread count is less than that of percale sheeting made with a finer yarn. ("Coarse" and "fine" here refer to yarn diameter, not yarn quality.) All else being equal, closely woven cloth is stronger and more durable because it contains more yarns than

---

THREAD COUNT AND DURABILITY

The durability of cloth is a function of many factors besides thread count, including the weight of the cloth, the type and quality of the fibers comprising the fabric, the overall construction of the cloth and its yarns, the nature and quality of the weave, and the types of finishes used. Do not assume, therefore, that you are getting the most durable sheets or shirts when you pick those with the highest thread count. Higher thread count means greater durability only when the comparison is between similar fabrics woven with the same type of yarn. If the yarn used to produce the higher thread count is thinner and weaker, the fabric is not necessarily stronger. A satin weave is less durable than a twill, and heavier cloth wears better than lighter. Thus coarse, heavy-duty cotton fabrics used for work clothes wear longer than sateen fabric of combed Egyptian cotton and a thread count of 400 or more.

a loosely woven one. A tight weave also shrinks less than a looser one and holds its shape better in laundering.

The thread count may also be expressed in one number; that is usually how it is done for sheets, pillowcases, and other household linens. The number given on the package labels is obtained by adding together the number of warp yarns and the number of filling yarns per square inch. This style of expressing the thread count is chosen because most such household items have a "balanced construction"—that is, they have roughly equal numbers of warp and filling yarns. A thread count of 220 in a balanced construction, for example, indicates that there are about 110 warp yarns and 110 filling yarns per square inch. When fabrics have an unbalanced construction (unequal numbers of warp and filling yarns)—say 100 × 60—it is more informative to see the numbers separately because the properties of balanced and unbalanced constructions are different. The yarns in a balanced construction take wear evenly, so, other things being equal, the fabric tends to wear more evenly and thus to be more durable than fabric with an unbalanced construction. But other things are not always equal. One authority gives this rule of thumb: A fabric with a high thread count but poor balance will wear better than one with a low thread count but good balance.[1]

If you want to determine the thread count of a fabric, you can try to count the yarns yourself, but this can be difficult with high-thread-count cloth. Using a ruler and a pin (and a magnifying glass if you need to), count off the number of either filling or warp yarns in a quarter-inch square of fabric and— if it is a sheet or other fabric with a balanced construction—multiply the number by eight; you will end up with a figure that roughly represents the thread count. If it is not cloth with a balanced construction, you count both the warp and filling yarns in a quarter-inch square, and multiply each by four—say 25 × 4 and 20 × 4. You end up with the two numbers of a thread count, in this case 100 × 80.

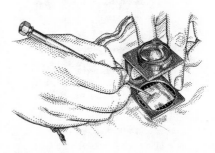

Taking a thread count (or fabric count) with a professional's pick and magnifying glass

A fine weave of a fabric ordinarily has a better "hand"—it feels better on the hand—and is more expensive than a coarser one.

Plain Weave, Twill Weave, and Satin Weave. There are only three basic weaves, of which most other weaves are variations: plain weave, twill weave, and satin weave. They vary in the way the lengthwise (warp) yarns are crossed by the filling (weft) yarns. Each of them can be found in looser and tighter and in coarser and finer versions, made of virtually any type of fiber or blend of fibers.

In plain weave, each filling yarn alternates over and under successive warp yarns across the fabric, and on its return across the fabric the filling yarn goes under and over alternate warp yarns. Plain weave appears identical on both sides and has no right side or wrong side unless it is napped or printed or otherwise finished differently on one side. Plain weave is used in dozens of fabric types, including broadcloth, calico, cambric, challis, percale, seersucker, blanket cloth, and tweed. Most sheets are plain weave. (But there are also sateen and twill-weave sheets as well as knitted-fabric sheets.) Plain-weave fabrics will generally be quite durable when the thread count is high. They may wrinkle more than twills.

There are several variations on the plain weave, of which the most common are the basket weave and ribbed or corded weaves. The basket weave creates fabrics that are usually loosely woven. It is often used for draperies and other furnishings because it hangs well. It is also somewhat wrinkle-resistant and flexible. It is not particularly durable, however, because it is of loose construction and contains yarns with little twist. Thus it is less suitable for many kinds of clothing than a balanced plain weave. Ribbed or corded fabrics (such as poplin, taffeta, faille, or ottoman) are created by using double the number of

Plain weave: Each filling yarn goes over and under each warp yarn, making a pattern of squares

Plain-weave handkerchief with lace trim

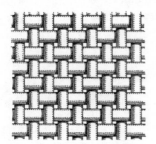

Basket weave: Two warp yarns pass over and under two filling yarns

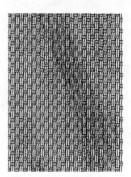

Fabric woven in basket weave

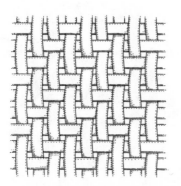 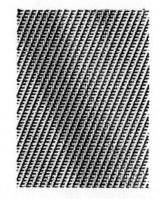

Twill weave: One or more warp (or filling) yarns go over at least two filling (or warp) yarns. The next warp (or filling) yarn(s) do not go over the same yarns as their neighbors. Instead the point of intersection is moved up or down by one or more yarns, creating the characteristic diagonal in the twill weave.

Herringbone twill

warp yarns as filling yarns, with larger filling than warp yarns; they are less durable than balanced plain-woven fabrics because of the increased abrasion to which the raised cords or ribs are exposed.

The twill weave has a characteristic diagonal pattern that can be varied to form attractive patterns by changing the direction of the diagonal, as in the herringbone weave. When the diagonal is more prominent on one side than the other, this side will be the face of the twill. A twill weave is more durable than a comparable plain-woven fabric; usually the steeper the diagonal of the twill line, the greater its strength and durability. Suits and coats are often made of fabrics in a twill weave. The long-favored denim, famous for its hardiness, is also a twill weave, as are gabardine, foulard, many tweeds, and serge. While twill fabrics are not perfectly wrinkle-resistant, they are more resistant to wrinkling than are plain-woven fabrics.

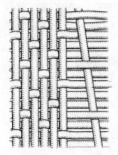

Satin weave: The warp yarns float over two or more filling yarns, creating a smooth, lustrous surface.

Satin weave fabric

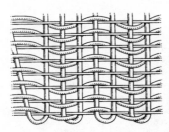

Gauze weave used in marquisette

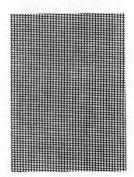

Marquisette

A satin weave tends to be less durable than plain and twill weaves because the yarns are given less twist—in order to make the fabric smoother and more lustrous—and because the long floating yarns on the fabric surface are more subject to snag and wear. (Floats are the length of the warp between the filling yarns.) Satin weave, however, is valued for this smooth, lustrous surface, which is desirable for elegant clothes. The shiny side of the satin weave is its face. Satin weaves also drape well. They are warmer and more absorbent because they are compact weaves: a great amount of fine yarn is woven into a small space. This gives satin weaves high thread counts despite their lower durability.

Other Common Weaves. Besides the three basic weaves, there are a few others with which it is useful to be familiar.

Double-woven cloth is usually chosen for its greater warmth and body. Double-woven cloth is made on a loom capable of simultaneously weaving two layers of fabric and joining the layers so as to create a single fabric. Double-woven fabrics may have different weaves on their two sides—for example, plain weave on one side and twill on the other. Many double-woven fabrics are reversible.

Leno weave is done on a loom capable of crossing two adjacent warp yarns. It is used to make lightweight, open-mesh fabrics, such as marquisette. This weave is also called gauze weave.

Dotted swiss cloth is a familiar example of a fabric created by swivel weaving, in which decorations such as circles or dots are woven into the surface of the cloth. Swivel weaves create the same design on both sides of the cloth. These fabrics typically are delicate enough that rough treatment in the laundry or elsewhere can pull the decorations out. Similar decorations are produced by lappet weaving, a method in which additional warp yarns are used to create small designs that are not the same on both sides of the cloth. Lappet-woven fabrics tend to be more durable than swivel-woven fabrics because the ends of the decoration threads are more securely fastened.

The dobby weave creates simple designs by means of a mechanical attachment to a plain loom. Bird's-eye is the name of a typical fabric having dobby weave. The jacquard weave creates fabrics with highly intricate designs. Jacquard weaving is done on a jacquard loom, which uses punched cards that control the movements of the warp yarns. This intricate type of weaving is used to make fine linen damasks, upholstery fabrics, silk brocades, and tapestries.

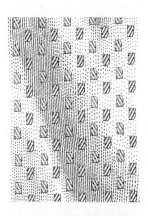

Two dobby-weave fabrics: The right-hand sample shows a dobby-weave fabric with a moiré.

Two jacquard-weave fabrics

Many weaves that were associated entirely with one sort of fiber a hundred years ago are now often available in virtually any sort of fiber one might wish. Serge, for example, once meant a very strong worsted (that is, a fabric of combed wool fibers) in a twill weave. Now serge may be made of wool, rayon, silk, or other fibers, and "worsted" refers to any type of yarn spun of longer, smoother, stronger yarns. Velvet originally meant a fabric made of silk, but now the word refers to any pile fabric with a plain or twill back and warp yarns forming the pile—silk, rayon, nylon, cotton, or synthetic. Flannel was once a wool fabric, but it is now more typically made of cotton and may be any napped, soft, loosely woven cloth of either plain or twill weave.

Knits. Knitted fabrics have characteristics unlike those of woven ones. Although woven ones, in general, hold their shape better, knitted ones tend to drape better and be less susceptible to wrinkling. By and large, knits deserve their reputation for being good travel choices. Knitted fabrics are usually more stretchy or elastic than woven fabrics and thus are famous for fit and comfort. But, because they are stretchy, they may bag, sag, or lose their shape if not well constructed. Knits are particularly prone to pilling and snagging because of their loose construction and the low twist of their yarns. Unless treated, knits, especially those made from cotton, have a strong propensity to shrink. Synthetic fibers are often used in knits, exclusively or in blends with natural fibers, to resolve such problems. When made of absorbent fibers, knits are exceptionally absorbent. They are highly air-permeable, and for that reason they are not good wind breakers. They are ideal for cool weather when they are thick and made from fuzzy, crimped fibers such as wool. Such knitted fabrics trap warm air near the skin very effectively. On the other hand, thin knits such as cotton T-shirts are especially comfortable for warm-weather wear.

Commercial knitwear is made by one of two processes: weft knitting or warp knitting. Weft knitting, like hand knitting, creates fabric by moving yarns horizontally back and forth across the fabric. Weft knitting permits rapid changes of design, but weft knits will run and unravel if a loop gets broken. Warp knitting creates fabrics in which the yarns run vertically in the fabric. Warp knits have less stretch than weft but will not run or unravel.

Weft Knits. Plain knit, also called jersey, is the basic knit stitch. (This is called stockinet when you do it at home by hand, knitting alternating rows of knit and purl stitches.) Jersey fabrics stretch both lengthwise and widthwise, but considerably more in the width. They are smooth on the right side (unless made with nubby yarns), showing vertical rows of Vs, and slightly nubby on the wrong side. They are commonly used for T-shirts, men's underwear, sweaters, socks, gloves, and other apparel. Jersey knits will unravel at the ends and form runs, too. Unless steps are taken to prevent it, they tend to curl up crosswise, or across the width, toward the face of the fabric and lengthwise

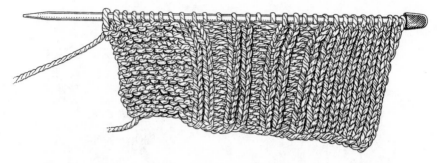

Front side of hand-knitted sampler: From left to right, plain knitting (or garter stitch), rib knit, and stockinet

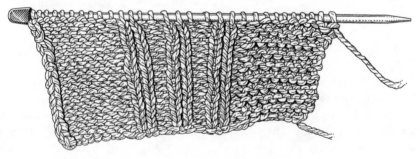

Reverse side of knitted sampler: From left to right, stockinet, rib knit, and plain knitting

toward the back side of the fabric. The more stitches per inch, the better a jersey knit holds its shape.

Links-links, or purl knit, looks like the fabric a home knitter creates doing garter stitch (knitting entirely in knit stitch or purl stitch), or plain knitting. It looks the same on front and back. Raised rows alternate with indented rows, which are only clearly visible if you stretch the material lengthwise. It is often used for babies' and children's clothes because it stretches both lengthwise and widthwise, but more in the length. Purl fabric is also commonly used for sweaters and other apparel. Like jersey knits, it unravels at both ends and can develop runs.

A rib knit produces alternating raised and indented rows ("ribs"), each consisting entirely of knit or purl stitches. In rib knits, the ribs run vertically and the stretch comes from their crosswise extension. (In hand knitting you make ribs by alternating a fixed number of knit and purl stitches, creating alternating columns of stockinet and garter stitch.) Because rib knit stretches more in the width than in the length, it is good for waists and wristbands in sweaters: it will stretch to allow you to put on the garment and then contract to fit your wrist or waist snugly. Rib knit is also used for the bodies of close-fitting sweaters and hats. Some ribs do, and some do not, look the same front and back.

Cable stitch

Raschel knit fabric

Cable stitch is used to make the plaited, interweaving decorative columns that appear on many sweaters and afghans.

Double knits are rib knits with two layers of loops. They are similar to double-woven fabrics. They are produced on knitting machines that have two sets of needles working simultaneously. The fabrics produced have a firmness and stability of shape that is comparable to that of woven fabrics. At the same time, double knits, like all knits, are naturally wrinkle-resistant. Double knits are used for women's suits and dresses, some menswear, and much sportswear.

Warp Knits. Tricot knits are the most common type of warp knit. They are produced on the tricot knitting machine, which can use very fine yarns such as those used to make lingerie fabrics. It can also produce a wide range of designs but does not easily permit changes of design or complex designs. Tricot knits look like rows of chains on the right side and rows of Vs or zigzags on the back (reverse) side. (You might need a magnifying glass to see this.)

Tricot fabrics drape well, are soft, have good wrinkle-resistance, and are elastic and strong. They are also open enough that air and moisture can pass through, promoting comfort.

Raschel fabrics are the second main type of warp knit. They are produced on the raschel knitting machine, which permits more versatility and complexity in design patterns and quicker change in design than tricot machines. The raschel knitting machine, for example, can produce heavy blankets, bedspreads, carpets, pile fabrics, fine laces, and veils, using any type of fiber whatsoever.

Both tricot and raschel knitting machines are used to make elasticized fabrics and waistbands, swimsuits, stretch foundation garments, and the like.

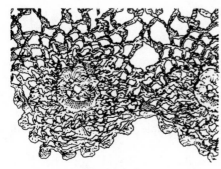

Handmade lace

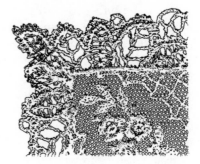

Machine-made lace

Lace. Lace is an openwork fabric of yarns that are twisted, looped, braided, stitched, or knotted together to form patterns. Although handmade lace is still produced for sale, almost all lace today is machine-made (usually on warp knitting machines). Machine-made lace is usually much less expensive and much more durable than handmade lace. Any lace pattern that can be produced by hand can also be produced by machine. Most patterns produced by machine today can be found in design anthologies that feature lace patterns owned by kings and queens centuries ago.

By its nature, lace tends to be delicate and easy to tear. Handmade lace should generally receive exceedingly gentle care. Laces can sometimes be machine-washed but often require hand-washing. The proper care of lace, like other fabrics, depends on the type of fiber of which it is made. Cotton, linen, silk, rayon, polyester, and other fibers are all commonly used for making lace today.

Yarn Construction

Carded and Combed; Staple and Filament Yarns. In the case of wool and cotton, the process of spinning raw natural fibers into yarns begins with carding or combing the fibers. Carded fibers are arranged in parallel fashion by a carding machine. The ropelike structure formed is called sliver; it can be spun to form carded yarn. Combing is a process in which the sliver is carded again, rendering the fibers more parallel to each other and removing the shorter fibers. Yarn made from combed fibers is called combed yarn. Combed yarns, of whatever fiber, produce superior fabrics that are stronger and smoother than those made of carded yarns. Articles made of combed cotton yarns, therefore, are so identified on labels to enable the buyer to know that they are of higher quality. Fuzzier woolen yarns are made from carded yarns; wool worsted, a smoother type of wool fabric, is made from combed yarns. See chapter 21, "The Natural Fibers." Linen yarns, too, are spun out of both short-staple fibers, called tow, and long-staple fibers, called line. Fine linen articles are always of line.

Silk is the only natural fiber that comes in filament lengths—that is, very long strands of up to a couple of thousand feet—as well as short (staple) lengths produced as waste in the process of reeling the long silk from cocoons. Whereas the staple-length silk fibers are spun into yarns the same way that cotton is, reeled silk filaments are twisted together in a process called throwing.

Synthetic fibers may be manufactured as staple that will be spun into yarns like cotton or wool fibers or as filaments of indefinite length that will be thrown like silk filaments. Rayon exists in both staple and filament forms, but it is mostly used in staple form.

Filament (or thrown) yarn may have strikingly different properties from spun yarn of the same fiber. For example, spun nylon would be used for sweaters and blankets, but filament nylon is necessary for silky lingerie and undergarments. Spun silk is less lustrous, strong, and elastic than thrown silk and tends to become fuzzy in use because the staple fibers rub up. Generally speaking, fabrics of spun yarn usually have a better hand and are fuzzier and softer, less smooth or slick, less lustrous, more adsorbent (because of a greater surface area—see page 294), more water-vapor permeable, warmer, and more insulating; they trap dirt more easily, produce more lint, pill more, slip less when you are sewing with them, and snag less than filament yarns of the same fiber and size.

Filament yarns, in turn, can be manufactured in different forms that result in fabrics of widely varying properties. Synthetic "textured" filament yarns (made of filament fibers that do not lie straight, close, and parallel) give greater comfort than older types of synthetic fabrics, which were made of flat multifilament yarns (made of straight filaments that pack close together and lie straight and parallel to one another). Thus, newer textured yarn fabrics do not lie so flat on the skin and do not feel as hot and clammy as flat yarn fabrics. They let more water vapor and air pass through, have greater adsorbency, and, in general, feel more comfortable. They also have a better hand, one more similar to that of spun yarns. Today, most clothing fabric made of synthetic fibers uses textured yarns.

Twist. In all types of yarn, the tightness of the twist in the yarn has a major effect on the characteristics of the finished fabric. Fabrics of harder-twisted yarns, other things being equal, are stronger, smoother, more elastic, more resilient, more abrasion-resistant, more absorbent and adsorbent, less prone to pilling or snagging, and even more comfortable on the skin. Up to a point, hard-twisted yarn also tends to shrink less, but both very low-twist and very high-twist yarns will shrink more—sometimes much more—than yarns with a moderate to high twist. Extremely hard-twisted yarns may also begin to weaken from the stress of the twist. Very fine, hard-twisted yarns are used for sheer fabrics, such as georgette, chiffon, and voile. Soft-twisted yarns are necessary for soft woolen fabrics. Crêpe fabrics are created when hard-twisted yarns with both right-hand and left-hand twists are woven into the fabric.

When the fabric gets wet, the yarns kink in different directions, producing the crêpey look. Many other effects can be created by using different twists, both hard and soft.

Fiber Content

The strongest determinant of a fabric's properties is the type or types of fiber of which it is made. A fabric's coolness or warmth, durability, strength, washability, dry-cleanability, absorbency, cleanliness, softness, smoothness, resilience (proneness to wrinkling), hand, and many other properties, as well as its cost, are affected as much or more by the fibers it is made of than by construction, weave, finish, dye, or any other single factor. How you clean and care for garments and furnishings is affected more by fiber content than by any other factor. (Chapters 21 and 22 give details on the characteristics and care of each type of fiber commonly used in clothing and furnishings in the home.)

Natural Versus Synthetic Fibers. Some people insist on using only "natural" fibers, but "natural" is a term of doubtful meaning in this context as in so many others. Applied to fabrics, it denotes fibers of plant or animal origin, such as cotton, linen (flax), silk, or wool. These, the major natural fibers, are derived, respectively, from the downy coverings of the seeds of cotton plants, the stalks of flax plants, silkworms' cocoons, and sheep's wool. Other fairly common plant, or "cellulosic," fibers used to make clothes and household furnishings are jute, hemp, and ramie. All other fibers, such as rayon, nylon, polyester, acetate, acrylic, and spandex, are termed "synthetic," "man-made," or "manufactured." But the distinction between natural and synthetic fibers is somewhat strained. The plant and animal substances from which the "natural" fibers are derived are indeed naturally occuring, but wood pulp, coal, and petroleum products are provided by Mother Nature, just as flax and cotton are. Flax and cotton, moreover, are subjected to repeated mechanical and chemical treatments that alter their appearance, shape, color, and other qualities. When we refer to the products of these enormously complicated manufacturing chains as "natural" and regard nylon as "synthetic," we are saying more about our own preferences for the familiar and the traditional than about the characteristics of the cloth.

This is not to say that preferences for natural fibers are necessarily arbitrary. Natural fibers have characteristics that really make them, in many instances, the best choice for furnishings and clothing, especially clothing to be worn next to the skin. For one, they are all hydrophilic (water-loving or -attracting), whereas most manufactured fibers (except for rayon, a cellulose-based fiber, and its cousins) are hydrophobic (water-hating or -repelling). This is what makes the natural fibers more absorbent, which is, as we shall see, a prime factor in their superior comfort under many circumstances. But by and large, the best choice of fiber for a particular function cannot be based on the thin distinction between natural and synthetic. A synthetic carpet backing that is rot-proof is preferable to a jute one that is not. A drape made of light-resistant synthetic fibers will last much longer and cost less than a silk one that will all too soon fall to pieces from the effects of ultraviolet radiation; the synthetic might even look as good. But the prejudice against synthetics is not easily removed because it has been infected with status perceptions. Wrongly but persistently, synthetics are associated with bright, unfading colors, smoothness, neat creases, durability, and cheapness, and they are disdained. Meanwhile clothes that wrinkle, fade, shrink, bleed, and develop holes become signs of superior taste and class, and deeper pockets, as these characteristics, equally mistakenly, are identified as the attributes of "natural" fibers such as cotton.

Sometimes the prejudice goes the other way, too, in favor of synthetics when they make little sense. People may sometimes choose synthetics for certain types of exercise and sportswear only because they feel that shiny, stretchy, "high-tech" fabrics are the right fashion statement for the exercise club, or because the symbolic value of synthetics rises in the sports world. Predictably, too, when natural fibers are chosen out of a sense of moral superiority, a backlash in favor of fun and self-indulgence cannot be long in coming, and this, as well, partly explains certain trends in favor of synthetic fibers where they are not necessarily better. The production of newer, high-priced, luxury versions of older synthetics is another development that has probably done more than anything else to erode prejudice against synthetics.

Environmental concerns have tended to push people toward buying natural fibers, but the facts do not present us with a clear-cut choice for one or the other on environmental grounds. Environmental issues in the textile industry are exceedingly complex. You must weigh not only the effects of elaborate agricultural, production, and manufacturing processes, but also the finishes and dyes that are likely to be used on both sides; the number of years the two kinds of fabrics are likely to survive; whether they are likely to be dry-cleaned or laundered, how they will be laundered, and the relative advantages and disadvantages of those processes environmentally; any waste or disposal problems created by a particular fiber; whether the fabric will be recyclable; and what reforms are ultimately possible in each case. There are studies that suggest that cloth makes its biggest impact on the environment not during the manufacturing process but while we own it, as a result of dry cleaning and laundering.

Most synthetics are made of petroleum products, a nonrenewable resource. Natural fibers are made of renewable resources. But the agricultural and manufacturing processes that produce cotton, for example, create staggering amounts of pollution in the form of pesticides (common estimates are that from 25 to 50 percent of the world's pesticides are devoted to cotton crops); defoliants and other herbicides; fungicides; chemical fertilizers such as nitrates; enormous poundages of bleach, softeners and fading agents, and sizing agents such as polyvinyl acetate; resins, including polyurethane resin, acrylic, and formaldehyde resins; dyes (the excess goes down the drain and, unless biodegradable, passes into the soil and surface water); and the large quantities of energy and water needed to carry out these processes. Pollution from these substances affects the earth, water, and air. Similar concerns have been raised about other natural fibers, although the problems associated with silk, wool, and linen appear to be smaller, in part because smaller quantities of such fibers are produced. Sheep for wool require millions of acres of land for grazing and sheep dips containing phosphorus or chlorine. Chromium mordant dyes used on wool in underdeveloped countries can create toxic sludge.*

Industry and government have not been indifferent to these environmental problems. Reforms have been instituted, and more are likely to come, both formally, through environmental regulations, and informally, both through manufacturers' attempts to clean up their production processes and the production of "transitional," "green," and organic cottons. "Transitional" cottons are those grown without pesticides but on soil that has not been clear of pesticides and chemicals long enough to qualify as organic. "Green" cottons are not organic—that is, they have been grown with pesticides and chemicals—but they are "minimally processed": they may have used low-impact or nontoxic dyes or closed-system dyeing; they may be unbleached or undyed; they may be stonewashed (which is considered environmentally better than using chemical softeners) or enzyme-softened (which may be better than both). Preshrinking may be done by washing, with no chemicals; starch may be used rather than polyvinyl acetate. There are even naturally colored cotton fibers—mostly in green and brown—that require no dyeing.

Some environmentalists favor the increased use of hemp for fabrics because it can be grown without pesticides, fertilizers, and other chemicals required for cotton growing. Unfortunately, laws in this country make it difficult to be a legal hemp grower because of hemp's great similarity to the marijuana plant, which is illegal to grow. The type of hemp plant used in textiles is a different strain, however, and cannot be used for drugs. In many states, laws to make it easier to grow this type of hemp have been proposed in recent years. The push to grow more hemp has also coincided with a push toward developing better and more attractive types of hemp fabrics. These have been given some attention by clothes designers in recent years, and the number of imported hemp garments on sale in the United States appears to have increased considerably.

Because the manufacture of viscose rayon (which constitutes 95 percent of the rayon currently marketed) has always been a highly polluting process, the pressure of environmentalism has led to the introduction of a new rayon fiber, brand name Tencel and generic name lyocell, that is now being pro-

---

*Only about 50 percent of raw wool by weight is in fact fibrous material. The rest is oils or fats, excrement, dirt, and other matter, which all goes into the sludge. From this unsavory potpourri lanolin is extracted and subsequently used in the manufacture of such items as peppermint cremes and lipsticks.

moted as environmentally favorable or low-impact. Like all rayon, lyocell is made of cellulosic polymers derived from wood pulp, which is a renewable resource that uses little fertilizer or pesticides. But lyocell is said to be taken from sustainably harvested tree farms; and, unlike conventional rayon, it is made in a solvent spinning process that is "close-looped," meaning that the dissolving agent is used over and over rather than being discarded as waste with each batch. The Achilles' heel of this product, as with all rayon, is the pulp-making process, which releases massive amounts of natural and unnatural chemicals into the environment.

Other attempts to make natural fibers available without harmful pollution include various kinds of recycling. Wool has always been recycled (see chapter 21). Cottons, however, have not been; only recently have some companies begun shredding and respinning cotton fabrics into yarns by relatively clean processes.

It is difficult to find any objective evaluation of the effects of all this. The environmental regulations are said to have brought about real improvements. But none of the organic or low-impact fibers so far constitutes a significant share of the market. (Of about 13.5 million acres of cotton planted in the United States in 2003, only about 4,000—less than .03 percent—were dedicated to organic and transition cotton.)* They cost considerably more than conventional cottons and rayon. Unless a product is labeled to show that it is both organically grown and processed, moreover, the buyer often does not know which improved procedures were actually used. All of these products and procedures offer real benefits, or at least could make a real difference if they amounted to somewhat more than a small drop in a large bucket. Alas, the sacrifice required on the part of a buyer determined to purchase only environmentally virtuous natural-fiber products, in terms of variety, cost, and quality, is still immense.

Spokespeople for synthetic fiber manufacturers argue, with some justice, that the production of low-impact cotton and even expensive organic cotton has a greater negative environmental impact than polyester production, both because of the enormous amounts of water and energy that cotton growing consumes and because the manufacture of even these virtuous products typically creates chemical pollutants as by-products. They point out that the manufacture of synthetics involves no growing or raising process to complicate matters, and synthetic fiber manufacturing continually reuses solvents rather than discarding them as waste. Dyeing synthetic fibers (other than acrylics) does not require prior bleaching, which uses massive amounts of

---

*Despite hopes that a new (2002) Department of Agriculture National Organic Program would promote an increase in organic cotton farming, these figures represent a significant decline in United States organic cotton production. At the same time, however, United States and worldwide demand for organic cotton fabrics is increasing, and organic cotton production in other countries outstrips ours.

water to prepare the fibers; synthetic fibers are already white. Although there are as yet no efforts toward recycling synthetic textiles (and these are unlikely anytime soon because of the complications presented by textiles made of blended fibers), plastic beverage bottles have been recycled and used to manufacture synthetic fabrics that are made into outerwear. In 2002, the FTC recognized a new synthetic fiber that, like lyocell, was designed to be more environmentally favorable than its predecessors. This fiber, called PLA and trade-named Ingeo, is in some respects like polyester but, unlike polyester, uses plant sources, such as corn and sugarbeets, for raw material where polyester relies on petrochemical sources. PLA is also said to be compostible in industrial composts. See pages 362–63. So far, PLA is available in few goods for the home.

Those who wish to fight pollution with their textile-buying habits might sensibly try buying goods manufactured only in countries with expensive pollution-control regulations—our own, many Western European countries, Canada, Australia, and Japan. Many other Asian, African, and Central and South American countries do not have such laws. Avoiding overfrequent laundering and dry cleaning of clothes and furnishings is environmentally prudent too. But perhaps the surest bet of all, at least for the time being, may simply be not to buy so much. (An academic specialist in textiles told me that the annual rate of consumption of textiles is about 40 kilograms per person in the United States, 20 kilograms per person in Europe, and 2 to 3 kilograms per person in Asia.) This would mean buying things that last longer and learning how to clean, preserve, and mend them so as to extend their lives. So far there has been no call for the really revolutionary solution: an end to fashion, the pleasant habit that keeps most of us buying new clothes and furnishings when old ones are quite serviceable.

Effect of Fiber Content on Fabric Performance; Interplay with Other Determinants

Comfort Is Partly Subjective. Fiber content strongly affects how comfortable a fabric feels. Some types of polyester now have a pleasing silky or cottony hand, but older types had a slight harshness, and many types still do. Wool can be scratchy. Coarse weaves of many fibers are literally painful when worn against the skin. Medieval penitents who donned coarse sackcloth undershirts chose an effective means of self-torment.

Some scientific bases for the comfort factor of various kinds of fabrics are discussed below, but the reader should remember that the final test is in the wearing. If you find a fabric comfortable (or not), that is all that counts. Comfort depends not only on the characteristics of the fabric but on those of the wearer—how much you perspire, your skin sensitivity, your bodily responses to environmental factors, and so forth. In addition, some places on the body are more sensitive, warmer, or cooler than others; and some people's bodies are overall more sensitive, warmer, and cooler than others'. Dressing for comfort means juggling a lot of subjective factors with the objective ones.

Comfort Effects of Absorbency and Permeability of Fibers; Dressing for the Weather. A fabric's comfort in different kinds of weather depends largely on the extent to which it is permeable to air and water vapor. In fact, the interactions of skin, perspiration, air, fabrics, and environmental heat and moisture are so complicated that scientists only now feel they are beginning to unravel their mysteries, which would require whole books to explain thoroughly.

At temperatures around 85°F, so textile scientists tell us, the amount of heat produced by the human body and the amount lost to the environment are in equilibrium, and you will feel warm enough without clothes. Although the naked body can accommodate cooler temperatures to some extent by contracting its blood capillaries or shivering, it will start feeling chilly and uncomfortable at temperatures only a little lower; you will begin to want something on. At slightly higher temperatures, the body dilates the capillaries and sweats to cool itself; you may find yourself wanting to remove layers of clothing. But although wet skin is less comfortable than dry, it does not follow that in very warm weather no clothing is more comfortable than light clothing. Clothing can cool you down and protect you from the heat of the sun.

Whether a fabric holds heat well or poorly is a profound determinant of the comfort it affords. Relatively recently, people thought that the comparative warmth or coolness of different fabrics was mostly a function of how well, comparatively, their fibers conducted heat. I was taught as a girl that it was because linen was a good heat conductor (it conducted heat away from the body) that it was cool, and that wool was warm because it was a poor heat conductor (it did not conduct heat away from the body). This was not accurate.

In fact, all textile fibers are rather poor heat conductors, and fabrics can be excellent insulators. Metals will conduct heat a thousand times better. But the air warmed by your body is trapped by the textile material. Woven textiles, being nothing more than a latticework of air and textile fibers, thus create an extremely effective and lightweight insulation, holding heat near your body and preventing it from being lost to the wind or the surrounding cooler air. The thicker a fabric and the more air pockets it has, the better it holds heat. (Note that a thick fabric may or may not also be heavy.) The coolest fabrics, therefore, are the thinnest, smoothest, most loosely constructed ones, for these are least effective in holding a layer of warmed air around you. Napped, pile, and fuzzy fabrics, of whatever fiber, tend to be warmer than smooth ones because they hold air in the interstices between the fibers that make up the fuzz. Linen (flax), whose fibers are extremely smooth and are readily woven into very fine and air-permeable fabrics that are nonetheless strong, is thus highly valued as summer wear. Flannel sheets, which have a fuzzy surface that traps air, feel warmer than regular sheets. Wool fibers, which are even fuzzier and are scaly and quite crimped, trap a great deal of air and thus make an extremely warm fabric. Yet because wool worsteds that are smooth and fine can be woven, there are summer-weight wools too (although they could never compete with linen for coolness). Silk is often warm, but it is usually considered summery because it can be woven into lightweight and highly breathable fabrics—fabrics that permit air to pass in and out. Even linen yarns can be knitted into a rather spongy, dense material fit for cooler weather. Thus, although fiber content is quite important to how cool or warm a fabric is, it is by no means the whole story.

The way a fabric reacts to moisture is almost as important as the way it holds heat in determining whether people feel that it is comfortable. A complicated interplay occurs among the effects of moisture, air and other factors, and fabrics. The comfort goal in moisture management is to keep your skin neither too wet nor too dry. Dry skin feels scratchy, and it itches. Wet skin is uncomfortable too. Fabric acts on it more abrasively; it is more vulnerable to infections from funguses or other microorganisms; if your feet are sweating you are more likely to get blisters. Your skin naturally and constantly loses moisture— through perspiration—even when it feels perfectly dry. In a hot environment, you will notice when you begin to sweat. You feel cooler when the perspiration evaporates from your skin. Usually what you want your clothing to do is let your perspiration move away from your body; usually, therefore, absorbent fabrics are far more comfortable against the skin than unabsorbent ones.

The so-called natural fibers (cotton, linen, silk, wool, ramie, hemp) and the cellulosic man-made fibers (rayon and lyocell) are all absorbent and hydrophilic or water-attracting. Synthetic fibers such as polyester, nylon, acrylic, and polypropylene are all unabsorbent and hydrophobic or water-repelling. When an absorbent fabric is placed on your skin, water evaporating from your skin surface will be taken right into its fibers. Highly absorbent fabrics can often hold great quantities of moisture before they become saturated; thus they can keep you quite comfortable unless you perspire a great deal. When the fibers and the air trapped in and near their interstices all begin to fill with moisture, the insulating ability of the fabric will be decreased, and you may also start to feel cooler. As the saturation point of the fabric is reached, for example, on a very hot day when you are exercising actively, your skin may begin to feel wet again. If a fabric releases absorbed water readily through evaporation, it is less likely to become or stay saturated and it is likely to remain more comfortable. How readily the moisture evaporates from the fabric depends only partly on fiber content; fabric and yarn construction and garment construction are also extremely important, as are the environmental temperature and humidity. Wool, by the way, has extraordinary advantages in cold, damp weather. Not only does it take in enormous quantities of moisture before becoming saturated, it actually releases enough heat as it becomes wet to help you feel warm.

Fabrics also remove moisture from the skin by mechanisms other than absorbency. Synthetic fibers as well as natural ones, for example, may adsorb or wick. (The latter term, still absent from many dictionaries, gradually worked its way from textile-industry jargon into advertisements for the public.) "Adsorbency" refers to a fabric's capacity to attract water to its surface. The more surface area a cloth has, the more water it can hold on its surface, which partly explains the longer drying time for cotton towels with looped-fiber surfaces compared to those with cut pile (velour)—the former simply have a greater surface area to adhere to. When fabrics "wick" moisture, they draw it off the skin surface and pass it along their interstices (without absorbing it), where it evaporates into the air at a rate determined by fiber type, the atmospheric relative humidity, and other factors. If you put the edge of a cotton towel in water, you can watch the water wick up the cloth.

Such hydrophilic fibers as cotton, linen, and rayon tend to hold moisture longer than the hydrophobic ones such as nylon, polyester, and polypropylene, which dry more readily; this slight dampness contributes to their keeping you feeling cool in warm weather. On a hot summer day, you will love the coolness—hence the ever-popular cotton T-shirt for a summer's jog. It's better than bare. But if you are cross-country skiing on a frigid day and sweat to the point of soaking your cotton undershirt, you put yourself at risk for dangerous hypothermia. That is why sports experts often recommend that for cold-weather sports you wear a wicking type of fiber next to the skin—to get perspiration off the skin and let it evaporate rather than saturate the fabric. Not all synthetic fabrics wick, however, or wick sufficiently to make you comfortable in the extremes of cold weather or warm, humid weather, particularly when you are exercising heavily. And not all forms of exercise produce enough perspiration to make high wickability the chief desideratum of next-to-skin clothing. Wearing ordinary polyester, nylon, or other synthetics in the summer can make you feel hot and clammy or itchy. Among synthetics, polypropylene naturally wicks well. Some synthetics are constructed so as to wick well; the fibers in one type are actually hollow tubes through which perspiration can pass. There are also finishes applied to synthetic fabrics that promote wicking.

A fabric's "breathability," as the retailers call it, really refers to its permeability to water vapor; this is another factor that strongly affects comfort. Various coatings applied for waterproofing, for example, render fabrics impermeable to water vapor in the way that vinyl upholstery or rubber and plastic are impermeable. As your perspiration evaporates, it cannot pass through such fabrics into the surrounding air; you feel wet and uncomfortable. The hotter it is, the more water-vapor permeability you will want in your clothes and the less you will enjoy sitting on a vinyl car seat or upholstery that is completely impermeable. The most comfortable rain gear is impermeable to moisture from the outside but permits water vapor from the inside to pass through, so you do not become wet from your own perspiration. Fabrics such as Gore-Tex are designed to do this.

Garment construction also matters greatly to your comfort. Never underestimate the simple effect of unbuttoning your coat or of loose or vented clothing that lets air in. Unzipping can be far more effective than wicking. Close-fitting garments are warmer than loose ones just because they do not let the air inside them move around much. Tight cuffs and collars and waists also keep the air in and restrict its flow. Double-breasted garments insulate better than single-breasted ones. Unbuttoning your collar, loosening your tie, removing your scarf, taking off one insulating layer—all are actions that can overpower the effects of fiber content and construction. On the other hand, no amount of loosening and unbuttoning is going to make your Norwegian wool sweater endurable on the beach in August.

Aesthetics: Look and Feel. In the world of textiles, a fabric's "hand" refers only to its feel on the hand, not to its feel on other parts of the body and not to its feel, in general, on the skin. In fact, your hands and other parts of you can respond quite differently to the same fabric, which explains why the sheet or shirt that feels so lovely when you handle it in the store can give quite an ugly sensation when pressed against your back. To say that a fabric has a good hand is a purely aesthetic evaluation. Yet the fabric's hand contributes significantly to its comfort.

Fiber content strongly affects how smooth, rough, silky, soft, hard, or luxurious a fabric feels. The satiny feel of some silks can never be matched by wools, no matter how finely woven. Many 100 percent polyesters lack the pleasant sensations of linen and cotton on the skin. The softness of good wool cannot be achieved with cotton or linen. Each of the major fibers, as rendered in an ordinary plain-weave construction, has a unique, all but indescribable hand that is so familiar to us that we tend to use the fiber names archetypally and to speak of cottony, woolly, silky, and linenlike sensations. Still, remarkable things can be done in the process of constructing the fabric. Cottons can feel flannelly. Synthetic yarns can look and feel woolly or cottony.

The look of a fiber can be as variable as its hand. Some fabrics are lustrous; some have a dull surface. Luster is produced by a number of factors. Very smooth fibers, such as silk, are highly lustrous. Linen, which is also smooth, has a pleasing subtle luster; cotton, a rougher fiber, generally has little unless it has received a treatment to give it luster. Synthetics can often be produced in both lustrous and dull versions. (There are various chemical treatments and weaves that will produce a luster too.) Drapability—how well a fabric falls into pleasant folds—is strongly influenced by fiber content. Wool, silk, and nylon drape softly and gracefully, but for crispness you need cotton or linen. How successfully a fabric dyes is also mostly a matter of fiber content. Linen is hard to dye, and silk is famous for dyeing with gorgeous colors. (But for the same reason, linen resists staining, and silk stains outrageously easily.) Acetate takes no ordinary dyes; special ones had to be developed for it. Many synthetics not only dye well but resist fading—an important factor in determining how long upholstery or a garment or curtain will be serviceable.

Resilience. Fiber content strongly affects a fabric's resilience, or how read-ily it wrinkles. Manufactured fibers other than rayon tend to have excellent resilience. Nylon is the most popular material for carpets because, among other things, it is highly resilient, springing back after being crushed under-foot. Wool, another traditional fiber for carpets, is also highly resilient but costs much more than nylon. Everyone knows that cotton wrinkles—and linen wrinkles horribly—unless they have received a treatment that controls wrin-kling. A simple test for resilience is to crush a bit of the fabric in your hand for a few seconds and see whether it emerges wrinkled.

Durability. The durability of fabrics depends on many factors, including yarn and fabric construction and finishing treatments. Fiber content is a major determinant of tear strength, that is, resistance to ripping when the fabric is pulled in opposite directions. But a fabric's abrasion resistance (how well it resists rubbing or friction) is another strong determinant of durability, and fab-rics with excellent tear strength may have little abrasion resistance. Silk is con-sidered a durable fiber because it is strong, in fact stronger than cotton, but it has less abrasion resistance than cotton. Durability is to some extent relative to use; a weaker fiber with good abrasion resistance might outlast a stronger fiber with poor abrasion resistance if it is used in such a way that it is subjected to little pulling but much rubbing (say, as a handbag lining or a polishing cloth). Spandex, the weakest of all fibers, has good durability not only because of its high resistance to abrasion but also because it is elastic. If a fabric is somewhat weak but elastic, such as spandex or to a much lesser degree nylon or wool, the danger of tearing is reduced because the fabric will give before the pull pro-duces a tear. Generally speaking, thicker fabrics are more durable than thin-ner ones of the same type. Even the degree of smoothness of the fabric can affect its durability; a smooth fabric, all else being equal, may last longer because it will not pull and snag on surfaces it comes in contact with.

Some fabrics deteriorate readily with exposure to sunlight, and others will fade. Lightfast fibers, obviously, are more durable choices for draperies. See "Choosing Ultraviolet Light–Resistant Fibers" in chapter 13, pages 183–84. Susceptibility to moths and mildew strongly affects the durability of fabrics. A rough rule of thumb is that natural fibers may be damaged by insects and mildew, while synthetics usually are not. (The susceptibility of various nat-ural fibers to silverfish, moths, and mold is discussed in chapter 21.)

Cleanliness. Some fibers have an inherent tendency to stay clean. Fabrics that tend to soil less may have a longer life because washing and cleaning gradu-ally wear out cloth. Smooth fabrics such as linen tend to be cleaner than other fabrics because rough surfaces trap and hold dirt more readily; cotton's rougher surface means that it soils more than linen. Unabsorbent fabrics do not readily attract dirt and resist staining simply because matter that would otherwise stain remains on the surface of the fabric, where it is more easily removed. That is why upholstery fabrics often benefit from some synthetic fiber content—most synthetics are unabsorbent—or stain-repelling treatment. However, several synthetic fibers have a tendency to build up static electricity, which tends to attract lint and dirt. Many synthetics also tend to be oleophilic and hydrophobic—they attract oil and repel water—which means that they tend to oil-stain and to resist getting thoroughly wet and clean in the laundry. Napped and pile fabrics also tend to resist stains because their construction prevents the soil from easily penetrating the cloth; it stays on the surface where it can more readily be removed. Of course, napped and pile fabrics are by no means stain-proof.

Launderability. Launderability is determined greatly, although not solely, by fiber content. Because most soaps, detergents, and laundry solutions are alkaline, fabrics that tolerate alkalinity well are typically highly launderable, and those that do not tolerate alkalinity usually require dry cleaning or special handling. This is why fabrics composed of plant fibers, such as cotton, linen, and ramie, are often launderable while those derived from animal matter, such as wool and silk, are more problematic. Plant fibers are made of cellulose polymers, which are sensitive to acids but can tolerate a fair degree of alkalinity. Silk, wool, and other hair fibers are composed of protein polymers, which are more resistant to acids but less resistant to alkalies than cellulosic fibers. Although many silk and wool articles can be washed with mild or nonalkaline soaps or detergents if special care is taken, more often than not they should be dry-cleaned—for this and other reasons. (For laundering instructions for each type of fiber, see chapters 21 and 22.)

The vulnerability of particular fibers to acids and alkalis may be increased with heat or may not be present at all except at high temperatures; that is one reason why laundry instructions sometimes recommend using cold or lukewarm water. There are other substances besides soaps and detergents—such as foods, household cleaning products, household chemicals, and medicines—some of which are strongly alkaline or acidic, that may damage fabrics they come into contact with.

Synthetics may have chemical vulnerabilities to alkaline solutions or dry-cleaning fluids; thus some are either not launderable or not dry-cleanable, although many are both.

GLOSSARY OF FABRIC TERMS

Abrasion resistance. The ability of a fabric to withstand rubbing without suffering damage to its appearance or function.

Art linen. Closely woven, round-thread (not calendered or beetled; see chapter 21) linen, used mainly for embroidery in plain weave. It is also used for dresses and table linens.

Bark crêpe (krape). Fabric with rough, barklike surface, used for coats and dresses. Of wool, rayon, or manufactured fibers.

Batiste (buh-TEEST). Sheer, fine, combed cotton or cotton blend in plain weave, used for soft dresses, shirts, infants' wear, nightgowns, lingerie.

Bedford cord. Heavy, corded fabric with the cords running along the warp. Used for coats, suits, uniforms, upholstery.

Bengaline (BEN-guh-leen). Lustrous corded fabric with ribs running in the direction of the filling, like grosgrain but heavier. Used for dresses, coats, ribbons.

Bisso. A fine, crisp, sheer linen made of wiry yarns, which is sometimes called altar cloth because it is used for that purpose.

Boiled wool. Very densely felted wool fabric; used for coats, jackets, slippers.

Bouclé (boo-KLAY). Cloth knitted or woven with a novelty yarn that has protruding loops or curls.

Broadcloth. Originally meant a high-quality, closely woven woolen worsted fabric wider than 27 inches, in a twill or plain weave. Now refers to cotton and cotton/polyester plain-weave fabrics in solid color or print.

Brocade (bro-KADE). Heavy jacquard-woven fabric with raised floral or figured designs. Often has a satin-weave figure on plain- or twill-weave ground. Originally was a heavy silk with gold or silver thread, and often still has that appearance.

Brocatelle (brock-uh-TELL). A stiff upholstery fabric, similar to brocade, with raised or puffed figures, usually in silk, rayon, or cotton.

Buckram (BUCK-ruhm). A plain-weave, coarse cotton fabric given a stiff starched or sized finish.

Burlap. A coarse plain-weave fabric usually of jute.

Calico (KAL-ee-ko or KAL-i-ko). A plain weave printed with small designs, of cotton or cotton blend.

Cambric (KAME-brik). A soft, plain-weave linen or cotton fabric, calendered to give it luster, often used for dainty and delicate things such as handkerchiefs, underwear, aprons, and blouses, but it comes in heavier weights as well. It is also called handkerchief linen, linen lawn, or linen batiste.

Camel hair. Lightweight, warm, soft-napped fabric, made from the natural-colored hair of a camel. Frequently mixed with wool. Used for coats, sweaters, blankets.

Canvas. Any strong, firm, heavy plain-weave fabric. Usually of cotton, sometimes of linen or hemp.

Cashmere. Soft, fine fabric made entirely from the soft undercoat of cashmere goats or from fine wool mixed with the soft hair. Widely used in coats, suits, sweaters, shawls.

Cavalry twill. A twill-weave fabric with a steep, double twill line. Used for uniforms, sportswear, riding habits.

Challis (SHAL-ee). A lightweight, soft wool, cotton, rayon, or combination of fibers in a plain weave, usually printed with a small design. Used for dresses, blouses, pajamas. Originally wool or silk.

Chambray (SHAM-bray or SHAM-bree). Usually cotton, but may be made with a combination of fibers. Yarn-dyed fabric, plain weave, with colored warp and white filling thread (or contrasting color in filling thread, which produces an iridescent effect). Depending upon weight and quality, used for shirts, dresses, and work or play clothes.

Chamois cloth (SHAM-ee). Cloth of cotton or synthetic fiber that has been napped so as to resemble chamois leather.

Charmeuse (shar-MOOZE). Lightweight, soft fabric that has a semilustrous satin front and a dull back, with hard-twisted warp yarns and crêpe filling yarns. Made of silk, cotton, or synthetics. Sometimes refers to cloth that is given a somewhat lustrous finish, for example, by mercerizing.

Cheesecloth. Very open, plain-weave, lightweight fabric of carded cotton yarns.

Chenille (shen-EEL). The term refers to two types of fabric. One is made by tufting, a process in which yarn is "punched" through a backing fabric. Chenille robes and bedspreads are made this way. This type of chenille fabric can show a pattern or may have a "velvet" pile surface. The other type of chenille fabric is made of chenille yarn, which has pile protruding all around it, so as to show patterns in pile.

Cheviot (SHEV-ee-uht). Twill weave, in wool or worsted yarns, with a rough, hairy surface, good for sportswear.

Chiffon (shiff-ON). Very lightweight, sheer silk or silky synthetic, made in a plain weave with a very fine, hard-twisted yarn. Its surface is dull; it is used for dressy blouses, scarves, dresses, veils.

China silk. A soft, lightweight, plain-weave silk, used for blouses, linings. Rayon imitations of china silk are common.

Chino (CHEE-no). Sturdy plain- or twill-weave cotton used for sportswear; dyed a khaki color.

Chintz. A glazed, crisp cotton in close plain weave, usually in bright prints, often big florals. It is used for draperies, slipcovers, and, in light weights, summer dresses.

Clear finished. Worsted whose yarns and weave are clearly visible because the fuzz and nap are singed or sheared.

Corduroy. A strong, durable pile fabric with lengthwise ridges of cut pile called wales. Usually of cotton. Used for casual clothes and sportswear.

Covert (KUHV-ert or KOH-vert). Twill-weave fabric woven with yarns of two shades of the same color, usually tan and brown, so that the fabric looks speckled or mottled. Of wool, cotton, or other fiber.

Crash. Relatively coarse plain weave, medium weight, made of uneven, slack-twisted yarns in various qualities. In cotton or linen, often with colored borders. Used for toweling, table linens, draperies.

Crêpe (krape). Any fabric with a grained, crinkled, or textured surface.

Crêpe de chine (krape-d'SHEEN). Very light, fine, plain-weave silk with a fine-textured crêpe. It is woven with filament silk yarn in the warp and hard-twisted filament silk yarn in the filling. It is also made with spun yarns in warp and filament yarn in the filling.

Cretonne (KREE-tahn or kri-TAHN). Like chintz, but with an unglazed, dull surface. Usually in big florals and used for interior decorating purposes such as upholstery, draperies, slipcovers.

Crinoline (KRIN-uh-lin). Any of a variety of stiff, plain-weave fabrics used for support, for example, to hold out full skirts. Lighter-weight than buckram.

Crocking. The transfer of color from a fabric to other surfaces as a result of rubbing.

Damask (DAM-uhsk). Cloth with jacquard-woven floral or geometric designs, used for

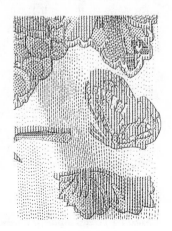

Damask

tablecloths, towels, bedspreads, and other household linens, as well as upholstery and drapes. Usually in white or one or two colors.

Denim. A sturdy, twill-weave cotton used for work and play clothes, blue jeans. Often has blue (indigo-dyed) warp and white filling threads.

Diaper. A woven pattern that shows repeated units of design that are all connected to one another or cover the whole surface of the cloth.

Dimity (**DIM-i-tee**). A thin, sheer, plain-weave cotton, with cords in the warp, often in stripe or check. Used for dresses, aprons, bedspreads.

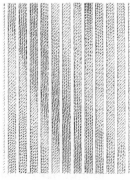

Dobby. Any fabric woven on a dobby loom. These fabrics have small woven-in geometric figures such as bird's-eyes, diamonds, and so forth. See illustrations on page 281.

Doeskin. Fine quality, smooth finish, satin-weave wool fabric with a slight nap, or similar napped fabric of other fibers. Used for coats, pants, uniforms.

Dimity

Donegal tweed (**DON-i-gall**). Woolen tweed of medium to heavy weight, originally handwoven in the county of Donegal, Ireland, but now any Irish tweed. In a plain or twill weave with a single color in the warp and a mix of colors in the filling yarns. Used for suits and coats.

Dotted swiss. Any fabric with dots created by swivel weave, lappet weave, or flocking. It is usually crisp, with a lawnlike background. Used for summer clothes, children's wear, curtains.

Double cloth. Fabric with two layers joined in weaving. Used for overcoats, sweaters, blankets, upholstery.

Drill. A durable, closely woven, medium-weight cotton twill used for khaki and ticking.

Duck. A closely woven, durable, heavy cotton plain-weave fabric. Used for belts, bags, tents, awnings, sails. Also called canvas, but usually lighter than canvas.

Duvetyn (**DYU-vuh-teen or duv-TEEN**). A very softly napped, drapable fabric that looks suedelike or like a compact velvet.

Faille (**file**). Somewhat shiny, closely woven silk, cotton, rayon, or synthetic fiber fabric with a flat, crosswise, fine ribbed surface, similar to grosgrain. Used for dresses, suits, coats.

Filament. A fiber of indefinite length or of very great length. Filament yarn is made of one or more filament fibers gathered together.

Flannel. Napped plain-weave or twill cloth originally of wool, now usually of cotton.

Flannelette. A lightweight cotton flannel, often used for nightwear or baby clothes.

Fleece. A heavyweight, bulky woolen fabric with a long, fleecy nap, used for coats.

Fleur-de-lis (flure-d'LEE or flurr-d'LEE). Floral design resembling an iris.

Foulard (foo-LARD). Lightweight, plain-woven or twill silk or rayon fabric, soft, usually printed in small figures. Popular for neckwear, soft dresses, blouses, robes.

Frosting. Change in, especially lightening of, fabric color as a result of abrasion or rubbing.

Full-fashioned knit. A garment made from pieces that have each been knitted to a given shape. Such garments usually have a better fit.

Gabardine (GAB'r-deen). Sturdy, firm, clear-finished fabric in twill weave, with steep diagonal lines on the face of the cloth. Made of worsted, cotton, and other fibers. Used in suits, coats, sportswear.

Georgette. Thin, lightweight, crinkly silk fabric with a pebbly crêpe surface as a result of its hard-twisted yarns. The fabric has stiffness and body despite its light weight. Sometimes made of synthetics. Used for dresses, blouses, gowns, hats.

Gingham (GING'm). A plain-weave, medium-weight cotton fabric with a check (sometimes plaid or striped) design. Varies from coarse to fine, light fabrics. Commonly used in summer dresses and play clothes.

Gingham

Greige (grazhe, rhymes with "beige") or gray goods. Undyed, unfinished fabrics.

Grenadine. Open-weave dress fabric made of silk or synthetic fibers.

Grosgrain (GRO-grane). Closely woven, ribbed fabric with heavier crosswise ribs than poplin. Familiar in ribbons. Made in silk, cotton, rayon, polyester.

Hand. The tactile qualities of fabrics, or those perceived by touching, squeezing, or rubbing them with one's fingers.

Herringbone. A twill with rows of alternating left- and right-hand twill lines. Usually seen in coats, jackets, wool dresses. (See illustration on page 279.)

Holland. Plain-weave linen or cotton, heavily sized and sometimes glazed. Used for window shades. (Formerly referred to a fine, plain-weave linen shirting fabric, especially from Holland.)

Homespun. Cloth woven at home rather than a factory. Or any loosely woven, fairly heavy plain weave, with coarse, uneven yarns, which looks hand-loomed.

Honeycomb. A dobby-woven fabric with a textured pattern of raised squares or diamonds that look like a honeycomb. Also called waffle cloth. Used for clothes and furnishings.

Hopsacking. Actually burlap, but the term also refers to any coarse, rough cloth in a basket weave or other weave with a similar look. Used primarily for sportswear, suits and coats, draperies.

Houndstooth check. A variant of the twill weave in which yarns of two different colors produce a jagged check effect.

Huck towel. A towel in a dobby weave, usually woven with borders or names, in color, such as the sort of towel you see at hotels or clubs.

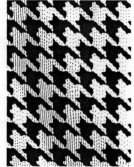

Huckaback. Cotton or linen toweling in bird's-eye or honeycomb dobby weave, or with a rough, pebbly surface, and with loosely twisted filling yarns or long floats to increase absorbency. See Huck towel.

Houndstooth check

Hydrophilic. Tending to attract water; absorbent (of water).

Hydrophobic. Tending to repel water; unabsorbent (of water).

Irish tweed. Tweed made in Ireland, usually with white warp and colored filling yarns.

Jacquard (JACK-ard). Any fabric woven on a jacquard loom. The jacquard loom creates intricate designs woven into the cloth by means of punched cards that enable it to handle far more threads than other looms. Brocades, damasks, and tapestries are all types of jacquard fabrics.

Jersey. A smooth, plain-knit fabric of wool, cotton, rayon, or synthetic blends. Used for dresses, shirts, sportswear, underwear. Called stockinet in handknitting. See illustration on page 283.

Lace. An open-network fabric of twisted, looped, or knotted threads, usually forming intricate patterns.

Lamé (la-MAY). Any fabric with metallic threads woven in for decorative purposes.

Lawn. Fine, sheer, crisp-finished cotton or linen of plain weave. Less crisp than organdy or voile. Used for children's clothes, summer dresses, sleepwear. See "Cambric."

Madras. Cotton from the Madras region in India, either in natural color or vegetable dyed, often in colored plaids, stripes, or checks. Its tendency to fade and bleed as a result of the dyes used is periodically the object of faddish admiration.

Marled. Made of yarns of two different colors twisted together.

Marquisette (mar-ki-ZETT). Leno-weave open-mesh fabric, very light in weight, of cotton, silk, or synthetics. Used for curtains, dressy evening fashion. See illustration on page 280.

Matelassé (mat-el-lass-AY or mat-luh-SAY). Double-cloth woven on a jacquard loom to create a quilted or stitched surface. Used for bedspreads and draperies. Originally made of padded silk.

Melton. A dull, smooth, heavy, very short napped, quite durable wool fabric used for coatings and outerwear. Looks somewhat like felt. Also comes in fibers other than wool.

Mohair. Fibers from the hair of the angora goat, or a soft, woolen fabric made from mohair, in plain or twill weaves.

Moiré (mwah-RAY or mah-RAY). Any fabric with a wavy, watermarked design. Taffeta fabrics often receive a moiré finish, and some plain-weave fabrics are printed with the design.

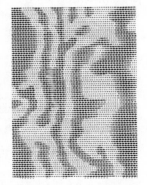

Moleskin. A napped cotton fabric with a suede-like hand. It is made in a strong, heavy weave of coarse, carded yarn. Used for sportswear and work clothes.

Monk's cloth. Loosely woven, heavy basket weave cotton, usually in brownish or oatmeal colors. Often used for upholstery, drapes, or other fur-nishings.

Fabric with moiré finish

Mousseline (moose-uh-LEEN). The French term for muslin; refers to a finer fabric than our own cotton muslin. Used in the United States, it denotes any of several lightweight, sheer, crisp fabrics of a variety of fibers. "Mousseline de soie"—literally, "silk muslin"—is a lightweight, plain-weave, sheer, crisp silk or rayon that resembles chiffon. It is used primarily for evening wear.

Muslin. Originally a substantial plain-weave cotton, fairly strong and heavy. Now also refers to similar fabrics made from blends of cotton and other fibers.

It exists in various weights and qualities and has highly varied uses, from heavy sacking to light dresses.

Nainsook (NANE-sook, rhymes with "look"). Plain-weave, soft, lightweight cotton fabric of varying grades, usually dyed in pastels. Made from the same gray goods that are turned into batiste and cambric. Used for ladies' blouses and babies' clothes.

Net or netting. Any fabric made of threads, string, or twine worked into open mesh. Of any fiber.

Organdy. A sheer, stiff, transparent plain-weave cotton, treated to make it permanently stiff.

Organza. Thin, transparent, stiff fabric of rayon or silk, used for evening wear.

Ottoman (OTT-uh-muhn). A crosswise-ribbed fabric similar to faille or bengaline but with heavier ribs. Wool, cotton, silk, or synthetic fibers may be used.

Oxford cloth. A plain- or basket-weave cotton, used for shirting. Usually has a double-yarn warp and a single filling thread. Oxford chambray is oxford cloth with colored warp and white filling yarns.

Paisley. Any fabric printed with a traditional paisley design. The paisley design, which originated in Paisley, Scotland, has a teardrop shape with a curving point.

Paisley design

Peau de soie (po-d'SWAH). Literally "skin of silk," denotes a soft, good-quality silk (or silky synthetic) satin cloth with a dull surface. Used for dresses.

Percale (purr-KAL, rhymes with "Al"). A closely woven, plain-weave cotton, used for dresses, blouses, sheets. Percale has a thread count (fabric count) of 180 or higher.

Pile fabric. Any fabric in which one set of yarns (pile yarns) stand vertical to the base fabric. May be made by weaving, knitting, and tufting. May have a looped or velvety surface. Examples are terry-cloth, velvet, velveteen, and corduroy.

Piqué (peek-AY or pik-AY). Any woven or knitted fabric with a raised pattern or quilted-looking surface. Usually of cotton; sometimes of synthetics. Woven piqués are usually medium- or heavyweight, rather stiff fabrics with raised crosswise cords, often used for collars, cuffs, dresses.

Plissé (pliss-AY). Has a puckered or blistered surface appearance in stripes created by a chemical treatment. In cheap goods, it may wash out. Looks like seersucker.

Pointelle. Any ribbed knit with tiny holes or openings in a pattern. **Polished cotton.** A plain-weave cotton with a glazed finish.

Pongee (pahn-GEE). Raw silk fabric often in a natural tan color, with a rather uneven, crude texture. The term is also used to refer to cotton or rayon cloth of a similar weight and texture.

Poplin. Plain-weave dress goods in which the filling is heavier than the warp, producing a fine, crosswise rib surface appearance. Most commonly a medium- or heavyweight cotton fabric, but also in wool, silk, synthetics.

Ragg. Formerly a fabric made from waste clippings of wool or used wool. Now may refer to new wool fabrics or garments made with multicolored yarns or made to resemble rough fabrics or garments of waste, used, or recycled wool.

Rep. Fabric with narrow, lengthwise ribs made with unbalanced plain weave.

Resilience. Ability of a fabric to spring back to its original state after being crushed or wrinkled.

Rib or ribbed fabric. Any woven fabric with a cord or ridge either lengthwise or crosswise, such as poplin, grosgrain, and rep. Any knit fabrics with lengthwise ribs on both sides.

Sailcloth. Strong, durable fabric of linen, cotton, jute, or nylon or other synthetics. Used for sails, play clothes, upholstery.

Sateen. A cotton fabric in a lustrous satin weave with filling yarn floats.

Satin. Originally referred to silk fiber in a satin weave, but now may refer to man-made fibers in a satin weave too. Highly lustrous, slippery. Used for evening wear, lingerie, linings. Any fabric made in a satin weave.

Seersucker. A dull-surfaced, medium-weight fabric with crinkly rows woven in. A variation of a plain weave. It is used for summer clothes. Classically of cotton fiber, but now made from synthetic fibers too.

Selvage. The edges of cloth that are finished in a tighter weave, sometimes with a different weave or heavier threads, to prevent their raveling. (Note, however, that some modern-weave selvages do not look this way anymore.) Sheets usually have selvages along the sides, with hems at the foot and head.

Serge (surj). Smooth twill made from heavy worsted yarns, clear finished.

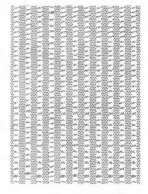

Seersucker

Shantung (shan-TUHNG). Rough silk in plain weave with irregular filling yarns that give it a slubbed or textured effect; originally of wild silk. Sometimes refers to similar-looking fabrics in fibers other than silk.

Sharkskin. Medium- to heavyweight sleek fabric with slightly lustrous surface. Usually in a basket weave, of wool, rayon, silk, or synthetic fibers. Used for tailored suits, slacks, and sportswear.

Sheeting. Fabric of size, construction, and weight suitable for bedsheets.

Slub. A thick place in yarn caused by uneven twisting or irregularities in the fibers. Sometimes slubs are intentionally created for a fashion effect. Otherwise they constitute a flaw.

Novelty yarn with slubs

Staple. Fibers of medium or short length. Used to make spun yarns.

Suede cloth. A plain-weave fabric napped on one side. Made of cotton or other fibers.

Suiting. Any fabric suitable for coats or suits.

Surah (SORE-uh). Lustrous twill weave of silk, rayon, or synthetic fibers suitable for soft-tailored garments and neckwear. Available in solids, prints, plaids.

Taffeta (TAFF-et-uh). Any of a group of fabrics, all plain weave, fine, smooth, and crisp, usually with a fine crosswise rib. Originally of silk, now of almost any fiber.

Tattersall. A style of English plaid; usually has crossing lines in two colors forming squares on the background of a third color.

Tear strength. Ability of fabric to resist tearing.

Terry-cloth. Cotton-pile woven or knitted fabric with uncut loops on one or both sides.

Ticking. A type of drill cloth with alternate stripes of white and colored yarn. Used mainly for mattress, upholstery, and pillow covers. Term may be used to refer to any strong, durable, closely woven fabric used for such purposes.

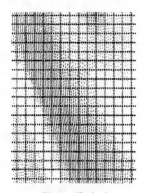

Tattersall plaid

Toile (twhal). The term means, simply, cloth or fabric, or more particularly a linen cloth. It has come to be associated with "toile de Jouy," which are printed linens made in Jouy, France.

Tricot (TREE-koh). A fine-waled warp-knit fabric, often used for underwear, sleepwear, and gloves. Of cotton or synthetic fibers.

Tulle (tool). Fine, soft, sheer silk (or silky synthetic) net fabric, usually with tiny hexagonal mesh. Used for veils, gowns, bridal gowns, dance costumes.

Tussah (TUHSS-uh). A sturdy, rough or coarse, loosely woven silk fabric, especially fabric made from Tussah silkworm (wild silk) fibers.

Tweed. Any rough-surfaced woolly fabric, usually woven in two or more colors, either plain or patterned. Originally a rough homespun fabric of heavy woolen yarns, today almost any fabric that is nubby and rough with mixed colors. Now of wool or almost any other fiber.

Twist. The number of twists or turns per inch given a thread or yarn. Hard-twisted yarns have many twists, soft-twisted yarns few. But in Beatrix Potter's *Tailor of Gloucester,* the cry "No more twist!" refers to a specific kind of firmly twisted thread, the "buttonhole twist" that is needed to make the last of the twenty-one buttonholes in the mayor's new waistcoat.

Union cloth. A fabric with cotton warp and filling of reused wool, usually heavily napped. Used for heavy overcoating.

Union linen. A fabric with cotton warp and linen filling. Sometimes this is called union cloth.

Velour. Thick, soft woven or knitted fabric with a deep pile (deeper than velvet). Mainly used as a suit or coat fabric.

Velvet. Fabric with short, thick, smooth pile. Originally of silk, now of many types of fiber.

Velveteen. A cotton velvet. It has a short, thick pile and a dull surface.

Voile (voil, rhymes with "oil"; or vwahl). Plain-weave, lightweight, sheer, crisp fabric made of hard-twisted spun yarns, loosely woven. Used for dresses, blouses, and curtains. Of cotton, silk, rayon, worsted.

Waffle cloth. Any fabric woven on a dobby loom in a wafflelike pattern, such as honeycomb or waffle weave.

Waffle knit. Knit fabric with a pattern of wafflelike squares.

Waffle weave. See "Waffle cloth."

Whipcord. A fabric made from worsted. Similar to gabardine but with a steeper twill. Has a hard, wiry hand. Used for riding clothes and other highly tailored garments. Now may be seen in many fibers other than wool.

Zibeline (ZIB-uh-leen). A woolen coating fabric with a long, lustrous, hairy nap of straight fibers laid in one direction.

20

Transformations

Synthetic vs. natural dyes . . . Colorfastness . . . Vat dyes . . .
Fiber or stock dyeing, piece dyeing, garment dyeing . . . Crocking
and frosting . . . Pigments and prints . . . Finishing treatments
for absorbency, antisepsis, antistatic, antiwrinkling . . . Beetling,
bleaching, calendering, and crêpeing and similar procedures . . .
Flame resistance . . . Glazing, mercerizing, mothproofing,
nanotechnologies, napping and sueding, preshrinking, resin
treatments, soil resistance, ultraviolet protection, stiffening
treatments, and water resistance

What happens to cloth after it is woven may substantially transform its look and behavior and, more often than not, is what matters most to us when we go looking for clothes or furnishings. We tend to take the structure and fiber quality of the cloth for granted. What we want to know is what color it is and whether we have to iron it or wash it separately. The answers often depend on what dyes and finishes have been used.

Inferior dyeing can wreck the appearance of the finest cloth and greatly reduce its usable life, or cause expense in dry cleaning or the inconvenience of separate or hand-washing. Modern finishing treatments, from resins that prevent wrinkling to napping that creates a warm, fuzzy surface, significantly affect how you care for the cloth, what you can use it for, and how it looks.

Dyes

Almost all dyes used on textiles today are synthetics, derived from coal-tar distillates or petrochemicals rather than from plants, minerals, or animals. Functionally, synthetic dyes are available that are considered superior in almost every respect to natural ones. Environmental and health issues have occasionally been raised concerning synthetic dyes, however, and some synthetic dyes have been found to be potentially carcinogenic and banned from use.[1] Natural dyes, on the other hand, are hard to find and expensive, and they may present environmental problems of their own as a result of the use of toxic metals, such as chrome, copper, tin, and zinc, to improve colorfastness and light resistance. Aluminum and iron may be relied upon as substitutes for these metals, but they are less effective. The production of natural dyes also requires the use of much agricultural land.

Colorfastness, the resistance of color to removal or extraction, is a complex set of behaviors. Fastness may be tested against different substances used in laundering, such as soap or detergent, bleach, and water (cool, warm, and hot), or in dry cleaning (a variety of solvents); light; acidic and alkaline solutions; heat; and perspiration. Some colors withstand laundering of any sort but fade in the light; these, obviously, should not be used for drapery or upholstery. Some fade or bleed in laundering but not in dry cleaning. Vat dyes, so called because the first of them, indigo, was steeped in a vat, are widely used on cellulosic fibers such as cotton, linen, or viscose rayon. They result in color with excellent fastness to washing—even with the strong bleaches used by professional laundries—and to light. (Among dyes commonly in use today, indigo, used for blue jeans and other blue denim cloth, inevitably fades, and is valued for this property. I know of someone who refused to wear a pair of inexpensive blue jeans that had a herculean resistance to fading: they looked like new even after half a dozen launderings with chlorine bleach.)

A dye's performance is determined not only by the type of dye but also by what fabric and fiber it is used on and the method used to apply it. Dye (or pigment) can be applied at almost any point in the manufacturing process. It may be added to the solution out of which man-made fibers are produced (referred to as "solution dyed" or "producer dyed") or to the fibers out of which yarn will be spun ("fiber dyed," "stock dyed," or "top dyed," tops being the long fibers out of which wool worsted is spun). Or it may be applied to the yarn out of which fabric is woven ("yarn dyed"); or the woven fabric may be dyed in the piece or after the garment is made ("piece dyed" and "garment dyed"). Tweeds are stock dyed; the fibers are dyed before they are woven into yarn. Gingham, chambray, and denim are yarn dyed, as are most fabrics containing two or more colors of yarn, such as plaids or checks. The dyeing of already made-up articles is fraught with dangers. Poor penetration by the dye at seams, discoloration of trim, uneven color, and similar problems all become more likely. As a rule of thumb, the earlier in the production process the color is added, the more likely the product is to have uniform coloring, good penetration, and good colorfastness, but these are likelihoods, not guarantees.

Colorfastness and uniform color are not the only important characteristics of a good dye or dyeing process. Good dyes will not readily yellow or otherwise discolor. Good color will neither crock (transfer color to other surfaces when rubbed against them) nor frost (show areas where color has been rubbed off by abrasion). When jeans are stonewashed, they are subjected to abrasion to create frosting intentionally, but ordinarily this effect is unwelcome. Frosting can result unintentionally when the dye has not penetrated the fabric thoroughly. As the outside of the fabric wears off from abrasion, so does the dye, and light areas begin to show.[2] Bleeding of dyes is also a headache for home launderers. Manufacturers are required to warn you on care labels to wash items likely to bleed separately from others, which might otherwise pick up the color left in the wash water by the bleeding articles. But this can be exceedingly inconvenient. (Remember that towels sometimes bear no care labels. If they have bright or deep colors, wash them separately a few times, after which, if they are the product of a good manufacturer, they will cease giving up color.)

Pigments—which do not actually unite with the fibers as dyes do, but are attached to their surface by means of resins—can be used on any type of fiber. They tend to be fast to light and bleach. When deep colors are achieved with pigments, however, the colors sometimes have a tendency to crock. Pigments have fair fastness to washing. Pigments are also used in a dyeing process for manufactured fibers called "mass pigmentation," in which the pigment is added to the spinning solution. This is as yet not a versatile method, and certain technical problems stand in the way of its widespread use. However, it is desirable for dyeing polypropylene satisfactorily. It provides lightfastness not available by other means in nylon and polyester.

Prints are fabrics with colored designs (usually created with pigments) that are applied to their surfaces. The design can be screened, heat-transferred, rolled, or stamped onto the cloth or applied to it in still other ways. In poor-quality prints, you may see bits of pattern askew or off their proper place, areas that have not received color, a lack of fine detail, fuzzy edges, and similar imperfections.

As the case of the unfading blue jeans illustrates, we should not assume that fading of fabrics after a few launderings is natural and unavoidable. Care and skill in the use of dyes can produce products that resist fading, bleeding, crocking, frosting, and discoloration. Unfortunately, once the ordinary buyer has examined a fabric for good appearance, he or she has no way of judging further how the dyeing will perform with use and with laundering or dry cleaning. Catalogues sometimes announce that a garment is yarn dyed; or occasionally a tag boasts of "only pure natural dyes"—a probable contradiction in terms, according to one expert in textile dyes. But aside from what you can learn by performing some simple home tests for colorfastness (see chapter 1, "Gathering, Storing, and Sorting Laundry," pages 21–22), you are usually forced to glean bits of information from the fabric's appearance and care label. It is truly a case of caveat emptor, for not even the principle that you get what you pay for holds at the retail level; many expensive items fade. Your best bet, which is by no means infallible, is to get what information you can from your retailer and to buy from reputable manufacturers and those whose products have proved colorfast in your home laundry. (In a store recently I saw a stack of knit tops displayed with the sign "Garment dyed!" As garment dyeing is typically a sign of lower rather than higher dyeing quality, the management of this store either labored in ignorance of its stock-in-trade or believed that its customers did.)

Finishing Treatments

When you purchase nonwrinkling shirts or blouses, mercerized thread for your sewing box, flame-resistant potholders, jeans with a suedelike hand, chintz upholstery fabric, or soil-resistant tablecloths, you bring home fabric that has been subjected to a certain finishing treatment through chemical or mechanical means. These and other finishing treatments can profoundly affect how well the fabric will function, how durably it will do so, and how you will have to care for it during its useful lifetime. Thus when you understand finishing treatments you can choose fabrics more wisely and take better care of them. Immediately below, descriptions are set forth of finishing treatments commonly applied to fabrics used in clothing and furnishings in the home. Chapters 21 and 22 take up in detail proper care for fabrics subjected to wrinkle-resistance and other resin finishes.

Finishing Treatments Commonly Applied to Fabrics

Absorbent Finishes. The natural absorbency of cotton, rayon, and linen may be increased by the use of absorbency treatments. Underwear and towels are sometimes treated for absorbency. Some treatments, applied to sanitary napkins, tampons, towels, and other materials used for drying and absorbing moisture, may increase absorbency dramatically. A variety of chemicals and resins are employed, depending on the fiber being treated and the use intended. Nylon and polyester may also be subjected to treatments to increase their absorbency. Sometimes they may be specially manufactured to increase their wicking capacity. Synthetics so treated are said to feel more comfortable against the skin, especially in warm and humid weather. But such claims are regarded skeptically by some, and I have been told that they have not stood up to double-blind trials. Mercerization (see "Mercerizing" on page 319) increases the absorbency of cotton (although that is not its purpose). The absorbency of natural fibers is decreased by resin treatments, fabric softener, and constructions using extremely tightly twisted yarns or weaves.

Antiseptics; Mildew Control. Antiseptic finishes may be used to help prevent athlete's foot or to control odors in shoe linings, bedclothes, diapers, underwear, and socks. There are also finishes that can help prevent mildew damage to fabric and rotting on shower curtains, carpets and rugs, and elsewhere. The presence of various antimicrobial substances is indicated by the use of words such as these in labels: "antiseptic," "bacteriostatic," "antibacte-rial," or "mildew-resistant." (Linen, cotton, and rayon are particularly suscep-tible to mildew. Silk and wool will also mildew, although somewhat less readily. Most synthetics will not mildew, but some tend to retain body odors, and for this reason receive antiseptic finishes.)

Antistatic Treatments. Many synthetic fibers, especially polyester and nylon and their blends, are prone to building up static electricity when subjected to friction. (Olefin—polypropylene—an exception, tends to be low-static.) Garments made of these fibers gather static electricity when you wear them or tumble them in the dryer; carpets become charged when you walk over them. Among the natural fibers, wool and silk may develop static cling, too, particularly when the humidity is low, but not to the extent that synthetics do. Clinging, climbing, and minor electrical shocks and sparks that may be painful or even dangerous (for instance, in the presence of flammable gases) or destructive (to delicate electronic equipment) are some potential conse-quences of static electricity in clothing and furnishings. Static may also cause fabric to attract dirt. To prevent static buildup, manufacturers sometimes use antistatic finishes, but these are not durable. New forms of certain synthetic fibers have been developed with built-in resistance to static. If you are buy-ing nylon carpeting, this is a feature to insist on.

At home one can use antistatic sprays or fabric softeners to reduce static effectively. Or one can choose naturally low-static or nonstatic fibers. Humid-ity reduces the amount of static electricity produced by friction.

Antiwrinkling Treatments. Antiwrinkling treatments rely on the use of resins that combine with two or more adjacent molecules of the fibers of cel-lulosic cloth in a chemical process called cross-linking. (See "Resin Treat-ments," pages 321–22.) Cross-linking is what diminishes wrinkling. If a fabric has been subjected to a wrinkle-resistance resin treatment, it may need some ironing after laundering but will tend to resist wrinkling during wear, and any wrinkles acquired during wear will tend to fall out when the article is hung up. Fabrics so treated are referred to by a variety of familiar names: "permanent-press," "wash and wear," "durable press," "easy care," and "minimum care."

Because cross-linking weakens cotton fabric, most permanent-press fab-rics are cotton/polyester blends. The polyester in the blend is not weakened by the treatment, and treated blends thus have more strength than all-cotton fabrics. (The polyester confers other advantages too. See chapter 22, "The Man-Made Fibers and Blends.") Some newer treatments, however, cause less deterioration in the strength of cottons, and more durable easy-care 100 per-cent cottons are becoming more common. These are not yet as strong or as resistant to wrinkling as the blends.

Antiwrinkling treatments are of two major types: precured and postcured. Precured treatments are applied to fabrics before they are sewn into garments, with the result that they may be hard to work with. It is precisely their wrinkle-resistant properties that make it difficult for them to contour properly to body shape or to be pressed into creases. Drip-dry clothes have been precured; you hang them to dry and they regain their shape and smoothness with little or no ironing. You see few drip-dry clothes nowadays, however, as most clothes are postcured.

The postcured wrinkle-resistance treatments are applied after the fabric is sewn into garments or other finished products. One problem with postcured treatments is that articles treated with them are difficult to alter: creases, pleats, curves, seams, and the like are built into the fabric's "memory" and cannot readily be moved around. A second problem is that the crease lines are even weaker than the rest of the fabric: they may lighten or abrade.

The durability of any wrinkle-resistant resin finish depends on a number of factors: the type of resin, the quality and type of application procedure, the degree of saturation, the care used in applying the treatment, and the care of the wearer in following the instructions on the garment label. Resin anti-wrinkling treatments are not permanent, but they are fairly durable, lasting for up to fifty washes. Such treatments usually reduce wrinkling without preventing it entirely; the amount of wrinkling you actually get also depends on such factors as the type and amount of resin used, the skill and care with which it has been applied, and how the garment is laundered and dried.

Antiwrinkling treatments are not applied to synthetics except in blends because many of these fibers have built-in wrinkle-resistance.

There are "durable-press" treatments that create permanent creases and pleats in wool and wool blends. These rely on resin or chemical treatments, and they are of varying durability.

A nonresin wrinkle treatment for cellulosic fibers, without the negative side effects of resin treatments, also exists. The liquid ammonia durable-press treatment, which is used only on cloth that is made of 100 percent cellulosic fiber, involves placing the fabric in an ammonium hydroxide bath in which temperature, fabric tension, time, ammonia concentration, and other factors are carefully controlled. It is a sensitive and expensive process and therefore not widely used. It is fairly durable, lasting for between forty and fifty launderings. The buyer, however, will find no indication on tags that it has been applied.

Wrinkle-treated garments should usually be machine-washed and tumbled dry on the permanent-press cycles. See chapter 4, "Laundering." But note that the application of antiwrinkling resins has been combined with nanotechnologies to create cloth that is both wrinkle-resistant and stain-repellant. Cloth subjected to such nanotreatments may require significantly different care from cloth that has merely been treated with resins. In such cases, read care labels carefully. See "Nanotechnologies," below.

Beetling. Beetling is the process in which linen fabric is pounded with wooden mallets until the yarns are permanently flattened and the weave of the cloth is closed. Table linens are usually beetled. Because beetling makes the yarns smoother, it increases luster. Beetling will give linen cloth a uniform thickness and render it more flexible. Ironing with hard pressure renews the flattened look of the yarns after laundering.

Bleaching. Unless it is to be used in its natural color, cloth must be bleached to whiten it or to prepare it for dyeing. Substances used for this purpose include chlorine bleaches—sodium hypochlorite (also used as a household bleach, as in Clorox) or sodium chlorite—hydrogen peroxide, and sodium perborate (the household bleach Snowy or Clorox 2), but a number of other chemicals may be used at various points in the bleaching process. Some Irish linen is still whitened by bleaching in the sunlight, a process called "grass bleaching." Bleaching by any means generally weakens the cloth to some degree. Sunlight, however, is considerably more gentle than chemical bleaching. Manufacturers sometimes also apply optical brighteners to fabrics, which simply alter the way the fabric reflects light, creating an appearance of brightness and masking yellowish hues. Most all-purpose detergents contain optical brighteners too.

Calendering. The term "calendering" refers to any of several processes in which fabric is subjected to great pressure and/or heat, in a type of ironing using large rollers. Calendering renders fabric smooth and lustrous. It is not a durable treatment when applied to cotton without resins. But when resins are used with calendering to create glazed, ciré, embossed, moiré, or Schreinerized fabrics (see the following paragraph), or when calendering is applied to thermoplastic fibers such as polyester, it is durable.

Crêpeing, Plissé, Embossing, Moiré, Schreinering. The use of heat, pressure, or acids, bases, and other chemicals on textiles can produce decorative effects. Crêpe can be produced either by weaving techniques and yarn construction or by passing fabric between specially engraved rollers. Crêpe produced by engraved rollers will eventually wash out, whereas the former methods render the crêpeing permanent. Embossing and moiré are also done with engraved heated rollers. Embossing produces a design by raising a pattern on the fabric or causing a depression in certain portions of it. It is permanent on thermoplastic fibers but not on cotton unless the cotton is treated with resins that are resistant to water and dry cleaning. Moiré is permanent only on thermoplastic fibers, such as acetate, polyester, and nylon, or on natural fibers treated with resins. Nylon can be chemically treated to crinkle it. The use of sulfuric acid on sheer cotton produces organdy; it stiffens the fabric and makes it translucent. But if the acid treatment is not properly done, it can seriously weaken the cloth.

Plissé (a crêpe effect) is the result of the application of caustic soda (sodium hydroxide). The chemical shrinks the area to which it is applied—mercerizing the area, in effect—and produces puckers. Chemically produced plissé is less permanent than real seersucker, which is produced by weaving. Plissé may come out under ironing, but seersucker will not. Seersucker can be distinguished from plissé by its clearly defined, alternating crinkled rows and smooth rows. By stretching the fabric and seeing how persistent the decorative effect is, you can gain some indication of how permanent it may be.

Embossing. See "Crêpeing."

Emerizing. See "Napping."

Flame-Resistance Treatments. There are only two flameproof fibers, both inorganic: glass and asbestos. Organic fibers are at best flame-resistant; that is, after the fiber is ignited, flaming is prevented, terminated, or inhibited, whether or not the ignition source is removed. Flame retardants are substances that render fabrics flame-resistant; they slow or stop the eruption and spread of flames but do not entirely prevent burning. Most treated fabrics will extinguish as soon as they are removed from the ignition source. The idea behind flame-resistant treatments is that they provide enough time to extinguish or to escape a fire before grave harm occurs. Wool and silk are naturally somewhat flame-resistant, but various finishes may render either of them less so. Some modacrylic is also naturally flame-resistant. Some synthetics can be rendered permanently flame-resistant during the manufacturing process without the use of flame retardants.

Unless treated, cotton, linen, rayon, acetate, nylon, and polyester ignite and burn readily. In all cases, the construction of the fabric, as well as fiber content, affects flammability; napping, pile weaves, loose weaves, soft-twisted yarns, and light weight all increase flammability.

Prior to the passage of legislation in 1953, there had been tragic fires and injuries caused by highly flammable fabrics and wearing apparel. Some of these involved napped or pile fabrics of viscose rayon that would flash-burn and engulf a wearer in flames in an instant following contact with a spark. The 1953 law, as later amended, prohibits the sale of highly flammable fabrics as apparel but requires that fabrics be flame-resistant only when used in children's sleepwear, rugs and carpets, mattresses, and mattress pads. Small rugs and carpets need not meet the standards if they bear a label stating, in part, "Flammable . . . Should Not Be Used Near Sources of Ignition." Upholstery is governed only by voluntary industry standards. The law on children's sleepwear requires it to be durably flame-resistant, that is, able to undergo at least fifty launderings without losing its flame-resistant qualities.

Before you take too much comfort in the existence of this limited law, you should know that the test—known as the 45-degree-angle test—for whether a textile is "dangerously flammable" (as provided in the federal Flammability of Clothing Textiles Standard) is widely regarded as inadequate. This test requires, among other things, that you hold a piece of fabric at a 45 degree angle and apply to it a flame of a specified size for one second. If it burns at a certain rate within a certain time, then it is banned for use in apparel in this country. Unfortunately, as one text points out, dry newspaper would not fail this test. Cotton/polyester blends, untreated for flame resistance, are often more dangerous than either 100 percent cotton or 100 percent polyester. Yet such blends are not "dangerously flammable" under the 45-degree-angle test. (They are difficult to treat for flame resistance because the treatments—heavy back-coatings—tend to yield materials with an unpleasant hand.) Moreover, some fabrics pass this test that might melt or emit toxic fumes or suffocating amounts of smoke when exposed to a flame. These characteristics can render them more dangerous than a textile that fails the test and thus legally counts as "dangerously flammable." Melting synthetic fabrics may adhere to the skin, causing worse burns than flaming fibers; heavy fumes and smoke can be lethal. Better regulations to remove these and other irrationalities, however, are resisted by interests in the textile industry. A proposed molten drop test, for example, that various types of synthetic cloth would have failed (even though they passed the 45-degree-angle test) was dropped.

Flame-resistance treatments have been problematic in other respects as well. One of the flame retardants widely used earlier was subsequently determined to be a carcinogen. A substitute developed for it was then found to be mutagenic. Some flame retardants, when they burned, were found to produce toxic fumes or large amounts of smoke, which were hazards in themselves. Some flame-resistant finishes tend to worsen the fabric's hand, producing harshness and stiffness, or they weaken the fabric. Excessive dirt can defeat flame retardants, making it important to keep items clean. Bleaches and soaps as well as fabric softeners and detergents containing carbonates (which can build up in fabrics and render it more flammable) should also be avoided.[3] All this means that it is important to carefully follow care labels on garments treated with flame retardants. In addition, to reduce the possibility of skin reactions, you should wash articles treated with flame retardants before wearing them.

In 1996, the Consumer Products Safety Commission amended the rule requiring that all children's sleepwear be flame-resistant, effective as of June 8, 1998. The amendment to the rule, which has aroused fierce opposition, contains two major provisions. First, it exempts from the flame-resistance requirements all sleepwear for infants under nine months of age. Second, it permits sleepwear for children of any age to be made of untreated (non-flame-resistant) cotton so long as it is snug fitting or contacts the skin at all points. (Snug-fitting clothes ignite less easily and burn less readily than loose-fitting or flowing ones.) Aside from these two categories, cotton sleepwear must still be treated to render it flame-resistant. So far as I am aware, United States manufacturers no longer make children's sleepwear that is treated with flame retardants, but some imported cotton pajamas are. In addition, flame-resistant pajamas of synthetic fibers continue to be widely available. But if you find pajamalike cotton garments for children older than nine months that are neither treated to render them flame-resistant nor snug fitting, they will continue to be labeled "Not intended for sleepwear."

When cotton sleepwear has been treated with flame retardants, this typically is done with tetrakis hydroxymethyl phosphonium (THP) salts, which are said to be both effective and safe from a general health standpoint. Such treatments last for fifty or more launderings. But clothes so treated cannot be washed with chlorine bleach or any product containing chlorine bleach or with ordinary nonphosphate detergents. This can be a problem in those areas that ban phosphate detergents, although there are nonphosphate detergents on the market that state that they will not harm flame-resistant finishes. Unfortunately, THP-treated cloth produces fumes and heavy smoke when it burns.

Nowadays, however, most children's sleepwear is made of synthetic fibers that have some degree of intrinsic flame resistance—at least for legal purposes (that is, they pass certain tests)—and need no treatment with flame retardants. These include polyester, modacrylic, and, according to its manufacturer, the new synthetic, PLA. There are also inherently flame-resistant variants of rayon, acrylic, and olefin (polypropylene). Experts point out, however, that given the insufficiencies of the legal standard, no matter what you buy, all you can be sure of is that the fabric passed the test, not that the fabric is necessarily safer than another. One authority[4] gives the inherent burning characteristics of fibers as follows, ranking them from most hazardous at the top to least hazardous at the bottom of the list:

Less Safe

COTTON/LINEN

Burns with a hot, vigorous flame, light-colored smoke, and leaves red glowing ember after flaming stops. Does not melt or draw away from the flames.

RAYON/LYOCELL

Burns similarly to cotton and linen, except that it may shrink up and become tighter to the body.

ACETATE

Burns with a rapid flame and melts when burning. May melt and pull away from small flames without igniting. Melted area may drip off the clothing, carrying flames with it. When flames have died out, the residue is a hot molten plastic and is difficult to remove from any surface.

ACRYLIC

Burns similarly to acetate, except that it burns with a very heavy, dense, black smoke. It drips excessively.

NYLON, LASTOL, OLEFIN (POLYPROPYLENE), POLYESTER,
AND SPANDEX

Burns slowly and melts when burning. May melt and pull away from
small flames without igniting. Melted area may drip off clothing,
carrying flames with it, but not to the extent of acetate and acrylic.
Residue is molten and hot and difficult to remove. May self-extinguish.

WOOL AND SILK

Burns slowly and is difficult to ignite (especially in winter garments).
May self-extinguish.

MODACRYLIC AND SARAN

Burns very slowly with melting. May melt and pull away from small
flames without igniting. Self-extinguishes.

More Safe

Glazing. Glazing creates a stiff, shiny appearance. Chintz and polished cotton
are familiar glazed fabrics. Older-style glazes of starch or wax are not durable.
Some modern glazes are created by baking or calendering resins onto the fabric, and these are more lasting.

Mercerizing. Mercerizing is used principally on cotton yarns and fabrics.
They are treated with a solution of caustic soda, causing the fibers to shorten
and swell up into a round shape. The effect is that the fabric or yarn becomes
stronger, more lustrous, and easier to dye. The fabric also acquires an improved
hand and drape. Cotton sewing thread purchased for use in the home should
always be mercerized.

Mildew. See "Antiseptics; Mildew Control," pages 312–13.

Mothproofing. Silk, wool, fur, and other hair fibers are susceptible to damage by insects that feed on the protein in such fibers. Moth larvae eat wool and
fur; carpet beetles eat wool, fur, and silk. Wool blends are vulnerable in the
same ways that wool is and should receive the same treatment. Insect-proofing
that will not come out with laundering or dry cleaning is built into some wool
fabrics, such as carpets and upholstery and, apparently, some clothes. Some of
these treatments kill the larvae when they try to eat the fibers; others render it
indigestible by the larvae. According to one authority, however, none of the
substances presently being used for such purposes is completely effective.

Less durable mothproofing can also be applied during dry cleaning. If
woolen articles have not been treated, preventive measures should be under-
taken at home. See the discussion of mothproofing in chapter 21 on pages
351–52; see also chapter 18, "Closets for Clothes and Linens."

Nanotechnologies. Nanotechnologies are rapidly being developed that permit new approaches to creating water repellancy and resistance to wrinkles, stains, abrasion, and shrinking. (Nanotechnology is the science of manipulating materials that are only billionths of a meter wide.) Such treatments, it is claimed, can be permanent and often leave the hand and other characteristics of the fabric unaltered. It is hoped that nanotechnologies will also permit improved treatments for, among other things, flame retardance, ultraviolet-radiation blocking, and antistatic effects. "Nano-treatments" involve the application of polymers or other substances at the molecular level in such a way as to cause them to bind permanently to the fibers of cloth, producing the desired effects. In addition, their manufacturers claim, the fabrics remain breathable, and the way it feels to the hand does not change because the nanotechnology attaches to the fabric at a nano- or sub-micron level.

Nano-treated fabrics now available in stores include wool that is washable and resists shrinking; cotton that is stain-, water-, and wrinkle-resistant; and synthetic fibers that are oil- and water-repellant and have enhanced wicking ability. There are also nano-products that are said to improve colorfastness, durability, softness, and drape. (In the case of cottons, new nano-treatments may be combined with older-style resin treatments for antiwrinkling.) Keep in mind that nano-treatments are no guarantee against staining; ink, mud, dyes, mustard, and other staining substances may still stain after nano-treatment. But because the treatment helps keep the stain material on the surface and prevents it from soaking in too deeply, it gives you a window of opportunity for wiping it off before it does much damage. Similarly, water will eventually penetrate items that have been nano-treated for water resistance, but more slowly.

Nano-treated fabrics may need laundering and other care that is significantly different from what you would otherwise give them. Fabric softeners may not be recommended. Dry cleaning may not be recommended. You may need an extra rinse cycle to get good performance; you may be told that steam ironing enhances the performance of the fabric. Always obey the care label on nano-treated fabrics.

Napping; Sueding; Sanding; Emerizing. Napping gives fabrics a fuzzy surface. It is accomplished by giving the yarns from which the fabric is woven a slack twist when they are spun, then passing the woven fabric over a roller covered with wires ending in small hooks. The hooks pull fiber ends out of the fabric and create the fuzziness or nap. (In brushing, brushes are used to raise the nap.) Napping creates air pockets in which warmth can be trapped; thus napped fabrics, such as flannels, are warmer. Napped fabrics are also more stain-resistant because the nap prevents substances from penetrating deep into the fabric. Napping should not be confused with pile, in which additional threads have been woven into the cloth, creating raised loops (which are sometimes cut) on the surface.

Sueding, or sanding, is similar to napping except that the roller that the cloth moves over has a sandpaper surface that abrades the cloth, producing the familiar suede finish. Like napping, sueding can render cloth weaker. In sandwashing, sand is put in a wash bath to abrade and soften the fabric. Emerizing uses gentler, emery-covered rollers to produce the sort of suedelike surface you find on many garments of polyester microfiber.

Plissé. See "Crêpeing."

Preshrinking and antishrinking. Whenever you can, buy preshrunk finished goods. You can usually buy preshrunk fabrics for home sewing as well, but when you cannot you should usually wash them before sewing so as to preshrink them yourself. Unfortunately, continued shrinking of any preshrunk goods may occur, and this shrinking may continue in small increments over many washings.

There are many antishrinking procedures, ranging from simple washing to mechanical, chemical, and resin treatments, and combinations of these. The familiar "Sanforized" trademark indicates that the cloth, woven cotton and rayon, was subjected to a standardized, highly effective method of compressive shrinkage, and that additional shrinkage will not exceed 2 percent. (Compressive shrinkage subjects fabrics to a controlled shrinking process that results in uniform shrinking and ensures that additional shrinkage will not exceed a given percentage.) There are other trademarks reflecting compressive shrinkage and other antishrinking treatments.

Wools are subjected to a similar variety of preshrinking methods using water, chemicals, or thermosetting resin treatments. Fulling is a laundering process to which wool may be subjected to clean it and to produce a controlled degree of felting, or drawing together of the wool fibers. Fulled fabric is smoother and fuller, denser and more compact, which makes it warmer. Thus fulled woolens such as melton (which is a heavily fulled, napped, closely woven fabric) are used to make overcoats. Worsteds are only lightly fulled, if at all. If an antishrinking effect in wool is derived from the use of chemicals, shrinking may develop after several launderings when these are finally washed away.

The "Superwash" trademark indicates that wool has received treatments that render it durably shrink-resistant and machine-washable. The wool is exposed to chlorine, which dissolves fiber scales and reduces felting shrinkage, and then coated with resin. The process makes wool feel different (less appealing, to my taste) and decreases its absorbency. The use of chlorine in the process raises environmental issues.[5]

Resin Treatments. Textile resins are "pre-polymers" that are applied to cellulosic fibers (cotton, linen, rayon) or blends containing them to produce a variety of effects: permanent creases or wrinkle-resistance, resistance to shrinkage, permanent stiffness or crispness, shine or luster, water repellancy, and decorative effects such as ciré, moiré, embossing, and so on. The resins most commonly used for these purposes are urea, glyoxal, carbonate, and melamine formaldehyde compounds. Resins work not by coating the fibers but by linking adjacent cellulosic molecules so that the resins actually form part of the structure of the cloth.

When resins were first used, years ago, health questions were raised about them because they were found to emit formaldehyde fumes. The odor was often unpleasant; some people are allergic to formaldehyde or can become sensitized by it; formaldehyde is classified as a "probable carcinogen" by the EPA. Newer, lighter application procedures and low- and non-formaldehyde-emitting resins, however, have by and large answered these concerns. (Newer resins still emit an extremely low amount of formaldehyde, but documented cases of sensitivity to resin-treated cloth in this country are rare.) Various experts seem to agree that resin-treated cloth is safe, recommending simply that you launder resin-treated articles once before using them to remove the tiny amount of free formaldehyde they may contain. There are also resins that contain no formaldehyde, which are often used on infants' and children's wear (because younger folk are more sensitive), but these tend to be more costly and less effective.

The application of resins, however, is not without other side effects, bad and good. On the negative side, they will render fabrics less absorbent, which means they are less comfortable, particularly in hot, humid weather. The cloth will also have a less pleasant hand and be weaker—up to 50 percent weaker—and less resistant to abrasion. Treated cloth will also develop a tendency to oil-stain, just as synthetic fibers do, and may develop static cling. Resin-treated fabrics may require different, milder laundry treatments. (See chapter 21, "The Natural Fibers," pages 349–50.) On the other hand, besides reducing shrinking and wrinkling, resins will cause the cloth to dry faster and will act as a stiffener, which renders many cotton garments more attractive. And both the positive and negative side effects of resin treatments are reduced by newer resins and lighter applications.

See also "Antiwrinkling Treatments," pages 313–14.

Sanding. See "Napping."

Schreinering. See "Crêpeing."

Skin Protection from Ultraviolet Rays. More protection is naturally provided to your skin against the ultraviolet rays of ordinary sunlight by clothes that are made of thicker, tighter weaves. Darker clothes are more protective than lighter-colored ones (although they feel hotter) because they absorb more ultraviolet radiation. Dry clothes are more protective than wet ones because the latter are more transparent. As far as cloth construction and color go, therefore, in warm weather you have something of a Hobson's choice between comfort and protection.

Some fabrics are manufactured to provide extra protection from the dangerous rays of the sun, through chemical treatments—called "sun-protection" or "ultraviolet (UV) blockers"—or cloth construction or a combination of these. Such cloth tends to be fairly light and cool yet offers at least as much protection as dark, tight weaves. Check hang tags and labels to see whether garments have received sun-protective treatments. See also chapter 13, "Fabrics That Work," pages 183–84.

Soil-Resistance Treatments. Apparel, tablecloths, upholstery fabrics, and other textile goods used in the home can receive treatments or finishes that make them more accident-proof and soil-resistant. Soil-resistance treatments are of two types: soil release and soil repellant. See also "Nanotechnologies," above, on new soil- and stain-resistance treatments using nano-treatments.

Soil Repellants. A soil-repellant fabric has received a treatment that renders it resistant to soil by causing water and/or oil to bead on its surface rather than penetrate immediately. This gives you a chance to wipe dirt and spills off before they can do damage. Such treatments are now available for both wool and synthetic carpets. There are many different kinds of soil repellants, and they do not all do the same thing. Some repel only water. Fluorocarbon polymers such as Scotchgard Dual-Action and Zepel repel both oil and water. Soil repellants generally will reduce the absorbency of fabrics but not their breathability. Soil-repellant treatments are applied to both natural and synthetic fibers as well as their blends.

Soil release. Soil-release fabrics have received a treatment that causes them to come cleaner during laundering. Check labels and hang tags to see if an article has received a soil-release treatment, e.g., Visa, Come Clean, or Scotchgard Stain Release. Soil-release treatments are applied only to synthetic fibers and their blends or to durable-press fabrics—that is, to oleophilic/hydrophobic fibers or to those that, as a result of resin treatments, resist thorough wetting, and thus thorough cleaning, during laundering. Without soil-release treatments, any of these fabrics may need some laundering pretreatment to ensure against "ring around the collar (or cuff)" or to help remove soil in areas of the garment that are particularly likely to pick up body oils or greasy food stains, such as collars, cuffs, and the midriff area.

Soil-release treatments are not all the same. Fluorocarbons work by making a film that prevents the oil from making direct contact with the fibers, so that a detergent-and-water solution can more easily wash it away. Others work by trying to make the surface of the fabric more hydrophilic through the application of chemicals. According to one textiles authority, those soil-release treatments that create a more hydrophilic fabric surface have various beneficial side effects: they can improve the garments' comfort level by increasing their moisture takeup, soften the hand, reduce static buildup, decrease soil redeposition during laundering, and reduce pilling. This expert points out, however, that soil-release treatments actually seem to cause fabrics to soil more heavily than nontreated ones.[6] Soil-release treatments have varying degrees of durability; some will last the life of the garment.

Combination soil-repellant and soil-release finishes. Note that the application of fluorocarbon copolymers (Scotchgard and Zepel) renders fabric both more soil repellant and more soil releasing.

Stiffening. Cottons and linen may be given temporary stiffness or crispness by the use of starches or sizing. These terms are often used interchangeably, but "sizing" should properly refer to any substance used to stiffen a fabric, and "starch" only to starch solutions, that is, solutions containing $C_6H_{10}O_5$. A wide variety of substances may be used for temporary stiffening—from starch to resins. Starches tend to be crisper and sizings softer. Both will wash out and, if the original crisp look and feel are to be retained, must be replaced on laundering. Overstarching or oversizing may be used to conceal inferior goods. If goods after washing become hopelessly limp, they may have been overstarched. If you suspect overstarching, before you buy the garment, rub the fabric between your hands to see whether any starch will powder off. (For a discussion of starching or sizing at home, see chapter 6, "Ironing," pages 111–12.)

Many more or less permanent stiffening treatments are also in use. These work by altering the structure of the fiber with resins. The application of resins has a variety of side effects, good and bad. See "Resin Treatments," above.

Sueding. See "Napping."

Water-Resistance Treatments. Fabrics that are absolutely impermeable to water are called waterproof. Those that are called water-repellant have a coating of some hydrophobic chemical that causes water to bead up on their surface rather than soaking through immediately. These fabrics have varying degrees of resistance to water but sooner or later are penetrated. Waterproof articles are made of or coated with a continuous layer of some water-insoluble material such as plastic, rubber, vinyl resins, and the like; thus they are impermeable to air as well as water. Waterproofing is generally permanent. Water-repellant treatments, however, have varying degrees of durability. Some lose their effectiveness with washing or dry cleaning or both. Durable water-repellancy treatments are possible using any of a number of chemicals and resins that will withstand both laundering and dry cleaning. Many of them confer other advantages such as wrinkle-resistance and stain resistance. Silicone treatments, while economical and highly effective, do not launder as well as they dry-clean. Fluorochemical water-repellants, such as Scotchgard or Zepel, which also function as soil repellents, to some extent repel oil as well as water. When water-repellant garments become less effective as a result of cleaning or washing, they may be retreated by the dry cleaner. Labels and the occasional knowledgeable sales clerk are your only sources of information about water-resistance treatments.

21

The Natural Fibers

Advantages of understanding fibers . . . Linen fabric manufacture . . . Judging damask . . . Properties of linen . . . Why we are more careful with linen fabrics today . . . Laundering delicate vs. sturdy linen fabrics . . . About bleaching, avoiding shrinking, drying linen . . . Cotton fabric manufacture . . . Properties of cotton fibers and fabrics . . . Caring for cotton fabric . . . Manufacture of wool fabrics . . . Judging quality in wool . . . Worsted vs. woolen yarns . . . Properties of wool . . . Caring for wool fabrics . . . Hand-washing and machine-washing wool fabrics . . . Manufacturing silk fabrics . . . Raw, pure dye, duppioni, and wild silk . . . Properties of silk fiber and fabrics . . . Caring for silk fabrics . . . Bast fibers and their properties and uses . . . Permanent-press and resin-treated cotton, rayon, finer fabrics, and their blends . . . Washable antiques, heirlooms, and other fragile or valuable linen . . . Mothproofing wool

Imagine two shirts of identical bright color and cut, indistinguishable except that one is made of cotton and the other of polyester. One may fade, and the other almost surely will not. One may pill, the other won't. One will wrinkle, the other will hardly wrinkle at all. One will be cool and comfortable in hot, sticky weather, the other may not be. These examples by no means exhaust the list of differences, all of which are functions of the fiber content of the two garments.

When you buy clothes, linens, towels, drapes, or other cloth goods for the home, you unavoidably choose one kind of fiber or blend of fibers over another. That choice determines how well the cloth will function in the role you envision for it, how it will feel, how long it will wear, how attractive it will remain as it ages, and how you will have to clean and care for it. To choose on the basis of style or look alone can lead to repeated experiences of frustration and unnecessary expense. To help you choose wisely and increase your awareness of how different fibers behave, in this chapter and the next I summarize the nature of the major fibers used in clothing and furnishings and offer a summary of how fabrics made from each of them are best cared for.

The natural fibers have a long and distinguished history. Linen, cotton, silk, and wool have each been used in clothmaking for millennia. They have been so important in our history that our language carries dozens of phrases and ideas borrowed from the manufacture and use of cloth of natural fiber—from calico cats and gingham dogs to getting fleeced, wearing sackcloth, and buying shoddy work or goods. Sometimes a restaurant disappoints you with its run-of-the-mill food. You might prefer tweedy friends to homespun ones, but certainly you want no sleazy ones.* The same richness of connotation cannot be expected of the synthetics, which are so recent. A young woman might be glad that her hair is flaxen and her skin like satin, but she will not cotton to being compared to polyester.

We draw upon the rich meanings of the natural fibers in a different way when we choose to put one rather than another on our backs or in our homes. Linen is dignified, and it often seems capable of heights of refinement and elegance that cotton cannot reach. Cotton is whatever you want it to be—plain or fancy, sensible, businesslike or whimsical, as you wish. Its very versatility works against its being a symbol of anything. Wool is comfortable, protective, warm, and prudent. Silk, as the fiber of true velvets, satins, and flowing chiffon scarves, retains an image of luxury and sensuousness. In each instance, these associations are derived from something in the way the fiber actually works or feels. A better acquaintance with the cloth made of these fibers will enable you to do more with fabrics in your home and to care for clothes and furnishings more successfully.

Linen

About Linen. Linen is so highly venerated that people tend to think of it as precious and delicate. But linen is available in sturdy constructions as well as fine. While some linens are fit for royal boudoirs and fragile lace on christening gowns, others are suitable for hard work as towels, bandages, everyday sheets, and other ordinary items. Flax is a remarkably strong, durable, and functional fiber. Linen is chosen for the finest damasks and the most delicate

---

*"Shoddy" refers to wool that has been reused or reprocessed. Run-of-the-mill goods are goods before they have been inspected or sorted for defects or flaws. When sheets and pillowcases were sold as "run of the mill," therefore, you were not guaranteed first quality. Applied to cloth, "sleazy" means flimsy, limp, or loosely constructed when it should not be. A loosely woven sheet, for example, would be sleazy.

laces partly because it is lustrous and smooth but also because it has superior strength, launders so well, and lasts so long. Linen towels, handkerchiefs, clothes, nightgowns and nightshirts, sheets and pillowcases, and upholstery are often both lovely and exceptionally serviceable.

Linen fabric is made from fibers of the flax plant's stem, which, like other plant fibers, are made of cellulose polymers. Good-quality linen is expensive, especially in the United States, which imports all of its fine linen and uses only small quantities of it each year. Linen is produced in many European countries. Traditionally, Belgian, Irish, and Italian linen are the most prized. Courtrai flax, grown in Belgium, creates the strongest and finest yarns, but Irish workmanship has long been regarded as superior. Belgian linen has a faint yellow cast; Irish linen is often skillfully sun-bleached to a prized degree of whiteness. French linen, also of high quality, is characteristically woven of round yarns, that is, it has not been put through the beetling process that is used to flatten linen. See "Beetling" in chapter 20, pages 314–15.

Not all linen produced in these countries is of the highest quality, however. The Confédération Européenne du Lin et du Chanvre, known as CELC, is an association of linen producers from Austria, Belgium, France, Germany, Italy, the Netherlands, Spain, Switzerland, and the United Kingdom (including Northern Ireland). CELC, through its promotional organization, Masters of Linen, authorizes the use of its international linen trademark by producers who agree to meet its standards. The logo's presence indicates that the linen originates in the European Union, in accordance with its social and environmental policies, and that it meets the Masters of Linen quality standards of construction, strength, dimensional stability (resistance to shrinking), and colorfastness. The logo is also an indication that you will find reliable care information—often a boon on tablecloths and other household fabrics because United States laws do not require care labels on articles other than apparel. Hang tags bearing the logo denote the fiber content of the linen fabric, that is, pure (100 percent) linen, minimum 50 percent linen, or linen union (cloth with cotton warp and linen weft). Although the Masters of Linen logo is helpful, you must still judge the quality of individual pieces for yourself.

Manufacture of Linen. A process called hackling separates flax into long fibers and short fibers, or staple. The fibers are then spun into yarn for weaving or knitting. Only long staple, called line, is used for fine linens—handkerchief linen, fine tablecloths, fine lingerie, and dresses. Thus the label "pure linen" is not necessarily a guarantee of high-quality fabric. For very fine linen, hackling is done by hand to produce longer fibers than can be obtained by machine-hackling. Short fibers, called tow, however, might be used in a very thin, smooth, closely woven fabric. Dish towels that are 100 percent linen but have a bumpy, slightly rough texture are of tow, as are linen draperies and upholstery. If it were possible to untwist and examine the length of the fiber in linen fabric, you could determine for yourself whether the fiber is line or tow: line fibers are twelve to twenty inches long; tow fibers are shorter than twelve inches.

The characteristic smooth texture of line linen reflects the smoothness of flaxen yarn. Usually linen yarns used for table linens (but not those used for dress linens) are also subjected to beetling, which gives the fabric its characteristic flat, lustrous appearance. Beetling also renders linen more flexible and gives it a uniform thickness.

In its natural state, flax fiber ranges in color from pale yellow or cream to dark brown. To get white linen, the fibers or fabric must be bleached. The more the cloth is bleached, unfortunately, the weaker it becomes. The traditional Irish method of bleaching it by laying it out on the grass in sunlight is less damaging than the chemical bleaching that is more commonly done. Whatever method is chosen, linen may be bleached a little or a lot. (There are four grades of bleached linen: fully bleached or full white, three-quarters bleached, half or silver bleached, and quarter bleached.) Bleaching is used not only to produce lighter cream and white shades but to make it easier to dye the linen fibers to intense hues. Flax fibers' hard, nonporous surface resists taking color. Brightly colored linen will have been much bleached and therefore may be weaker and have a shorter wear life than linen that has been less bleached. Nonetheless, if it is vat dyed or if it bears the Masters of Linen logo, it will have good colorfastness.

Fine linen is characterized by close and regular weaving and a smooth surface, free of bumps or knots. Fuzziness of any degree indicates either lower quality or the presence of another fiber blended in. Linen is available in many different weights, from very sheer to very heavy, and in very tight to very loose weaves. The heavier the weight of a linen fabric, the more durable it tends to be and the better it stands up to laundering. Fine flax cambric, for example, is delicate, while linen duck (a canvaslike fabric) is hardy.

Fine table linens are almost always jacquard-woven in single damask or double damask. Damask's woven patterns show on both sides. Double damask has twice as many filling yarns as warp yarns, which makes its pattern show more distinctly. The thread count of double damask ranges from 165 to 400. In single damask, which usually has a balanced construction (equal numbers of warp and filling threads), the thread count is from 100 to 200. The higher thread counts are more desirable in both kinds of damask. You can assure yourself that you are getting good quality by examining the cloth with eyes and hand, by relying on reputable manufacturers, and by obtaining knowledgeable sales assistance when it is available.

Properties of Linen. Flax fibers are strong and can be rendered into hardy, durable linen fabrics as well as delicate ones. The strength of the best linen is equaled only by fabrics made of nylon and polyester. Flax is considered a durable fiber both because of this strength and because of its good resistance

JUDGING DAMASK

Double damask is not necessarily superior to single damask. If low-quality yarns are used for double damask and high-quality for single, the single may be better. To be of better quality than single damask, double damask should have a higher thread count, superior yarn, and careful design and weaving. In durable, high-quality damask, the yarns are very even and the weave very close; otherwise the yarns will slip and the floats will wear out sooner. In general, longer floats are more beautiful, shorter floats more durable. The most beautiful, high-quality damasks are made of linen rather than cotton because the long, smooth flax fibers, when woven into damask's long floats, do not pull out, fuzz up, and wear out as readily as cotton fibers do.

to abrasion (rubbing) and to the deteriorating effects of sunlight. However, wrinkle-resistance treatments and bleaching, especially strong chemical bleaching, will weaken it. (Antiwrinkling treatments will also render it less absorbent and affect its hand; see pages 313–14 and 321–22.) As it ages, it softens in a way that many people particularly enjoy.

Flax fibers' smooth surface neither attracts nor holds dirt and stains as much as less smooth fibers, including cotton, do. Linen clothing feels cool and comfortable in hot weather—more so than fabrics made from any other fiber. This is both because flax fibers are so smooth and flat and because they are one of the most absorbent of all fibers. (Even a linen garment will not be cool, however, if it is lined with a hot or inabsorbent fabric, so be sure to check the fiber content of linings.) Linen also dries quickly—faster than cotton fabric—and does not lint. Thus it makes excellent towels, handkerchiefs, and bandages. Linen is naturally crisp. It has more body than cotton and drapes better. Linen fabrics may shrink a bit when washed (unless they have been treated or are labeled "nonshrink"), but they shrink less than untreated cotton. It is always best to buy linen fabric preshrunk if possible. The presence of the Masters of Linen logo indicates that that linen fabric will resist shrinking.

Linen is not resilient—that is, it will wrinkle readily—unless treated to prevent wrinkling or blended with a less wrinkle-prone fiber. It is inelastic, too; linen clothes should be carefully fitted, for they will not "give" in wear. Because linen is stiff, a crease should not be repeatedly pressed in firmly or eventually the linen will actually crack there. Articles that are stored folded, such as sheets and tablecloths, may weaken along the fold line if they are always folded in the same way or if they are left folded for long periods, so periodically refold them or roll them on tubes. (See "Caring for Linen," below.)

Linen is vulnerable to mildew but not to moths. It has good light resistance, more than cotton, eventually deteriorating only with long exposure to light. Concentrated acids, or even dilute acids if they are hot, can damage cellulosic fibers like linen. Over time, acid perspiration will also weaken it. If linen is stored in a starched state, silverfish may attack the starch and harm the linen.

Despite its fine qualities and its various superiorities to cotton, linen is often so expensive that you are better off investing in cotton if your budget is limited. And although linen compares favorably with cotton in so many respects, it is considerably less versatile. There are fewer types of linen cloth, and it bears many fewer constructions. Linen is available in quite a few excellent blends with both natural and synthetic fibers. Look for the Masters of Linen trademark for assurances of quality with respect to colorfastness, shrinkage, strength, and cloth construction. Or, for colorfastness, look for a label that says "Colorfast" or "Vat dyed."

Is Linen Delicate? Those Times and These Times. Household linens, such as sheets, towels, and lingerie, are likely to have care labels that prescribe laundering. All other linens today tend to have care labels that call for dry cleaning.

When it comes to highly tailored garments such as linen suits and jackets, and furnishings such as draperies, upholstery, and the like, take the drycleaning prescription very seriously. By home-laundering a dazzling linen summer suit whose care label prescribed dry cleaning, I turned it into a limp, shrunken, crooked-threaded mess. There are times, however, when both manufacturers and home launderers are a bit too timid about laundering linen. It is, after all, in principle, a strong, durable fabric. Not so long ago people did not hesitate to bleach, boil, and scrub linen vigorously, using strong chemicals like washing soda, to ensure that it was white, germ-free, and gorgeously gleaming. But today, even a care label that instructs you to wash the linen article does so in a way that makes you nervous. When you stop to consider why this change has taken place, it may help you to decide how you wish to treat your own prized linen fabrics.

In part, today we need to use more caution because our linens are less sturdy than linens were in the old days, when they were much heavier in weight, resin-free (resin treatments weaken cloth), and often made of the finest-quality flax. However, the gentle treatments recommended for linen today are not always addressed to its fiber content. For example, linen can take a lot of heat—hot wash water and a very hot iron—without damage. (A strong fiber by nature, linen is even stronger when wet.) Yet you are usually told not to wash it in hot water, and certainly not to boil it! One reason for the change is that dyes in colored modern linens may bleed or fade, whereas in the old days linen wasn't dyed at all but came in shades of white, tan, and brown. Another reason is that the manufacturer thinks you will be angry if the article shrinks, whereas people expected and allowed for some shrinking in the old days. They did not use fitted sheets (there were no fitted sheets); rather, they got their sheets—and nightgowns, chemises, shirts, and tablecloths—big enough to shrink somewhat and still fit. And whereas today people tend to buy linen for its looks, in the old days people valued it as much for function as for its beauty. It was inconceivable to the sanitarily minded Victorian that you should not render your bed and body linens germ-free by boiling or that you should not do everything in your power to render them snowy white. It was precisely because linen resisted staining and soil and because sturdy linen could endure strenuous laundering that it was used for bedding, tablecloths, towels, underwear, and nightgowns.

A final difference that matters is that in the good old days people were expert ironers and used very hot irons. Today's manufacturer is worried about what the home launderer will do when faced with the job of restoring a flat rectangle of a tablecloth—let alone a garment of complicated construction—to its smooth, prelaundered appearance. Many modern irons do not get quite hot enough to do linen well. Most people just don't expect to iron or even know how to do fine or complicated ironing of an article that has to be very damp, requires a very hot iron, and may need starch, so the manufacturer shrugs and writes on the care label, "Don't even try." But you can certainly learn this simple and satisfying skill, and quickly too, if you are willing to practice and survive less than stellar results until you pass beyond the beginner's stage.

It is, of course, always safest to follow the care labels. There are many reasons why care labels on linen articles might call for dry cleaning or very gentle laundering, even though linen is in principle a sturdy, highly washable fabric. To summarize and provide a few other examples:

Heirloom and antique linens always require special handling. (See pages 350–51.)

Linens may have water-soluble finishes that will dissolve in the wash, leaving you with a hopelessly limp, unsightly garment. If linen is not preshrunk—and it often is not—it may shrink significantly when washed, especially if the fabric has a loose weave.

Linen articles may have trims or linings that are not washable. Many colored linens are prone to fading and bleeding.

The manufacturer may fear that the skill required to iron some linen garments properly, especially heavyweight ones, will exceed the talents of the average person.

Ironing dark and bright-colored linens might cause seams and dart lines to turn white.

The fabric may be a blend that includes some fiber that requires a more conservative treatment than flax.

Loosely or delicately constructed linens might unravel, tear, snag, or shrink in the wash. Linen damasks that are not of the highest quality may be loosely woven with low-twist yarns and long floats.

Any construction or weaving factors that render other fabrics delicate may be present in linen fabrics. (See pages 267–80 and 330.)

Because of such contingencies, it is risky to disregard care labels on linen. And of course any risks are magnified by the premium in price that you pay for good linen. The high cost is enough to drive any of us to extreme caution.

Caring for Linen

Choosing a Good Laundering Technique. Laundering linen differs from laundering cotton in several respects. First, bleaching will usually be unnecessary, and chlorine bleach should usually be avoided. Second, shorter or gentler agitation is called for. Third, linen is best dried out of the dryer. In laundering any type of off-white linen, be cautious about the use of laundry detergents. Most contain optical brightening agents, which can change the color or create a dappled effect on some off-whites. (One manufacturer of linen damasks also advises against using detergents or other products that contain optical brighteners on white damask because, the manufacturer says, this will detract from the appearance of the subtle pattern. See "Optical brighteners," pages 83–84, and "Detergents and soaps, mild," pages 78–80, in the Glossary of Laundry Products and Additives.)

Cautious, conservative laundering is required for antique or heirloom linens; linens of very fine or delicate construction; less sturdy or lower-quality damasks; sheer fabrics; loose weaves or weaves with long floats or low-twist yarns; lace; embroidered (especially hand-embroidered) fabrics; cutwork; and similar linens. If you do not want to tackle the laundering of such linens, there are businesses that specialize in laundering antique and fine linens of all sorts.

The experts disagree on the best ways to launder linen. To a large extent, the disagreements reflect different ideas about how long you should expect linen to last. If you really wish and expect washable sturdy linen to last a lifetime, you should give it the gentle treatment described below as suitable for washable delicate linens. But if vigorous cleaning is more important, consider whether you should choose the method directed for washable sturdy linens. (To clean antiques, heirlooms, and other fragile or valuable cottons and linens, see pages 350–51. The instructions immediately below are not appropriate for such items.)

Cautious Laundering Methods for Washable Delicate Linens

These instructions apply to washable delicate linens that have not become fragile through age and are not being preserved for posterity.

Washable delicate linens may be hand-laundered in mild detergent in the manner described in chapter 4, "Laundering," pages 62–63. Or they will do fine on the gentle cycle of your washing machine, set for a short wash. If you have no gentle agitation setting, you might consider machine-washing delicate linens very briefly on regular agitation, but this requires you to exercise your judgment as to just how delicate the articles are. For protection while machine-washing, especially if the pieces have fringes, ties, or loose trim, place them in a mesh bag or an old pillowcase and fasten it closed. Use warm water for white linens and lukewarm for colored (or cool if the colored linens bleed readily). Use a mild detergent (preferably one without optical brightening agents if you are laundering off-whites or white damask). If you prefer a mild soap to a detergent, be sure that you have soft water. Rinse very thoroughly with plain cool water. (Those who are uncertain how to choose a mild detergent should read "Detergents and soaps, mild," in the Glossary of Laundry Products and Additives, pages 78–80.)

To remove spots or stains or general dinginess or yellowing, first try soaking the fabric overnight in warm water with mild detergent. (However, protein stains—blood or egg, for example—get a cool-water soak; see the Guide to Stain Removal that begins on page 163.) Next, resort to sun bleaching and then to oxygen bleach, as described below. (I myself am willing to chance even chlorine bleach to cure stains or dinginess in delicate linen when I reach the point at which I feel I have nothing to lose.)

To dry linen, do not wring; roll it in a towel to remove excess moisture, then dry flat away from sources of heat. Hanging to dry can stress delicate fibers but will be fine for a sheer linen nightgown or blouse (one that you wear—not an antique). Use your judgment.

You can avoid ironing delicate lace if you gently pull it to its proper shape and then pin it to the towel or weigh it down around the edges with something harmless to prevent its curling up or drying crooked. Watch out that you do no harm with the pinning; put the point of the pin through holes in the lace.

If ironing will be safe and is necessary, take the linen up while it is still fairly damp. Then iron sheer or delicate linens on the wrong side with a medium iron; iron less sheer, less delicate linens on the wrong side with a hot iron. (See "Ironing Linen" in chapter 6, "Ironing," pages 108–10.)

Laundering Washable Sturdy, Nonshrink, Colorfast, or White Linens

The following instructions apply to washable sturdy tablecloths, sheets, woven towels, clothes, and similar linens. Linen that has not been Sanforized or preshrunk may shrink moderately, and the hotter the water the more shrinking you may expect. (See "About Shrinking of Linen," below.)

Use hot water and regular laundry detergent unless you need to avoid optical brighteners (on certain off-whites or on white damask; see "Optical brighteners" in the Glossary of Laundry Products and Additives, pages 83–84).[1] If you use soap, make sure you have soft water. Set the machine for gentle or slow agitation or—if you have only one agitation speed—a short agitation period. (Although some experts think regular agitation is fine, my experience suggests that linen's brittle fibers last longer if they are not beaten about too much. A front-loading washing machine would probably be less damaging on "regular" than an agitating top-loader.) Use a fast spin. Rinse thoroughly; using the extra-rinse option on your washer is a good idea. Do not wring. When you are having trouble getting linens clean with the fore-going procedures, add a long presoak, overnight if the problem is stubborn, with hot water initially.

Woven linens can be hung to dry; knits should dry flat. See "About Drying Linen," below. Iron with a hot iron. (See pages 108–10 in chapter 6, "Ironing.")

About Bleaching Linen. If you launder linen well and rinse it well, it is not likely to need bleaching. But sometimes dinginess develops or stains or spots occur. If bleaching becomes necessary, sun-bleaching is gentlest. To whiten linen and help remove spots, sun-bleach by laying the freshly washed, damp article in the sun, putting a sheet or some other protection under it. Make sure it will not be injured or soiled by animals or children. (The habit of laying stained fabrics on a bush to bleach them gave rise to the expression, "If that doesn't take the rag off the bush.")

City dwellers may cautiously resort to chemical bleaches on whites. On colorfast colored and white linens, try oxygen bleaches if you feel the linens need bleaching. If you need to avoid the optical brighteners or bluing that oxygen bleaches typically contain, consider using plain hydrogen peroxide (see pages 70–71). Chlorine bleach is generally unnecessary, but I have made occa-sional use of it, without mishap, on white, sturdy, washable linen that grew dingy. I use chlorine bleach on linen dish towels at each laundering; after sev-eral years, none has developed holes or any other apparent weaknesses.

About Shrinking of Linen. If you wish to use hot water, be sure to buy sturdy, well-made linens that are Sanforized or preshrunk or that are big enough to undergo some shrinkage and still fit. (The presence of the Mas-ters of Linen logo indicates that the fabric should be dimensionally stable.) If you are deliberately shrinking non-preshrunk linens, however, be alert to size and to decorative patterns, such as those that are meant to track the edge of the table. If linen is not preshrunk and you cannot permit any shrinkage, you might consider dry-cleaning it, because even washing it in cool water and dry-ing it flat or on the line will produce a bit of shrinking on each laundering until it is finally completely shrunk. But sooner or later—usually sooner—dry cleaning produces grayness, dinginess, or limpness in white or light linen. So be sure to search for a reliable dry cleaner and make your standards known when you deliver your linens.

About Drying Linen. Tumbling in the dryer causes linen fabric to become terribly wrinkled; all the tumbling is hard on the fabric, and for many house-hold linens it is quite unnecessary as they dry quickly and you must iron them very damp. Flax, keep in mind, is a rather brittle fiber. Thus good care for linen fabric includes not bending and jerking it too much, especially when it is dry. One manufacturer actually recommends removing linen from the washer after the spin cycle and ironing it right away. This manufacturer probably has in mind the front-loading type of washing machine common in Europe but not the United States, which spins laundry much dryer than ours do. However, the advice does make a point: you want linen to be quite damp when you iron it, so there is no reason to risk damage by tumbling it dry. If you feel you must put sturdy linen in the dryer, keep the drying time short and be sure to remove the linen when it is still very damp. If you are concerned about shrinkage, dry the linen on a low setting.

It is best, however, to hang an article made of linen to dry or to dry it flat. When it is the proper degree of dampness for ironing, roll it up tightly, place it in an airtight plastic wrap or bag, and put it in the refrigerator or freezer if you do not intend to iron it within a few hours. If you are going to iron it soon, wrap it so that the dampness does not evaporate in the meantime.

On ironing linen, see chapter 6, "Ironing," pages 108–10.

Cotton

About Cotton. Cotton is the true "miracle fiber." It is the fiber of democracy: it can be anything it wants to be, ambitious or humble, and its qualities can be enjoyed by rich and poor alike. More cotton is used in the United States than any other fiber.

Cotton, like flax, is a cellulosic fiber. It is derived from the fuzzy fibers surrounding the seeds of the cotton plant. It has many of the virtues of flax. It is absorbent, cool, crisp, smooth, and strong, even if, in each case, less so than linen. The quality of cotton fabric, like that of linen, is determined by the closeness and regularity of the weave and the construction of the fabric as well as the kind of cotton plant that provided the fibers from which it was made. The cotton plant determines the fiber's color, strength, luster, fineness or coarseness, and the length of the staple—short, medium, long, or extra long. (Long-staple cotton is 1⅛ inches or more in length; extra long is 1⅜ inches or more.) In general, the longer the staple, the better and the more costly the cotton fabric made from it and the more strength, smoothness, softness, luster, and durability it has.

Measured by these criteria, the best kind of cotton fiber is said to be Sea Island cotton, first grown off the coast of Georgia and now grown in the West Indies. This is a lustrous fiber with the finest and longest staple of all cottons (from 1½ to 2½ inches), and therefore it is used to manufacture the very finest cotton fabrics. It is now available only in small quantities, and you are unlikely to find many fabrics made of it. I have encountered men's shirts and pajamas made of Sea Island cotton, and I have bought Sea Island cotton fabrics in a piece goods store.

Pima cotton, another superior type of cotton, is a crossbreed of American and Egyptian cottons that is grown in Texas, the Southwest, and southern California. Pima cotton, like Sea Island cotton, is extra-long staple (its staple length ranges from 1⅜ to 1⅝ inches), uniform, very fine, lustrous, strong, and light in color, which means it needs less bleaching than darker cottons. The Supima Association is an organization of pima cotton farmers that promotes pima cotton and authorizes the use of the Supima trademark only on fabrics of 100 percent pima cotton. (The Supima Blends trademark indicates that the fabric contains at least 60 percent pima cotton. The other 40 percent may be composed of other types of cotton or other types of fibers.)

Egyptian cotton, grown largely in the Nile Valley, is a third extra-long staple, better-quality cotton, with a staple length running from 1½ to 1¾ inches. It comes in a number of varieties; although all are long or extra-long staple, only some are of the highest quality, and you cannot rely on labels announcing "Egyptian cotton" as a guarantee that you are getting the best. Egyptian cotton fibers range from light cream to dark tan; they are said to be less uniform than pima cotton fibers.

When purchasing goods bearing labels indicating that they are made of "Sea Island" or "Egyptian" cotton, look to see whether they are said to be of 100 percent of this type of cotton; otherwise they may be made of a mixture of fine and less fine cottons or other types of fiber. When purchasing pima cotton goods, look for the Supima trademark or for a statement about the percentage of pima cotton the article contains.

Most United States cotton, however, as well as most of the world's cotton, is upland cotton; most cotton goods, including clothes, towels, sheets, and diapers, are made of upland cotton. The Seal of Cotton, with its familiar cotton boll, is a registered trademark of Cotton Incorporated, an industry organization supported by growers of upland cotton. This seal indicates fabric made of 100 percent upland cotton; the Natural Blend trademark indicates that the fabric contains at least 60 percent upland cotton. Upland cotton, too, comes in a number of varieties and staple lengths, and these are of different quality, but none are as long and strong as Sea Island, fine Egyptian, or pima cotton; its staple length averages ¹³⁄₁₆ to 1¼ inches. Yet quality in cotton is to some extent relative to purpose. In towels, for example, my preference is for upland cotton, which seems to me to be most absorbent and soft.

South American cottons are to be found on the market in a wide range of quality. Asiatic cotton imported into the United States is almost always of relatively short staple and is usually used only for lower-quality cotton goods.

Fine-quality cotton goods will often be labeled "Combed cotton." Combed cotton fabric is made of combed yarns that contain the longest of the long-staple cotton fibers. Combed yarns are stronger, smoother, and more durable than carded yarns and make higher-quality fabrics.

Properties of Cotton. Cotton fibers are naturally very absorbent, and so are fabrics made of them. Cotton fabrics are often preshrunk. If they are not, they tend to shrink; the more loosely woven the fabric, the more it will shrink. Cotton cloth wrinkles, but not quite so much as linen. The cotton knits that have been so deservedly popular for so long wrinkle less than cotton wovens. In addition, much cotton fabric on the market, including cotton in blends, has been subjected to wrinkle-resistance treatments. (But these tend to alter the cloth's hand, weaken it, and render it less absorbent. See "Resin Treatments," pages 321–22, and "Antiwrinkling Treatments," pages 313–14.)

Cotton fabric is cool, but not quite as cool as linen because its fuzzier, less smooth surface holds warmed air. Although cotton fabric is highly absorbent, it dries more slowly than linen. It can be delightfully cool on a hot summer's day, therefore, as it grows damp from perspiration. Cotton is also strong and durable, although, once again, a bit less so than linen. Cotton fabrics are generally crisp and hold their shape well. Cotton fiber is inelastic but cotton fabrics may acquire "give" or "stretch" from their construction or that of their yarns, for instance, through crêpeing or knitting. And because cotton fibers have a relatively rough surface, cotton fabrics are not quite as dirt- and stain-resistant as linen. One of cotton's chief advantages over linen, however, is that it takes dyes very well, although colorfastness varies from poor to excellent depending on the dye and the dyeing process. Cotton fabrics generally have low luster, but those made of long-staple cotton fibers have higher luster.

Like linen, cotton fabric is stronger wet than dry. It has fairly good resistance to degradation by light, but it will yellow and weaken with prolonged exposure to sunlight. It mildews readily if left damp but will not be attacked by moths. (In cotton/wool blends, however, moths might attack the wool.) Like all fabrics made of cellulosic fibers, cotton fabric is vulnerable to strong acids. Acidic perspiration has a slightly deteriorating effect on cotton over time. Certain other acids occasionally used in the home, such as hydrochloric, sulfuric, and oxalic acid, will quickly do damage; the hotter and stronger the acidic solution, the greater the damage.

Cotton fabrics are available in every conceivable quality, coarse and fine; in a huge variety of woven and knitted constructions; and in blends with both natural and synthetic fibers.

Caring for Cotton. Subject to the usual caveats regarding finishing treatments, dyes, loose or otherwise delicate weaves, trims, and linings, cotton garments are in principle machine-washable, withstand vigorous and strong detergents, and are also dry-cleanable. Cotton clothes, bedsheets, and tablecloths can be laundered on the regular wash cycle, unless the care label indicates otherwise or unless the article in question is delicate in some respect. Unless treated or preshrunk to prevent it, woven cotton fabrics shrink modestly, and knitted cotton fabrics less modestly. Avoiding hot water and high dryer temperatures reduces shrinkage of cotton knits.

Cotton fabrics may safely be bleached with ordinary household bleaches as long as this is done properly and they are rinsed thoroughly. Chlorine bleach, used according to the manufacturer's directions, is usually safe on white and colorfast cottons. (But prolonged use weakens the fabric. See "Bleaches," pages 70–74, and "Optical brighteners," pages 83–84, in the Glossary of Laundry Products and Additives.) Cotton that has been resin-treated to make it wrinkle-resistant is weaker, however, and may last longer if you avoid bleaching it with a chlorine bleach.

Cotton fabrics tend to yellow with age or long exposure to sunlight. For this reason, you often hear these days that if you line-dry cotton you should put it in the shade. Keep in mind, however, that this is the long-term effect of sunlight. The short-term effect is that sunlight bleaches cotton—whitens whites and fades colors. If I had a clothesline, I would put white cotton in the sun if I wanted to whiten it, but I would not leave it there for more than a few hours, and I would always put colored cottons (and other colored fabrics) in the shade. If your cotton has yellowed from sunlight, by the way, you can usually bleach the color out. (My mother tells me that boiling for forty-five minutes or an hour with detergent will do the trick, too, but no one today has facilities for boiling, so I do not recommend this for bulky items.) Another problem with line-drying cotton is that some cotton is treated with optical brightening agents that yellow in the sunlight. But this problem seems to be rare. Yellowing from either cause tends to show up only on white or light cottons—for instance, on a pastel blue that turns dull. If your sturdy white cottons or linens have yellowed from unknown causes, try the remedy in "Yellowing of White Cottons or Linens," page 168.

Cotton fabrics can take a hot iron, and woven cottons usually need ironing unless they have received a resin treatment to reduce wrinkling, in which case the warm or permanent-press setting is usually recommended. Use starch or sizing for added crispness.

On the care of permanent-press cotton and cotton blends, see pages 349–50. See also pages 369–70 in chapter 22, "The Man-Made Fibers and Blends."

Wool and Other Hair Fibers

About Wool. Nature designed wool for comfort. Wool fabric, woven from sheep's fleece, offers you a bit of what it gave the sheep: warmth, softness, cushioning, protection from dampness, and absorbency. Almost all wool fabrics that you can buy are made from sheep's wool, but the term "wool" on a garment's label can also refer to fibers obtained from the fleece of Angora or cashmere goats and to fibers drawn from the coats of the camel, alpaca, llama, and vicuña. Wool fibers are the warmest of all natural fibers. They can absorb a great amount of moisture without feeling damp and are naturally water-repellant. Wool fabric will not keep you dry in a pouring rain, but it will easily keep a sprinkle or a chilly mist at bay. Moreover, as wool fibers absorb water they actually release heat. This means that in cold, damp weather wool fabric will feel remarkably warm and comfortable, a fact that has been well appreciated for millennia. Wool fibers can also be woven into fabrics that are so lightweight and porous that they are considered suitable for summer wear. Wool is also widely used for furnishings, especially upholstery, carpets, and rugs. Wool fabric can be smooth or rough, fine or coarse. Although raw wool fibers are the weakest of the natural fibers (and grow still weaker when wet), wool fabrics can be constructed to be extremely durable. Wool fabrics are generally more expensive than either cotton or linen because of wool's expensive production process, beginning with the breeding of sheep.

Wool fibers are classified in two main ways: according to the kind of sheep the fiber comes from and according to the kind of fleece. Merino sheep are the source of merino wool fibers, the finest, softest, strongest, and most elastic wool fibers; because of these qualities, merino wool is the warmest type and spins into yarns well. But merino is not the most durable. The names of the sheep whose wool is most durable are not likely to appear on labels. ("Shetland" and "Botany" refer to places the sheep are raised—the Shetland Islands in Scotland and Botany Bay in Australia.) There is a wide variety in the quality of wool fibers, but quality is relative to function; the coarse, durable wool that makes a good carpet would make a rough, uncomfortable sweater.

Classification by type of fleece reflects the age and condition of the sheep and its fleece. Lamb's wool is a fleece of very fine quality. Fabrics of lamb's wool are the softest of all, but less strong than those made of mature wool. Hogget wool, the first shearing off year-old sheep, is highly desirable because it is still quite soft yet stronger than lamb's wool. Later shearings, from older (and dirtier) sheep, are progressively less desirable for clothing fabrics. Other decidedly inferior classes of fleece are taken from slaughtered or badly nourished sheep. Taglocks are the inferior (torn or discolored) pieces of any fleece.

New Wool and Recycled Wool. Previously manufactured wool yarn and fabrics may be recycled and used in new products. When recycled wool, known also as "shoddy," "reclaimed," "reused," or "reprocessed" wool, is added to new wool, it can add durability, especially if it was of a good grade, but at the cost of some warmth, softness, and resilience. Although the term "recycled" may be relatively new, the practice of recycling wool is quite old. Products containing recycled wool may well be of good quality, and they are generally less expensive than 100 percent new wool fabrics. The Wool Products Labeling Act requires that labels state what percentage, by weight, of wool is con-

American Wool

Pure New Wool Woolmark

Harris Tweed Certification Mark

tained in a fabric and how much of it is new (or virgin) and how much recycled. A label guaranteeing 100 percent new wool does not, however, and is not intended to, guarantee a wool fabric of superior quality, let alone one superior to all fabrics containing recycled wool. Even very inferior grades of wool, such as pulled wool (from slaughtered sheep), might properly be identified as 100 percent new wool. A fabric made of a high-grade recycled wool would be superior to one made of low-grade new wool.

Evaluating Wool. The Wool Products Labeling Act does not require any indication of the breed of sheep or the type of fleece used in a garment or other wool product. Thus it can be difficult to determine the quality of the wool fiber used. There are several trademarks you can look for that help in assessing the quality of wool fibers and fabrics. The Woolmark is the trademark of The Woolmark Company. It may be used only on fabrics of 100 percent new wool that meet The Woolmark Company's quality specifications. The Woolmark Blend symbol, created in 1971, indicates quality apparel yarns of wool blends containing at least 50 percent new wool (80 percent for carpets and rugs; 60 percent for furnishings and bedding). The Wool Blend symbol, introduced in 1999, identifies quality apparel yarns containing at least 30 percent but less than 50 percent new wool. The presence of the logo of the American Wool Council, a division of the American Sheep Industry Association, indicates that the article contains a significant percentage of wool that originated in the United States—at least 20 percent in all-natural-fiber articles or 30 percent when blended with synthetics. As a condition of receiving permission to use the logo, the manufacturer agrees to use it only on goods of highest quality, samples of which it agrees to supply to the American Wool Council. Genuine Harris tweeds, which are known for their quality of construction, durability, and exclusive designs, can be identified by the symbol of the Harris Tweed Authority.

Tags or labels indicating that the fabric is of merino wool are one means of determining good quality. But use common sense. Recently, I have seen some not inexpensive merino sweaters of mediocre to poor quality. The sweaters were knitted very thinly in a latticework pattern (with lots of holes). Thus for your money you got little cover, little warmth, and little wool—but what you got was indeed merino. The indication on the label of the proportions of new and recycled wool fiber tells something about the relative durability and resilience of the fabric, but, unless you know about the quality of both, this information is of limited use. A "Superwash" or "H$_2$O Wools" (J. P. Stevens Company) label indicates that the wool fabric has been resin-treated to render it machine-washable. Machine-washable Woolmark fabrics are labeled "Easy Care." You should be sure to read the care label to see whether handwashing or dry cleaning is going to be necessary. Labels may also indicate preshrinking treatments, other treatments rendering wool washable, antiwrinkling treatments, permanent creasing, and so forth.

Much can be learned by sight and touch. If wool feels harsh and stiff, it is of an inferior grade for use in clothing. If it feels very soft and resilient (that is, it does not wrinkle when crushed in the hand), it is of a high grade for this purpose. But softness and resilience are not a guarantee of strength. The addition of some reprocessed or reused wool may indicate increased durability. Napping tends to weaken any fabric; if wool is highly napped it may not be strong. Tightly twisted yarns are stronger than loosely twisted yarns; and yarns in two or more ply are progressively stronger than single-ply yarns. Always observe the quality of the weave. You can usually rely on the representations of reputable retailers and manufacturers and knowledgeable sales clerks, but I find that many sales clerks are as much in the dark as I am.

Different grades of wool may be blended during the manufacturing process to make a hardier or less expensive fabric. Wool/synthetic blends (the percentage of each fiber will be noted on the label) often combine beauty with comfort, serviceability, and economy. Wool fiber contributes softness, warmth, absorbency, and drapability while synthetic fibers can add increased wrinkle-resistance, crease retention, or strength to the fabric and help prevent sagging, bagging, or stretching. Wool/microfiber blends have been particularly praised as giving the appearance and hand of a fine-quality wool.

Cashmere, a type of goat hair, is synonymous with luxury and costliness, but cashmere, like all other types of wool, can be of better or worse quality. The best-quality cashmere, with its exceptional silky softness, is made only of the longest and finest fibers. You will find many garments accurately labeled "100 percent cashmere" that, however, are made only of the less desirable short fibers. If you are inexperienced with cashmere, stop into a good shop and run your hand over its best cashmere sweaters; you will quickly learn what fine cashmere really feels like. One textiles expert advises you to notice, in addition, whether the fabric wrinkles or creases after you scrunch it or returns to its original smoothness, as high-quality goods should do. Test cashmere blends in the same way.[2]

Worsted and Woolen Yarns. Wool yarns fall into one of two types: worsted and woolen. Long wool fibers are used for worsted yarns. They are separated out from short ones and laid parallel (by several processes, including carding and combing) before spinning. The long wool fibers spin into a smoother and firmer yarn. Short wool fibers are used for woolen yarns. They are not combed and are rendered nonparallel so they will spin into fuzzier yarns than worsted yarns.

Worsted fabrics have the flat, hard, smooth feel of tailored wool suits and dresses. Worsted fabrics are usually found in twill rather than plain weave. Worsteds are considerably stronger and more wrinkle-resistant than woolens, and they resist dirt better because they are not fuzzy. However, they can develop unattractive worn, shiny spots.

Woolen fabrics feel soft and fuzzy. Their fuzziness renders them warmer than worsteds but less durable. They are often napped, which gives even more softness but means they hold dirt more readily. Woolens are familiar in sweaters, blankets, sportswear, and jackets.

Oiled wool has had more natural lanolin left on the fibers than usual, which creates extra water-repellancy, and thus might be used in heavy, water-shedding sweaters.

Properties of Wool. Wool is a soft—not crisp—fabric. Although technically wool is a weak fiber, fabrics made from it are exceedingly durable. Wool fabrics have good resistance to abrasion, and both woven and knit wool fabrics can be constructed so that they have excellent strength. Hard-twisted wool yarns, in two or more ply, make very durable fabrics. Wool has fairly good resistance to pilling, which increases its durability in uses such as carpeting. (Although wool fabrics pill, the pills break off and thus do not accumulate as they do on fabrics made of synthetic fibers.) Wool fabrics drape gracefully.

Wool fabrics tend to be warm because wool fibers have scales and crimps that create air pockets that trap body warmth. It is also highly absorbent. It can hold great quantities of perspiration and atmospheric moisture while still feeling dry. Moreover, as wool absorbs water it liberates heat and makes the wearer feel even warmer; thus it well deserves its reputation as the fiber of choice for cold, damp climates. Wool fabric is resilient (resists wrinkling). Wrinkles will disappear when the garment or fabric is steamed. But because its resilience is reduced when it is wet, you should not walk on a wet wool carpet or wear a wool garment you have just steam-pressed.

Wool fabrics shrink in water unless treated. Woolens shrink more than worsteds, but both shrink. Look for the "Superwash" or "Easy Care" marks on tags or for some other trademark or label indication that the wool will resist shrinking in water. Wool/synthetic blends may be more resistant to shrinking in water than 100 percent wool that has received no nonshrinking treatment, but such blends are sometimes more prone to pilling. Wool ordinarily has low static buildup but in a very dry atmosphere can become quite static-charged. It is stain-resistant; liquids will run off wool or penetrate it slowly, giving you time to blot them up. Dust and dirt often brush off wool. But it can also absorb and hold odors.

Wool fabrics are highly vulnerable to damage by moths. Sometimes they are given a mothproof finish.

Although wool resists mildew, it may succumb if left damp for a long period. Wool has low resistance to ultraviolet radiation.

Caring for Wool. Wool tends to hold dirt. Because of wool's elasticity, wool garments should be allowed to "rest" for twenty-four hours in order to return to their proper shape before they are worn again. According to one authority, wool garments should also be left to rest for a few days after dry cleaning or washing. If wool fabrics are left to rest, their fibers age or "anneal." The wool molecules actually rearrange themselves into more energy-efficient configurations.[3] To prepare a garment for resting, empty the pockets, button or zip it up, and hang it straight on a hanger with broad shoulders or fold it and lay it in a drawer or on a shelf. Brush wool garments after wearing and allow them to air, properly hung on a hanger or folded, before replacing them in your closet or dresser. Brushing not only helps keep the cloth clean, it is also good protection against moths; airing will reduce odors. Wool, however, does not hold body odors the way synthetics sometimes do and can actually help get rid of underarm odors by absorbing them. To freshen and unwrinkle wool garments, hang them in a steamy bathroom or use a steaming device. You will help wool garments stay clean longer if, after brushing and before airing, you simply wipe them down with a barely damp white, lint-free cloth. Make sure you let them air-dry before replacing them in the closet or drawer.

Wool fabrics are usually dry-cleaned. Some (including some cashmere) are washable, but wool is softened by moisture and heat, and shrinking and felting may occur when the fabric is washed, especially in alkaline solutions. Because shrinking and felting are much less of a problem with dry cleaning, most care labels call for this. For instructions on hand-washing and machine-washing wool, see page 345.

Even washable wools require careful laundering. Because ordinary laundry detergents all create an alkaline wash-water solution, wool should be washed with special detergents. Use a gentle soap or detergent that is nonalkaline or near-neutral pH. (See "Detergents and soaps, mild" in the glossary at the end of chapter 4.) Make sure the soap or detergent is effective in cool water. Hot or warm water with detergent can cause astonishing shrinkage: your size 38 sweater can emerge toddler-sized. Washable white wool may be bleached, if you are careful about it, with hydrogen peroxide but not chlorine bleach. (See pages 70–71.) Do not dry wool in the sunlight, especially white wool, as this can render it yellow or dull.

Store wool clothes, blankets, and carpets out of light and dampness, and make sure they are perfectly clean when they are put away; moths and other insects will be attracted to soils. On protecting wools from moths, see "Mothproofing Wool," pages 351–52.

Do not iron wool; press it, using a damp press cloth. (See chapter 6, "Ironing," page 104.) Ironing wool dry will make its fibers brittle and damage them.

Silk

Sumptuary laws in sixteenth-century England forbade the wives of poor men to wear silk gowns or French velvet bonnets. Such finery was considered suitable only for the wives of men who had at least a horse to ride in the king's service. For centuries, silk has been regarded as the most desirable, elegant, and luxurious of all fabrics, and it continues to hold that status despite keen competition from synthetics and blends.

WASHING WOOL

Hand-washing. Before washing a sweater or other garment, draw its outline on a piece of sturdy paper or cardboard. To control shrinking, use cool water (but not icy-cold water) with a mild, neutral soap or detergent suitable for wool and for cool-water laundering.* You might try lukewarm water if the item is heavily soiled. Soak for three to five minutes. Then lift from beneath the article and gently squeeze suds through the material. Leave the garment in the water for as short a period as possible; the longer it is in, the more its fibers swell and weaken. Since wool loses strength when wet, wool fabrics should never be pulled, twisted, or wrung while wet. Rinse the article thoroughly in clear, cool water. To dry, roll it in a towel and squeeze gently. Then, using your drawing as a guide, block the garment to its original shape. If you need to, pin it to the shape. Let it dry flat on a towel or other clean surface away from direct heat or sunlight.

Machine-washing. Most wool blankets require dry cleaning. Some wool blankets, afghans, and certain wool sweaters and other garments can be machine-washed. Be sure to check the care label before proceeding. Before machine-washing a sweater or other garment that might lose its shape, draw an outline of it on a piece of paper or cardboard. Test for colorfastness before laundering any colored wools, especially prints. On machine-washable wool blankets, see chapter 8, pages 124–25.

"Superwash," "Easy Care," and similar labels on wool garments indicate a wool fabric that can be machine-washed and, sometimes, machine-dried because it has undergone chemical and resin treatments that eliminate felting and shrinkage. Such treatments are usually permanent.

To reduce pilling from abrasion during laundering, use plenty of water. Set the machine on "gentle" or "delicate" to reduce abrasion and pilling, but use a medium or fast spin so as to get the wool as dry as possible. Use cool wash water (lukewarm if the item is heavily soiled) and a mild detergent safe for wool and suitable for cool water and machine-washing. Dissolve the detergent before adding the wool item. Fabric softeners are unnecessary. Wash each item briefly. Never leave wool to soak for more than a few minutes; keep the wash as brief as possible. Rinse with cool water.

Dry flat, blocking as for hand-washing, unless the care label instructions permit machine-drying, in which case you will probably be instructed to use a low temperature. Superwash wools can be tumbled dry; be careful not to overdry. When you have air-dried blankets, sweaters, and other soft wools, you may then wish to put them in the dryer for a few minutes on the air-fluff cycle, which uses cool air, to fluff them up.

*One acquaintance recommends using shampoo on wool. This course is a bit risky, however, as some shampoos are alkaline and some contain medicines, colorants, conditioners, and extras that could harm or discolor your wools. However, it is true that a neutral or slightly acidic, gentle shampoo that contains no colorants or additives might clean wool nicely. Be sure to test first, and avoid products that look milky rather than clear, that contain conditioners or other additives, or that have bright or unusual colors.

Silk is made of the filament secreted by the silkworm, the larva of a moth, to form its cocoon—the only natural fiber that comes in filament form. It is smooth, soft, lightweight, lustrous, strong, and resilient, with excellent drapability. Because it has only moderate resistance to abrasion, it is not an ideal choice for upholstery fabrics that are to take hard wear, but it may be quite durable in other uses. Silk takes dye—and, alas, stains—more readily than any other natural fiber, and today, as in the past, much of the appeal of silks lies in the gorgeous colors and patterns applied to them.

Production; Types of Silk. After silk cocoons are sorted and softened, several silk filaments unwound from a cocoon are combined and wound onto a reel, forming a long, raw silk strand called reeled silk. Reeled silk is then "thrown." Throwing is a kind of twisting of the reeled-silk filaments into threads. Thrown silk is used to make fine and sheer fabrics, such as georgette, taffeta, voile, crêpe de chine, organza, and grenadine.

Spun silk is produced when short lengths of silk filament are carded, combed, and spun into threads just as wool, cotton, and linen are. Because of the short staple of spun-silk yarn, spun-silk fabric tends to become fuzzy with wear (the short fibers rub up). Spun-silk fabrics have less strength and elasticity than thrown-silk fabrics but otherwise have the same characteristics. Spun-silk fabrics are usually less expensive than filament (thrown) silk fabrics. Spun-silk fibers are used in blends and in pile fabrics such as velvet.

The gum that covers the natural silk fibers is boiled off, ultimately resulting in fabric that weighs less and has less body. Manufacturers may "weight" silk by adding metallic salts that make up for the lost weight and give the silk more body and better drape. But heavily weighted silk is less elastic and more vulnerable to damage by sunlight, perspiration, and dry cleaning. It may crack or split. Because heavily weighted silks were once a problem, federal regulations require that heavy weighting be disclosed on the label.

Raw silk is silk that has not been processed to remove the gum. Fabric woven of raw silk is bumpy and irregular, and is less expensive.

Pure dye silk is silk that contains no metallic weighting, although it may contain limited amounts of water-soluble substances such as starch or gelatin used in dyeing and finishing processes. Good pure dye silk is superior to and more durable than weighted silks; not only does it retain its natural elasticity, but it usually has a greater amount of silk yarn woven into it, rendering it stronger than weighted silk.

Duppioni silk fabric is made of fibers from the double or interlocking cocoons that can occur when two silkworms spin the same cocoon or spin cocoons side by side. Since these fibers are irregular, the fabric made from them has a thick-and-thin look.

Most silk fabric is made from cultivated silk fiber—silk fiber from the cocoons of silkworms raised especially for the production of silk filaments. Wild silk or tussah comes from a wild species of moth, usually the tussah silkworm. Wild silk is not the same as raw silk, and may or may not be raw. It is less lustrous and coarser than cultivated silk. Wild silk fabrics—such as pongee or shantung—are both more durable and less expensive than pure dye silks.

Properties of Silk. Silk fabrics are generally considered summery. Filament silk can be woven into sheer cloth that air readily penetrates, which makes it comfortable on all but the hottest and most humid days. But spun silks can be made into fairly warm garments. Silk is also highly absorbent and, like wool, can take in much perspiration and atmospheric moisture and not feel damp. This makes it a more sensible choice for undergarments and lingerie than silk-like but inabsorbent synthetics. Silk is naturally somewhat wrinkle-resistant.

Because it is somewhat elastic, silk has a comfortable give when worn and does not readily stretch out of shape. Silk does not pill and has moderate abrasion resistance. It has a very slight tendency to build up static, especially in a dry environment. Carpet beetles will attack silk. It has poor resistance to the effects of ultraviolet radiation. It does not readily mildew but may do so if left damp for a long time. Silk, like cotton and wool, is woven into a great variety of fabrics and blends.

Caring for Silk. Silk does not attract or hold particles of dirt readily because it is so smooth. But it is perhaps the most readily stainable of all fibers. Most care labels for silk recommend dry cleaning. Silk is significantly weaker when wet and, because it is a protein fiber like wool, is vulnerable to alkalies, even mild ones.

On the other hand, some silks that have had chemical treatments to render them washable cannot be dry-cleaned. Read care labels carefully. Such silks do not appear lustrous and smooth in the manner of classic silk, and according to one text that I consulted, their proper laundering is a matter of debate. Some say that machine-washing will permanently alter them (presumably for the worse) and recommend only hand-washing in cool water with gentle soap or detergent. Others say you can machine-wash them. Both groups caution that these articles must be washed separately because their dyes bleed. As for drying, tumble them on a cool setting in the dryer, or hang the garments to dry. Iron them while still damp.[4]

Some silk fabric that has not been chemically treated to render it washable can nonetheless be laundered, but this must usually be done with special care. Never wash glossy, dressy silks; if you do, it is all too likely that they will never look that way again. Some of us at times successfully wash silk despite care labels saying not to, but we do this at our own risk. If the silk is not a pure dye silk, the weighting may wash out, leaving you with an irremediably limp garment. Or the colors may run—always test for colorfastness in an inconspicuous area before attempting to launder silk. Silk crêpes must always be dry-cleaned, as they shrink disastrously when wet. Skill is required in both the washing and ironing of silks at home.

Washable silks that have not been chemically treated to render them washable should be washed gently by hand in lukewarm water and mild soap or detergent. Regular laundry detergents are alkaline; the hotter and more concentrated the alkaline solution, the more damage will be done to silk. Chlorine bleach will cause silk to disintegrate. Hydrogen peroxide or sodium perborate bleaches may be used on white silks with caution. Do not leave silk soaking for long periods. Because silk weakens a little when wet, it might be harmed by wringing or rough tumbling.

Water often leaves spots on silk (as a result of sizings and other finishes applied by manufacturers), but the spots generally come out upon laundering. Iron silk on the reverse side when it is still damp, or use steam and a press cloth on a medium setting. Wrinkles that develop in wear will often come out as the garment hangs.

Perspiration weakens and discolors silk, and the aluminum chloride in some antiperspirants and deodorants also harms it. The use of dress shields is therefore advisable. Wash out perspiration as soon as possible, before it has a chance to do damage. If yellow areas develop in the underarm area of white silks, try an oxygen bleach. (See chapter 9, "Common Laundry Mishaps and Problems," "Perspiration," pages 138–39, and "Yellowing," pages 142–44.)

Bast Fibers

Bast fibers are strong fibers obtained from the inner bark of a variety of plants. Linen is a bast fiber. There are three others that may show up at home in clothes, furnishings, or utilitarian objects of various sorts: jute, ramie, and hemp.

All the bast fibers are cellulosic, like cotton and linen, and thus have similar physical and chemical properties. For example, they are absorbent, they are vulnerable to acids but not to mild alkalies, and they can usually be bleached, if care is taken (but jute, being one of the weakest cellulosic fibers, can be damaged by bleaching). If washable, they can be laundered, usually, as linens and cotton are.

Jute. Jute is derived from the jute plant, grown in Bangladesh, India, Thailand, and China. It is the stiff, inelastic fiber from which burlap, bags, rope, and similar comparatively inexpensive, rough goods are made. It also finds some uses in carpentry, as a backing fabric, and as a binding thread. It must be kept dry—it rots if left damp.

Ramie. Ramie, also called China grass, is grown in the Philippines, China, Brazil, and many other places. Its fiber is white or cream-colored, very strong, and lustrous. Ramie fabric is similar to linen but more brittle, which limits its use for apparel and furnishings. Increasingly, however, it is being included in blends used for such products. Unlike linen and cotton, ramie resists mildew, although it will eventually mildew if left damp for a long time. In blends with cotton, rayon, nylon, and polyester, it contributes strength and benefits from the flexibility of the other fibers. It is used for clothing (especially in blends), for twine, and for upholstery fabrics.

Hemp. Italy has traditionally grown the best hemp, which is a stiff, rough, and durable fiber taken from the inner bark of the hemp plant. Hemp is used to make cords, twine, and ropes (especially for use on ships because hemp is strongly resistant to rotting or weakening in water), and canvases and tarpaulins. It is also used in carpet manufacture and some furnishings. Lately it has been used more and more for clothes too. Environmentalists and environmentally alert designers have forwarded its use because hemp, compared to cotton, can be grown with little water and few chemicals. (See page 289.)

Miscellaneous Issues in Caring for Natural Fibers

Permanent-Press (Durable-Press, Wash-and-Wear, or Wrinkle-Resistant): Resin-Treated Cottons, Rayons, Linens, and Their Blends. For several reasons, laundering can be problematic for permanent-press or durable-press cottons, rayons, linens, and blends containing these and other natural or man-made fibers. First, cotton, rayon, and linen fabrics, including cotton, rayon, or linen blends, that have been subjected to resin treatments to create wrinkle-resistance or permanent creases or pleats are significantly weaker than those that have not; hence harsh washing procedures may significantly shorten the fabric's life. Second, permanent-press fabrics tend to take up and hold soil that gets deposited in the wash water and emerge from the laundry gray or dingy. Third, such resin-treated fabrics are particularly prone to oil-staining and, in some cases, to retaining body odors.

Despite such problems, home laundering is the cleaning procedure of choice for permanent-press clothes. Commercial laundering is usually too harsh. You should wash all new clothes and linens before using, but it is especially important to wash those that have been subjected to a resin treatment, so as to remove any remaining formaldehyde. (However, not all permanent-press garments have the problem today.) Permanent-press washing and drying cycles should always be used. Use plenty of water and make smaller loads, as overcrowding in the washer will also tend to cause wrinkling. The permanent-press cycle cools off the washed clothes with cool water so that when they spin they do not take a wrinkled imprint; it also spins them more slowly for the same reason. The permanent-press dryer setting includes a cool-down period at the cycle's end so that clothes do not wrinkle from sitting, heated, when the dryer stops tumbling.

Before washing, examine the usual wear areas: collars and cuffs, pleats and darts, creases, the seat of pants. If necessary, make repairs before washing. If wear is apparent, you may prolong the life of the garment by using the gentle washing cycle with a warm or cool wash, cool rinse, and slow spin. Because the fold and crease lines on permanent-press articles tend to be even weaker than the rest of the fabric, it is often a good idea to wash and dry permanent-press articles turned inside out.

Frequent washing is the key to keeping permanent-press clothes clean and fresh-smelling. Use pretreatments on pillowcases and cuffs, collars, and other areas that take up body oils and odors; the use of pretreatment products that contain solvents is a good idea. Also use plenty of detergent and warm or even hot wash water (when it is safe for the fabric), not cold, to keep permanent-press clothes clean.

Tumbling dry, followed by prompt removal from the dryer, is necessary to get the full benefit of wrinkle-resistance treatments on permanent-press articles. But drip-dry clothes should usually have no spinning in the washing machine, no wringing, and no machine-drying; their care labels will prescribe hanging to dry or drying flat. In some cases, mild soap should be used; check the care labels. Hang clothes carefully, "finger ironing" them—smoothing and straightening them with your hands—especially at seams. Sometimes a quick touch with an iron will be necessary to reduce a bit of puckering.

Chlorine bleach may not be recommended for permanent-press cloth because the cloth has been weakened. In addition, some permanent-press clothes will yellow if exposed to chlorine, although this problem appears to be unusual nowadays. In any event, use chlorine bleach with caution. In my experience, though, an occasional light bleaching does no harm.

Washable Antiques, Heirlooms, and Other Fragile or Valuable Linen. Extremely delicate and aged fabrics cannot be washed at all. You can at times vacuum these by using a protective screen and the low setting, with open vents, on your vacuum cleaner. (See chapter 16, "Textile Furnishings," pages 228–29.)

Sometimes washable antiques and heirlooms will be sufficiently cleaned by merely soaking for half an hour or so in plain, soft, lukewarm water. To avoid potentially damaging handling, you can lay the piece on a nylon screen or in a plastic colander and gently immerse it in the plain-water bath. This will dissolve dust and acids that may have collected on the fibers and thus extend the life of the fabric. After the soak, pour off the water and gently add another bath of pure, soft, cool water for rinsing. Then raise the screen or colander out of the water and let the piece drain and dry while still resting on it.

If more cleaning is necessary, add some very mild, neutral detergent to your water bath and let the article soak for a few minutes. Orvus WA Paste (manufactured by Procter & Gamble) is often recommended for this purpose by museums and conservators. (If you choose instead to use a mild soap, be sure that your water is soft and that you rinse thoroughly.) Then pat the piece gently to get water to pass through it. Or you may lay it on a nylon screen or colander, as described above, and gently raise and lower the screen to get the water to run through the cloth. If the piece does not come clean, repeat. Pour off the wash water. Then rinse gently with plain, cool water in the same manner until absolutely all soap or detergent residues, along with any dirt that has been removed, are rinsed away.

Use no bleach of any sort, including sun bleaching, on very fragile pieces. If you are determined to get spots or stains out of a fragile piece, you can try additional soaking in a solution of lukewarm water and mild detergent. If the piece is neither valuable nor very important and if its appearance is marred, you might escalate to sun bleaching, then to the more risky expedient of stronger detergent (one without optical brighteners or bluing).

As for chemical bleaching to remove stains or to lighten a dingy piece, try it only if you have nothing to lose or if the piece is not too important or valuable. Avoid commercial oxygen bleaches, as these contain laundry boosters, optical brighteners, and bluing. If you wish to try an oxygen bleach, consider using plain hydrogen peroxide. (See pages 70–71.)

To dry, blot or press with a towel and then let dry flat on the screen or colander if you are using one or, if you are not, on a clean white towel. Dry away from sunlight and heat.

Mothproofing Wool. The most important thing you can do to keep your clothes and carpets free of moth damage is to keep them clean. Moths will be attracted to grease and food stains on clothes. Frequent vacuuming and occasionally cleaning or shampooing will give carpets in use all the protection they need. Clothes that are frequently worn and laundered will also not be moth damaged. You should make sure that clothes and carpets in storage are perfectly clean, but they will also require additional protection.

Brushing wool articles frequently, and always after wearing, and cleaning them before they are stored will help remove any eggs that may have been deposited. Storage in an airtight compartment at or below 40°F will prevent eggs from developing and hatching. Ironing at temperatures greater than 130°F kills them.

Home chemical treatments work by either repelling or killing the insects. Repellants may prevent the deposit of eggs but will not destroy eggs already deposited, and they do not last long. The most popular repellant, cedar, is at best modestly effective, in my experience. It has been determined that cedar oil will kill young larvae (not older ones or eggs), but it is hard to see how cedar-lined closets or cedar chips, blocks, hangers, and chests are going to expose the young larvae to a lethal dose of cedar oil. The hope is that moths will not wish to lay their eggs in a cedar-scented environment, but I have seen moths flutter happily out of my cedar-laden closets and found moth holes in cedar-surrounded garments. So far as I have been able to determine, there is no scientific evidence—at least not yet—for the theory that moths will avoid cedar-laden areas.

Some people tout dried orange peel and various spice mixtures and potpourris as repellants. These have scents that will appeal to many people, but, again, I have found no scientific evidence that any of them really works as a moth repellant. (My Italian grandmother used both lavender and dried orange peel, but only for their scent, not to repel moths.) As for commercial moth repellants that may use secret or unnamed ingredients, their effectiveness is also a mystery. Of course, it does not hurt to try any nontoxic products that interest you.

Naphthalene and paradichlorobenzene, typical ingredients in mothballs and other antimoth devices today, will actually kill moths, larvae, and eggs, provided the storage is airtight and compact so that the atmosphere can be saturated; if it is not, the chemical released is not strong enough to do the job. The chemical-containing device should be hung above the clothes because the vapors, which are heavier than air, will flow downward. Unfortunately, both naphthalene and paradichlorobenzene are toxic to humans. Paradichlorobenzene is a carcinogen, and naphthalene is classified by the U.S. Environmental Protection Agency (EPA) and other authorities as a possible carcinogen. The EPA recommends that you use devices containing paradichlorobenzene only in areas sealed off from your living space, such as garages or attics. I would follow the same advice when using naphthalene mothballs, crystals, or flakes. See also "Mothproofing," page 319.

The Man-Made
Fibers and Blends

Viscose rayon, cuprammonium rayon (cupro), high wet-modulus
rayon (Modal), and lyocell and their care . . . Acetate and
triacetate and their care . . . Nylon (polyamide) and its
care . . . Polyester and its care . . . PLA and its care . . . Acrylic
and modacrylic and their care . . . Spandex (Elastane) and its
care . . . Polypropylene and its care; lastol . . . Microfibers . . .
Blends . . . Caring for hydrophobic synthetic fibers

M an-made or manufactured fibers have been used to make fabric for more than a century. Rayon, invented in the late nineteenth century, was first commercially produced in this country in 1910; acetate was commercially produced by the 1920s. Both of these are based on plant, or cellulosic, fibers. When nylon was introduced, with great fanfare, in 1939, it was the first fiber made entirely from synthesized or manufactured chemicals. Many other entirely synthetic fibers followed in short order. By 1960, acrylic and modacrylic, olefin, polyester, and spandex fibers were all well known, and fabrics composed of innumerable blends of two or more synthetics or of synthetics and natural fibers became popular. These new fibers constituted a revolution.

Man-made fibers other than rayon and acetate—the synthetics—are unabsorbent and hydrophobic. (Rayon and acetate fibers are based on cellulose and are therefore absorbent.) The synthetics are also thermoplastic—that is, they melt or soften when enough heat is applied and harden when they are cooled. As a result, creases or smoothness can be programmed into the cloth by a process called heat setting. If the cloth is smoothed when hot enough, it stays smooth unless it is rendered that hot once more. Thus such cloth needs little or no ironing. Similarly, if a fabric made of synthetic fibers is creased when at the right temperature, it will stay creased unless it is once more brought to that temperature. Care labels on clothes made of synthetic fibers often call for low to moderate temperatures in washing and drying and a cool-down period in the dryer; this is to avoid setting in wrinkles. Likewise, these fabrics should be ironed at low to medium settings.

Rayon

Rayon is made of regenerated cellulose derived from cotton fiber or wood pulp. The variety of rayons on the market makes it difficult to generalize about its properties. Not only are there different types of rayon, but each type can be produced in both thrown or filament yarn and spun yarn, and the characteristics of these spun and filament yarns may be markedly different. Rayon filament yarns produce silklike fabrics. Spun rayon can be napped, finished, and constructed to resemble fabrics of cotton, linen, and wool. (Such rayon fabrics, however, will function quite differently from the fabrics of natural fibers that they resemble.) Rayon fibers can be effectively blended with many other fibers, natural and synthetic.

Viscose Rayon. Most of the rayon you buy is viscose rayon. Its name derives from a step in its processing in which a cellulose mixture is transformed into a viscous solution. This type of rayon is usually identified on the fiber content label merely as "rayon" or, often, "viscose."

Fabric made from viscose rayon is usually soft and drapable with a pleasant cottony hand. It is weaker than silk, linen, cotton, and wool. It is highly absorbent—even more than cotton or linen—and cool, characteristics that make it one of the most comfortable of fibers, especially in warm weather. Viscose rayon fabric may stretch when it gets wet and shrink as it dries, and may even stretch and shrink with changes in atmospheric humidity; thus it is usually a poor choice for draperies. Unlike cotton and linen, rayon fabrics lose much strength when wet, so laundering may not be recommended or may have to be done with gentle agitation. Unless given a shrink-resistant treatment, viscose rayon fabrics tend to shrink more than comparable cotton fabrics. Viscose rayon fiber is modestly more elastic than cotton or linen but less elastic than silk and wool. Rayon fabric tends to be rather limp or lacking in body.

Viscose rayon fabric tends to lack the resilience of silk and wool and therefore wrinkles readily. Its inherent tendency to wrinkle is one of its biggest disadvantages, but this may be reduced by wrinkle-resistance treatments and by careful engineering of the construction of the yarn and fabric. When buying an item made of rayon fabric, crumple it for a few seconds in your hand and then release it to determine how much it wrinkles.

Prolonged exposure to sunlight may cause weakening or yellowing of viscose rayon fibers and fabrics. Viscose rayon fabric mildews if left damp. It is vulnerable to silverfish but not to moths. Like all cellulosic fibers, viscose rayon fiber is vulnerable to acids but has good resistance to alkalies.

Cuprammonium Rayon. Cuprammonium rayon, also known as cupro, Bemberg, or cupra rayon, is named after a step in its processing in which cellulose is dissolved in a cuprammonium hydroxide solution. The buyer may be told only that it is "rayon." Cuprammonium rayon is soft, lustrous, and silky, and usually it is produced as filament rayon. Fabrics made from cuprammonium rayon tend to be more resilient than viscose rayon—that is, they do not wrinkle so easily. Cuprammonium rayon fabrics also tend to have greater abrasion resistance than viscose rayon. Thus they make excellent linings as well as women's dresses and blouses.

Modal (High Wet-Modulus Rayons). Rayon fibers have been developed which have greatly increased strength when wet, comparable to that of cotton; they can be mercerized and rendered shrink-resistant with compressive shrinkage treatments. These fibers are known as Modal (or high wet-modulus rayon, modified rayons, high-performance, or polynosic rayons). Fabrics made from Modal often look and feel like high-quality cotton fabrics and tend to have more body and stiffness than viscose rayon fabrics, but they can also be silky or woolly. Because they have better wet strength, these types of rayon are more readily launderable than viscose rayon and can usually be machine-washed (subject, of course, to the usual caveats). Acid perspiration will cause some types of high wet-modulus rayon to deteriorate.

Caring for Rayon Fabrics. The buyer of clothes or furnishings made of rayon fabrics should be sure to check care labels before purchasing. Many inexpensive pieces of rayon sportswear may require the inconvenience of hand-washing or the expense of dry cleaning. High wet-modulus rayons, however, are usually machine-washable.

Many, but not all, types of viscose rayon have a smooth surface that sheds dirt readily. Theoretically, viscose rayon may be both dry-cleaned and laundered. For many reasons, however, dry cleaning is more frequently recommended. Viscose rayon fabrics weaken greatly when wet and often shrink, bleed colors, go limp, and wrinkle badly after washing. Laundering more quickly wears them out. Viscose rayon fabrics are frequently given water-soluble finishes and sizings that may dissolve in laundering, resulting in changes for the worse in the fabrics' hand and drape.

Launderable viscose rayon should be handled very gently during laundering. It is more vulnerable to all sorts of chemicals than cotton, including alkaline laundry solutions. It should usually be hand-washed in mild detergent and warm water, then squeezed—not wrung or twisted—to remove excess water, unless the garment care label explicitly permits machine-washing. When it does, it usually calls for using a shorter, delicate agitation cycle. Viscose rayon knits should be dried flat; woven viscose rayon fabrics should be hung to dry. White viscose rayon will ordinarily not turn gray or yellow with cleaning or laundering and therefore usually needs no bleaching, but household bleaches may be used, with care, on white viscose rayon, so long as it is not blended with another fiber that cannot be bleached. Some types of rayon are much sturdier than regular viscose rayon, so do not hesitate to take advantage of vigorous laundering methods when you find them prescribed on a rayon fabric care label.

Viscose rayon fabrics should usually be ironed damp with a low to medium iron or with a steam iron. Some rayon fabrics develop a shine from ironing, so use a press cloth or iron the fabric on the wrong side. (See chapter 6, "Ironing.")

Lyocell (Tencel)

Lyocell is the generic name of a new (FTC approved in 1996) rayonlike, cellulosic fiber that is more wrinkle-resistant, shrink-resistant, durable, and strong than viscose rayon. It is absorbent, with an appealing soft, luxurious hand. Like rayon, it is derived from wood pulp, but it is produced through an environmentally more favorable process. It tends to be more expensive than viscose rayon. Lyocell is used both alone and in blends with linen, cotton, rayon, and wool fibers. Lyocell fabrics are noted for their comfort.

Lyocell may be treated with antiwrinkling resins. Although this treatment weakens the fabric, it also reduces wrinkling, shrinking, and fuzzing. Lyocell burns like rayon.

Follow the care label on garments made of Lyocell; the care procedures called for may be necessary to protect finishes on the fabric, and you may otherwise get excessive shrinking or wrinkling. Lyocell may shrink slightly in laundering but it does not "exhibit the progressive shrinking of rayon fabrics." Lyocell fabrics should be washed on the gentle cycle or dry-cleaned. Gentle washing decreases "the chance of causing uneven color, fuzziness, pilling, and unacceptable hand."[1] Lyocell weakens when wet. Lyocell fibers can be bleached with chlorine or oxygen bleaches.

Acetate and Triacetate

Properties of Acetate and Triacetate. Acetate, or cellulose acetate, is made in a process that begins by treating cellulose, derived from wood, with acetic acid. Acetate fabrics are often lovely. They are smooth, very lustrous, and silk-like in appearance and hand. Triacetate, acetate's chemical cousin, is more versatile and may be constructed into fabrics that resemble those made of rayon, cotton, wool, or silk fibers. Both acetate and triacetate fabrics drape attractively. They tend to be more expensive than those made of cotton, rayon, or polyester.

Acetate and triacetate, however, are both weak fibers, and fabrics made of them have poor abrasion resistance. Acetate fabrics become significantly weaker when wet, which means that they must usually be dry-cleaned; when launderable, acetate fabrics must be washed with great care. Triacetate is less weakened by wetness and can usually be machine-washed and -dried. Fabrics made from acetate and triacetate are more elastic, warmer, and more wrinkle-resistant than rayon; they also shrink less. Triacetate is quite wrinkle-resistant—more so than acetate—and when wrinkles do form in a triacetate garment they tend to fall out when it is hung for a while.

Acetate and triacetate have a little absorbency, but much less than fibers classified as hydrophilic. Both are classified as hydrophobic, and fabrics made of them may feel uncomfortable in hot, humid weather. They are useful in items such as raincoats or shower curtains that need some water resistance. Both are used in dresses, blouses, and other clothes, as well as draperies and curtains, but not in articles that will receive hard wear. Although linings are often made of acetate, its weakness and poor abrasion resistance mean that otherwise durable coats with acetate linings will need new linings long before the rest of the coat wears out. Acetate's low absorbency can interfere with the comfort of summer garments lined with it.

Both acetate and triacetate are thermoplastic, triacetate more so than acetate. Triacetate can receive permanent heat-set pleats and creases; acetate cannot. Triacetate can take much more heat than acetate before melting. Acetate will melt and stick to a hot iron, but triacetate melts at a higher temperature than irons reach.

Both acetate and triacetate have good pill resistance. They do not mildew and will not be attacked by pests (except that silverfish might harm the cloth in the process of devouring any starch in it). Both fibers, but triacetate more than acetate, tend to build up static unless they have received antistatic treatments. Acetate and triacetate have moderate resistance to the ultraviolet radiation in sunlight. Concentrated solutions of alkalies or acids will harm them. Acetate and triacetate and their blends will be destroyed by nail-polish remover, paint remover, and other solvents that contain acetone.

Special acetate dyes are used on acetate, and they may bleed, fade in laundering or in contact with atmospheric gases (a phenomenon known as "fume fading"), or discolor with perspiration. Solution dyeing solves these problems; the color of solution-dyed acetate is fast to washing, atmospheric gases, perspiration, and light. Triacetate is less likely to be discolored or weakened by perspiration and is less prone to fume fading and fading during washing than acetate.

Caring for Acetate and Triacetate. Dry cleaning is usually recommended for acetate fabrics because acetate fibers are fragile, lose strength when wet, and are highly temperature-sensitive. Triacetate, however, is usually machine-washable. When acetate is launderable, either gentle machine-washing or hand-laundering will be recommended. Lukewarm water, not hot, is usually recommended—or acetate fabric will shrink and wrinkle—and mild soaps or detergents. Bleaches will not ordinarily be necessary on white acetate because it tends to stay white, but if there are stains, household bleaches may be used cautiously. Bleaches may also be useful on white fabrics that are blends of acetate with other fibers that do not stay white. Colored acetate fabrics should not be soaked because they will bleed. (Solution-dyed acetate, however, will have color that is fast to laundering.) If you hand-wash acetate or triacetate fabrics, do not wring, twist, or rub them. You may wish to use a fabric softener now and then.

Roll acetate items in a towel. Dry knits flat and hang wovens to dry, unless the care instructions permit machine-drying. Usually you can tumble dry triacetate; use the permanent-press cycle (at medium to low temperatures) to take advantage of the cool-down period, and remove the items promptly. If either of these fabrics is left to sit warm in a dryer, it will wrinkle. Triacetate will need little to no ironing, but it can take a hot iron. (It may be billed as wash and wear.) Acetate fabric will need damp ironing on its wrong (back) side at low to medium temperatures, or on the right side using a press cloth.

Nylon (Polyamide)

On May 15, 1940, in a remarkable marketing event, nylon hose were offered for sale throughout the United States following an extraordinary advertising campaign addressed to a public already disposed to admire rather than disdain man-made fibers. It is difficult for us today to imagine how a mere article of clothing could cause such a stir in the world, or how eager women were to get rid of silk hose that ran, sagged, and bagged.

The word "nylon" refers to any member of a group of similar compounds (polymers) called polyamides. These polymers are made from coal, petroleum, air, water, and sometimes cereal waste products such as oat hulls or corncobs.[2] On the fiber content labels of goods produced outside the United States, nylon is often called "polyamide."

Properties of Nylon. Nylon fiber comes in many chemical forms that are sold under a variety of trade names and differ greatly in their properties. Spun and filament yarn nylons also differ significantly from each other. However, the various types of nylon fiber share some common characteristics. Nylon fibers are light and strong and highly resistant to abrasion. They are also extremely elastic—second only to spandex and rubber. Such qualities make nylon fibers exceptionally well suited for use in hosiery and sheer fabrics. Nylon fibers are also resilient, so nylon fabrics resist wrinkling, and wrinkles that develop during use or wear fall out easily. In looks and hand, fabrics made of nylon often have a silky luster, but nylon fabrics can easily resemble those made of cotton, wool, or other fibers in their appearance and hand.

Nylon can be made into warm fabrics. It is low in absorbency (although it is more absorbent than other hydrophobic fibers such as polyester, poly-propylene, or acrylic), and nylon fabrics can feel hot and sticky in warm, humid weather. A tightly woven, light, filament nylon, which is impermeable to air, heat, or moisture, makes an excellent windbreaker or raincoat, but it may trap moisture inside and make you feel cold and clammy in winter or hot and sticky in summer. Spun nylon, used in sweaters and socks, is warmer than filament nylon because its fuzziness traps additional heat. And because nylon can be rendered into exceptionally fine, sheer, and light fabrics that air readily penetrates, it is also used for summer wear.

Newer types of nylon fabrics and new treatments applied to nylon (and other synthetics) have been developed to solve some of nylon's problems with moisture and comfort. There are now a few types of nylon that wick moisture quite effectively. Fabrics made from nylon microfibers may be waterproof yet breathable, with a pleasant hand. Such fabrics therefore have a different com-fort profile from those made of older types of nylons.

Nylon is not damaged by mildew, moths, or other pests. It is much weak-ened by exposure to sunlight, but neither sunlight nor laundering causes dyes used on nylon fabrics to fade. Perspiration can discolor it. Many types of nylon tend to have annoying problems with pilling and static buildup. Modifications of nylon fiber that render it static-resistant, however, are available.

Nylon's resilience, elasticity, and spectacular strength are relied on in a vari-ety of highly desirable blends with both natural and synthetic fibers.

Caring for Nylon Fabrics. Care labels usually recommend laundering nylon, although in principle it is dry-cleanable. But nylon is somewhat diffi-cult to launder well. As a hydrophobic fiber, it holds oily soils and stains rather tenaciously but at the same time needs gentle treatment. To avoid a buildup of oily soil or odor, follow the methods recommended on pages 369–70, "A Note on Caring for Synthetic (Hydrophobic) Fibers": frequent washing, pre-treating, presoaking, plenty of detergent, warm water, and so on. Being sta-tic-prone, nylon attracts dirt and lint. It also tends to take up dirt from the wash water when it is laundered. You can use ordinary soap or detergent to launder nylon. Always wash white nylon separately from any colored fabrics, no matter how pale, because of the strong propensity of white nylon to pick up any hint of color and turn dingy. Once this happens, you will probably not be able to remove the dinginess. Bleaching is usually unnecessary. If you feel you need to use a bleach, you might try an oxygen bleach. Do not use chlorine bleach; it tends to yellow nylon. If nylon yellows from other causes or from unknown causes, you have nothing to lose by trying the remedy sug-gested in "Yellowing of White Nylon," page 168.

When laundering, use gentle (slow) agitation and a slow spin (or a brief spin, if you have no choice of spin speed), with warm wash water and a cool-down rinse. Thorough rinsing is advisable. Set the dryer at low temperature using the permanent-press cycle, which has a cool-down period, and remove promptly when dry to avoid setting in wrinkles. (Nylon is thermoplastic.) Iron at a low to medium setting.

Use a fabric softener to reduce static problems and wrinkling and to improve the hand.

To reduce pilling, turn articles inside out for washing and drying, use plenty of water, and keep the agitation and tumbling periods short.

Polyester

If nylon is the king of synthetics, polyester is the queen. Like nylon, it is produced from substances derived from coal, petroleum, air, and water. Like nylon, its introduction was heralded by an enormously successful advertising campaign whose most memorable moment was the exhibition at a press conference of a man's suit that had been worn for sixty-seven days, immersed twice in a swimming pool, machine-washed, and never pressed. The suit was still wearable.

Polyester fiber comes in many chemical and structural varieties, each with characteristics different from the others, some expensive and some inexpensive. Polyester filaments of different shapes may be created, and these will have distinct properties in use. The basic solution out of which the filaments are made may be modified by chemical additions that produce various effects, or special finishes may be applied to the filaments. As with other synthetics and silk, the fibers can be rendered into filament yarns or spun yarns. Because so many variations exist, only rough generalizations about polyester are possible.

Properties of Polyester. Many polyester fabrics are crisp and light, but they can be found in medium and heavy weights too. Polyester fabrics are made in both lustrous and nonlustrous versions, napped and not napped, with and without bulk, and in knits and wovens. They tend to drape fairly well. (Fabrics made from spun polyester yarns drape better than those made from filament yarns.) Their hand can be slightly harsh, but in some types, especially newer ones and in "microfiber" versions, the hand can be soft, silky, or satiny, and generally pleasant to the touch. An outstanding characteristic of polyester fabric is its great resilience (wrinkle-resistance); it needs little or no ironing. A highly thermoplastic fiber, polyester readily heat-sets into permanent creases. Ordinary polyester is an inabsorbent, low-wicking, hydrophobic fiber; but modern variants and treatments have been developed to alter these characteristics.

On average, polyester fabrics are quite strong and durable, but they range from relatively weak to exceptionally strong. None of them weakens when wet. Polyester fabric is highly abrasion-resistant, but it tends to pill. There are pill-resistant variants. (These, however, lose some abrasion resistance.) Polyester fabrics have some elasticity but much less than nylon; they do not stretch or bag or shrink.

Polyester fabrics can be warm or cool to wear, depending on their construction. New variants are vaunted as having state-of-the-art heat-insulating capacities. The inabsorbency and nonwicking character of most unmodified polyester, however, means that many find it uncomfortable worn next to the skin, as it traps moisture. There are new types of polyester designed to wick moisture well—some actually have tubes or channels in the fibers through which moisture can pass—and these are said to be more comfortable. There are also variants that are more absorbent. Polyester's inabsorbency, however, means that it dries quickly and does not stain easily, except by oil, which stains it readily. Most polyester accumulates static electricity, but there are static-resistant variants.

Polyester fabrics are resistant to damage from both alkalies and most acids. Polyesters have good resistance to damage by sunlight, are unaffected by mildew, moths, and other insects, have good colorfastness, and are usually quite impervious to damage by perspiration.

Like some other hydrophobic fabrics, polyester tends to retain body odors. Polyester athletic wear has sometimes received antimicrobial treatments that help to reduce the odor problem. Soil-resistance treatments are sometimes used to help achieve better laundering results.

Caring for Polyester Fabrics. Polyester fabrics may be dry-cleaned or laundered. Because polyester fiber often holds static electricity, it also tends to attract and hold dirt and lint. Any ordinary laundry detergent can be used to launder it, and any ordinary household bleach can be used. But white polyester very often stays white without bleaching. Fairly warm water is safe to use. To reduce pilling, turn garments inside out for laundering and, in top-loading agitator-style washing machines, use plenty of water and less vigorous agitation. To reduce wrinkling, set the machine on the permanent-press cycle or manually set it for slower spin speeds and a final cool-down rinse.

To conquer the oil-stain and odor problems, wash frequently, pretreat the problem areas, and use a presoak or prewash period, plenty of detergent, and warm or hot rather than cold water. (See "A Note on Caring for Synthetic (Hydrophobic) Fibers," pages 369–70.) One text particularly recommends using pretreatment products that contain organic solvents and detergents that contain grease- or soil-release agents. (See "Pretreatments and prewash stain removers," in the Glossary of Laundry Products and Additives, page 84.)

When polyester is properly dyed, it is highly colorfast in laundering. But if residual dye remains in the fabric, it can bleed into the laundry water and badly stain certain other fabrics, such as acetate and nylon. To test for this, touch some acetone (acetone nail-polish remover will do) on an out-of-sight spot on a new polyester garment. If you get color removal, wash the garment separately at first.

Drying polyester in a dryer is recommended because the fluffing helps prevent wrinkling, but clothes should be removed promptly from the dryer or wrinkles may be set in. Use the permanent-press cycle, which has an automatic cool-down. Use fabric softener if necessary to soften or reduce static cling. It will probably not be necessary to use it at every laundering.

If properly laundered, polyester fabrics do not wrinkle much, but if any ironing becomes necessary, they should be ironed at a low to medium setting. They will melt with excessive heat.

To reduce pilling, wash and dry polyester garments turned inside out, reduce agitation and tumbling time as much as possible, and use plenty of water; do not crowd the load.

PLA

PLA, trade named "Ingeo," is a new generic fiber, approved by the FTC in 2002. PLA is the acronym for the polymer from which the fiber is manufactured—polylactic acid or polylactide.[3] Although PLA fibers are synthetic, they are derived from renewable natural resources, including agricultural crops such as corn and sugar beets, and for that reason are sometimes said to be composed of "biopolymers." According to its manufacturer, Ingeo is compostable in any industrial composting facility. Using PLA rather than petrochemicals, the manufacturer says, requires 20 to 50 percent less energy and produces 50 percent less carbon dioxide. For these reasons, PLA is touted as being more environmentally favorable than polyester.

PLA, or Ingeo, has been described as "advanced polyester," but, while it shares various characteristics with polyester, the differences between them are substantial. Like polyester, PLA is not absorbent, but it is said to wick moisture better than polyester and to have better overall "moisture management" than polyester, better resistance to ultraviolet light, a lower melting point, and better flame resistance.

PLA, like other synthetics, is versatile and can be manufactured with a silky or a cottony hand. Low dye uptake and poor colorfastness are said to be among its disadvantages. It is used in blends, especially with cotton and wool, as well as in 100 percent Ingeo textile goods.

Qualities said to make PLA suitable for various apparel uses, especially in active sportswear, include its good wicking and moisture management, soft feel or hand, shape retention, strong wrinkle-resistance (resilience), and a high level of overall comfort. Two advantages claimed for PLA, especially in active sportswear uses, are that, unlike polyester, it is not odor-retentive and is less prone to pilling and oil-staining than polyester. But, like polyester, it tends to pick up static electricity in wear and in tumbling dry. It withstands moderately strong acids and the alkalinity of normal laundering.

PLA is also suitable for use in furnishings (where, its manufacturer points out, its UV resistance and lower flammability are advantages), blankets, and throws. It is used to make a fiber fill for pillows and comforters. (Like other synthetic fibers, PLA is also used to make a large variety of nontextile materials, including many types of packaging.)

Caring for PLA. PLA is both launderable and dry-cleanable. As with any new fiber or fabric, follow care labels at least until you gain some familiarity with it. Ordinary laundry detergents are safe for PLA. Wash in cool water (to protect its dyes) with medium to slow spin speed to avoid setting in wrinkles. Turn garments inside out for laundering to reduce any chance of pilling. Do not use bleach. Tumble dry on medium to low and, as with other synthetics, use your dryer's antiwrinkle option. PLA is quick-drying. Should you encounter problems with static, try a fabric softener. Iron, if necessary, on low.

Acrylics

Acrylic (polyacrylonitrile) and modacrylic are made from petroleum derivatives. The modacrylics are modified acrylics with slightly different properties.

Acrylic tends to be used as a staple fiber in fabrics that are soft and woolly, fluffy, or fuzzy; most acrylic fabrics look and feel like wool. But there are some smooth acrylics and some that feel like cotton fabrics. Acrylic fabrics are made into a wide range of garments and furnishings, from sweaters and sportswear to rugs and draperies. Modacrylics, which can be soft and fleecy or furry, are often used in fake furs, wigs, carpets, and draperies; because they have good flame resistance, they are also used in children's sleepwear. Both acrylics and modacrylics are well suited to napped and pile constructions.

Properties of Acrylic and Modacrylic. The various types of acrylic and modacrylic fibers bear a family resemblance to one another, but the two fiber families also have some significant differences. Used often as a wool substitute, both have the virtue of being light and warm yet stronger and less expensive than wool. Their strength, however, is less than that of linen, cotton, or silk. Acrylics weaken when wet; modacrylics do not.

Fabrics made from these fibers have fair to good abrasion resistance and very good to excellent resilience (wrinkle-resistance). They tend to pill, but not always. All have little elasticity and do not stretch (unless the yarn is crimped) or sag. They will not shrink unless exposed to high temperatures or steam. Acrylic and modacrylic fibers are thermoplastic and can be heat-set to retain pleats and creases.

Acrylic and modacrylic fabrics have low absorbency and can be uncomfortable in muggy weather. All will hold static electricity unless treated. All are oleophilic—oil-loving—and prone to being stained by oil. They have good to excellent resistance to ultraviolet radiation and usually have good resistance to perspiration. They are unaffected by mildew or by moths or other insects. They have good colorfastness. Modacrylics are flame-resistant. Pilling is a problem with many acrylics. For those who find wool irritating, acrylics are an excellent alternative. Acetone and acetone-containing substances such as nail-polish removers will harm modacrylics.

Caring for Acrylic and Modacrylic Fabrics. The suggestions that follow are generally applicable, but particular finishes or constructions might require different treatment. Pay careful attention to care label instructions on acrylic and modacrylic fabrics. A "Dry-clean only" instruction on a care label may mean that the fabric has been given a water-soluble finish that, if removed by laundering, will leave the fabric with a harsh hand.

Acrylics tend to hold oily soil and body odors. Because they develop static electricity, these fibers also tend to attract and hold dirt. Frequent cleaning, pretreating, presoaking, and using plenty of detergent will help resolve any such problems. Dry cleaning is not usually recommended, but in principle almost all types of acrylic and modacrylic may be dry-cleaned. They may also readily be laundered with mild soap or detergent in cool water—acrylics are highly heat-sensitive and will shrink—on the gentle cycle or by hand, without wringing, rubbing, or twisting. But modacrylic fabrics with a pile construction should usually be dry-cleaned only or treated with a fur-cleaning process. Household bleaches may be used. To avoid static problems, reduce wrinkling, and give a good hand, use a fabric softener.

For those acrylic or modacrylic fibers that are prone to pilling, the problem may yield to the usual precautions: turn such articles inside out for laundering and drying, use plenty of water, and keep the agitation and tumbling periods short. More delicate articles should be hand-washed. If the article is being hand-washed, avoid rubbing or wringing.

Woven and firmly knitted acrylic fabrics should usually be dripped dry. Heavy acrylic knits should be dried flat. Sometimes you can tumble them dry on a low heat, but you must include a cool-down period. Be careful to keep the dryer temperature low.

Ironing may not be necessary at all. If it is, use a low iron setting.

Spandex (Elastane)

Spandex, developed in the 1950s and early 1960s, is the generic name for a group of fibers made of different types of polyurethane. In Europe, and, increasingly, in the United States, fiber content labels often refer to spandex as "elastane." Spandex fibers are "elastomeric," that is, very stretchy. And, as everyone knows who has worn fabrics that contain spandex, it is stretchy in a different way from nylon or other stretch fabrics. The fibers of the latter do not really stretch much; their elasticity comes from the straightening out of crimps in the filaments. Spandex, by contrast, can pull out to five or more times its own length and promptly contract to its original size. Its stretchiness makes it ideal for athletic clothes, tights, knits, sportswear, foundation garments, support hose, and swimsuits.

Properties of Spandex. Spandex fibers are rather weak. Nonetheless, they are durable because they have good abrasion resistance and such great elasticity that in ordinary wear they are never stretched far enough to reach their breaking point. They are extremely resilient and flexible, so fabrics of spandex appear smooth, unwrinkled, and neat. Spandex itself does not pill, but fabrics containing spandex often pill because they contain other fibers that do.

Spandex is highly inabsorbent, even more so than polyester. Spandex fabrics are virtually all blends that include only a small percentage of spandex. The other fibers usually make up more than 90 percent of the fabric by weight. Exercise clothes, for example, might be made with a small amount of spandex and a large amount of cotton, producing a fabric that is at once cool, absorbent, and stretchy. It is because these blends have so little spandex that they are so comfortable. Foundation garment and swimsuit fabrics usually include a larger percentage of spandex—from 15 percent to 50 percent.

Spandex has good resistance to light. All types of spandex are unaffected by mildew or by moths or other insects. Colorfastness varies from poor to good. All types of spandex resist damage from seawater, perspiration, body oils, cosmetics, and suntan lotions, which is important in fabrics used for exercise, foundation garments, and swimwear.

Caring for Spandex Fabrics. Because spandex is almost always found in blended fabrics that include much more of the other fibers than of spandex, it is important to read the care and content labels carefully. A rule of thumb in laundering blends, aside from following care instructions, is to use the most conservative procedures required by any fibers present. The suggestions offered below are applicable to spandex alone, not to any fibers it might be blended with.

All spandex fibers can be both dry-cleaned and laundered. They are machine-washable with ordinary soaps and detergents in warm, not hot, water; high heat will damage the elasticity. Wash whites separately. Some care labels on spandex-blend garments recommend drip-drying; if you are careful, you can machine-dry on a low setting. Delicate articles, however, should be hand-washed and line-dried.

White spandex may be yellowed by body oils, perspiration, chlorine bleach, and smog. To avoid yellowing, launder frequently and use a nonchlorine household bleach. Spandex fibers might be weakened or yellowed if exposed to a chlorine bleach. The spandex in swimsuits gradually deteriorates—and loses elasticity—after repeated exposures to the chlorine in swimming pools. (The spandex is usually hidden, however, so that if yellowing also occurs, it often cannot be seen.) Your spandex-blend swimsuits will last longer if you rinse them out after you wear them to swim in chlorinated water. Sodium perborate bleaches are safe for spandex. (See "Bleaches" in the glossary at the end of chapter 4.)

Spandex fibers do not shrink in water, but some will lose elasticity and weaken if exposed to hot water. Avoid high temperatures in the dryer and on the iron. If ironing is necessary, iron quickly on a low setting.

Olefins (Polypropylene)

Olefins are produced from ethylene and from propylene, petroleum by-products that are inexpensive and available in great quantities. The olefin fiber most used in the home is polypropylene. It is a fiber with many excellent traits, as well as a few negative ones that limit its uses. Currently it is used for, among other things, rugs, upholstery fabrics, rope, disposable diapers, and apparel, especially sportswear and activewear. Polyethylene, which is used for furnishings, car upholstery, blinds, and awnings, is omitted from the discussion that follows. It differs substantially in character from polypropylene and is much more limited in use.

Properties of Polypropylene. Polypropylene is extremely lightweight—the lightest of any fiber. It can be made into very lightweight, warm sweaters and blankets. Among its other merits are that it can be made into fabrics that are strong, abrasion-resistant, and wrinkle-resistant. Polypropylene fabrics can be heat-set into creases that are permanent, so long as they are not exposed to high temperatures. Polypropylene fibers are extremely inabsorbent (the least absorbent of all the synthetic fibers). Some assert that polypropylene wicks extremely well, and it has become a popular choice for active sportswear. Whether or not polypropylene fibers actually wick well, however, is a matter of debate. Unlike a fabric made from a hydrophilic, absorbent fiber such as cotton, polypropylene fabric will not become soaked with perspiration and lose its heat-insulating ability; thus it has been favored for cold-weather sportswear. And unlike many other synthetic fibers, it resists static buildup. Polypropylene is not harmed by mildew or by moths or other insects. Pilling is often a problem for polypropylene fabrics.

Other problems that afflict polypropylene fabrics are poor dyeability (which producers have made slow progress in improving), strong sensitivity to heat and light (it has the lowest resistance to ultraviolet radiation of all fibers), extremely low absorbency, and ready susceptibility to oil-staining and odor-holding. Its heat and light sensitivity can be substantially reduced with chemical additives, resulting in fibers with adequate resistance for most uses. Its laundering problems, especially those caused by polypropylene's oleophilic tendencies, are less tractable.

Caring for Polypropylene Fabrics. Like other hydrophobic, oleophilic fibers, polypropylene is prone to retaining oily soils from, for instance, food spills or the body. On the other hand, it is quite resistant to water-based stains, which can sometimes just be wiped off—a real virtue in carpeting. Dry cleaning is not usually recommended for polypropylene because it shrinks in perchlorethylene, the most commonly used drycleaning fluid; if dry cleaning is recommended, an alternative solvent will be specified on the care label. If dry cleaning is necessary, the cleaner should be made aware of the item's fiber content.

Unfortunately, polypropylene does not readily launder clean, as it can take neither hot water (it shrinks) nor vigorous agitation. Polypropylene may be washed only in warm or cool water, with gentle agitation. Most soaps, detergents, and bleaches may be used. Because it is prone to oil-staining and holding body odors, getting it really clean and fresh is difficult. Polypropylene tends to be low in static, but if you do have a static problem, use a fabric softener. Because it is quite heat sensitive, line-dry or tumble dry polypropylene with cool air or at the lowest dryer setting followed by a cool-down period. It dries very readily, so do not be tempted to turn up the heat out of fear that otherwise it will take forever to dry. Be most careful with irons! If an iron touches polypropylene fabric, it may melt; using a press cloth with a cool iron is wise.

"Lastol" is, technically, a generic subclass fiber name (approved by the FTC in 2003) that may be used as an alternative to the name "olefin." This means that it is different enough from olefin to merit separate identification on fiber content labels. Lastol is a stretch fiber that is both considerably more elastic and more heat- and chemical-resistant than olefin. Lastol also has the advantage of being resistant to drycleaning chemicals that harm olefin. Its manufacturers describe it as having a cottony hand with a natural feel to it. So far, it is used in easy-care stretch apparel, cotton shirts, garment-washed denim, casual and quality shirts, blouses, professional wear, and uniforms.

Lastol is dry-cleanable and readily launderable. Its manufacturers say that it will not shrink or lose its shape or stretch recovery even after multiple launderings or dry cleanings. Hot water, tumbling dry, and bleach are all safe for lastol, but, as with any new fiber or fabric, follow care labels until you gain experience with it.

Microfibers

Microdenier, or microfiber, fabrics are woven from superfine fibers. You will sometimes see the term "microfiber" used to refer solely to polyester microfibers, these being the most familiar in apparel, but there are also rayon, nylon, and acrylic microfibers.

Only in the past decade have manufacturers begun to produce superfine fibers or microfibers, generally defined as those of less than one denier. The sizes of silk and man-made fibers are specified in "deniers," or in terms of their linear density.[4] One denier of a given fiber is defined as the weight in grams of 9,000 meters of the fiber. For example, if 9,000 meters of polyester weighed 1 gram, this polyester would be 1-denier; if 9,000 meters of it weighed 3 grams, it would be 3-denier. (A "tex" is ⅑ of a denier, or the weight in grams of 1,000 meters of fiber.) Higher deniers (or tex numbers) imply bigger (greater diameter) fibers, but because different kinds of fibers have different weights, you cannot conclude that 1-denier nylon is the same diameter as 1-denier polyester. The first microfibers were 1-denier, or about the same denier as silk. Now manufacturers sometimes use even "ultrafine" microfibers, with a denier of 0.3 or less. Until these developments, man-made fibers were either fine (less than or equal to 2.2 denier), medium (2.2 to 6.3 denier), or coarse (between 6.3 and 25 denier).

A yarn composed of microfibers contains more filaments and has more surface area than yarn with the same diameter that is composed of regular fibers. This produces a number of effects. All microfiber fabrics tend to have a very soft, silky hand, excellent drapability and strength, and great abrasion-resistance. They are warmer (because they trap more air) and have improved moisture wicking, which contributes to improved comfort. They resist pilling. They are well suited for outerwear, providing both excellent water-repellancy and good breathability. They can also show superb color contrasts in prints. Microfibers frequently contribute to excellent blends.

Despite the improvement in hand, some observers say that microfibers still look synthetic and lack the beauty of natural fibers. They tend to be expensive—often as expensive as silk—and they tend to retain the general characteristics of whatever synthetic they are made of. For example, polyester microfibers are inabsorbent, may oil-stain, and may develop static unless they receive modifications or treatments to control such problems. Microfibers may be more heat sensitive because their thin fibers are more readily penetrated by heat. One reliable source recommends that you use only a cool iron on polyester and nylon microfibers to avoid glazing or melting the fabric and that you avoid applying heavy pressure with an iron, which can cause shine and ridges on the fabric.[5]

Blends

Blends are fabrics that contain two or more fibers, which may be natural, synthetic, or both. The qualities of blends depend on the proportions of each fiber in the blend and on the finishes and treatments that are applied to it. In judging the characteristics of blends, a rule of thumb is that the resulting fabric will have the properties of each fiber in the degree to which that fiber is present in the blend. The most successful blends unite the best qualities of the blended fibers, but there are often trade-offs. Cotton/polyester blends are more wrinkle-resistant than 100 percent cotton fabrics and more comfortable than 100 percent polyester fabrics. However, they can pill (like polyester) and overall may be more likely to stain than either polyester or 100 percent cotton because they may contain the vulnerabilities of both fibers. Blends improperly made or cared for may lose shape or pucker if one fiber shrinks and the other does not. Skillfully made blends, however, often unite superb looks, easy care, and excellent performance.

Examples of deservedly popular blends are far too numerous to list. Cotton/rayon blends often have better crispness, luster, sheen, and hand than a fine 100 percent cotton fabric. With the proper treatments, cotton/rayon blends may also have better shape retention, washing properties, and strength than 100 percent cotton given similar treatments. Rayons with good resistance to alkalies can be mercerized in cotton blends, and wrinkle-resistance treatments weaken them less than they weaken cotton or other types of rayon. Rayon or cotton will contribute good hand, looks, and absorbency when blended with polyester, acrylic, triacetate, or nylon.

A polyester/rayon or polyester/cotton blend is likely to look and feel better than 100 percent polyester but will often fall short of the comfort and good hand of a fabric containing all cotton or rayon or a fabric with a higher percentage of cotton or rayon. The more polyester the article contains, the more wash-and-wear properties it will have, but a higher percentage of cotton or rayon than polyester will give the fabric greater absorbency and a better hand. When cotton/polyester blends are given wrinkle-resistance treatments, polyester's strength is important because cotton is weakened by the finishing process.

Blended with wool, polyester and other synthetics enhance abrasion resistance and easy-care properties (wrinkle-resistance, crease retention) and help to prevent sagging, bagging, and stretching. The wool adds beauty, warmth, and elasticity. The greater the percentage of wool, the warmer the blend will be and the less likely to pill (but not all such blends are prone to pilling). A garment of wool and triacetate is cooler, more wrinkle-resistant, and holds its shape better than wool alone.

A Note on Caring for Synthetic (Hydrophobic) Fibers and Their Blends

Hydrophilic fibers (all the natural fibers as well as rayon and lyocell) absorb both oily and water-soluble soils, but since they also absorb water and detergent very readily, they tend to give up both types of soil easily too. Man-made fibers such as polyester, nylon, triacetate and acetate, spandex, polypropylene (olefin), acrylic, and modacrylic are all, to one degree or another, hydrophobic. Polypropylene and polyester are exceedingly hydrophobic, and nylon is moderately so. Hydrophobic fibers do not readily absorb water; they may even repel it, and it takes them longer to get wet. They do, however, readily retain oil (they are oleophilic) and do not readily give it up. On the positive side, this means that they shrink less and tend to repel water-based stains, such as coffee and sugary stains, just as they tend to repel water. On the negative side, because it is so hard to get them good and wet, it can also be hard to get them good and clean—especially when it comes to oily dirt and stains, such as greasy tomato sauce. They may retain body odors and oils. Fabrics made from synthetic fibers tend to pill.

Synthetic fibers, for the foregoing reasons, in most ways require the same type of laundering as resin-treated cottons and cotton blends. Laundering frequently, pretreating (particularly with solvent-containing pretreatment products), using plenty of detergent and water, and using the warmest water the fiber will tolerate—all the procedures recommended for resin-treated cloth—help conquer the oily soil and odor problems that you sometimes experience with synthetics. Turning garments made of synthetic fibers or their blends inside out helps too, as this reduces pilling. Use the permanent-press cycle on your washer, with its cool-down rinse and slower spin, with plenty of water, and avoid overcrowding so as to reduce or avoid wrinkling and excess abrasion in the washer; the dryer's permanent-press setting, too, includes a cool-down period so that hot clothes do not sit and wrinkle.

Because hydrophobic fibers resist wetting, the main trick in laundering them is to leave them in the water for a longer time than you ordinarily need with cottons and linens. The best way to do this is with a good long presoak with plenty of detergent or a presoak product in the hottest water safe for the fiber. You can also increase the wash/agitation period, but this increases the amount of abrasion the fabric is exposed to and hence may increase pilling too.

If oil stains will not respond to laundering, drycleaning solvents or stain removers containing drycleaning solvents, whether used professionally or at home, will often work. If you use them yourself, observe all cautions on labels. They are highly flammable.

Soil-release treatments are often applied to synthetic and wrinkle-treated fibers. These are chemical finishes that make the fibers more absorbent and hence more wettable. They work well at improving the washability of these fabrics for as long as they last, but such treatments tend to become less effective over time. Some last longer than others. If treated with soil-release finishes, permanent-press clothes will generally wash free of both oil- and water-based stains in ordinary home washing procedures. Some types of durable-press and wash-and-wear fabrics are treated with antimicrobials to reduce odor problems.

NOTES

Chapter 3. Washers, Dryers, and Other Laundry Room Equipment

PAGE 40. 1. Soap and Detergent Association. *Consumer Update: Laundry Products and High-Efficiency Washers.* 1997.

PAGE 43. 2. www.energystar.gov/index.cfm?c=clotheswash.pr_clothes_washers

Chapter 4. Laundering

PAGE 65. 1. *Maytag Encyclopedia of Home Laundry.* Western Publishing, 1969, pp. 86, 145, 153. The manual for my old top-loading Maytag washer cautioned: "Although some sources suggest turning down the hot water heater, 140°F *at the faucet* [emphasis added] is necessary for cleaning soiled items." (*Maytag Laundering Guide,* Form No. 60FE-0390, Part No. 2-05914, undated, p. 2).

Chapter 10. Sanitizing the Laundry

PAGE 149. 1. Eduard Smulders. *Laundry Detergents.* Wiley-VCH, 2002, p. 81.

PAGE 149. 2. There is now a line of hydrogen peroxide products called $H_2Orange_2$, marketed as an industrial sanitizing cleaner, which has a far longer shelf life than drugstore hydrogen peroxide and, according to its manufacturer, works in cold or warm water. (Some $H_2Orange_2$ cleaners are EPA registered sanitizers.) It is citrus scented and comes in concentrated form that you dilute. A representative of $H_2Orange_2$'s manufacturer, EnvirOx, told me that "$H_2Orange_2$ Grout-Safe" can be used in the laundry as a bleach and that the product is environmentally and otherwise safe. (Terry Freeman, EnvirOx LLC, personal communication, August 26, 2004.) At the time of this writing, $H_2Orange_2$ Grout-Safe and information about it are still hard for people at home to get, and I am not able to offer comparisons between it and other products as to effectiveness in sanitizing or bleaching.

PAGE 151. 3. See R. Sporik et al. *New England Journal of Medicine.* August 23, 1990, pp. 502–507, quoted in "House-dust mites may cause childhood asthma," Child Health Alert, October 1990.

Chapter 12. Science for the Laundry

PAGE 177. 1. Philip Dickey, Washington Toxics Coalition, personal communication, August 18, 2004; "Criteria for Good Environmental Choice: Laundry Detergents, Stain Removers, and Bleaches," Swedish Society for Nature Conservation, 2002.

PAGE 177. 2. Apart from its use in the laundry, chlorine bleach is important as a general household disinfectant for which nonpolluting and equally effective substitutes are not easy to find, especially when the other substantial advantages of chlorine bleach are weighed in the balance. Many scientists, for example, favor chlorine bleach as a home disinfectant because its mode of action precludes any possibility of its breeding disinfectant-resistant microbes (an alleged possibility on which the jury is still out with respect to certain other disinfectants). One promising candidate as a replacement for household chlorine bleach is called $H_2Orange_2$ Grout-Safe. See note 2 in Chapter 10.

Chapter 15. Beds and Bedding

PAGE 213. 1. D. P. Strachan and I. M. Carey, "Home Environment and Severe Asthma in Adolescence: A Population-Based Case-Control Study," *British Medical Journal,* 311 (1995):1053–1056.

PAGE 213. 2. Kathryn V. Blake, "Asthma Management," *American Druggist,* July 1998, p. 57.

Chapter 19. The Fabric of Your Home

PAGE 277. 1. Kathryn L. Hatch. *Textile Science.* West, 1993, p. 320; Bernard P. Corbman, *Textiles: Fiber to Fabric.* McGraw-Hill, 1982, p. 78.

Chapter 20. Transformations

PAGE 310. 1. Germany and the Netherlands have banned the import of certain dyed goods whose colors might, if subjected to reduction treatments, produce carcinogenic dye degradation products.

PAGE 311. 2. Frosting tends to plague some permanent-press clothes made of cotton/polyester blends. In such clothes, the cotton fibers tend to be a bit darker than the polyester ones, and, when weakened by the resin treatment that creates the resistance to wrinkling, the cotton fibers also tend to wear away faster than the polyester. In areas subject to abrasion, such as the knees, a lighter area may appear.

PAGE 317. 3. "Facts about Fabric Flam-mability," North Central Extension Service Publication 174, revised July 2003. www.extension.iastate.edu/Publications/NCR174.pdf

PAGE 318. 4. "Facts about Fabric Flam-mability," North Central Extension Service Publication 174, revised July 2003. www.extension.iastate.edu/Publications/NCR174.pdf

PAGE 321. 5. Sara J. Kadolph and Anna L. Langford. *Textiles,* 9th edition. Prentice-Hall, 2002, pp. 299–300, Kathryn L. Hatch. *Textile Science.* West, 1993, p. 416.

PAGE 324. 6. Kathryn L. Hatch. *Textile Science.* West, 1993, p. 417.

Chapter 21. The Natural Fibers

PAGE 334. 1. Fergusons Irish Linens, manufacturer of linens and damasks, recommends hot water, a "color care" detergent free from optical brightening agents, and no bleach on sturdy washable linens. The following *maximum* wash-water temperatures are suggested (I have converted from centigrade to Fahrenheit): (1) White linen without special finishes, 200°F. (2) Linen without special finishes, where colors are fast, 140°F. (For 1 and 2, a temperature of 122°F is generally sufficient.) (3) Linens that are colorfast at 104°F but not at 140°F should be washed at 104°F. (Test first for fastness at different temperatures.) (4) Fine hand-embroidered linen should be hand-washed at 104°F.

PAGE 342. 2. Fashion Institute of Technology professor Ingrid Johnson, quoted by Morris Dye in a Scripps-Howard news service story, November 11, 2003.

PAGE 344. 3. Kathryn L. Hatch. *Textile Science.* West, 1993, p. 147.

PAGE 347. 4. Kathryn L. Hatch. *Textile Science.* West, 1993, p. 417.

Chapter 22. The Man-Made Fibers and Blends

PAGE 356. 1. Kathryn L. Hatch. *Textile Science.* West, 1993, p. 483.

PAGE 358. 2. Bernard P. Corbman. *Textiles: Fiber to Fabric.* McGraw-Hill, 1982, p. 347.

PAGE 362. 3. *Federal Register.* February 1, 2002, vol. 67, pp. 4901–4903 (designating a new generic fiber name and describing PLA).

PAGE 367. 4. The natural fibers other than silk, the only natural filament fiber, are measured by their diameters, stated in micrometers. Sheep's wool ranges from 17 to 40 micrometers (17 being fine and 40 coarse), cotton from 16 to 21 micrometers. Flax is slightly finer than cotton, from about 15 to 20 micrometers. Only filament fibers are measured in deniers, and what counts as a filament fiber is determined by its length, which is indefinitely long. See Kathryn L. Hatch, *Textile Science,* pp. 90–91.

PAGE 368. 5. Joyce A. Smith. Ohio State Extension Factsheet (ohioline.osu.edu/hyg-fact/5000/5546.html).

ACKNOWLEDGMENTS
AND SOURCES

I owe a great debt to the many people who helped me to write this book—my family, friends, colleagues, and all the delightful people whom I met during the course of my research. Every page of the book benefited from the attention of Edward Mendelson, my most astute reader. James Mendelson's editorial acumen has also contributed to clarity throughout.

Never was an author more fortunate in her editors than I have been. Without the generous support of Maria Guarnaschelli and Nan Graham, this book would never have been completed. They edited with genius and sensitivity, and they always had a clear view of the forest when I got lost in the trees. Rica Allanic's ideas benefited the whole book enormously. Alexis Gargagliano was simply indispensable, and Mia Crowley-Hald is simply a genius. The illustrations by Harry Bates clarify much that I was unable to say in words. My agent, Michael Carlisle, helped make this book's passage into the world as painless as possible.

Any errors that may remain in the book are my sole responsibility, and I will be grateful to readers who inform me of possible corrections and additions, which may be sent in care of the publisher.

Many individuals and organizations read or helped confirm information contained in one or more chapters of this book. Among those who gave generous help with large portions of the book were Professor J. Richard Aspland of Clemson University and Professor Kathryn Hatch of the University of Arizona. Patricia Bauer repeatedly came to my aid with scientific knowledge, domestic skill, friendship, and the operating manuals for her washer and dryer (which I swear I will return to her). I am also indebted to Professor Ingrid Johnson of the Fashion Institute of Technology.

Invaluable advice was also provided by Jane Borthwick; Sandy Sullivan of the Clorox Company; Damon Jones, Beverly Larkin, and Ron Smith of Procter & Gamble; Andy O'Hearn of Reckitt Benckiser Inc.; Richard Owen of Redox Brands Inc.; Jana Starr of Jana Starr Antiques, New York; and Bridget Weigel of Cargill Dow LLC; as well as employees and officials of many other companies, including the American Society for Testing and Materials, Rowena DeLeon of Unilever, Fergusons Irish Linens, Inchcape Testing Services, Schweitzer Linens, Bergdorf Goodman, and Bloomingdale's. Brian Sansoni of the Soap and Detergent Association was a storehouse of useful names and sources, and he was unfailingly generous with his time and knowledge.

Among the many experts who helped on the science of the laundry and related subjects, I want to offer special thanks to Dr. Israel Lowy; Professor William Rutala, University of North Carolina; Professor Thomas A. E. Platts-Mills, University of Virginia; Dr. Elaine Larsen, Columbia University; Cheryl Wrightmeyer, Iowa State University; and Philip Dickey of the Washington Toxics Coalition.

I am especially indebted to the Cooperative Extension Services of many states; these services, established by federal law, disseminate information derived from agricultural experimentation stations and other departments of land-grant colleges and universities. Answers to many questions on textiles, laundering, and related matters may be found at extension service Web sites; many local extension services may be found in the county government listings in telephone directory blue pages.

Books used as sources include *1997 Annual Book of ASTM Standards* (American Society for Testing and Materials, 1996; the figure on page 35 has been reproduced by the Simon & Schuster Consumer Group under license from ASTM. This figure is reprinted from ASTM Standard D 5489-96C, Standard Guide for Care Symbols for Care Instructions on Textile Products, copyright 1996 American Society for Testing and Materials, 100 Barr Harbor Drive, West Conshohocken, PA, 19428, USA [phone: 610–832–9585, fax 610–832–9555]. Copies of the official standard should be obtained directly from ASTM.); J. R. Aspland, *Textile Dyeing and Coloration* (American Association of Textile Chemists and Colorists, 1997); Bernard P. Corbman, *Textiles: Fiber to Fabric* (McGraw-Hill, 1982); Françoise de Bonneville, *The Book of Fine Linen* (Flammarion, 1994); Kathryn Hatch, *Textile Science* (West, 1993), and its 2000 supplement, *Lyocell*; Judith Jerde,

Encyclopedia of Textiles (Facts on File, 1992); Marjorie L. Joseph, *Essentials of Textiles* (Holt, Rinehart and Winston, 1988); Sara J. Kadolph and Anna L. Langford, *Textiles,* 9th edition (Prentice-Hall, 2002); J. J. Pizzuto, *Fabric Science Swatch Kit* (Fairchild, 1990); Arthur Price and Allen C. Cohen, *J. J. Pizzuto's Fabric Science* (Fairchild, 1994); Eduard Smulders, *Laundry Detergents* (Wiley-VCH, 2002); Phyllis G. Tortora, ed., *Fairchild's Dictionary of Textiles* (Fairchild, 1996); Isabel B. Wingate, *Textile Fabrics and Their Selection* (Prentice-Hall, 1976); Frank L. Wiseman, *Chemistry in the Modern World* (McGraw-Hill, 1985); *Maytag Encyclopedia of Home Laundry,* 3rd ed. (Western Publishing, 1969).

Other books that were especially useful include the following: American Chemical Society, *ChemCom: Chemistry in the Community* (Kendall/Hunt, 1988); Seymour S. Block, *Disinfection, Sterilization, and Preservation* (Lea & Febiger, 1991); Thomas R. Donovan et al., *Chemicals in Action* (Holt, Rinehart and Winston, 1987); Paul D. Ellner and Harold C. Neu, *Understanding Infectious Disease* (Mosby Year Book, 1992); John R. Holum, *Elements of General and Biological Chemistry* (Wiley, 1975); Frank A. Oski, *Pediatrics* (Lippincott, 1990); Hermione Sandwith and Sheila Stainton, *The National Trust Manual of Housekeeping* (Viking, 1991); Frank L. Wiseman, *Chemistry in the Modern World* (McGraw-Hill, 1985); *Good Housekeeping's Guide to Successful Homemaking, Revised Edition* (Harper & Row, 1961).

Among the many valuable articles that I relied on were E. R. Bischoff et al., "Mite Control with Low Temperature Washing, I: Elimination of Living Mites on Carpet Pieces," *Clinical & Experimental Allergy,* August 1966; "Mite Control with Low Temperature Washing, II: Elimination of Living Mites on Clothing," ibid., January 1998; Morris Dye, "Beware of

Counterfeit Cashmere," Scripps-Howard News Service, November 11, 2003; Lindy G. McDonald and Euan Tovey, "The Role of Water Temperature and Laundry Procedures in Reducing House Dust Mite Populations and Allergen Content of Bedding," *Journal of Allergy and Clinical Immunology*, October 1992; G. Schober et al., "Control of House-Dust Mites (Pyroglyphidae) With Home Disinfectants," *Experimental and Applied Acarology*, August 1987; R. Sporik et al., "Exposure to House-Dust Mite Allergen (Der p I) and the Development of Asthma in Childhood: A Prospective Study," *New England Journal of Medicine*, August 23, 1990 (cited in *Child Health Alert*, October 1990); M. S. Thakur, "Chemicals and Raw Materials Used in the Soap and Detergent Industry," *Chemical Business*, May 31, 1999; T. Vandenhove et al., "Effect of Dry Cleaning on Mite Allergen Levels in Blankets," *Allergy*, May 1993; Donna L. Wong et al., "Diapering Choices: A Critical Review of the Issues," *Pediatric Nursing*, January-February 1992; "On Your Mind: Dust-Mite Control," *Consumer Reports on Health*, May 2000; "Nanofinishing," *Advances in Textiles Technology*, November 1, 2002; "Abrasion and Wrinkle Resistance," ibid., January 1, 2003; "Nanotechnology Applies Protein Sheathing to Fibres," ibid., May 1, 2004.

David Bardell, "Survival of Herpes Simplex Virus Type 1 on Some Frequently Touched Objects in the Home and Public Buildings, *Microbios*, no. 256–57, 1990; B. Bean et al., "Survival of Influenza Viruses on Environmental Surfaces," *Journal of Infectious Diseases*, July 1982; Kathryn V. Blake, "Asthma Management: What You Need to Know," *American Druggist*, July 1998; Chris Borris, "The Hidden Life of . . . Laundry," *Sierra Magazine*, September-October 2002; Clive M. Brown et al., "Asthma: The States' Challenge," *Public Health Reports*, May-June 1997; Jacque-

lynne P. Corey, "Environmental Control of Allergens," *Otolaryngology: Head and Neck Surgery*, September 1994; P. Cullinan et al., "Asthma in Children: Environmental Factors," *British Medical Journal*, June 18, 1994; G. D'Amato et al., "Environment and Development of Respiratory Allergy: II. Indoors," *Monaldi Archives for Chest Disease*, December 1994; Rupali Das and Paul D. Blanc, "Chlorine Gas Exposure and the Lung: A Review," *Toxicology and Industrial Health*, May-June 1993; Leonard R. Krilov and S. Hella Harkness, "Inactivation of Respiratory Syncytial Virus by Detergents and Disinfectants," *Pediatric Infectious Disease Journal*, July 1993; Patricia A. Kuster, "Reducing Risk of House Dust Mite and Cockroach Allergen Exposure in Inner-City Children with Asthma," *Pediatric Nursing*, July-August 1996; John N. Mbithi et al., "Survival of Hepatitis A Virus on Human Hands and Its Transfer on Contact with Animate and Inanimate Surfaces," *Journal of Clinical Microbiology*, April 1992; Gerd Reinhardt, "Bleach—Meeting the Challenges of the Market," *Household and Personal Care Today*, supplement to *Chemica oggi/Chemistry Today*, 2004; William A. Rutala, "APIC Guideline for Selection and Use of Disinfectants," *American Journal of Infection Control*, August 1996; William A. Rutala and D. J. Weber, "Uses of Inorganic Hypochlorite (Bleach) in Health-Care Facilities," *Clinical Microbiology Review*, October 1997; William Schulz, "The Many Faces of Chlorine: [C. T.] Howlett and [Terence] Collins square off about one of the most evocative chemicals," *Chemical & Engineering News*, October 18, 2004; Elizabeth Scott and Sally F. Bloomfield, "The Survival of Microbial Contamination via Cloths, Hands, Utensils," *Journal of Applied Bacteriology*, March 1990; D. P. Strachan and I. M. Carey, "Home Environment and Severe Asthma in Adolescence: A Population-Based

Case-Control Study," *British Medical Journal*, October 21, 1995; C. Howard-Reed and R. L. Corsi. "Volatilization of Chemicals from Drinking Water to Indoor Air, the Role of Residential Washing Machines," *Journal of Air and Waste Management*, October 1998.

Arm & Hammer ("Super Solutions for Tough Day-to-Day Chores from Arm & Hammer Super Washing Soda," "Baking Soda Basics").

Association Internationale de la Savonnerie, de la Détergence et des Produits d'Entretien ("Benefits and Safety Aspects of Hypochlorite Formulated in Domestic Products, Briefing Document, December 30, 1997").

DHI Water & Environment ("European Eco-label: Revision of Eco-label Criteria for Laundry Detergents," May 2003).

National Asthma Education and Prevention Program ("Expert Report II: Guidelines for the Diagnosis and Management of Asthma").

Soap and Detergent Association ("Household Cleaning Facts," "A Handbook of Industry Terms," "Soaps and Detergents").

Swedish Society for Nature Conservation ("Laundry Detergent, Stain Removers and Bleaches 2002").

University of Newcastle upon Tyne, Honours Programme in Sustainable Engineering, background notes on household laundry detergents, surfactants, etc.

Washington Toxics Coalition (Philip Dickey, "Safer Cleaning Products.")

I found detailed, reliable information in pamphlets and Web pages provided by corporations, extensions services, governmental and private organizations, especially the following:

Arizona Department of Water Resources ("Water and Energy Saving Horizontal Axis Washer 'Wash Wise' Program—Tucson, Arizona, Final Report, February 26, 1999," prepared by Christine Bickelmann).

Centers for Disease Control, National Center for Infectious Diseases, Hospital Infection Program ("Laundry"), and Office of Safety Information ("Guidelines for Laundry in Health Care Facilities").

Environmental Protection Agency ("Energy Star: Clothes Washers").

Federal Trade Commission ("FTC Consumer Alert: Buying a Washing Machine?"); 10 CFR Part 430, January 12, 2001 (FTC amends energy-conservation standards for clothes washers); 16 CFR Part 303, February 1, 2002 (also *Federal Register*, vol. 67, p. 4,901; FTC establishes new generic fiber "PLA"); 16 CFR Part 305, July 14, 2002 (FTC amends the appliance labeling rule to eliminate the "front-loading" and "top-loading" subcategories); 16 CFR Part 423, August 2, 2002 (also *Federal Register*, vol. 65, p. 47,261; FTC amends the care label rule definitions of "cold," "warm," and "hot" water); 16 CFR Part 303, January 27, 2003 (also *Federal Register*, vol. 68, p. 3,813; FTC establishes new generic fiber subclass "Lastol").

Kansas State University Cooperative Extension Service ("Reducing Bacteria in Clothing and Textiles").

Michigan State University Extension ("Kinds of Soil and Appropriate Cleaners").

Mississippi State University, Cooperative Extension Service ("Stain Removal Guide," revised by Dr. Everlyn S. Johnson).

University of Missouri-Columbia, University Extension ("Stain Removal from Washable Fabrics," by Sharon Stevens).

New Mexico State University, College of Agriculture & Home Economics ("Getting Clothes Clean").

North Central Extension Service, "Facts about Fabric Flammability," North

Central Extension Service Publication 174, revised July 2003, www.extension .iastate.edu/Publications/NCR174.pdf, North Central Extension Service Publication 174, revised July 2003.

Ohio State University Extension ("Lyocell—One Fiber, Many Faces," by Joyce A. Smith; "Microfibers: Functional Beauty," by Joyce A. Smith; "Quick 'n Easy Stain Removal," by Janis Stone; "Rayon—the Multi-Faceted Fiber," by Joyce A. Smith).

Arm & Hammer ("Super Solutions for Tough Day-to-Day Chores: Super Washing Soda," "Arm & Hammer Baking Soda: The Little Yellow Box with a House-full of Uses").

Dial Corp. Consumer Information Center ("20 Mule Team Borax Laundry Booster: A Guide to Laundry and Household Uses").

DowBrands ("Your Guide to Tough Laundry Problems from the Stain Removal Experts at Dow-Brands").

Economist Intelligence Unit ("Textiles and the Environment," by Jack Watson).

Fergusons Irish Linen ("Fergusons Care Guide for their Genuine Irish Linen").

Frigidaire ("TumbleAction Washer Owner's Guide," "Stackable Dryer Owner's Guide").

General Electric ("Profile Dryers Owner's Manual and Installation Instructions," "Profile Washers Owner's Manual and Installation Instructions," "Spacemaker Washers Owner's Manual and Installation Instructions").

International Fabricare Institute ("Clothing Stains," and the "Professional Cleaners Care" series of pamphlets on a variety of subjects).

Lever Brothers ("Optical Brighteners," "Dirty Secrets and Clean Facts: The Wisk Laundry Guide," "Home Laundering Guide: Deterioration of Laundry Items," "Get It *All* Clean").

LG Electronics ("Owner's Manual Washing Machine WM2432HW [etc.]," "Owner's Manual Electric and Gas Dryer DLE5977W [etc.]").

Maytag Company ("Maytag Laundering Guide," "Special Baby, Special Cleanup: How to Care for Baby Laundry," "Automatic Washer Model A9800 User's Guide," "Automatic Dryer Model D9700 User's Guide," "Maytag Neptune Washer Model MAH7500 User Guide," "New Maytag Neptune Dryer Model MD5500 User Guide," "Maytag Neptune TL Washer Model FAV-2 Use & Care Guide").

Ohio State University Extension Service ("Conserving Water in the Home: Washing Clothes," by A. Koester).

Procter & Gamble ("Stain Removal Guide for Water Washable Items," "Laundry Tips," "Home Fabric Care Made Easy," "What Causes Color Loss in Fabrics?").

City of Santa Barbara Water ("Horizontal Axis Washing Machines").

Soap and Detergent Association ("Removing Stains from Washable Items," "Laundering Facts from the Soap and Detergent Association," "Laundry Detergent Package Directions," "Sorting It Out," "Soaps and Detergents," "Laundry Detergent Package Directions," "A Handbook of Industry Terms," "Laundry Products and High-Efficiency Washers").

Seymour Housewares ("Handbook on Laundry Care and Ironing").

Whirlpool U.S.A. ("Automatic Washer With Calypso Wash Motion Use & Care Guide," "Duet HT Front-Loading Automatic Washer Use & Care Guide").

Woolite ("Caring for the Clothes You Care About").

Chapter 21, "The Natural Fibers," includes logos and other symbols reprinted by permission of la Confederation Europeene du Lin et du Chanvre and Masters of

Linen (P.O. Box 1630, New York, NY 10028, 212–734–3640); Cotton Incorporated; the Woolmark Company; the American Wool Council; and the Harris Tweed Authority.

General sources that I found useful include, among many others, Witold Rybczynski, *Home: A Short History of an Idea* (Viking, 1986); Margaret Horsfield, *Biting the Dust* (St. Martin's, 1998); Laurie Abraham et al., *Reinventing Home* (Plume, 1991); Caroline Davidson, *A Woman's Work Is Never Done: A History of Housework in the British Isles 1650–1950* (Chatto & Windus, 1982); Jane and Leslie Davison, *To Make a House a Home* (Random House, 1994); Dorothy Hayden, *The Grand Domestic Revolution: A History of Feminist Designs for American Homes, Neighborhoods, and Cities* (MIT Press, 1981); Elizabeth Wayland Barber, *Women's Work: The First Twenty Thousand Years* (Norton, 1994); Glenna Matthews, *"Just a Housewife"* (Oxford, 1987); Laura Shapiro, *Perfection Salad: Women and Cooking at the Turn of the Century* (Farrar, Straus & Giroux, 1986); Ruth Schwartz Cowan, *More Work for Mother: The Ironies of Household Technology from the Open Hearth to the Microwave* (Basic Books, 1983); Susan Strasser, *Never Done: A History of American Housework* (Pantheon, 1982); Katherine Kish Sklar, *Catharine Beecher: A Study in American Domesticity* (Norton, 1973).

Older books that remained fascinating or useful include Mary Randolph, *The Virginia Housewife* (1824), ed. Karen Hess (University of South Carolina Press, 1984); Catherine Sidgwick, *Home* (James Munroe, 1835); Catharine E. Beecher, *A Treatise on Domestic Economy for the Use of Young Ladies at Home and at School* (T. H. Webb, 1841); Harriet Beecher Stowe, *House and Home Papers* (Ticknor and Fields, 1865), and *Motherly Talks with Young Housekeepers* (J. B. Ford, 1875); Catharine Beecher and Harriet Beecher Stowe, *American Woman's Home* (J. B. Ford, 1872); *Cassell's Book of the Household* (4 vols., Cassell, 1875); Eunice Beecher, *All Around the House; or How to Make Homes Happy* (Appleton, 1879); Annie Fields, *Life and Letters of Harriet Beecher Stowe* (Houghton Mifflin, 1897); Julia McNair Wright, *The Complete Home* (J. C. McCurdy, 1879); Marion Harland, *House and Home* (Clawson Brothers, 1889) and *The Housekeeper's Week* (Bobbs-Merrill, 1908); Mrs. C. E. Humphrey, ed., *The Book of the Home* (6 vols., Gresham, 1912); Marion Talbot and Sophonisba Preston Breckinridge, *The Modern Household* (Whitcomb & Barrows, 1912); L. Ray Balderston, *Housewifery* (Lippincort, 1928); Henry Humphrey, *Woman's Home Companion Household Book* (P. F. Collier, 1950).

INDEX